Constellation

Constellation

FRIEDRICH NIETZSCHE
AND WALTER BENJAMIN
IN THE NOW-TIME OF HISTORY

James McFarland

FORDHAM UNIVERSITY PRESS   *New York*   2013

THIS BOOK IS MADE POSSIBLE BY A COLLABORATIVE GRANT
FROM THE ANDREW W. MELLON FOUNDATION.

Copyright © 2013 Fordham University Press

All rights reserved. No part of this publication
may be reproduced, stored in a retrieval system, or
transmitted in any form or by any means—electronic,
mechanical, photocopy, recording, or any other—
except for brief quotations in printed reviews,
without the prior permission of the publisher.

Fordham University Press has no responsibility for the
persistence or accuracy of URLs for external or third-
party Internet websites referred to in this publication
and does not guarantee that any content on such
websites is, or will remain, accurate or appropriate.

Fordham University Press also publishes its books
in a variety of electronic formats. Some content that
appears in print may not be available in electronic
books.

Library of Congress Cataloging-in-Publication Data

McFarland, James (Philip James)
  Constellation : Friedrich Nietzsche and Walter
Benjamin in the now-time of history / James
McFarland.
       p. cm.
  Includes bibliographical references and index.
  ISBN 978-0-8232-4536-9 (cloth : alk. paper)
  1. Nietzsche, Friedrich Wilhelm, 1844–1900.
2. Benjamin, Walter, 1892–1940. I. Title.
B3317.M43 2013
193—dc23
                                    2012027017

Printed in the United States of America

15 14 13 5 4 3 2 1

First edition

CONTENTS

Preface vii
Abbreviations xiii
A Note on Citations xvii

Introduction: Walter Benjamin, Friedrich Nietzsche 1
The Förster House 1—Affinity 4—Excelsior! 9

1. Mortal Youth 16
   A Youthful Facies 16—The Friend 33—Conversation 43—
   Heinle 49—*Abstand* 59

2. Presentation 67
   Philology 67—Tragedy 74—Hamlet 83—Socrates 89—
   Silence 93

3. Inscription 103
   Pseudomenon 103—Untimeliness 113—Muri 130—
   "We Philologists" 143—Asyndeton 155

4. Collaboration 167
   Shadow 167—Wanderer 174—Correspondence 180—
   Demon 190—Caesura 198

5. Mad Maturity 208
   "Born posthumously" 208—Conspiracy 219—
   Eternal Return 227—*Glück* 237—Now-Time 241

   Conclusion: Friedrich Nietzsche, Walter Benjamin 249
   Transcendental Medicine 249—The Pawnshop 255—
   The End of All Things 258

Notes 263
Bibliography 301
Index 311

PREFACE

> The Trauerspiel therefore knows no hero, only constellations.
> —WALTER BENJAMIN, *The Origin of German Trauerspiel*

In his essay "A Portrait of Walter Benjamin," reprinted in the collection *Prisms*, Theodor W. Adorno gestures toward a methodological congruence between the work of his friend Walter Benjamin and the work of the philosopher Friedrich Nietzsche. "The later Nietzsche's critical insight," Adorno writes, "that truth is not identical with a timeless *universal*, but rather that it is solely the historical which yields the figure of the absolute, became, perhaps without his knowing it, the canon of [Benjamin's] practice."[1] Adorno's understanding of the relationship between the thought of Nietzsche and Benjamin situates it at a fundamental level of significance, for it holds between an original insight of Nietzsche's and the very principle governing Benjamin's speculations, the irreducible presence of history in Benjamin's thought. At the same time, with his cautious qualification Adorno concedes that the relationship does not have the philological guarantee that would bolster more robust readings. Perhaps Benjamin was hardly aware of this Nietzschean precedent.

An account detailing which of Nietzsche's writings Benjamin had read and a characterization of what he had said about those texts and the man who wrote them—this basic philological excavation—had not yet been attempted in 1950 when Adorno offered his comparison. Beyond the dispersed condition of Benjamin's writings and the practical difficulties their study presented, the reasons for this lack of interest are not far to seek. In the wake of a genocidal European fascism that had claimed Benjamin as its victim a decade before, the great tension in his thought between Jewish messianism and Communist commitment seemed prima facie to preclude much sympathy for the antidemocratic and atheist Nietzsche who derided both tendencies and who had found such enthusiastic parrots among the Nazi intelligentsia. Though none of Benjamin's close survivors could or would take the fascist grotesque of Nietzsche's thought seriously, Nietzsche's general proximity to reactionary discourses in the twentieth century meant that articulating Benjamin's more nuanced attitudes and responses toward him was a project that lacked urgency.

And yet Adorno's indication of an affinity at work between Nietzsche and Benjamin was never entirely forgotten. As more of Benjamin's writings reached print in subsequent decades and the textual foundation for such philological investigation took shape in the *Gesammelte Schriften* under the direction of Adorno's students Rolf Tiedemann and Hermann Schweppenhäuser, it became clear that Adorno's qualification of Benjamin's familiarity with Nietzsche was hardly necessary. Benjamin knew Nietzsche, early and late. From his juvenilia through his scholarly work to his avant-garde journalism and radio broadcasts in the 1930s, Benjamin consistently oriented his own position with respect to Friedrich Nietzsche's, whether he took him to be the avatar of an ardent "youth" or the diagnostician of mortal tragedy or the exiled wanderer through an anachronistic Europe, witness to the hopeless temporality—new and always the same—of bourgeois imperialism. Benjamin's central treatise *The Origin of German Trauerspiel* presents itself as the overcoming of Nietzsche's *Birth of Tragedy*; *The Arcades Project* that orients Benjamin's exiled career pulses to the historical rhythm of a Nietzschean Eternal Return. By the 1980s it was clear: In no period of his theoretical career did Benjamin fail to identify a nihilistic limit to his own developing reflections with the views and the example of Nietzsche.

Even as this part of the philological foundation for a comparison of the two writers was setting through the last third of the twentieth century, the significance of Nietzsche's philosophy was emerging from the shadow that National Socialism had cast upon it midcentury. The ontological and existential emphases governing interpretations of Nietzsche by Heidegger and Jaspers, conducted in Nazi Germany but at a skeptical remove from official enthusiasm for the Superman, redirected postwar reactions to Nietzsche toward celebration of his commitment to the particular, the accidental, the unrepeatable, and his insubordinate attitude toward received "tables of values" and their public advocates. Reappraisals of Nietzsche's philosophical and political significance outside of Germany in France and Italy, as well as in the United States,[2] gained in self-confidence and interpretive power. Gilles Deleuze's seminal 1962 *Nietzsche et la philosophie* conveniently dates the renewed sensitivity to the anarchistic political consequences of Nietzsche's radically nonconformist example and its incompatibility with totalitarian normativity.

The philological consequences of these reassessments were reflected in the decomposition of Nietzsche's putative magnum opus *The Will to Power*, an amalgam of passages from Nietzsche's notebooks arranged without regard to chronology or context by Nietzsche's dubious executors Elisabeth Förster-Nietzsche and Heinrich Köselitz, called Peter Gast. The book was less a testament to Nietzsche's mature philosophy than a monument to the intellectual pretensions of the Nietzsche Archive, the institution his sister had built to house his mute insanity and publicize his ferocious ideas, pretensions that could not long survive the catastrophes of the twentieth century. After the Second World War new editions of Nietzsche's works edited by Karl Schlechta and then by the Italian scholars Giorgio Colli and Mazzino Montinari brought Nietzsche's texts up to an academic standard of credibility, rectifying the textual interventions by Nietzsche's immediate heirs and restoring the elements of *The Will to Power* to their original draft positions among the voluminous notebooks Nietzsche obsessively filled with his insights and periods. The result was a Nietzsche much closer to the act of inscription but without the closure of an authoritative culminating statement, a thinker who bears the very possibility of philosophical communication into the yelping silence of his madness.

As early as 1978, under the influence of this antiauthoritarian Nietzsche reception in France, Helmut Pfotenhauer reviewed the role of Nietzsche in Benjamin's work and found much more than the Marxist caricature of reactionary bourgeois irrationalism. Pfotenhauer's essay "Benjamin und Nietzsche" locates the two foci of Nietzsche's orbit through Benjamin's thought: the theory of tragedy in the first part of Benjamin's *Origin of German Trauerspiel* and the remarks on the eternal return of the same in the late notes around Benjamin's *Arcades Project*. In explicating this material, Pfotenhauer uses Nietzsche as a common ancestor to draw suggestive connections between Benjamin's notion of origin and Michel Foucault's concept of genealogy, Benjamin's notion of allegory and Jacques Derrida's concept of writing. Nietzsche's philosophy is subordinated to its contemporary reception in order to illuminate the possibility of a contemporary Benjamin interpretation less beholden to the revolutionary orthodoxies so attractive to the postwar student movement in Germany. But that actual interpretation is only suggested. "Shouldn't one consider Benjamin's remarkable Nietzsche reading and the contemporary references that appear from that perspective as a stimulus to reading Benjamin himself in a new way?"³

Pfotenhauer's call for a new mode of reading was ambitious, and though essays by Irving Wohlfahrt in 1981⁴ and Renate Reschke a decade later⁵ reinforced the sense that Benjamin's entire attitude exhibited profoundly Nietzschean characteristics, neither of these readings made any claim to navigate the broad methodological dislocations implicit in Benjamin's Nietzscheanism. Wohlfahrt celebrated a centrifugal Nietzsche creatively resisting reactive resentment and informing both Benjamin's self-confident rejection of academic authority and his eventual validation of the destructive character. Reschke, writing in an East German intellectual milieu still reluctant to renounce entirely the class-based critique of Nietzsche's amoral destructiveness, identifies a maelstromic Nietzsche, the seductive pole of barbarism calling out to Benjamin's nihilism, but held at bay by an essential tact on Benjamin's part. The last attempt at a comprehensive analysis of the relation between Nietzsche and Benjamin, an analysis centered on Nietzsche's deeply destabilizing doctrine of the eternal return as it appears in Benjamin's *Arcades Project*, was Stéphane Moses's essay "Benjamin, Nietzsche, et l'idée de l'éternel retour" from 1996. For Moses, Nietzsche's eternal return is in the first instance a theoretical limit in the present at which any possibility of historical novelty disappears, where "the vision of the deterministic world that dominated the nineteenth century is elevated to the status of myth."⁶ Benjamin does not endorse this mythic elevation but presents it as "an antithesis to his own vision of history" (156), a contrasting historical-philosophical limit in the present that registers what Moses ventures to call "une temporalité non-diachronique" (155).

The following study builds on this prior work and its demonstration that beyond the decadent traditions within which they think, Nietzsche's presence in Benjamin and Benjamin's presence in Nietzsche together uniquely triangulate potentials inscribed in the present moment in history. The one premise of the treatise, then, is a simple one: the relation between Benjamin and Nietzsche is a historical relation. But in relating two historical acts of thinking, each of which is situated, though differently, at the boundary of what is thinkable, there is no refuge from the radicality of those acts themselves. To claim that the relation between them is historical is not to posit a neutral space within which they both can be unproblematically set and maneuvered but is to indicate the stakes for which they themselves were playing. What question more pressing to Nietzsche than the effect of thinking on what succeeds it? What problem more urgent to Benjamin than the origins of the present in the tempest of the past? The intuitions governing influence studies must fail us here. "But just as it is the way of natural springs to feed on obscure trickles, on nameless damp, on barely moist veins of water, so it is with spiritual sources," Benjamin himself writes in *Deutsche Menschen*. "They live not only on the great passions from which spring seed and blood, and still less on the 'influences' so often invoked, but also on the sweat of daily toil and the tears which flow from enthusiasm: drops soon lost in the stream" (*SW* 3:189–90; *GS*, 4:186). Benjamin's engagement to Nietzsche is elusive not because it is superficial or trivial but because it is profound. When Benjamin speaks about André Gide's relation to Nietzsche, he could just as well be describing his own.

> If . . . , in an account of his debt to German literature, Gide omits the name of Nietzsche, this may be explained by the fact that to talk about Nietzsche would imply talking about himself in an overly pointed and responsible way. For anyone who was unaware that Nietzsche's ideas meant more to him than the outline of a philosophical *Weltanschauung* would know very little about Gide. "Nietzsche," Gide remarked once in conversation, "created a royal road where I could only have beaten a narrow path. He did not 'influence' me; he helped me." (*GS*, 4:498–99; *SW*, 2:81)

Not influence but assistance. That is the relation between Walter Benjamin and Friedrich Nietzsche.

This book is the work of many years. It would certainly not exist had not Stanley Corngold, with remarkable personal and professional generosity, opened the doors of serious scholarship to me. In its original form the study was guided with exemplary discernment and patience by many conversations with Michael Jennings, who set a standard of interpretive clarity and textual mastery when working with Walter Benjamin's writing that continues to animate my reading. I am immensely grateful to both of these scholars and friends. At the more recent end of the project, I am indebted to Henry Sussman and two anonymous readers for Fordham University Press for sympathetic, challenging, and helpful reactions to a preliminary version of the book. Professionally, my colleagues at Connecticut College and then at Vanderbilt University have been invariably encouraging and inspiring. Outside the academy, my old friends Mark Shea, Benjamin Powers, and John Fred Bailyn have continually demonstrated the irreducible meaning of friendship, which is, in its way, the subject of my book. What I know about loyalty, humor, and integrity I learned from them. My friendship and conversation with Barbara Hahn is one of the great good fortunes of my life, introducing me into the reality of an intellectually vital and historically informed existence. Without her patience, guidance, and encouragement the book would still be binary fragments on a hard drive. My uncle Thomas McFarland, who embodied for me since childhood the most uncompromising standards of scholarly discipline and passion, passed away before this book could be completed. Whatever scholarly value this study may have derives ultimately from the existential honesty of his example. My brother, Joseph, and my parents, Philip and Patricia, have had every reason to doubt that this book would ever be finished but never have. I have learned much from all of them. But it is my wife, Leah, who has endured the most and given the most in getting to this point; the book is gratefully offered to her.

ABBREVIATIONS

The following abbreviations are used to identify citations in the text. References are provided to both the German texts and to published translations where available. The translations have in places been silently amended.

AA   Immanuel Kant. *Werke*. Akademie-Ausgabe. Edited by the Royal Prussian Academy of Sciences. 11 vols. Berlin: Walter de Gruyter, 1968.

ABB   Theodor W. Adorno and Walter Benjamin. *Briefwechsel 1928–1940*. Edited by Henri Lonitz. Frankfurt am Main: Suhrkamp, 1994.

ABC   Theodor W. Adorno and Walter Benjamin. *The Complete Correspondence 1928–1940*. Edited by Henri Lonitz. Translated by Nicholas Walker. Cambridge, Mass.: Harvard University Press, 1999.

AC   Friedrich Nietzsche. *The Anti-Christ*. Translated by R. J. Hollingdale. New York: Penguin Books, 1968.

AGS   Theodor W. Adorno. *Gesammelte Schriften*. Edited by Rolf Tiedemann. 20 vols. Frankfurt am Main: Suhrkamp, 1997.

AP   Walter Benjamin. *The Arcades Project*. Translated by Howard Eiland and Kevin McLaughlin. Cambridge, Mass.: Harvard University Press, 1999.

BAW   Friedrich Nietzsche. *Jugendschriften 1854–1869*. Beck'sche Ausgabe Werke. 1933–1940. 5 vols. Munich: Deutscher Taschenbuch Verlag, 1994.

BGE   Friedrich Nietzsche. *Beyond Good and Evil: Prelude to a Philosophy of the Future*. Translated by Walter Kaufmann. New York: Vintage Books, 1966.

BT   Friedrich Nietzsche. *The Birth of Tragedy.* Translated by Walter Kaufmann. New York: Vintage Books, 1967.

CB   Walter Benjamin. *The Correspondence of Walter Benjamin, 1910–1940.* Edited by Gershom Scholem and Theodor W. Adorno. Translated by Manfred R. Jacobson and Evelyn M. Jacobson. Chicago: University of Chicago Press, 1994.

D   Friedrich Nietzsche. *Daybreak: Thoughts on the Prejudices of Morality.* Edited by Maudemarie Clark and Brian Leiter. Translated by R. J. Hollingdale. Cambridge: Cambridge University Press, 1997.

EH   Friedrich Nietzsche. *Ecce Homo.* Translated by Walter Kaufmann. New York: Vintage Books, 1989.

EW   Walter Benjamin. *Early Writings: 1910–1917.* Translated by Howard Eiland et al. Cambridge, Mass.: Belknap Press, 2011.

GAB   Gretel Adorno and Walter Benjamin. *Briefwechsel 1930–1940.* Edited by Cristoph Gödde and Henri Lonitz. Frankfurt am Main: Suhrkamp, 2005.

GB   Walter Benjamin. *Gesammelte Briefe.* Edited by Christoph Gödde and Henri Lonitz. 6 vols. Frankfurt am Main: Suhrkamp, 1995–2000.

GF   Gershom Scholem. *Walter Benjamin: Die Geschichte einer Freundschaft.* Frankfurt am Main: Suhrkamp, 1975.

GHA   Johann Wolfgang von Goethe. Werke. *Hamburger Ausgabe in 14 Bänden.* Edited by Erich Trunz et al. Munich: Deutscher Taschenbuch Verlag, 1988.

GKB   Georg Lukács. *Geschichte und Klassenbewußtsein: Studien über marxistische Dialektik.* Darmstadt: Luchterhand, 1968.

GM   Friedrich Nietzsche. *On the Genealogy of Morals.* Translated byWalter Kaufmann and R. J. Hollingdale. New York: Vintage Books, 1967.

GS   Walter Benjamin. *Gesammelte Schriften.* Edited by Rolf Tiedemann and Hermann Schweppenhäuser. 7 vols. Frankfurt am Main: Suhrkamp, 1992.

GSc   Friedrich Nietzsche. *The Gay Science.* Translated by Walter Kaufmann. New York: Vintage Books, 1974.

Abbreviations

HA	Friedrich Nietzsche. *Human, All Too Human: A Book for Free Spirits.* Translated by R. J. Hollingdale. Cambridge: Cambridge University Press, 1986.
HCC	Georg Lukács. *History and Class Consciousness: Studies in Marxist Dialectics.* Translated by Rodney Livingstone. Cambridge, Mass.: MIT Press, 1971.
KGW	Friedrich Nietzsche. *Werke: Kritische Gesamtausgabe.* Edited by Giorgio Colli and Mazzino Montinari. 30 Vols. Berlin: Walter de Gruyter, 1967–77.
KSA	Friedrich Nietzsche. *Kritische Studienausgabe.* Edited by Giorgio Colli and Mazzino Montinari. 15 vols. Berlin: Walter de Gruyter, 1988.
NER	Karl Löwith. *Nietzsche's Philosophy of the Eternal Return of the Same.* Translated by J. Harvey Lomax. Berkeley: University of California Press, 1997.
NEW	Karl Löwith. *Nietzsches Philosophie der ewigen Wiederkunft des Gleichen.* Berlin: Verlag die Runde, 1935.
OFE	Friedrich Nietzsche. *On the Future of Our Educational Institutions.* Translated by Michael W. Grenke. South Bend, Ind.: St. Augustine's Press, 2004.
OH	Walter Benjamin. *On Hashish.* Translated by Howard Eiland et al. Cambridge, Mass.: Belknap Press, 2006.
OT	Walter Benjamin. *The Origin of German Tragic Drama.* Translated by John Osborne. London: Verso Press, 1977.
PTG	Friedrich Nietzsche. *Philosophy in the Tragic Age of the Greeks.* Translated by Marianne Cowan. Washington, D.C.: Regnery Publishing, 1962.
SB	Friedrich Nietzsche. *Sämtliche Briefe.* Kritische Studienausgabe. Edited by Giorgio Colli and Mazzino Montinari. 8 vols. Berlin: Walter de Gruyter, 1984.
SE	Franz Rosenzweig. *Der Stern der Erlösung.* Frankfurt am Main: Suhrkamp, 1993.
SF	Gershom Scholem. *Walter Benjamin: The Story of a Friendship.* Translated by Harry Zohn. New York: New York Review of Books, 2001.
SR	Franz Rosenzweig. *The Star of Redemption.* Translated by Barbara E. Galli. Madison: University of Wisconsin Press, 2005.

SW   Walter Benjamin. *Selected Writing*. 4 vols. Edited by Howard Eiland and Michael W. Jennings. Cambridge, Mass.: Belknap Press, 1996–2003.

TI   Friedrich Nietzsche. *Twilight of the Idols*. Translated by R. J. Hollingdale. New York: Penguin Books, 1968.

TSZ   Friedrich Nietzsche. *Thus Spoke Zarathustra: A Book for None and All*. Translated by Walter Kaufmann. New York: Viking Penguin, 1966.

UO   Friedrich Nietzsche. *Unfashionable Observations*. Translated by Richard T. Gray. Stanford: Stanford University Press, 1995.

UW   Friedrich Nietzsche. *Unpublished Writings from the Period of* Unfashionable Observations. Translated by Richard T. Gray. Stanford: Stanford University Press, 1999.

WC   Friedrich Nietzsche. "We Classicists." Translated by William Arrowsmith. In *Unmodern Observations*, edited by William Arrowsmith. New Haven: Yale University Press, 1990.

WM   Friedrich Nietzsche. *Der Wille zur Macht: Versuch einer Umwertung Aller Werte*. Edited by Peter Gast und Elisabeth Förster-Nietzsche. Stuttgart: Alfred Kröner Verlag, 1996.

WP   Friedrich Nietzsche. *The Will to Power*. Edited by Walter Kaufmann. Translated by Walter Kaufmann and R. J. Hollingdale. New York: Vintage Books, 1968.

WuN   Walter Benjamin. *Werke und Nachlaß: Kritische Gesamtausgabe*. Edited by Christoph Gödde and Henri Lonitz. 21 vols. Frankfurt am Main: Suhrkamp, 2008–.

A NOTE ON CITATIONS

The bulk of Nietzsche's posthumous papers are housed at the Nietzsche Archive in the Klassik Stiftung Weimar in Germany. Walter Benjamin's posthumous papers, dispersed across continents by wars hot and cold, now reside largely in the Akademie der Künste in Berlin and the Hebrew University in Jerusalem. Among these papers in both Nietzsche's and Benjamin's cases are the fragments of an uncompleted magnum opus: Nietzsche's *Will to Power* and Benjamin's *Arcades Project*. The status of these virtual books, ontologically situated in a nimbus of possibility, brings to a point the larger interpretive question of archival remains as such and their relation to published work. These private and preliminary writings both enjoy the authority of immediate candor and suffer the defect of unconsidered approximation; they reside in history differently from finished works. A sensitivity to the historical contrast between completed works and fragmentary documents was fundamental to Benjamin's historical philosophy, whereas Nietzsche's reception has wrestled persistently with the significance of his voluminous notebooks for an accurate understanding of his thought. The less than self-evident historical status of the archival materials surviving from these thinkers is ultimately a consequence of the fact that each of them conceptualized matters of *philosophical* generality by reflecting on *philological* practice. This common philological orientation is a central object of the present study. In a citational practice derived from Benjamin's German editors, I mark visibly in the text this historical difference by rendering in *italics* quotations from Nietzsche's notebooks (volumes 7 through 15 of the *Kritische Studienausgabe*) and Benjamin's notes on the Parisian arcades (volume 5 of the *Gesammelte Schriften*) as well as fragmentary paralipomena, with their idiosyncratic punctuation reproduced as scrupulously as translation permits. This visualization is meant to remind the reader that here in these preliminary texts the public authority of the writers' signatures is not yet fully vested. Quotations from the finished works of both philosophers are given in the traditional way, between quotation marks or as block quotations in roman type. Though translations have in many places been adjusted from published versions for contextual accuracy, emphases within quotations have never been altered from the original German.

Introduction

Walter Benjamin, Friedrich Nietzsche

Against mediators.—Those who want to mediate between two resolute thinkers show that they are mediocre; they lack eyes for seeing what is unique. Seeing things as similar and making things the same is the sign of weak eyes.

—FRIEDRICH NIETZSCHE

THE FÖRSTER HOUSE

At 10 o'clock on 22 May 1934, in a dim Paris room, Walter Benjamin injected 20 mg of mescaline into his thigh, one of the last of the drug experiments he had engaged in since the late 1920s. A protocol of the trip was recorded by his friend Fritz Fränkel. It is an arresting document. The gestures of controlled empirical psychology provide a sober framework for the narrative: Fränkel administers Rorschach tests, describes Benjamin's gestures in minute detail, registers his disconnected remarks. But the strained objectivity cannot eliminate the bohemian resonances round this garret exploration and the man undertaking it. "At the same time, the test subject comments critically that the conditions for the experiment are unfavorable. An experiment of this sort ought to take place in a palm grove. Moreover, the dose administered is for B much too weak; this train of thought recurs throughout the experiment and occasionally finds expression in bitter indignation" (*OH*, 87; *GS*, 6:608).

Benjamin's mood throughout is volatile: "It is manifest outwardly in rather erratic motor phenomena, such as restless turning about, fidgety movements of the arms and legs. B crumples, begins lamenting his own state, the indignity of this state" (*OH*, 86; *GS*, 6:607–8). He at first petulantly refuses to participate in the Rorschach tests. "Meanwhile, the peevishness, the mood of discontent, keeps returning. B himself now calls for the Rorschach images once again in order to get over the bad mood" (*OH*, 88; *GS*, 6:609). Before long, graphology has intruded into his attempts at communication. He begins to scrawl words in embryonic coils across a piece of paper. He writes "veritable witches" ["*richtige Hexen*"] several times in several different handwritings, "in which the essence of the witches is supposed to be presented by the individual words" (*OH*, 89; *GS*, 6:610). The trip proceeds:

> Once again, darkness. During the next phase in the experiment, which marks the deepest stage of the intoxication, the test subject's hands assume peculiar positions. While lying down, the subject stretches out his forearm, the hand held open and the fingers slightly curled. Now and again the position changes, so that the hand is held upright. The different positions are often held for a long time—up to ten minutes. B supplements the observation of this phenomenon with important commentaries on understanding catatonic behavior.... The interpretation of catatonia is now as follows: The test subject compares the fixed position of his hand to the outline of a drawing which a draftsman has set down once and for all. (*OH*, 89–93; *GS*, 6:610–12)

At the nadir of his mescaline trip, Benjamin confronts catatonia. The stiff, cramped posture of a catatonic hand suggests to him a diagnosis: The catatonic figure has metamorphosed into a drawing, fixed by another for all eternity.

There is a photograph of this hand. In June of 1899, less than a year before Friedrich Nietzsche's death, the draftsman Hans Olde arrived in Weimar on commission to draw the notorious philosopher. Curt Paul Janz, in his biography of Nietzsche, tells us that in the course of the next two months Olde made seven oil paintings, one ink drawing, seventeen charcoal or pencil sketches, five etchings, and sixteen photographs of the invalid. "From this material Olde fashioned the now famous etching for [the Berlin art journal] PAN, an etching on whose plate so many so-called 'corrections' had to be made to the brow and chin at Frau Förster's insistence that later in a letter of 13 December 1900 to his wife Olde called the picture a 'botch.' Strictly speaking," Janz adds, "as a depiction of Nietzsche it is actually inaccurate."[1]

Olde's photographic studies for the etching show us Nietzsche on the Weimar balcony of Villa Silberblick, where he spent most of his final summers, his sister and mother changing his cushions to prevent bedsores and bringing him his food. The photographs are unposed, snapshots and not portraits. One such study captures an empty, catatonic gesture of Nietzsche's. His chin is sunken and the tilt of his head seems involuntary and ill. His right hand is raised to eye-level, hovering between a motion in self-defense and a corporeal memory of the act of writing: the fingers might be curled around an absent pen. The left hand clings helplessly to the coverlet, its wrist a taut, spasmodic curve into the patient's loose gown.

The image, if not the photograph, of the ruined Nietzsche who languished behind Olde's heroic etching was familiar to Benjamin. Two years before the mescaline experiment, he had reviewed a series of recent books on the philosopher, among them E. F. Podach's *Nietzsches Zusammenbruch* [*Nietzsche's Breakdown*]. Podach's harrowing reconstruction, through medical reports and letters, of Nietzsche's collapse in Turin and treatment in asylums in Basel and Jena had made a strong impression on Benjamin. Factual and relentless, the book was part of a concerted attack on Elisabeth Förster-Nietzsche and the Nietzsche Archive, an attack with which Benjamin sympathized strongly. Though he found Podach's own psychogenesis of Nietzsche's paralysis progressiva less than entirely convincing, Podach's debunking of the drug etiologies promoted by the archive was complete. "If, though, the attempt has recently been made to eliminate Podach's theses through such constructions," Benjamin concluded, "that was likely not only to avoid the conclusion 'that here a man was driven mad by his intellectual hubris,' but out of reticence at integrating into his thought-massif those abysses that opened up in the last weeks of Nietzsche's existence. For they are abysses that separate him forever from the spirit of pointless industry [*Betriebsamkeit*] and philistinism that dominates the Nietzsche Archive" (*GS*, 3:325–26). The abyss of Nietzsche's madness does not open beneath his philosophical work as judgment. Nor can it be cleanly separated from that work. It opens, for better or for worse, between Nietzsche and interpretive efforts.

In the dark Paris room, the catatonic Benjamin begins to revive. A shiver courses through his body; he hallucinates the sorrow and suffering of the world as a net dragged across his skin. And then Nietzsche enters explicitly.

> Introduced with a witticism: Elisabeth will not rest until the Nietzsche Archive has been turned into a Förster-House.[2] The image of the Förster House is vividly present to the test subject. In the course of his account, it appears now as a school, now as hell, now as a bordello. The test subject is a hardened, obdurate post in the wooden banister of the Förster House. What he has in mind is a sort of wood carving in which, among other ornamental figures, animal forms appear; these, he explains, are in effect degenerate scions of

the totem pole. The Förster House has something of those red-brick structures that appeared resplendent on sheets of cutout patterns in an especially dark, bloody red. It also has something of the building-block structures one made as a child. From the cracks between the building stones grow tufts of hair. (*OH*, 94; *GS*, 6:613–14)

The Förster House: school, hell, and brothel; a blood-red, childish structure, architectural and organic, into which Benjamin is physically incorporated as fetishized ornament. In his own notes, his position coalesces into a vulgar pun: "I am a spindle in its banister: an obdurate, hardened *Ständer* [post/hard-on]" (*OH*, 96; *GS*, 6:615). The hallucination is extraordinarily clear to him. "A chamois' foot in the Förster House: test subject refers with the greatest energy to Little Cock and Little Hen atop Nut Mountain and to the riffraff, since the Förster House would be found here too" (*OH*, 94; *GS*, 6:614). Arising against a ragged landscape of fairy-tale pastoral[3] tinged with urban ghetto; oscillating among temple, toy, body, and bourgeois interior; the demonic sexualized frame around a catatonic Nietzsche transformed into another's drawing—the Förster House gives a first glimpse of the unsettling geography where the meetings of Walter Benjamin and Friedrich Nietzsche occur.

AFFINITY

"The historical method is a philological method based on the book of life. 'Read what was never written,' runs a line by Hofmannsthal. The reader one should think of here is the true historian" (*SW*, 4:405; *GS*, 1:1238). This study ventures to read an unwritten book. Benjamin composed no major essay on Nietzsche's work, left no extended discussion in the letters, no authoritative summarizing statement. Casual mentions, quick references, brief citations of the philosopher move through Benjamin's prose; one catches, as it were, glimpses of Nietzsche, or what looks like Nietzsche, echoes of Nietzsche, or what sounds like Nietzsche, through the thickets of Benjamin's sentences. "I haven't yet had any time," Benjamin wrote to Scholem in 1932, "to concern myself with the question of what significance could be derived from his writings if one had to [*im Ernstfall*]" (*CB*, 394; *GB* 4:100). Such reticent gestures surround Benjamin's explicit mentions of Friedrich Nietzsche in his letters. "Do you know Zarathustra?" he writes to Ludwig Strauß as early as 1912. "For a variety of reasons in school I never dared approach him" (*GB*, 1:78). In 1919, before a performance of *Siegfried*, he reads *The Case of Wagner*, "only to be quite astonished by the simplicity and penetration of what it says," as he writes to his friend Ernst Schoen. "The second Wagner book (*Nietzsche contra Wagner*) I don't yet know, but this first one has made me quite enthusiastic, which is something I cannot on the whole say about all the writings of Nietzsche with which I am familiar" (*CB*, 137; *GB*, 2:10–11). Again, along with praise, professed ignorance and cautious distancing. "En attendent," he continues the above remarks to Scholem, as if to underline the reserve maintained even in a review of books on Nietzsche, "in the review you mentioned I did not commit myself as far as my opinion on Nietzsche himself is concerned" (*CB*, 394; *GB*, 4:100).

If this public coyness in the correspondence might seem a reaction to the overdetermined pregnancy of Nietzsche's name in the ideological cacophony of the twentieth century, an expression of "the horror . . . that comes over well-bred people at the thought of the workings of the Nietzsche Archive" (*GS*, 3:323), in Benjamin's 1932 phrase, this cannot explain why the reserve extends into his private papers. Only three of Nietzsche's titles appear in the fragmentary list of books read that Benjamin maintained intermittently throughout the 1920s and '30s; numbers 598, 722, 835: *The Case of Wagner, Beyond Good and Evil, The Birth of Tragedy*. And yet it can be specifically documented that Benjamin was familiar as well with *Human, All Too Human, Daybreak, The Gay Science, Thus Spoke Zarathustra*, the second *Untimely Observation*, and other less well known writings. But how familiar was he? In May 1918, enthusiastic over Bernoulli's *Franz Overbeck und Friedrich Nietzsche* ("a most exciting, almost too exciting . . . book"—so to Scholem [*GB*, 1:449]), Benjamin recommends it to Ernst Schoen: "If you have time and already know Nietzsche rather well, including his correspondence with Overbeck (which is most significant) then, but only then, perhaps read C. A. Bernoulli" (*GB*, 1:459). The implication would seem to be that Benjamin, the adviser, already knows Nietzsche rather well. This a year before his professed surprise at the late polemics against Wagner.

There can seem to be a repulsion at work between Benjamin and Nietzsche, a diffidence, a touch of distaste, a whiff of embarrassment, perhaps. But the absence of a finished statement here is not only a matter of missed opportunity, of not finding the right mood or the appropriate occasion. "Nietzsche's life is typical for someone who is determined by distances as such; it is the fate of the highest among complete human beings,"⁴ Benjamin remarks parenthetically near the end of the "Outline of the Psychophysical Problem" (*SW*, 1:400; *GS*, 6:87). An irreducible distance is part of this encounter, and brings Nietzsche paradoxically into the heart of Benjamin's thought, gives his name an "aura," "the unique apparition of a distance, however near it may be" (*SW*, 3:104–5; *GS*, 1:479). Repulsion remains a kind of concern, complementing a consistent attraction the philosopher also exercises over Benjamin, who for all his discretion is never indifferent to Nietzsche, or done with him. An "auratic" Nietzsche indigenous to Benjamin emerges from a far deeper affinity between the two thinkers than explicit references in Benjamin's writing can comprehend. An affinity not written in their texts but in the book of life.

The young religious scholar Gershom Scholem had been close friends with Benjamin for more than two years already when, in the last months of the First World War, he left Germany for Bern, Switzerland, where Benjamin was completing his doctorate on German Romanticism. There, Scholem recalls in his biographical memoir, *Walter Benjamin: The Story of a Friendship*, an increased intimacy revealed a troublesome discrepancy between the "radiant moral aura" of Benjamin's thought and "a strictly amoral element" in his everyday practical existence. "Benjamin's attitude toward the bourgeois world was so unscrupulous and had such nihilistic features that I was outraged," Scholem writes. "Benjamin declared that people like us had obligations only to our own kind and not to the rules of a society we repudiated. He said that my ideas of honesty [*Redlichkeit*]—for example, where our parents' demands were involved—should be rejected totally. Often I was utterly surprised to find a liberal dash of Nietzsche in his speeches" (*SF*, 66–67; *GF*, 70–71).

Years later, in 1934, Benjamin himself takes note of a conversation with Bertolt Brecht in Svendborg, Denmark, a contentious discussion of Benjamin's essay on Franz Kafka. "With a somewhat abrupt and forced transition in the conversation, he remarked that I, too, could not entirely escape the charge of writing in diary form, in the style of Nietzsche. My Kafka essay, for example" (*SW*, 2:786; *GS*, 6:527). Benjamin defends his essay, but the Nietzschean stylistic charge sticks: "I could not refute the criticism that it was a diary-like set of notes" (*SW*, 786; *GS*, 6:528). Scholem, Brecht—two in other respects quite antithetical friends of Benjamin's sense to their common dismay a touch of Nietzsche in their contemporary, Scholem recognizing it in the life that falls short of Benjamin's writing, Brecht in the writing that falls short of Benjamin's urgent vital circumstances. A third friend, a third testimony, here from a posthumous perspective: In the introduction to his 1955 edition of Benjamin's *Schriften*, which itself reintroduced Walter Benjamin to postwar efforts to revivify the intellect, Theodor W. Adorno concludes:

> [Benjamin] had an ability that in its power to please leaves all immediately pleasing characteristics far beneath it: the ability to give without reserve. What Zarathustra praised as the highest, the gift-giving virtue, was his to such an extent that it overshadowed all else: "Uncommon is the highest virtue and useless; it is gleaming and gentle in its splendor." And when he called his chosen emblem—Klee's Angelus Novus—the angel who does not give but takes, that too redeems a thought of Nietzsche's: "such a gift-giving love must approach all values as a robber," for "the earth shall yet become a site of recovery! And even now a new fragrance surrounds it, bringing salvation—and a new hope!" Benjamin's words testified to this hope, as did his fantastically quiet, incorporeal smile and his silence. (*AGS*, 11:581)

To read the book on Nietzsche Benjamin never wrote is eventually to describe and account for this Nietzschean aspect to his own historical posture. This is something other than a matter of external influence on Nietzsche's part or immanent reception on Benjamin's. The recognition by some of Benjamin's closest and most perceptive associates of a Nietzschean dimension in his life and work reminds us that any attempt to determine Benjamin's own understanding of Nietzsche as a historical figure and as a corpus of writings, however positively it grounds itself in Benjamin's texts and the archives that preserve them, does not encounter a stable philological object as much as a process of transformation. The Nietzsche Benjamin's friends detected was not Benjamin's own considered assessment of his problematic forebear but a certain impression he himself made, one that characterized his entire intellectual physiognomy, his theoretical commitment, his expressive style, his moral and political posture in the world. Such an affinity involves Benjamin's explicit understanding of Nietzsche but cannot be reduced to it.

And yet, if Benjamin's understanding of Nietzsche cannot exhaust the relationship between them, Nietzsche's philosophy directly can also not secure its foundation. The differences among Scholem's, Brecht's, and Adorno's assessments of this affinity—whether they see it in Benjamin's life or in his work, as a virtue or as a defect—recall the unique difficulty to which any calibration of Nietzsche's philosophy with a subsequent thinker is exposed. Famously unsystematic and blatantly self-contradictory, Nietzsche's writings solicit with an unprecedented intensity the very possibility of meaningful thought. The nihilism that haunts his philosophical experience and the displaced communicative strategies that he invokes to accommodate and circumvent that nihilistic threat preclude any simple paraphrase of Nietzsche's "position" against an impersonal and durable horizon. Nietzsche's writing does not simply preserve the content of a thought that later readers can appropriate but registers an experience of thinking later readers are called upon to realize if Nietzsche is to be "born posthumously" into human life. This is Nietzsche's historical explosion, communicated as a destructive shock through the material of thinking in the present. Thus the excess of Nietzsche's influence over Benjamin's settled intention must be correlated with an excess of Benjamin's receptive prerogative over Nietzsche's expressive authority if justice is to be done to the relation between these two writers.

Benjamin mediates Nietzsche into the future; Nietzsche mediates Benjamin into the past. This formula emphasizes the mutual implication at work in this relationship. Nietzsche's expressive impulse, which emerges from an ungovernable fracture in human self-conception, both inspires Benjamin's writing and simultaneously traverses that writing as an antithetical experience. From the start of his career, Benjamin is impressed by Nietzsche's rhetorical fearlessness and destructive energy. Yet if that intrepid energy returns to itself in Benjamin's writing, it is not where Benjamin adopts Nietzschean claims as his own but rather where he distinguishes himself from them and locates his own critical position over against Nietzsche's relentless disintegration of intellectual traditions. It is that perennial destructiveness in Nietzsche's work that eventually renders him for Benjamin both a character, like Charles Baudelaire, in whom what he comes to call "ur-history"[5] condenses, and a herald, like Karl Kraus, through which an alternative future is announced. Considered as a "reflection-medium"[6] within which Nietzsche's nihilistic concussion with thought appears, Benjamin's archival remains both retain their own integrity with respect to the oeuvre built from them and manifest uniquely and exclusively a constellation of motifs indigenous to Nietzsche's precedent. The concussion in this case just *is* the elaboration of this distinction. And as mediated through Benjamin's anthropological materialism, the meaning of Nietzsche's text is displaced from the apotheosis of Zarathustra at the apex of his oeuvre into the perishable evidence of *his* archival remains, the posthumous notebooks from which scholarship and advocacy assembled and then disassembled a work, *The Will to Power*. The philological legacy of Nietzsche's putative magnum opus reveals in the light of Benjamin's historical skepticism the crisis in the very possibility of binding authority that characterizes at its deepest level the present moment in history. Thus in each direction of this mediating process, the notion of intended significance inhabits and organizes but does not dominate or determine the ultimate meaning of what is at stake.

EXCELSIOR!

On 15 April 1876, Friedrich Nietzsche offered a sincere apology, in a short letter whose contrite tone contrasts sharply with the self-confident rhetoric of his public writings. "Most esteemed Fräulein," his note begins,

> you are large-spirited enough to forgive me, I feel it in the delicacy of your letter, something I genuinely do not deserve. I have suffered so much in thinking on my cruel violent behavior that I cannot thank you enough for this gentleness. I will explain nothing, and know of no way to justify myself. I merely have a final wish to express that, should you at some future point read my name or again encounter me, you not think exclusively on the fright I have caused you; I ask you above all to believe that I would happily make good the evil I have brought about. // Most Respectfully Yours, Friedrich Nietzsche. (SB, 5:154)

The recipient of this penitent epistle was twenty-three-year-old Mathilde Trampedach, a Dutch piano student living with her sister in Geneva. The "cruel violent behavior" for which Nietzsche apologizes here had taken the form of a different letter, sent five days before on 11 April. This was a week or two after he had first met the young woman. Mathilde Trampedach's piano teacher, Hugo von Senger, general director of the Geneva Orchestra, had been a friend of Nietzsche's since 1872. "On a sultry Spring morning," as Mathilde would recall much later, von Senger had brought the young and somewhat notoriously polemical Wagnerian philologist with him when he paid his student and her sister a call.

> The chambermaid knocked on the door and announced the visit of our protector Hugo von Senger accompanied by a stranger. "My friend Friedrich Nietzsche," was heard from the friendly lips of our

benefactor; "be sensible of the honor you have, children, in beholding him." Unfortunately we were unable to see as much of the famous man as we desired, since despite the dimmed light, he held a green-fringed umbrella above his head, no doubt because of his weak eyes.[7]

The two visitors spoke with the sisters until midday, about, among other topics, English poetry: Shakespeare, Lord Byron, Shelley, as well as the American Longfellow. Mathilde asked whether Professor Nietzsche were familiar with Longfellow's recently translated effort, "Excelsior"? No; and, certainly, he would be delighted were she to transcribe it for him. A few days later he joined von Senger and the two young women, chaperoned by their landlady, on an excursion to Villa Diodati on Lake Geneva, where sixty years earlier Mary Shelley, together with her husband and Byron, had begun her novel *Frankenstein*. There is no mention of an umbrella. Then on 10 April Nietzsche called to take his leave for Basel and his teaching duties. "He was introduced to our receiving room, where he greeted us with a gesture of somber ceremony. Turning to the piano, he began to call up with tempestuous feeling a surging expression that resolved into somber harmonies, fading away into the softest tones. We parted shortly afterwards, the parting silent."[8] But the next day she received the translation of the musical outburst:

> My Fräulein,
> This evening you write something for me, I wish to write something for you, as well—
> Gather together all the courage of your heart in order not to fear the question I pose to you: Will you be my wife? I love you and it is as if you were already mine. Not a word about the suddenness of my inclination! At least there is no guilt in it, so that nothing need be excused. But what I would like to know is whether you feel as I do— that we are not at all foreign to one another, not for an instant! Do you not also believe that a connection would let each of us become freer and better than would be possible alone, that is, excelsior? Would you dare to accompany me as one who most passionately strives for emancipation and improvement? On all the paths of life and of thought? (*SB*, 5:147)

We can only speculate on the convergence of elements that provoked Nietzsche to this precipitous offer. That Mathilde was in fact in love with von Senger and would soon become his wife certainly doomed Nietzsche's chances but probably lent an atmosphere of courtship to the group's supervised excursion to the Romantic landmark. Nor would Nietzsche have failed to notice the odd onomastic resonance between the poetry-transcribing Mathilde Trampedach and Mathilde Wesendonck, whose lyrics an infatuated Wagner had scored to great effect two decades before in the "Wesendonck Lieder," when she, too, was twenty-three years old.

Among the constellation of historical factors that condition this curious juncture in Nietzsche's life, alongside the letters and the memories, passing through translation and transcription, is the poem by Longfellow. Excelsior!—Ever upward! Longfellow had composed his ballad on 28 September 1841, finishing it at "Half past 3 o'clock, morning. Now to bed," as he punctiliously noted on the manuscript.[9] In the English neither Mathilde nor Professor Nietzsche could read, this is the poem:

> The shades of night were falling fast,
> As through an Alpine village passed
> A youth, who bore, 'mid snow and ice,
> A banner with the strange device,
>   Excelsior!
>
> His brow was sad; his eye beneath,
> Flashed like a falchion from its sheath,
> And like a silver clarion rung
> The accents of the unknown tongue,
>   Excelsior!
>
> In happy homes he saw the light
> Of household fires gleam warm and bright;
> Above, the spectral glaciers shone,
> And from his lips escaped a groan,
>   Excelsior!
>
> "Try not the Pass!" the old man said;
> "Dark lowers the tempest overhead,
> The roaring torrent is deep and wide!"
> And loud that clarion voice replied,
>   Excelsior!
>
> "Oh stay," the maiden said, "and rest
> Thy weary head upon this breast!"
> A tear stood in his bright blue eye,
> But still he answered, with a sigh,
>   Excelsior!
>
> "Beware the pine-tree's withered branch!
> Beware the awful avalanche!"
> This was the peasant's last Good-night,
> A voice replied, far up the height,
>   Excelsior!
>
> At break of day, as heavenward
> The pious monks of Saint Bernard

Uttered the oft-repeated prayer,
A voice cried through the startled air,
   Excelsior!

A traveler, by the faithful hound,
Half-buried in the snow was found,
Still grasping in his hand of ice
That banner with the strange device,
   Excelsior!

There in the twilight cold and gray,
Lifeless, but beautiful, he lay,
And from the sky, serene and far,
A voice fell, like a falling star,
   Excelsior!

Longfellow himself provided a paraphrase of the poem in a letter. It depicts, he wrote, "the life of a man of genius, resisting all temptations, laying aside all fears, heedless of all warnings, and pressing right on to accomplish his purpose. . . . Filled with these aspirations, he perishes; without having reached the perfection he longed for; and the voice heard in the air is the promise of immortality and progress ever upward."[10] The poem is thus about renunciation, and its final ambiguity, the contrast between the ascending vector announced by the refrain and the descending vector of the closing simile, finds a positive, comforting cast in the paraphrase. A falling star meets the blazon of renunciation, Longfellow says, as its confirmatory validation. This remains of course interpretation and cannot be verified by the poem itself. The movement of the falling star does not answer but contradicts what continues to be, after all, the mere assertion of ascent. The slogan "excelsior" survives its frozen advocate because it has no more content than its own reiteration, even where the voice that iterates it falls.

The interminability of the refrain is its birthright, for before it adorned Longfellow's banner it had been inscribed across the scroll of an actual crest, the Seal of the State of New York, where Longfellow noticed it and was inspired. The seal with its Latin motto had been designed in 1777, during the American Revolution, by John Jay, to replace the Crown Seal in use by the colonial administration. Its motto registers that original revolutionary perspective on tradition, anchoring the inherently retrospective aspect of an act of authoritative endorsement not in any actual aristocratic heritage but in a blank assertion of the future. This is what caught Longfellow's attention. Revolutionary rupture and not an educational deficit makes the Latin an "unknown tongue" in the polyglot Longfellow's poem. The impulse of an unprecedented initiation is caught by an image superficially imitating traditional heraldic authority. It is the echo of this revolutionary gesture that passes from the seal to a postcolonial appropriation of the European ballad stanza, and from there to mediate Nietzsche's proposal: "a connection [that] would let each of us become freer and better than would be possible alone, that is, excelsior."

Mathilde Trampedach and the marriage proposal that passed through the poem she transcribed disappear from Nietzsche's life, erased by the far greater personal catastrophe of his rejection by Lou Salome in 1882, the event that brings to a provisional close the aphoristic productions whose start had coincided with this earlier proposal. The motif "excelsior" and the pure impulse it encodes and makes visible, though, persists. The word labels aphorism 285 in the *Gay Science*, a text that begins—after the Latin title—with quotation marks, the distant paraphrase of Longfellow's series of admonitory and beseeching voices. "'You will never again pray, never again adore, never again recline into infinite confidence,—you deny yourself any halt before an ultimate wisdom, ultimate good, ultimate power, where you unharness your thoughts. . . . There is no avenger for you any more nor any final improver; there is no longer any reason in what happens, no love in what will happen to you; no resting place is open any longer to your heart." Renunciation, as in Longfellow, positions the revolutionary break with the past. "Man of renunciation [*Mensch der Entsagung*], all this you wish to renounce? Who will give you the strength [*Kraft*] for that? No one yet has had this strength!" Excelsior! The aphorism responds to this challenge with an image and a hypothesis. "There is a lake that one day failed to flow away and raised a dam where heretofore it flowed away: since then this lake has risen ever higher. Perhaps this very renunciation will also lend us the strength needed to bear such renunciation; perhaps a human being will rise ever higher when he ceases to *flow away* into a God" (*KSA*, 3:527–28; *GSc*, 229–30). Here the mere call for progress upward has become a self-reinforcing dynamic of restriction and increase. Renunciation begets the possibility of its overcoming: The lake rises behind an opponent of its own making. Not a confirming star from above but this self-sustaining constellation of force and its impediment produces the inexorable climb. What in the proposal of marriage had been the belief "that a connection would let each of us become freer and better than would be possible alone, that is, excelsior," has shifted into this self-referential antagonism.

This counterimpulse changes its valence but continues to attend the call for ascent because, without an authorizing origin or legitimizing telos, the riven impulse of excelsior can appear only against an intrinsic antagonism that registers its course. Where the dam appears in the aphorism, in the *Rede* or discourse of Zarathustra "On the Vision and the Riddle" early in the third book, the ascent is opposed and enabled by the Spirit of Gravity.

> Not long ago I walked gloomily through the deadly pallor of dusk—gloomy and hard, with lips pressed together. Not only one sun had set for me. // A path that ascended defiantly through stones, malicious, lonely, not cheered by herb or shrub—a mountain path crunched under the defiance of my foot. . . . [M]y foot forced its way upward. // Upward:—despite the spirit that drew it downward toward the abyss, the spirit of gravity, my devil and archenemy. // Upward:—although he sat on me, half dwarf, half mole, lame, making lame, dripping lead into my ear, leaden thoughts into my brain. (*KSA*, 4:198; *TSZ*, 156)

Zarathustra, himself the very impulse Excelsior designates, can and must oppose the countervailing Spirit of Gravity implacably. But for Nietzsche and for his readers, these two remain inextricable, conditioning one another beyond any confirmatory instance, any stellar blessing or revolutionary initiative that would decide between them.

This wizened spirit of surrender and failure whose hostile presence makes the most radical thinking possible reappears in a different guise in Benjamin's reflections. The aphorism that closes his autobiographical *Berlin Childhood around 1900*, "The Little Hunchback," recalls a motif from his formative years. Childhood glimpses through sidewalk gratings into the privacy of subterranean domiciles, glimpses of "a canary, a lamp, or a basement dweller," though fascinating to him, would provoke in young Benjamin disquieting dreams in which "looks, coming from just such cellar holes . . . froze me in my tracks. Looks flung by gnomes in pointed hats." The inhuman oneiric observers inverted the asymmetry of the boy's daylight voyeurism and embodied a return glance whose very absence was what made the glimpses into the human context of alien lives so compelling. These embodiments of absent gazes, unattended occurrences, unnoticed events outside the presence of awareness coalesce in Benjamin's memory into the figure of the "little hunchback" from *Des Knaben*

Wunderhorn, the early collection of German folk poems. The absurd nursery rhyme tells of a "little hunchback" who has always already intervened destructively in the quotidian activities of the speaker. "When I go down to my cellar stores / To draw a little wine, / I find a little hunchback there / Has snatched away my stein." For Benjamin the little hunchback personifies the lacunae in intentional existence, the contingencies, accidents, and discrepancies intruding into comprehensible history and exacting "the half-part of forgetfulness from each thing to which I turned." Only in dreams or at the margins of childhood existence can the little hunchback be discerned, for he is in principle a figure of distraction, an emissary from what in superhuman reality evades human awareness. "Whoever is looked at by this little man pays no attention. Either to himself or to the little man. He stands dazed before a heap of fragments" (*GS*, 7:430; *SW*, 3:385).

That the little hunchback knows something of Zarathustra's Spirit of Gravity is apparent in the fact that he resides upon the same landscape as the Förster-House: "It was 'riffraff.' Those night revelers Needle and Pin, who set upon Little Cock and Little Hen atop Nut Mountain . . . were the same ilk" (*GS*, 7:429–30; *SW*, 3:384–85). In his most idiosyncratic and personal moments of reflection, Benjamin touches, behind all its gaudy reception and pompous advocacy, the immortal strangeness of Nietzsche's passion. It is not difficult to document the influence Friedrich Nietzsche exerted on Walter Benjamin, and to demonstrate that this influence has been neglected by the contemporary speculation that perpetuates their thought into the future. But such a documentation and demonstration does justice to what is at stake in their relation only when it exposes itself to this dimension of their thought at which each becomes the other's other, the enabling antagonist who makes it possible for them to leave tradition behind and pass on to us glimpses, however fleeting, into the obscurity of our common future.

CHAPTER ONE

Mortal Youth

> The You is older than the I; the You has been sanctified, but not yet the I: thus man pushes himself toward his neighbor.
> —FRIEDRICH NIETZSCHE, *Thus Spoke Zarathustra*, "On Love of One's Neighbor"

A YOUTHFUL FACIES

Taking, for reasons that will prove to be not wholly arbitrary, 8 August 1914 as a *terminus ad quem* for the juvenilia in Benjamin's oeuvre, we face a heterogeneous body of material. Some twenty essays, a few primitive verses, the first pages of a novella, ninety-one letters, several travel diaries, scattered fragments on philosophical topics, a book review, a curriculum vitae. Only one piece is an academic assignment: a discussion of Grillparzer's "Sappho" written in connection with Benjamin's *Abitur*.[1] The two distinctive features that make a task instructional in this academic sense—inconsequence and standardization—are in fact what these texts ceaselessly denounce explicitly and by self-conscious example. The juvenilia resist and exceed, and are but indirectly beholden to the pedagogic context at their origin. Beyond the general vehemence of its extracurricular self-assertion, the assortment of prose and verse surviving from Benjamin's childhood exhibits no unified self-reflective relation to the extant genre categories in the culture: The orations do not render their author a politician, or the literary polemics a critic, or the abstract speculations a philosopher, or the verses a poet. This variety testifies both to remarkable expressive energy and profound formal ambivalence in the young Benjamin. The juvenilia are not the production of a dilettante at home in a plurality of fields but the traces of an unstable site of articulation.

Yet in another sense this instability—reconceived as pure receptivity and renamed "Youth"—is the very ideal these writings advocate.

Beyond their formal diversity the texts all participate in one way or another in Benjamin's antebellum Youth Culture Movement activism, and indeed their intrinsic coherence as a discrete phase in Benjamin's oeuvre rests in the strange reflexivity their proximity to this committed social engagement imposes on them. In the name of an exemplary youthfulness, these writings would like to promote juvenilia themselves to the status of an autonomous and equally legitimate cultural expression.[2] The desire is self-defeating. If an assertion betrays by its expressive insecurity its immature origin, it forfeits, with all juvenilia, mature authority. But juvenilia disappear in a different way if they achieve a fully adult poise, for they are then no longer juvenilia but simply a precocious adulthood. In either case, the normative reaction to youthful texts that sorts them into authoritative precocity or preliminary and nonbinding juvenilia itself remains securely situated on the adult side of that reflective divide. But just this situation is the ultimate target of Benjamin's quixotic intervention in the Youth Culture Movement. It is the perspective that produces the condescending term "juvenilia" that young Benjamin aspires to combat; but it is from the very ground that that perspective makes visible that he intends to combat it. He does this precisely by reactively challenging the normative precedence of adult reactions. That a specifically juvenile reactivity discriminates among cultural forces in an equally valid if wholly distinct manner is Benjamin's contention throughout these writings.

It is this paradoxical self-assertion that constitutes what Benjamin's editor Rolf Tiedemann could concede in 1991 was the "still in many respects puzzling physiognomy of the young Benjamin" (GS, 7:536), the obscure facies at the origin of his thought. That obscurity is not just historical but formal: The self-contradictory impulse traversing the juvenilia renders the youthful facies an impossible object.[3] As a bedrock of motifs that will continue throughout Benjamin's career, its contours define a foundational level for his thought; it is the autochthonous premise of his perseverant signature. As an immature physiognomy, its expression fails to transcend its local environment; it is the isolated particularity his entry into mature thought will entirely overcome. Interpretation hence must acknowledge the resulting fragility of these preliminary conceptualizations. But these texts are also the place in Benjamin's oeuvre where explicit references to Nietzsche most densely cluster. In Benjamin's early essay "Sleeping Beauty," for instance, he emphasizes what he takes to be correspondences between his contemporaries and the "youth-life [*Jugendleben*] of greats individuals: of a Schiller, a Goethe, a Nietzsche" (*EW*, 26; *GS*, 2:9). "I believe also that we have already had prophets: Tolstoy, Nietzsche, Strindberg," his avatar asserts in the "Dialogue on the Religiosity of the Present" (*EW*, 79; *GS*, 2:34). In the "Life of Students," the pantheon includes Plato, Spinoza, Nietzsche, and the Romantics (*SW*, 1:43; *GS*, 2:82).

But if, in one sense, these mentions would seem to make the philosopher a visible influence on the young Benjamin, in another and truer sense, they mark specific opacities in the eventual relation between the two writers. By their very nature such invocations of Nietzsche rest on extant investments in his iconic status, and where the name itself is a sufficient talisman, an engagement with the thinker cannot be said to occur. In "Sleeping Beauty," it is the meaning of the pleonastic neologism "youth-life" at issue, not the meaning of Goethe, Schiller, or Nietzsche. To this illustrative purpose authors and the characters they have fashioned can both contribute with equal facility; Schiller and Goethe represent youth because Karl Moor and Tasso represent youth. Nietzsche's name can appear in the mixed company of novelists, philosophers, dramatists, and poets less because his particular writings defy categorization than because these writings do not specifically intrude into the vague prestige he shares with these figures. Where Benjamin makes reference to individual Nietzschean doctrines, it is only in the most general terms: "We who want to be, with Nietzsche, aristocratic, different, true, beautiful" (*EW*, 104; *GS*, 2:45); "Our Gymnasium should refer to Nietzsche and his treatise *On the Advantage and Disadvantage of History*" (*EW*, 96; *GS*, 2:40). Because young Benjamin deploys cultural icons in this illustrative manner, where Nietzsche's name appears in these early writings is precisely where a uniquely Benjaminian engagement with the thinker is marshaled and simultaneously obscured.

For in the history beneath these stereotypical appeals, an engagement was taking place, even if the juvenilia are not autonomous enough to express it to us directly. It could hardly have been otherwise. By 1910 Nietzsche's repercussions had been spreading through Wilhelminian culture for more than twenty years, borne by the deliberate promotion of Elisabeth's Nietzsche Archive, by the contentious interpretations of his thought appearing in books, pamphlets, and the press, by the reactions of novelists, musicians, and other artists, and by the irrepressible ferocity of his texts themselves. This explosive response to Nietzsche's writings in the years before 1914 had not yet, however, produced a dominant interpretation of the thinker. Under Elisabeth's direction, the archive was never able to consolidate an authoritative scholarly image of Nietzsche upon a philologically secure textual foundation. Elisabeth subordinated the philological responsibility of the archive not, it must be stated, to a particular political agenda (though her political opinions were nationalist and authoritarian),[4] but to what she took to be its promotional responsibility to disseminate a respectable version of her brother's image as widely as possible. And in this effort, drawing on her experience both of Cosima Wagner's Bayreuth propaganda and her husband Bernd Förster's utopian colonialist recruitment, she had been impressively successful. As Steven Aschheim has clearly described, Nietzsche's challenge was appropriated by figures across the social scene, by anarchists and reactionaries, feminists and anti-Semites, by Zionists, youth groups, avant-garde reformers, and revolutionaries of all persuasions.[5] No significant cultural or artistic movement in the German-speaking world at this time was not to some extent contending with the relevance of Nietzsche's example for its situation, and more often than not quite vehemently, so that to survey Nietzsche's reception in these years is to discern the landscape of Wilhelminian culture itself. Where do young Benjamin's invocations place him in the resulting cacophony of Nietzscheanistic exhortation and pronouncement with which he was confronted?

Closer to home, the fact of Nietzsche's influence on the German youth movement is uncontroversial, but just how determinant he was remains a matter of debate. Thomas Herfurth finds "an affinity between the spirit of the Youth Movement and the doctrine of Zarathustra . . . because Nietzsche's philosophy in its essence is a philosophy of youth."[6] Christian Niemeyer's more historical approach leads him to a rather more skeptical conclusion, particularly with regard to the antebellum youth movement in which Benjamin participated. "The claim," Niemeyer writes, "that Nietzsche was the crucial prophet of the Youth Movement will continue to be insufficiently documented in the source material and moreover for logical as well as historical reasons must count as problematic."[7] And Hans-Georg Gadamer also remembers the youth movement and Nietzsche as an awkward pairing. "Access to 'Thus Spoke Zarathustra' was not easy in other respects as well," Gadamer recalled in 1984.

> There was the stylistic proximity to Wagner's music-drama and the overburdened mannerisms aping the Old and New Testaments, which

> repelled us from Nietzsche's "Zarathustra." The taste of the young generation I belonged to, not unlike today's taste, was quite distant from that stylistic epoch. It was the Youth Movement that determined our values, this protest against urban culture and bourgeois education, the escape into the woods with a guitar on one's back, long hikes, nighttime campfires—that was the climate of my generation.[8]

The scholarly examinations of Nietzsche's relation to the broader youth movement do demonstrate that many of the particular texts Benjamin mentions, most prominently *Zarathustra* and the second of the *Untimely Observations*, were widely cited at the time. (Unsurprisingly: Nietzsche's essay closes with a crescendo invoking "that youth of which I have spoken, . . . that first generation of fighters and dragon slayers" [*UO*, 164; *KSA*, 1:331].) But even in this localized context the name Friedrich Nietzsche evoked no consistent doctrine.

So there is no surprise but also small explanatory comfort in the fact that Benjamin's mentor at the time, the pedagogic reformer Gustav Wyneken,[9] also laid claim to a philosophical pedigree that included

> Kant, inasmuch as he relocated the Idea from the realm of theory into that of decision, Schopenhauer, inasmuch as he taught us the struggle of the intellect against the "will" and showed us our place in this struggle. And Nietzsche's fundamental demand, too, is no other [i.e. than Wyneken's own]: *be* the meaning of the earth; make its consequence turn out differently from what it would have otherwise.[10]

Even this most intimate influence throws little light into the obscurity of Benjamin's young Nietzscheanism. Wyneken's casual misquotation of Zarathustra (it is the superman, after all, and not the reader who is to be the meaning of the earth: "Let your will say: the superman *shall be* the meaning of the earth!" [*TSZ*, 13; *KSA*, 4:14]) is typical of Wyneken's blithe hermeneutic superficiality in matters philosophical. Whatever else Benjamin may have learned from him, such misprision he did not.

All of these examples of Nietzsche's prominence in Benjamin's cultural milieu no doubt help explain why the young intellectual was drawn to Nietzsche's writings. But none of them can directly illuminate what it was he found there. To answer that, we must reconstruct Benjamin's own thought-world at the time and observe how Nietzsche's authority and rhetoric participate in and overcome it.[11] For the particular Nietzsche to whom Benjamin relates would never be simply provided to him by the extant culture, which is as much as to say that Benjamin took Nietzsche seriously from the start, read him, and pondered him in the context of his own most profound concerns, and reacted to his writing and his example in these terms. Out of Benjamin's engagement with the Nietzschean precedent emerges an image of the philosopher that can be introduced to the monumental expositions produced contemporaneously by Heidegger and Jaspers that have largely secured Nietzsche's philosophical status in the present. Benjamin illuminates a Nietzsche whose nimbleness, recklessness, and irreducibly political intentions challenge and deepen those contemporaries' existential and ontological appropriations of Nietzsche's explosive movement.[12] The traces of this explosion in the youthful facies are the enduring truth content of Benjamin's early encounters with Nietzsche, which remains subordinated in the juvenilia to their material content, to the perishing historical specificity within which this juvenilia arose and about which in the first instance they speak. Only by reviving that material content in an account of Benjamin's Youth Culture Movement commitments can the truth content, and Nietzsche's role in it, be liberated from that occasion.

The origins of Benjamin's student activism lie in his two-year attendance as a boy of fourteen and fifteen[13] at the rural educational institute Haubinda (*Landeserziehungsheim Haubinda*), where he first came in contact with the school reformer Gustav Wyneken and the alternative pedagogic practices he championed. The activism itself, however, arises only later, once Benjamin has returned to the more traditional Gymnasium in Berlin. Benjamin's youthful facies appears in an oppositional posture toward its immediate cultural situation, representing not nascent tendencies within his audience but an ideal realized elsewhere—in this case, Wickersdorf, the school Wyneken had founded after leaving Haubinda.[14] The oppositional posture transcended any localized allegiance to particular educational institutions, when, after taking his *Abitur* in 1912 from the Kaiser-Friedrich-Schule, Benjamin continued his studies at the Albert-Ludwigs-Universität in Freiburg. The intellectual atmosphere in Freiburg was dominated by the neo-Kantian philosopher Heinrich Rickert and the historian Friedrich Meinecke, and Benjamin attended lectures by both men. But his interests, though intensely intellectual, were situated outside of the lecture hall. He had soon become a prominent participant in the activism of the "Free Student Movement," an uncoordinated network of reform-minded groups poised against the traditional *Korporationen* or dueling fraternities of the German university system. Among the loose amalgamation of extracurricular reform organizations was a "chapter" established the year before in sympathy with Wyneken and his theories: the "Detachment for School Reform."[15] This was the framework for Benjamin's thinking and writing in Freiburg throughout 1912, and continued to inform his sympathies when he returned to Berlin and enrolled in the Friedrich-Wilhelms-Universität late in 1913. In the months before the outbreak of the First World War, Benjamin moved back and forth between these institutions, while consistently promoting Wyneken's extracurricular Wickersdorf ideal, becoming one of the most prominent student activists of his day.

In later years, Benjamin would disavow the intellectual vacuity of the antebellum youth movement debates, and his later friends and eventual biographers have tended to share that assessment. But a scornful attitude toward the substantive goals of youth movement organizations—toward their shrill commitments to abstinence, coeducation, or Zionism, not to mention the darker nationalistic and anti-Semitic tendencies metastasizing through them—was in fact central to Benjamin's peculiar activism at the time, so his later disavowal is less straightforward than it might at first seem. Benjamin's involvement in the "Detachment for School Reform" throughout his student years was unconditionally emphatic, but his understanding of "Youth," the ideal for which he campaigned, was vested in such a generalized antithetical attitude toward the mature society and its recognized culture that any practical consequences of his efforts were difficult to distinguish from disengagement. Important for Benjamin were not the specific pedagogic recommendations implied by Wyneken's theories, such as the prefect system or an emphasis on music education—recommendations that would in any case have had but little relevance to the university. What compelled the youthful facies was the confrontational attitude that Wyneken himself exemplified toward preexisting pedagogic frameworks. "This constantly vibrating feeling for the abstractness of pure spirit is what I call Youth," Benjamin wrote to his friend Carla Seligson in 1913. "For only then (if we don't want to become mere workers for a movement) when we keep our view clear to perceive spirit wherever it may be, will we become those who realize it. Almost everyone forgets that *they themselves* are the site where spirit realizes itself" (GB, 1:175). What Benjamin called "Youth" simply *was* this antithetical posture, logically prior to any objective issue that might occasion it, and so potentially conditioning any issue whatsoever. In lieu of a common object of concern that would define a movement externally, Benjamin's activism aspired to the mutual recognition of those sharing that "youthful" posture as the precondition of an unspecific cultural renewal. The practical result was not a policy or program but a *site* in which programs and policies could contend and transform: the *Sprechsaal*, or "discussion forum" he founded in Berlin.[16]

The Berlin *Sprechsaal* brought Benjamin together with his university friends Herbert Blumenthal (later Belmore), Christoph Friedrich Heinle, Franz Sachs, Carla Seligson, her sister Rika Seligson, and other idealistic young people. Participation in the *Sprechsaal* reflected not allegiance to a positive program but rejection of any orienting commitment to determined goals in the name of an unconditioned openness to transformative currents in the present. The radicality of this posture removed the forum from substantive collaboration with socialism, Zionism, or any other actual political movement. In their uncompromising insistence on the alterity of youth over against the adult society, Benjamin and his allies risked its total practical irrelevance in the name of its absolute transformative potential. One immediate consequence of this shift of emphasis is that the encomium "Youth" as deployed in these texts can apply heedless of mundane chronology to sympathetic cultural figures at any stage of life. Wyneken himself, most obviously, participated in "Youth" from beyond the confines of its literal significance. Unmoored from its self-evident embodiment in those whose winters are few, Benjaminian youthfulness respects other criteria and celebrates other qualities. But just what those qualities and criteria are could not—so Benjamin felt—be explicitly stated without acceding to the adult cultural terrain with which they were in existential conflict. The antithetical principle of youth rests in an irreducibly reactive moment that precludes its positive definition and by the same token exposes all of culture to its mediating agency. The effect of this exposure does not appear in the mediated culture directly but as the profundity of the transformation this youthful reaction occasions in an exemplary group participating in it.

What Benjamin would later recognize, and what would sever his mature thought irrevocably from this initial foray into cultural politics, was that a site from which such an unconditional critique of culture can be conducted never simply appears in the society as a specific condition, such as youth, or a specific locale, a *Sprechsaal*. Rather, such *topoi* are entirely unpredictable and tangential, "the most endangered, excoriated and ridiculed creations and thoughts embedded deeply in every present," as he would say in his eventual farewell to the Youth Culture Movement, "The Life of Students" (*GS*, 2:75; *SW*. 1:37). Far from being an autonomous venue in which an ideal receptivity could reinterpret its entire social and cultural inheritance, the actual *Sprechsaal* was conditioned by all the moral inexperience and class myopia that characterized its attendees, and hence was intellectually irredeemable; this Benjamin would later insist upon. But the dislocation in the present that the *Sprechsaal* attempted to literalize topographically, a passive non-self-identity antithetical to the communicable present, this problematic site of articulation inhabits Benjamin's theoretical signature until the end.

This, then, is the historical context from which the youthful facies derives its expressive pathos. Youth, as its mute ideal, orients its juvenile enthusiasm. That ideal is mute not only in fact, because Benjamin's conceptions have not yet developed sufficiently to overcome their historical matrix, but also in principle, because the ideal emerges only as the condition and never as the result of communication. Benjamin posits youth as a receptive posture anticipating an actively expressive spontaneity, and consequently he must resist conceiving it as the active communication of already expressed content anticipating a receptive acknowledgment. As a condition of expression, youth, whatever it may be, is a possibility within silence. Nietzsche, says Benjamin, is a partner in this silence, a herald of this possibility. As we begin to extract the traces of the Nietzschean impact at the origin of Benjamin's efforts, we must recognize in this silence not only the vacancy of an expressive limitation but the commitment to an expressionless ideal. Neither the context of the ideal nor the technical insufficiency in its indirect evocation survives the juvenilia, but its principled situation as the possibility of an alternative within silence between contracted muteness and the transcendentally expressionless: This situated silence will prove—like the primal plurality anticipated by the youthful—to be a consistent rift in Benjamin's mature thought. Here, an essential silence renders youthfulness ultimately demonstrative, and it is as a demonstration that we should consider Benjamin's central statement of this time, the "Metaphysics of Youth" from 1913. The title's genitive is subjective, not objective: It does not promise a metaphysical determination of the meaning of youth, stabilizing a categorical content. Rather, here Benjamin offers a demonstratively youthful engagement with metaphysical generality, embodying an ultimate attitude.[17]

In accordance with this demonstrative intention, our reading remains largely in the descriptive mode of paraphrase. The text itself demands as much, for in pursuit of its metaphysical intentions it aggressively abjures any traditional philosophical terminology. Rather, the "Metaphysics of Youth" expresses itself through a violent rearrangement of everyday vocabulary. The terms it vests with categorical dignity—"conversation," "daybook"—do not inherit this dignity from the philosophical tradition but have it emphatically claimed for them. None of this terminology will outlast the youthful facies, but as the epitome of the juvenilia, the "Metaphysics of Youth" plots in its own terminology their youthful topology. A paraphrase of the text thus promises to organize the juvenilia in as intrinsic a way as possible, as a vital prerequisite for discerning across it the encounter with Nietzsche.

The original manuscript of "Metaphysics of Youth" has long since disappeared. The text comes down to us in two separate transcriptions Gershom Scholem (who would become friends with Benjamin only in 1915) entered at some later point into two different notebooks. One of these contains the initial two sections with the headings "Conversation" and "Daybook," while the other preserves a fragmentary continuation, "The Ball." The philological license to assemble the two transcripts into a single text derives in part from the manuscripts themselves: The first concludes with a horizontal line and the suspended titles: "Night: The Ball/The Criminal" (GS, 2:920). At the same time, even the authority of this anticipatory subtitle does not in fact align "The Ball" neatly with the earlier text, since the continuation we have is missing the contrasting "Criminal" and the contextualizing "Night"[18] promised by the segue, so that even the explicit connections between the two manuscripts would hardly permit such a wholesale grafting if the "Metaphysics of Youth" itself were not loosely enough conceived to tolerate the manipulation. In his letters Benjamin referred to it as a "cycle," resisting closure in the very designation (GB, 1:241). By the same token we do less violence to the work than it might at first seem when we here ignore the continuation and orient our investigation of the juvenilia through the first transcript and its motifs of "*Gespräch*" and "*Tagebuch*" alone. It is in this transcript that the juvenilia is epitomized.

These headings gesture in the first instance toward irreducible plurality—a plurality of conversing interlocutors, a plurality of written daybook entries. The effort to accommodate the differently decentering implications of these irreducible pluralities strains the form and the rhetoric of the entire text, and its two sections contrast generically: "Conversation" is an eight-part aphoristic sequence; "Daybook" is in three numbered sections, but these are each longer and together more continuous. Nietzsche's relevance for the text is perhaps already visible at this generic level, but we should be careful not to beg our question. Neither Nietzsche's name nor any characteristic terms from his writings appear in the "Metaphysics of Youth." His presence is in one sense obvious but just as obviously diffuse, and it can only be pursued in textual detail at one remove, among the localized juvenilia that a preliminary paraphrase of Benjamin's "cycle" promises to illuminate.

"Conversation," the aphoristic sequence, begins with abstract reflections on the dialogic character of meaning, pivots around a stilted central dialogue between the Genius and the Whore, and concludes at the silent limit of language among Sappho and her lovers. The sequence deploys as its fundamental rhetorical strategy what we might call a prosopopoetic investment in nominalized gerunds. The eight aphorisms emerge through an invocation implicit in the active voice of the *Sprechenden, Schweigenden, Fragenden, Hörenden*; he who speaks, stays silent, questions, or hears. These are the functionalized agencies Benjamin invokes, but in terms of contradictory predicates that prevent the rhetorical force of their impassioned designations from settling into conceptual content, and instead deflect it back into these active postures themselves, as the paradoxical conditions of whoever may ultimately adopt them. "Daybook," by contrast, is sustained through three longer expositions, which display a more discursive character. Here Benjamin pursues on behalf of an urgent first-person plural "we" the proper characterization of the relation between an "I" and its "time." This attempt to articulate an elusive theory of antagonistic temporalities promotes into terminological dignity in turn the *Tagebuch* (daybook), *Strahl* (ray), *Abstand* (interval), *Landschaft* (landscape), *Geliebte* (beloved), *Feind* (enemy), and, finally, death, *den Tod*. In the end, the "Metaphysics of Youth" aims to demonstrate a correlation between the active agencies invoked by the aphorisms and these patient termini provoked by the exposition.

In both sections, truth is not constituted within the private self-relation of a continuous reflection, but emerges in the exposure to an alien awareness.[19] This exposure is straightforwardly at issue in the aphoristic sequence "Conversation." The second aphorism begins:

> Conversation strives toward silence and the listener is really the silent partner. The speaker receives meaning from him; the silent one is the unappropriated source of meaning [*der Schweigende ist die ungefaßte Quelle des Sinns*].... For the speaker speaks in order to let himself be converted [*sich bekehren zu lassen*]. He understands the listener in spite of his own words; that someone is across from him whose features are ineradicably earnest and good, whereas he, the speaker, blasphemes against language. (*SW*, 1:6; *GS*, 2:91)

The conversing address is not directed toward an empirical hearer but anticipates along a reversed vector an idealized receptive instance, epistemologically and ethically secure, whose response would manifest a moment ineradicably serious and good. The speaker registers this ideal in himself as his own potential conversion, and since conversion is nothing if not an ordinal division into a before and an after, the ordinary locus of expressive wholeness relative to an address—its origin in the simultaneous intention of a speaker—is thereby riven, and the wholeness implicit in the act of addressing displaced into the moment of reception. This divisive registration in effect overlies the active expression and passive apprehension inherent in a communicative address with its inversion, situating at the site of the listener an actively truthful effectiveness and ascribing to the speaker its passive apprehension, "in spite of his words," as potential conversion. Truth and expression are perfectly noncoincident in the occasion of the address. In the silent purity of her potential, the addressee transfigures the significance of the address in the same gesture with which she denounces its actual source.

The anticipated addressee is intrinsic to the address, but not to the speaker, who thus surrenders ultimate control of the address to this eccentric virtual reference point. Radicalized in this way, conversation no longer rests comfortably within the larger practical context surrounding linguistic behavior, but gestures toward an immanent dialogic inexhaustibility within meaning. Benjamin underscores the difference between this intrinsic dialogic dimension of language and a pragmatic or performative understanding of discourse in the label he chooses for the receptive counterpoint to exposure: "*Schweigen*," staying silent. The grammatically active verb *schweigen* denotes a manifest absence of activity. This tension between the grammatical and the semantic recommends the term in this context, for strictly speaking it is neither the consequent moment of an actual interlocutor's active reply that constitutes the address nor her prior moment of passive audition per se, but that exposure understood as the potential to respond, the indifferent limit between passivity and activity. This limit can be illuminated in the act of not acting, the statement within silence. The dynamics of this situation are far from the give-and-take of actual discursive exchange; the constitutive dialogic instability resides in the actuality of the address as such: Its inherent perfection (to concede to a paradoxical formulation) lies outside of and beyond it, in the addressee.

When the station of the cycle "Conversation" itself assumes dialogue form, in the fifth aphorism, the voices are labeled "Genius" [*das Genie*] and "Whore" [*die Dirne*].[20] The figure of the whore accompanies Benjamin out of the youthful facies and on throughout his career, and the exploitative realities of the institution gain ever more significance.[21] But here at the outset she is hierodulic, and the commercial aspect plays no role. It is the prostitute's pure passive receptivity, her reduction to the occasion of an alien desire, that makes her the unexpected counterpart to the genius. Hence the liminal presentation in this brief dialogue: Neither the moments of solicitation nor of copulation, nor of compensation, with their active and passive distribution of roles definitive of the prostituted encounter, are here staged, but in an interim between them a point of identification is encircled. The depicted relation between Genius and Whore is a kind of equivalence. Discussing the actual institution in a letter to his friend Blumenthal, Benjamin insists: "You ask still too shyly: 'Either all women are prostitutes [*Prostituierte*] or none?' No: 'Either all human beings [*Menschen*] are prostitutes or none.' Now, give whatever answer you like. I however say: we all are. Or ought to be. We ought to be object and thing before culture [*Ding und Sache vor der Kultur*]. Verily: if we want to reserve for ourselves some sort of private personal dignity, we will never understand the whore [*Dirne*]" (*GB*, 1:128). The ingenious anticipation of the pure potential addressee, unclouded by actual particularity, finds its reflection in the anonymous availability of the prostitute, unclouded by indigenous desire.[22]

Outside of some appealingly flirtatious passages among the letters, such overt eroticism as "Conversation" displays is rare in the juvenilia. And yet it reflects a permanently relevant aspect of the youthful facies, an aspect whose theoretical centrality appears in Benjamin's long fascination with Plato's *Symposium* and its celebratory disquisitions on love. This Platonic dialogue is in a naive way a model to which young Benjamin's *Sprechsaal* aspires. But far more consequentially, throughout his productive life the unifying disparity of erotic love remains the privileged medium of truth in Benjamin, if not the inevitable condition of its expression. The fundamentally erotic dimension of Benjamin's thinking extends into his most austere texts; "On the Concept of History," for instance, where the enviable happiness whose light coordinates the past with redemption can be discerned "only in the air we have breathed, among people we could have talked to, women who could have given themselves to us" (*SW*, 4:389; *GS*, 1:693). And at a less immediately visible but more far-reaching level, Benjamin's oeuvre is inherently structured by his great, if often wrenching and melancholy, love affairs—with Jula Cohn, with Asja Lacis, with Gretel Karplus in the years of exile. Here in "Conversation," the perfect addressee is gendered (as Sigried Weigel has rightly emphasized) in order to capture this more encompassing eros that animates Benjamin's theoretical engagement. Ideal receptivity is feminized, and the aphoristic sequence terminates the truthful dislocation implicit in the address at an image of Sappho and her lovers. Silenced in the first instance through the vagaries of a poetic tradition that has forgotten everything but their reputation, Sappho's poems manifest a more profound silence at the end of expression. As the telos of Benjamin's dialogical displacement, the amorous address between idealized feminine instances leaves language and its expectations entirely behind. In Sappho's absent verse truth disappears into a space as inaccessible as the gap between mutually reflecting empty mirrors.[23]

Convicted of actuality, the dialogic speaker himself is called to account, his exposure opened to judgment. "Silence is the internal frontier of conversation," Benjamin's third aphorism had begun. "The unproductive person never reaches the frontier; he regards his conversations as monologues. He exits the conversation in order to enter the daybook or the café" (*SW*, 1:7; *GS*, 2:92). From conversation to daybook, the transformation of the dialogic problem is here explicitly sequenced. The passage from *Gespräch* to *Tagebuch* appears initially as a loss and a retrenchment. Abandoned to the critical force of the addressee's potential but unable to achieve a productive relation to her dialogic necessity, the actual speaker has nothing with which to answer the potential addressee's skeptical silence: He becomes unproductivity. He registers the silence as mere absence and falls from conversation into monologue. The pure transparency of potential round the ideal addressee clouds; her intimacy recedes; and unproductivity must choose between two monologic forms: the solipsistic privacy of the daybook or the self-dramatizing soliloquy of the café.

Coffeehouse self-dramatization exhausts itself in the immediacy of its performance, but the *Tagebuch* proves to open onto an even more fundamental dialogic dimension than did *Gespräch*, which rescues it from solipsistic closure and justifies its elevation to section heading. The dialogic position of the ideal addressee is no longer imagined within an interpersonal matrix but emerges as a purely temporal displacement. The daybook projects a future self for which it preserves a past incarnation. The unproductive author of the daybook imports into his very signature the dialogic moment as a temporal disparity between the actuality he records and a potential future reception he may or may not perform.

> This believer writes his daybook. He writes it at intervals [*Abständen*] and will never complete it, because he will die. What is an interval in a daybook? It does not occur in developmental time [*der Zeit der Entwicklung*], for that has been abrogated [*aufgehoben*]. It does not occur in time at all, for time has sunk away [*ist versunken*]. Instead it is a book *by* time [*von der Zeit*]: daybook. (*GS,* 2:98; *SW,* 1:11)

With the collapse of the conversation, the self in its preliminary posture as believer and not-yet-knower enters itself for a future day in the daybook. In so doing it inadvertently surrenders expressive authority over the entry, which is externalized into time itself. The daybook exposes the self to the authority of the temporal exterior of its expression.

The plurality of entries over time that defines the self-relation called "daybook" provokes a self-awareness Benjamin calls "*Strahl*," the beam or ray. He positions this figure as a correlated contrast to the interiority of an epistemological *Ich*: "Not the murky inwardness of that experiencer [*Erlebenden*] who calls me 'I' and torments me with his confidences, but the ray of that other which appears to oppress me but which is also myself: ray of time [*Strahl der Zeit*]" (*SW,* 1:11; *GS,* 2:97). Two senses of the word ray, the abstract directionality of a mathematical vector and the phenomenal illumination of a beam of light, are here subtly opposed in the same term. As the correlate to the interior temporality of the experiencing I, the ray emerges abstractly—as the figure for intentionality—at the position of the subject. But as the alternative to the tormenting confidences registered

Mortal Youth 31

in the daybook entries themselves, the ray shines from the intervals between those entries, from the vacant *Abstände* in the objective daybook conditioning the sequential displacements that each entry incidentally expresses. The interval between diary entries corresponds to an imperceptible displacement not in the self but around it across things as such. The daybook imbricates expression and temporality as inscription, but instead of understanding this as the preservation of positive content through time for a later awareness in a self-identical "I," Benjamin identifies a ray of potential awareness that would emerge from the intervals that pluralize that content into entries and so will exceed the "I" that they discretely preserve.

The site of this temporal relation between what disturbs the object and what exceeds the subject—a relation that contrasts with anything that might occur within the Cartesian theater—cannot be either the I or the daybook entries themselves. By the same token, the interval is not the space between the subject and its object, but a discrepancy within things themselves that undermines that traditional epistemological relation and decenters the subject that reigns there. "These books [that is, daybooks], then, are concerned with the accession to the throne of an abdicating self" (*SW*, 1:14; *GS*, 2:101). The relation between the ray and the interval in the daybook manifests an alternative to the "nature" idealist abstractions of subject and object circumscribe. This uncircumscribed alternative domain between ray and interval Benjamin dubs *Landschaft*: the landscape.

The landscape of discrepancy is the true historical dimension, where something superior to oneself can emerge. "Landscape conceives [*empfängt*] for us in the nakedness of futurity [*Nacktheit der Zukünftigkeit*] the greats [*die Größen*]. Exposed, the landscape responds to the shudder of temporality with which we storm it" (*SW*, 1:13; *GS*, 2:99). To the extent that it presents an alternative to the temporal self-relation of isolated individual subjectivity, the illumination of the ray from the intervals in the daybook conditions a collective expectation that here charges onto the landscape of potential superiority. And it is not as one of the promised greats but rather as an embodiment of that potential "we" of temporality to which the greats respond that the beloved, *die Geliebte*, appears. "The plunging nakedness which overwhelms us in the landscape is counterbalanced by the naked beloved" (*SW*, 1:13; *GS*, 2:100). She holds the promise of a collective realization of the ray across the unforgiving landscape of potential greatness. This promising pairing of the temporally fractured first-person confronts, however, an antithetical counterpart inhabiting the intervals in the daybook: the enemy.

> He is no less a manifestation of time than we are, but he is also the most powerful reflector of ourselves. Dazzling us with the knowledge of love and the vision of distant lands, he returns, bursting in on us, inciting our immortality to ever more distant missions.... We are always putting our immortality at risk and losing it. Our enemy knows this; he is the courageous, indefatigable conscience that spurs us on. (*SW*, 1:14; *GS*, 2:101)

The second section closes upon this configuration of the landscape, with an amorous alliance on the one hand confronting on the other an antithetical but not entirely antagonistic potential, an inimical displaced manifestation of the temporal I at work in the intervals that illuminate the landscape. It is this terminological juncture, the ambiguous appearance of the beloved and the enemy, that identifies the eventual site in the youthful facies where Nietzsche's Zarathustra will emerge.

But in the "Metaphysics of Youth" the possibility of that encounter is precluded by the comprehensive Death at which the daybook arrives. This Death, which dominates the third section, remains singular in its relation to the signature endorsing the work as a whole. And indeed, this is the neotenous premise of the "Metaphysics of Youth" and of the juvenilia per se: that youth does not contrast with maturity but with annihilation. It is this equation that makes "*Jugendleben*" (*EW*, 26; *GS*, 2:9) pleonastic. But when the daybook installs death as the paradigm of the interval, subsuming within it lover and enemy, Benjamin is drawn into a subtle complicity with that annihilation and the potentials it reveals.

> In death we befall ourselves; our deadness [*Tot-sein*] releases itself [*löst sich*] from things. And the time of death is our own. Redeemed [*erlöst*], we become aware of the fulfillment of the game; the time of death was the time of our daybook; death was the last interval, the first loving enemy, death which bears us with all greatness and the fates [*Schicksalen*] of our broad surfaces [*unserer breiten Fläche*] into the unnameable centerpoint of times [*die unnennbare Mitte der Zeiten*].... For immortality can be found only in dying [*im Sterben*], and time lifts up at the end of time. (*SW*, 1:15–16; *GS*, 2:103)[24]

This fatal imbrication of true awareness and death is what separates the youthful facies from the propaganda of the juvenilia. Beneath the emphatic hortatory commitment to youth in these writings lies a silent ambivalence, a sympathetic tension between youth and its opposite, which emerges beneath the swagger of these last lines. The word "*Tod*" marks the terminus of the juvenilia, but the edge of the youthful facies is defined not by language's posturing attraction to an abstract "death" it might mention and control but by the terrifying, silent alternative between survival and surrender, the suicidal promise whose threat provokes all the subtleties of indirection in Benjamin's mature presentation.

"The Metaphysics of Youth" thus does not address Nietzsche directly but prepares through its speculative terminology a place for Nietzsche as interlocutor in the heart of the youthful facies. Before the suicidal closure of death, the enemy in his inverted alliance with the beloved holds open a dialogic rift in meaning. After the real suicide of his friend and ally Christoph Heinle, the event that terminates the youthful facies and precipitates Benjamin's mature emergence in the essays on Dostoevsky and Hölderlin, in the speech "The Life of Students," his posture toward the morbid exterior inverts from passive acquiescence to implacable resistance, and the potential marked by the polarity of the enemy and the beloved reemerges beyond annihilation to condition Benjamin's resistance to the end. Across this dire inversion in the mortal authority of his signature Benjamin carries the force of Friedrich Nietzsche.

THE FRIEND

The name "Nietzsche" dots Benjamin's juvenile essays, but the most developed discussion of the philosopher in the youthful facies occurs in the correspondence that survives from this time. There we can see something more tenuous than the invocations in the juvenilia but at the same time more relevant to a reconstruction of their encounter: the contours of Benjamin's own reading experience at an exemplary moment. The passages that interest us here occur among the five letters Benjamin wrote between September 1912 and February 1913 to a new Freiburg acquaintance, Ludwig Strauß. Even before their definitive publication in 1995 these letters were attracting considerable interpretive attention, for in Strauß Benjamin was addressing an enthusiastic acolyte of Martin Buber's call for Jewish renewal,[25] which he understood as a personal commitment to a Zionist ideal. The letters provide a fascinating glimpse into young Benjamin's relation during his Youth Culture Movement period to that alternative political and theoretical tendency. As such they also promise an authoritative confession of Benjamin's early relation to his own Judaism, almost three years before he would meet Gerhard Scholem. Here, in these youthful missives—which "with regard to Zionism have a programmatic significance for me" (*GB*, 1:74)—Benjamin attempts to orient himself in the public milieu of his day.

Strauß's introductory letter has not been preserved, but Benjamin's response began from the promise of collaboration on a periodical, a "journal for Jewish Intellectual Life in the German language" (*GB*, 1:61). Thus Benjamin's first letter anticipated consensus and attempted to characterize his own Youth Culture Movement activism in terms broad enough to accommodate Strauß's Zionist allegiances. Whatever their political differences, both Strauß and Benjamin were committed "men of letters"—"*Literaten*"—and in this common cultural devotion to what transcends the practical they each exhibit the reactive unreservedness that Benjamin identifies with youth. Because youth as Benjamin understands it is a pure committed posture distinct from all adult doctrines, it communicates with Zionism only inasmuch as Zionism, too, can exemplify an unreserved commitment among the young. Youth encounters Zionism as a reactive posture prior to any practical involvement with its projects for political settlement. Where these two postures overlap, Benjamin discerns something he calls "Culture-Zionism," "that sees the Jewish values *everywhere* and works for them" (*GB*, 1:72). This deterritorialized Zionism is as close as Benjamin is able to come to Strauß's engaged perspective, but perhaps that is enough to found a journalistic alliance.

In fact the possibility of this collaboration was illusory, for the mere sincerity of a personal commitment abstracted from any concrete enterprise it might realize—and this is all, at this point, youth is for Benjamin—cannot accommodate the demands of an actual project such as Zionism. Benjamin seems to have thought initially that the concrete site of a collective journal would be enough to mediate these incompatible idealisms of youth and of Zion on the basis merely of the unconditional nature of the commitments they respectively occasion. But it soon became obvious to him that collaboration with Strauß would involve a decisive endorsement of localized Zionist goals that interfered with the unrestricted reactive scope of Benjamin's attitudinal Culture-Zionism, and the promise of cooperation faded. Benjamin's third letter to Strauß attempts to justify this disengagement, and it is here that the discussion of Nietzsche occurs. In resisting any alternate commitments that would mitigate his unconditional youthfulness, Benjamin invokes Nietzsche's authority. But then, returning to *Thus Spoke Zarathustra* at the close of the letter, he distances himself from Nietzsche's thought.

Between these two attempts to stabilize his own expression around Nietzsche's signed texts (if we respect for the moment the terms and aspirations of the youthful facies), an address to Nietzsche is implied, an address whose truth dislodges from Benjamin's explicit contentions and resides as a potential reply from the Nietzschean instance. This reply would not simply be a response to Benjamin's interpretation in its youthful insufficiency. In its pure potential Nietzsche's reply, initiated here, persists as the correlate to Benjamin's own persistent engagement with his predecessor throughout the tumultuous years of his mature career. Attending to this reply is, in a sense, the inquiry before us. What we are concerned with at this point, merely, but crucially nonetheless, is the tenor of that first address and the rubric governing it. For it is a rubric of singular relevance to Benjamin's example: the friend.

Where it is a question of preserving intellectual autonomy in the face of competing commitments, Benjamin gestures toward Zarathustra's "Nachtlied": "Everything Jewish that goes beyond what is self-evidently Jewish in me [*das selbstverständlich Jüdische in mir*] is dangerous to me," Benjamin writes. "An Idea rationalizes, makes life a good deal colder and purifies the instincts. There's a danger in this that is expressed quite beautifully in the 'Night-Song' of Zarathustra. I am not able to take up a second rationalizing, shaping Idea" (*GB*, 1:76). The "Night-Song," an elegiac interlude at the center of the second part of *Thus Spoke Zarathustra*, is Zarathustra's invisible lament beside the babbling night brook over the isolation his enlightening mission is imposing upon him. "Many suns revolve in the void: to all that is dark they speak with their light—to me they are silent. / Oh this is the enmity of the light against what shines: merciless it moves in its orbit. / Unjust in its heart against all that shines, cold against suns—thus moves every sun" (*TSZ*, 106–7; *KSA*, 4:137). Benjamin responds to the heroic isolation of the passage, in which he hopes to glimpse a dangerous analogy to his own exclusive commitment to the idea of youth. Because Benjamin in 1912 understands himself to be exclusively committed to the Wickersdorf idea, participation in other political movements, such as Zionism, is ultimately impossible for him.

In Benjamin's mature writing we find an echo of this Nietzschean lyric. When working out the implications of his theory of language in 1920, Benjamin returns to the astronomical image.

> Every essential being is a sun and relates to its equals in the same sphere, as suns in fact relate to one another. This also applies in the realm of philosophy, which is the only realm in which the truth becomes manifest, namely in a tone like music. And this is the harmonic concept of truth, which we must acquire so that the false quality of watertightness that characterizes its deceptive image vanishes from the authentic concept, the concept of truth. The truth is not watertight. Much that we expect to find in it slips through the net. (SW, 1:272; GS, 6:23)

In this mature passage, as we might expect, Benjamin plumbs far deeper into the Nietzschean precedent than he had in his letter to Strauß. The mutual exteriority implicit in the plurality of suns here hosts a radically alternative concept of truth, one available only intermittently at the very edge of thought. This concept of a porous and harmonic truth challenges the holistic orientation of the metaphysical tradition at a level much closer to the skeptical extremity that provokes in Zarathustra the "Night-Song." By the second book of his descent, Zarathustra's loneliness results not from any encompassing intellectual commitment but emerges precisely from his uniquely positive acceptance of the disappearance "in the void" of any external ideal worth committing to. In 1912, though young Benjamin is wrestling with his historical position in a deeply personal way, in relation to Wyneken and the Wickersdorf movement he is no isolated sun but an orbiting satellite: "My thinking starts always from my first teacher Wyneken, and always returns there again," he would write a few months later to Carla Seligson (GB, 1:108).

The invocation of Nietzsche's text remains fragile in the letter, but that at least in part is due to its proximity to the reading experience from which it derives. Benjamin is not demonstrating through a casual reference an achieved literacy but applying a text he had himself recently encountered or reencountered. A page or two later he unexpectedly returns to Nietzsche and reflects on that experience. "In recent weeks I've been reading in Zarathustra," he writes.

> As a complete work of art it cannot hold a candle to "Prometheus and Epimetheus," but it strives more powerfully for the Idea. The greatness [*das Größe*] of the book goes without saying—but it is boundlessly dangerous [*grenzenlos gefährlich*]; I mean that not in

> the banal sense that Nietzsche's tone might overwhelm the mediocre; rather it is boundlessly dangerous there where Nietzsche himself remains caught in a sublimated [*vergeistigten*] philistinism. Everywhere in the biological and most insidiously and perniciously in the concept of shame. He takes it to be something quite valuable, even sacred. And yet shame is utterly natural, it denotes precisely the site where the spiritual recoils from the natural. (*GB*, 1:78)

The comparison with Carl Spitteler, whom Wyneken held in higher regard than Goethe, indicates more than just Benjamin's allegiance to his master. Spitteler was a historical associate of Nietzsche's, corresponded with him and reviewed his work respectfully (though critically) as early as 1886.[26] Spitteler's long allegorical epics, which would earn him the Nobel Prize in 1919, were widely thought to resemble the rhetorical strategies of *Thus Spoke Zarathustra* and Nietzsche's poetry in particular. The comparison thus registers the historically accurate relevance of a specifically Swiss cultural setting from which Nietzsche speaks. And if the evaluation here asserted will not escape the youthful facies, Benjamin's sensitivity to the non-German national context within which Nietzsche's philosophy appears will only grow in significance for his mature reception of the philosopher.

Even here, though, the demotion of Nietzsche with respect to Spitteler is hardly straightforward. The aesthetic value derived from formal closure, the "complete work of art," is not synonymous but stands in tension with the strength of a work's relation to an ideal. And exceeding communicable form for the sake of a formless ideal is the template for young Benjamin's own commitment to what he calls youth. The greatness of Nietzsche's work stands beyond reach of formal justification because it partakes in the same emphatic receptivity whose pure embodiment as youth Benjamin understands himself to be promoting. Hence the danger Nietzsche represents is "boundless," not threatening from without but corrupting from within the relationship of the youthful to an infinite spiritual ideal. This danger Benjamin localizes in a reading of shame, one of the persistent motifs in *Thus Spoke Zarathustra*. As Benjamin reads him, Nietzsche endorses shame as revelatory posture, a trustworthy guide to the ideal. In so doing he betrays a broader endorsement of instinctive "natural" reactions that are in fact irreducibly historical and constricting.

At the interpretive level we can recognize a distortion and a simplification of the theme of shame, which is densely woven into Zarathustra's language, but which does not thereby become a unified phenomenon. From the start, when Zarathustra invokes the superman in terms of shame—"What is the ape to man? A laughingstock or a painful embarrassment [*schmerzliche Scham*]. And man shall be just that for the superman: a laughingstock or a painful embarrassment" (*TSZ*, 12; *KSA*, 4:14)—shame is positioned as a site of contention between antithetical orientations. For Zarathustra, there is a shame that is lacking in the human world, a shame his own discretion exemplifies. And yet there is also always a popular shame at work around him whose strictures Zarathustra defies. This ambivalence in the concept of shame opens within precisely the spontaneous reactivity Benjamin finds uniformly parlous. The "biological" simplification of Zarathustra's doctrines Benjamin proposes here will also not survive the youthful facies, but it nonetheless points to a specifically historical distance that Benjamin's mature reception of Nietzsche will consistently seek to maintain.

In its own immediate historical setting, Benjamin's critique of "social-biologists in the style of Nietzsche" (*GB*, 1:78) can be read as evidence of the contemporary cultural context informing Benjamin's early exposure to the philosopher. Benjamin appeals to Nietzsche's name and example to accommodate a specific cultural encounter. That encounter, as Anson Rabinbach has described convincingly,[27] was enabled by the stirring assertions in Martin Buber's seminal work *Drei Reden über das Judentum* from 1911. Buber's *Three Discourses* are Nietzschean in general format, with three impassioned exhortations recalling the three polemics composing Nietzsche's *Genealogy of Morals*, while invoking in their genre designation the "*Reden*" of Zarathustra's oracular communications. In their use of the "all-too-" prefix and such Zarathustrian phrases as the "stillest hour" in which the most momentous decisions are reached, the *Three Discourses on Judaism* exhibit a deep rhetorical affinity for Nietzsche's emphatic precedent. At the same time, Buber shifts the emphasis of Zarathustra's pronouncements when he invokes Nietzsche explicitly at the start of the last of his chapters, "The Renewal of Judaism." There, Nietzsche is presented as the "most tragic example" of the corrosive effect of contemporary cultural tendencies on the "superhuman confidence" (*übermenschliche Zuversicht*) in God's unconditional relevance that once sustained lives sufficiently heroic to renew, and not simply improve, something like Judaism. "And even the longing for a *new* heroic life was corrupted by these tendencies of the times; the most tragic example is probably that of a man in whom this longing was strong as in no other and who nonetheless could not wrest himself from the dogma of evolution: Friedrich Nietzsche."[28]

Nietzsche's consignment here to the ranks of nineteenth-century Darwinians anticipates Benjamin's rejection of a biological bias in Nietzsche's writing. But Buber's earlier, subtler transposition of the Nietzschean superman into a posture of "superhuman confidence," a displacement that makes room for the "consciousness of God" animating Buber's rhetoric, shows a far deeper affinity to Benjamin's eventual understanding of Nietzsche. That the meaning of the superman is not to be localized in any putative embodiment (whether ideal or historical) but recognized in the transformation of the human being that advocates this self-overreaching figure—this consequence of Buber's theological Nietzscheanism characterizes Benjamin's own engagement with Nietzsche as well. Beyond the youthful facies there is no "consciousness of God" in Benjamin that could instantiate the truth, but the "superhuman confidence" Buber uses Nietzsche to invoke remains in Benjamin poised toward the empty site where God would be. What Buber's presence behind Benjamin's reading experience reveals, in other words, is the messianic horizon against which Nietzsche appears to him.

Thus the encounter with Nietzsche that Benjamin's letter to Strauß preserves, for all the distancing and demurral, takes place at the very heart of the youthful facies, and inaugurates a relationship that will resonate with Benjamin's deepest intuitions and most consequential speculations. "No one has more need of a Zarathustra-mood—even an exaggerated one—than a mature and confident school-boy," Benjamin tells Strauß, qualifying his own reservations. And though he is claiming as a student to be beyond that need, the Zarathustra-mood and the suspicion of it traverse the breadth of the youthful facies. The posture of superhuman confidence that Nietzsche's rhetoric embodies will remain for Benjamin the defining problem his image raises. It is a posture related in fundamental ways to the poet's demythologized "courage" in Benjamin's discussion of Hölderlin, to the decisive refusal of fatal sacrifice by the "miraculous neighbor children" in his reading of Goethe's *Elective Affinities*, to the tragic hero's silent defiance of mythic judgment in the *Origin of German Trauerspiel*. The same posture is at work in Karl Kraus's lascivious attendance upon the *Dämon* in his campaign against the *Allmensch*, in the invincible concentration of Marcel Proust's *mémoire involuntaire*, and in the preternatural patience of Franz Kafka's nocturnal vigils over the origins of the Law.

Benjamin concludes his consideration here with a gesture that localizes his criticism of Nietzsche and invites further conversation: "Maybe sometime you could read the chapter 'On the Friend' in the first book; I mean in particular the passage on the sleeping friend," he suggests to Strauß: "it seems to me that he has misunderstood friendship there in as fundamental and dangerous a way as possible (inverted [*verkehrt*] it into what is most personal). Wyneken once said: Friendship is ethical comradeship of sentiment [*ethische Gesinnungsgenossenschaft*] and if that isn't the last true word on the subject, it is at least the first" (*GB*, 1:78–79). On the foundation of Wyneken's axiomatic counterauthority, Benjamin here develops his critique of Nietzsche's philistine naturalism in an idiosyncratic direction.

The Wyneken citation responds no doubt to the conclusion of Zarathustra's discourse on the friend: "There is comradeship [*Kameradschaft*]: let there be friendship!" (*TSZ*, 57; *KSA*, 4:73). Where Wyneken equates these two, Zarathustra's distinction subsumes under the former term any interpersonal relation that would maintain itself in opposition to enmity. "Friendship" in Zarathustra's sense by contrast labels a purely positional exposure to the other in which the friend and the enemy equally participate. "In a friend one should have one's best enemy" (*TSZ*, 56; *KSA*, 4:71). What this friendship excludes is any trace of the limiting asymmetries of slave or tyrant, where the mutual independence of partisan wills is neutralized, and what it thereby contrasts with is woman's discriminatory love, "blindness and injustice against everything she does not love" (*TSZ*, 57; *KSA*, 4:73). Zarathustra's friendship is thus a willed exposure beyond either pathetic affinity or mutual understanding, a self-overcoming equality sustained with respect to the friend outside of any transparent justification that would assimilate them.

This radicalized friendship thus endorses an unbridgeable interval between friends, a discrepancy that Zarathustra acknowledges with an inverted notion of "shame": "You wish to wear no garment before your friend? . . . / Yea, if you were gods, then might you be ashamed of your clothes! / You cannot groom yourself too beautifully for your friend: for you should be for him an arrow and a longing for the superman" (*TSZ*, 56; *KSA*, 4:72). It is in the context of this irreducible space of active self-display that Zarathustra turns to the sleeping friend as the passive antipode to that self-display. "Have you ever seen your friend asleep—to discover how he looks?" Zarathustra asks. "What more is the face of your friend? It is your own face in a rough and imperfect mirror. / Have you ever seen your friend asleep? Were you not shocked that your friend looks like that? O my friend, man is something that must be overcome." (*TSZ*, 56–57; *KSA*, 4:72). A failure of recognition and self-recognition in the face of the passive friend provokes Zarathustra in turn to address the reader as friend in a renewed commitment to superhuman self-overcoming. This transformation of friendship at its limit into self-overcoming is what Benjamin reads as Nietzsche's retreat into the personal. Friendship for Benjamin must not lose contact with the communitarian dimension in which its ideals are realized. By deflecting friendship back into a purely self-referential challenge, Nietzsche elides its exemplary role for the larger society as a demonstration of youth in collective reactive transparency.

Benjamin thus rests his criticism of Nietzsche on an insistence that a wholly external, reactive perspective has an irreducible relevance to the reciprocity inherent in friendship. Only from this external perspective does that reciprocity exhibit a broadly Kantian ideal of ethical transparency. In the juvenilia the relevant perspective is an antithetical contemporary adult world the example of youthful friendship challenges and potentially renews. The recursion of Zarathustra's reader into his own alienation dissolves the potential for a sympathetic external recognition that is, in the last analysis, what is at stake in friendship for young Benjamin. In Zarathustra's discourse, the sleeping friend does not awake, because, though they share a structural reference to an antagonistic instance, Nietzsche's *Kameradenschaft*, with its masculine institutional and leisured connotations, is not Wyneken's *Genossenschaft*, the personal solidarity behind effective political alliances. It is in effect a certain militancy that Benjamin misses in Zarathustra's discourse on the friend, the "ethical comradeship of sentiment" that renders friends, however radically defined, irreducibly allies.

It is not our place to take issue with the youthful facies, whose positions we are merely delineating and analyzing. Yet we can, in closing, note a consequence of Benjamin's approach to *Thus Spoke Zarathustra* here. Benjamin localizes friendship with respect to its larger setting, and this localization as a principle consolidates Zarathustra's vision of friendship around Nietzsche's historical intention. For young Benjamin the misunderstanding of friendship is Nietzsche's, and only incidentally Zarathustra's. But conflating Nietzsche and Zarathustra blunts the rhetorical sting of the remarks on the sleeping friend, the sudden apostrophe "O my friend" in Zarathustra's response to the misrecognition. A relation, friendship, that until this point has been treated abstractly or hypothetically and as a relation between human beings, is now asserted to hold between the reader and Zarathustra himself. "O my friend, man is something that must be overcome." This realignment of friendship to characterize the relation between the reader and the figure of Zarathustra alters the exposure at stake in the relation. The reader in the act of reading is suddenly the sleeper. Exposure to Zarathustra *is* friendship in this hypertrophic sense and so stands outside any interpersonal relationship. "Alas behold your poverty, you men," Zarathustra concludes, "and your avaricious souls! As much as you give the friend, I will give even my enemy, and I shall not be any the poorer for it" (*TSZ,* 57; *KSA,* 4:73). Zarathustra speaks from a perspective radically exterior to all extant human alliances, a perspective obscured for the time being by the adult world Benjamin is eager to reform.

But if an older Benjamin will be far less prone to conflate the textual figure of Zarathustra and the historical author Nietzsche, and so far more sensitive to the unmitigated extremism of the book whose title is in effect Zarathustra's disembodied signature, this does not mean his reading here falls short of an achievable ideal. All of us as readers are asleep and not yet ready to be a friend the way Zarathustra is a friend. But the earlier apostrophe, falling almost in the center of the discourse, suggests that we may, perhaps, be ready to be friends with Zarathustra. Such a friendship would not be an easy one. The connection to Zarathustra would involve the entire scope of human experience: "Your dream should reveal to you what your friend does while awake" (*TSZ,* 57; *KSA,* 4:72). It would require discretion, a tolerance for frustration and ambiguity, an acknowledgment of inevitable misconstrual, a suspicion of sympathy. It would not culminate in a union but in providing Zarathustra with the "pure air and loneliness" (*TSZ,* 57; *KSA,* 4:72) in which he can free himself from any and all fetters.

This irreducible loneliness at the site of the perfect friend corresponds to the invisible night in which Zarathustra sings. For though he claims in the "Night-Song" to be light, and garlanded with light, an inexhaustibly centrifugal illumination beyond reach of any compensatory centripetal reflection, Zarathustra sits, irreducibly, in darkness. Indeed the Night-Song is unleashed as an audible declaration precisely by the hushed obscurity of the setting. "Night it is: now all burbling springs speak more loudly. And my soul too is a burbling spring" (*TSZ*, 105; *KSA*, 4:136). This darkness at the source of Zarathustra's song, like the loneliness of his friendship, does not let itself be securely circumscribed by Nietzsche's intention. It falls behind Zarathustra's light as the inaccessible condition for inspired expression. "Night it is," Zarathustra closes; "alas that I must be light! and a thirst for the nocturnal! And loneliness! / Night it is: now like a well my craving bursts from me,—a craving for speech [*Rede*]!" (*TSZ*, 107; *KSA*, 4:138). Thus speaks Zarathustra, but the inaccessible night in which he speaks is not Herr Nietzsche's historical interior but an unlocalizable fracture in human history the speeches simultaneously call for and register. Beneath the "little sparkling stars and glow-worms up above," it is this invisible Zarathustra who awaits, in friendship, the consequences of Benjamin's mature self-recognition.

CONVERSATION

A dialogic principle, articulated and epitomized in the first part of the "Metaphysics of Youth," is productive across the youthful facies. It emerges not only in the actual dialogues, such as the "Conversation on Love" and "The Rainbow," but the undelivered oration "Romanticism" or the essay "'Experience,'" with their interjected objections and rhetorical questions, display a marked affinity for dialogue form. And this dialogic tendency opens a passage between the correspondence and the public writings. In letters to Blumenthal, to Carla Seligson, Benjamin performs the self-exposure that his public rhetorical efforts on behalf of youthfulness are designed to license. But the programmatic correspondence with Strauß first seems to have encouraged him to adopt the form explicitly to present his own position, and between the first and second letters to his new acquaintance (those same weeks, that is, when he was reading in *Zarathustra*), he brought to completion the "Dialogue on the Religiosity of the Present" [*Dialog über die Religiosität der Gegenwart*], the first of his writings with a self-consciously philosophical scope.[29] "Perhaps you don't need to give me much more of an answer about Zionism.—I've written a dialogue on the religious sentiment of our time. Maybe you could let me know what you think of it," his second letter concludes (*GB*, 1:73).

"The Dialogue on the Religiosity of the Present," like all of Benjamin's experiments in theoretical dialogue, is not composed as an argument but as the complementary explication of an object of common concern. These conversations do not proceed through gestures of refutation but through mutual clarification between sympathetic but discrepant perspectives on something at the limit of expression, whether the unity of love in "Conversation on Love" or the epistemological medium of fantasy in "The Rainbow" or the "religiosity" here in this first attempt. The absence of eristic tension diffuses any consequential dialectic in these texts; they do not move toward unequivocal conclusion but toward a mutually enriched silence. The expository technique is mobilized in an attempt, as Benjamin says in the "Dialogue on the Religiosity of the Present," "not to see everything so peacefully and self-evidently anchored in the 'I' as it customarily appears to be" (*EW* 72; *GS*, 2:27).

A certain naive naturalism is not least of the charms of the "Dialogue on the Religiosity of the Present," which begins as an earnest debate between an "I" and a "Friend" on the topic of the purpose of art. The first-person already mitigates the relation of the text to the genre of philosophical dialogue, and in the conversation we hear the continuation and refinement of actual discussions for which Benjamin's Berlin *Sprechsaal* was designed. The echoes of those historical exchanges in their vanished forum animate and thereby mitigate the juvenile pomposity of the conversation Benjamin records. The Nietzschean tropes in the dialogue operate in a space between the "I" and the "Friend" that exemplifies in idealized form that antithetical locale from which youth addresses the adult world. The Nietzsche we hear in this discourse is as intimate with the youthful facies in its historical specificity as we will find in the juvenilia. In this text, uniquely in the juvenilia, Nietzsche's terminology engages directly with Benjamin's theoretical efforts, assisting at strategic junctures the first-person responses to the Friend's proposals that articulate Benjamin's elusive position with respect to his contemporary circumstances.

Agreeing that art in the present cannot be subordinated to any external purpose, the interlocutors are soon led to consider why it is that the enthusiastic advocacy of that purposelessness in the doctrine of *l'art pour l'art* has become a symptom of narrow-minded philisitinism. This is because, Benjamin's first-person avatar suggests, the experience of art today has lost touch with the "persistent interiority and the persistent goal of all striving," and it absolutizes art only by isolating it from the rest of human endeavor. The simultaneous interiority and goal unifying all human effort is the "religiosity" of the title, its nominalizing suffix withdrawing the term from any external doctrinal profile beyond the seriousness that manifests it. Religiosity is thus synonymous with an emphatic "feeling" (*EW*, 79; *GS*, 2:34), and the conduciveness of the present to this orienting sentiment is what is at stake in the discussion. Historical religions themselves, the ontological status of their various comforts and prods, are not.

It is in fact the general collapse in the Enlightenment of any affirmative religious dogma that could substantiate a reference to God that has precipitated the contemporary crisis in religiosity. In a passage with a strong Nietzschean flavor Benjamin's "I" diagnoses the present as the result of this collapse.

> For us, the old religions have exploded over the course of the last centuries. But I daresay this has not been so entirely without consequences that we can innocently rejoice in the enlightenment. A religion would formerly have bound together powers whose free working is to be feared. The religions of the past concealed in themselves need and misery. These things have now come to light. (*EW*, 64; *GS*, 2:18)

This is for Benjamin no call to a return to those blasted religious doctrines. The direction of history is irreversible. Rather, what Benjamin's avatar advocates is a "future religiosity" (*EW*, 72; *GS*, 2:26) appropriate to contemporary circumstances that can render those ungoverned forces humanly productive again. This irreducibly progressive orientation renders the present moment in history a necessarily discontinuous transit between the disenchanting past and an unprecedented renewal in the future. Religiosity, as the anticipation of that renewal, arises in the challenge of that historical discontinuity.

The term through which the discussion moves in its search for this "new religion" is "pantheism." As answer to the contemporary religious crisis the more optimistic "Friend" proposes a pantheistic enthusiasm for nature in its immanent wholeness.

> In pantheism we've found the common soul of all particulars, of all that has been isolated. We can renounce all sovereign divine ends because the world, the unity of the manifold, is the goal of goals [*Zweck der Zwecke*]. (*EW*, 66; *GS*, 2:20)

Pantheism as Benjamin understands it here has no positive doctrinal implications, but labels through the examples of Spinoza and Goethe an exalted intellectual relation to the immanent totality of comprehensible appearances. "One should neither laugh at nor weep over the world, but rather seek to understand [*begreifen*] it: pantheism culminates in this saying of Spinoza" (*EW*, 67; *GS*, 2:22). But the "I" responds with skeptical hesitation to the Friend's proposal. "The times are no longer those of Goethe," he cautions. "We've had Romanticism and we are indebted to its powerful insight into the night side of the natural. At bottom, the natural is not good; it's strange, dreadful, frightening, repugnant—crude" (*EW*, 68; *GS*, 2:22). An undifferentiated endorsement of the totality of things risks either disingenuously overlooking this night-side or failing to take it seriously. "I'm well aware," the "I" asserts,

> that it is precisely this that makes pantheism so immensely comforting: one feels equally cozy in hell and heaven, in pride and skepticism, in superhuman striving (*Übermenschentum*) and social humility. For, naturally, without a little unpathetic—in other words, painless—superhuman striving, it won't come off. (*EW*, 69; *GS*, 2:23)

These "skeptical" (*EW*, 69; *GS*, 2:24) reservations do not contest the necessity of a pantheistic exposure to the world in favor of a substantive divinity beyond it. To the extent that the absolute immanence of the pantheistic attitude accurately characterizes the post-Enlightenment religious situation of the present, Benjamin's "I" recognizes its inevitability. What he here calls into question is the earnestness of those currently advocating such a disenchanted orientation. Contemporary self-conscious pantheism purchases its open-mindedness by failing to take seriously the demonic peril and skeptical disorientation the romantic reaction to a humanistic Enlightenment has revealed. In place of that seriousness, as the posture correlated with a comfortable rejection of moral and epistemological transcendence, Benjamin finds *Übermenschentum*, "superhuman striving." The proximity of Goethe's pantheism will recall the scornful words of the Earth-Spirit to Faust: "Da bin ich!—Welch erbärmlich Grauen / Faßt Übermenschen dich!" ["Here I am!—What pitiful horror / Seizes you, superman!"][30] But in the distance imposed by the diminutive Benjamin has attached to the word—"supermanity" it might be rendered—and in the larger context insisting on contemporaneity, Nietzsche, or a current version of him, inhabits this epithet, as well.

With the familiarizing suffix Benjamin degrades the Faust-Nietzschean posture into an inauthentically painless pose. At the same time, by distorting the term this way Benjamin skirts a direct critique of Zarathustra's call and preserves the silent possibility of a genuine, suffering relation to the superhuman dimension of the world. The denunciatory sarcasm of the Earth-Spirit, not the summons by a still-limited figure of the pre-Mephistophelean Faust, echoes in

Zarathustra's actual invocation of the superhuman. That contemporary Fausts fall far short even of Goethe's awestruck magus does not mute the challenge of that sarcasm or undermine its basic congruence with a Nietzschean posture. Benjamin's implicit critique remains at the "banal" level he had described to Strauß: "that Nietzsche's tone might overwhelm the mediocre," but it does not reach the point at which Nietzsche himself is "boundlessly dangerous" (GB, 1:78). Indeed, this more fundamental reservation is entirely missing from the "Dialogue," which concludes with the optimistic pronouncement that "I believe also that we have already had our prophets: Tolstoy, Nietzsche, Strindberg" (EW, 79; GS, 2:34). In this prophetic role Nietzsche does not exemplify a facile pose of comfortable supermanity, but participates in the "honorable sobriety" (EW, 65; GS, 2:19) that characterizes the properly youthful.

Initially, Benjamin claims, it will be artists who exemplify this authentic alternative posture. In its indiscriminate emphasis on totality, pantheistic exposure is already allied with aesthetic immediacy, and its experience has deep affinities with moments of artistic exaltation. But artists do not exemplify authentic religiosity by communicating pantheism to the society directly; they are no less distorted than the distorted society in which they participate and which in a certain sense they epitomize. Not their insights but their motivations illuminate the truth. It is through their intransigent insistence on their own individual relevance despite the pantheistic reduction of all transcendent values to positive nature per se that artists indirectly demonstrate what is at stake in contemporary pantheism. They are occasions for the realization of the coming religion elsewhere, in the youthful collective that recognizes the full consequence of the artist's self-destructive wager. With an ancient metaphor, Benjamin likens them to the yeast in the dough. "But a leavening is necessary," the I insists, "a fermenting agent. As little as we wish to be literati [*Literaten*] in this last sense, so much the more are they, the literati, to be regarded as executors of the religious will" (EW, 74; GS, 2:29). The role of youth is not to *be* the isolated artists responding to the fundamental needs of the day but to *recognize* with unconditional emphasis what is collectively at stake in the artist's individual response: the universal religious need that animates his exceptional expression.

This dislocation of truth from direct congruence with expression is, as we have seen, native to Benjamin's theoretical posture. But at this early stage of his thought the presentational difficulties inherent in this position have not yet been resolved. How this youthful recognition *itself* could in turn be expressed—what sense of literati these voices *would* accede to—is a question that slips beyond the scope of the discussion and resides entirely in its form. The dialogue demonstrates this expectant attitude but cannot define it discursively. Hence the naturalism of the text, and its distance from philosophical dialogue as a genre, carries more expository weight than might at first appear. Benjamin's emphatic invocation of Ibsen at one point is a kind of lens flare that shows the ambiguous position of the text itself between its illuminating philosophical and dramatic precedents. "Take the dramas of Ibsen. In the background always the social problem—certainly. But what drives the action are the people who must orient their individual being to the new social order" (*EW*, 73; *GS*, 2:28).

Thus the position in which the "Dialogue" itself is situated, and from which it speaks, remains inconceivable in its own terms, stranded between dramatic expression and conceptual representation. All the more revealing is it, then, that at the heart of the conversation, directly after the discussion of Ibsen's naturalism, when a self-reflective relation to literary expression is closest, Benjamin sidesteps into *Zarathustra*.

> And here is to be found the deepest, truly the deepest abasement to which the modern individual, punished with the loss of social possibilities, must submit: in the veiling of individuality, of all that which is inwardly in motion and in ferment. I would speak to you now of what is most concrete: religion will take its rise at this juncture. It will once again emerge from what is enslaved. But the class [*Stand*] that today endures this necessary historical enslavement is the class of the literati [*Literaten*]. They want to be the honest ones, want to give shape to their artistic enthusiasm, their "love of the farthest" (to speak with Nietzsche), but society repudiates them; and they themselves, in pathological self-destructiveness, must root out in themselves everything all too human needed by one who lives. (*EW*, 73–74; *GS*, 2:28–29)

The references to Nietzsche serve less a clarifying than a stabilizing function here. The first reference is in quotation marks, preserving Nietzsche's signature. But already the second is not, and Benjamin, speaking about the "all too human" *Literaten*, himself slips into Nietzsche's language. Thus Nietzsche's rhetoric is situated as a bridge between the youthful voices of the I and Friend Benjamin stages in conversation, on the one hand, and the discontinuous perspective of the adult literati in their distorted integrity whose recognition those voices are charged with performing, on the other. In this context, Nietzsche's terms fill in to characterize in a "youthful" way what is taking place at that adult locale. Whatever individual project the genuine artist imagines he pursues, from the point of view of youth it is an abortive instance of Zarathustra's "love of the farthest," one that for lack of an appropriate response inverts into self-destructive antihumanism.

Zarathustra had preached "love of the farthest" as an antidote to Christian "love of the neighbor." This discourse follows shortly upon and picks up motifs from Zarathustra's discourse on the Friend. "I teach you not the neighbor, but the friend," Zarathustra says. "Let the future and the farthest be for you the cause of your today: in your friend you shall love the superman as your cause. / My brothers, love of the neighbor I do not teach you: I teach you love of the farthest. / Thus spoke Zarathustra" (*TSZ*, 61–62; *KSA*, 4:78–79). In picking up the term, Benjamin retains the essential displacement of reciprocal local recognition into a mutually autonomous alliance for the sake of something higher. Zarathustra speaks quite generally, but in the context of the "Dialogue on the Religiosity of the Present" it is clear that the true object of that "love of the farthest," and what justifies Benjamin's use of the formula, is youth. In "speaking with Nietzsche," Benjamin asserts a fundamental sympathy between the philosopher's articulation of the contemporary cultural challenge, and the youthful expectation prepared to mediate renewal. Contemporary adult culture may be marred by facile superhuman posturing, but to the extent an idealized artist were ever accurately to comprehend his role in social renewal, he would speak with the voice of Zarathustra.

HEINLE

If Nietzsche holds out the possibility of an eventual articulation of his position, the figure who embodies conversation as a metaphysical principle for young Benjamin is Christoph Friedrich Heinle. It is "the figure of my friend Fritz Heinle," Benjamin himself later asserted, writing about his time in the Youth Culture Movement, "around whom all the happenings in the *Sprechsaal* arrange themselves and with whom they vanish" (*SW*, 2:604; *GS*, 6:477). Heinle's role is more than just intimacy of a personal kind. What constitutes the youthful facies as a discrete moment in Benjamin's development is the fact that the dialogic exposure to culture his juvenilia advocates is *realized* in the *Sprechsaal* relationships. This is why Heinle, and not the juvenilia themselves, is at the center of the youthful facies. For Benjamin, the paradigm of such exemplary theoretical friendship—the paradigm of "youth"—is the friendship between these two young men. The "Dialogue on the Religiosity of the Present" takes place between an "I" and a "Friend," but we can generalize the significance: Throughout the youthful facies, conversation is conversation with Heinle.

Such an assertion is complicated by the silence of the actual friendship: No letters between Heinle and Benjamin have come down to us. The young man appears in faint third-person profile in Benjamin's correspondence with others. This accidental silence is compounded by Benjamin's own reluctance to generalize about this specific friendship. "I will not respond to Guttmann's assertion about my relationship to Heinle," Benjamin insists in his 1914 open letter to Wyneken, "since this relationship seems to me to be neither simple nor in any sense an appropriate object of discussion, and no one who has even the slightest conception of the connection between me and Heinle will feel any differently" (*GB*, 1:204). This coy relation to expression gains depth and contour from two passages where Benjamin himself attempts to treat of the friendship explicitly. Both depict the two young men at odds. The first account culminates in a kind of reconciliation, whereas the second emphasizes their differences. But both accounts insist that the heart of the matter leaves language behind.

To Carla Seligson in 1913 Benjamin described overcoming a dispute with Heinle in the following terms:

> We spoke about trivialities. All at once he said: "Actually I have a great deal I could say to you." I asked him to do so at once, since it was high time. And since it was really he who wanted to say something to me, I wanted to hear it and at his request approached him [*ging zu ihm hinauf*].
>
> First both of us tormented ourselves about what had happened and tried to explain and so on. But we felt very quickly what was at stake and said as much: that we would both find it very difficult to part [*trennen*]. But I noticed the most important aspect of the conversation: he knew exactly what he had done, or rather, here it was no longer a matter of "knowing," he perceived our opposition really as strongly and as necessarily as I had expected of him. He opposed himself to me in the name of love and I countered him on behalf of the symbol. You'll understand the simplicity and relational plenitude [*Einfachheit und Fülle der Beziehung*] both of these have for us. A moment arrived when we both admitted we had reached fate

[*Schicksal*]: we said to one another that each of us could have stood where the other was standing. (*GB*, 1:181)

As in the "Dialogue on the Religiosity of the Present," if through a different venue, we hear an echo here of the committed conversations the *Sprechsaal* was meant to exemplify to the adult world. The epistolary paraphrase reveals starkly the same trajectory out of language that the literary stylization had performed. From trivialities to explanations to a reciprocal recognition of the common sincerity informing their fatal difference, the argument with Heinle here ends not in consensus but in the mute display of a confrontation between irreconcilable perspectives. Love and symbol name the termini at which these perspectives lose all internal difference and so gain the maximum of external relatedness. This limit status is far more significant than any residual content these terms may have; a content that in any case belongs to the perishable particularity of the youthful facies.[31] As limits, love and symbol in their opposition manifest fate, and by recognizing the arbitrariness of this ultimate boundary, Benjamin and Heinle contest the fate they respectively embody.

The second account was written much later, in 1932, as part of his autobiographical *Berlin Chronicle*. Again, Benjamin records a disputatious conversation. And though the scene, and so perhaps the quarrel, is different, these specifics are effaced beneath Benjamin's abstraction. "I think here of an altercation between Heinle and myself on an evening at *Die Aktion*," he recalls.

> Originally only a speech by me entitled "Youth" had been on the agenda.... The upshot was an ugly quarrel into which, as always happens on such occasions, the whole existence of each participant was drawn.... So it happened that on that evening at *Die Aktion*, before an astonished but less-than-captivated audience, two speeches with the same title and almost exactly identical texts were delivered; and in truth the latitude within which that "Youth Movement" had to maneuver was no larger than the area bounded by the nuances of those speeches. (*SW*, 2:605–6; *GS*, 6:479)

The existential extremity of the commitment each boy displays has not changed between the accounts, though what they had earlier understood as the cosmic immensity of fate at that limit has from the adult perspective contracted into the fragility of a juvenile nuance. Even so, whether a fatal identity beyond the irreducible difference between "love" and "symbol," or a nuanced difference beneath the contested identity of "Youth" and "Youth," the antithetical meaning of the friendship slips away from any language that would determine and preserve it. The accidental silence to which history condemned young Heinle thus echoes the more profound silence at this limit. The catastrophic event that redefined the relation for Benjamin and that separates these accounts from each other, occurred within this deeper silence.

In the 1913 letter, Benjamin concludes: "Sometimes I thought that we, Heinle and I, understand each other better than anyone else we know. That's not right as it stands. But it's this: Despite that each of us is the other one, each must of necessity persist in his own spirit" (*GB*, 1:182). Benjamin's paradox might be expounded thus: Their friendship exhibits a kind of negative identity—each is the other one, and the other's other—inasmuch as each recognizes their common positive necessity to persevere in his own spirit. The absolute difference between them expresses their common exemplification of an utter intellectual integrity. For Benjamin's later account the willful solidarity among "this last true elite of bourgeois Berlin" (*SW*, 2:605; *GS*, 6:478) marks not an existential exposure but the historical condition that this form of thinking could not transcend. But in both cases, the uncommunicative silence of the youthful friendship is registered as *commutative*. A reversible equivalence between the young men, whether it manifests fatal integrity or class myopia, is the ultimate foundation of the living friendship.

This dialogic symmetry between the two activists is not troubled by Heinle's other vocation, as lyric poet. Benjamin appreciates Heinle's verse and admires his facility. "Then there's Heinle," he had reported back to Herbert Blumenthal from Freiburg when he met him, "a fine fellow. 'eats, drinks, and makes poems.' They're supposed to be very beautiful—I'm going to hear some of them soon" (*GB*, 1:88). He identifies strongly with Heinle's lyrical voice and would write shortly later, again to Blumenthal, defending his new friend against initial Berlin skepticism:

> In Berlin I'll show you some poems of Heinle's that may win you over. Down here we're rather more aggressive, more pathetic, more im-prudent (literally!) Or better: he is and I echo the feeling and am often that way too. (*GB*, 1:149)

If Benjamin depicts himself here echoing his more aggressive colleague, it is nonetheless clear that in their best moments, they would be indistinguishable.

A monument to the inaudible equivalence between Benjamin and Heinle has survived, a series of eight brief verses at the edge of doggerel that they wrote together: "Urwaldgeister," "Spirits of the Primal Forest." "In dem Nebenraum daneben / Hört man einen König leben—/ Auf der Bahre ruhn die Kind / Die im Wind gestorben sind." ["In the side room to one side / One can hear a monarch living—/ On the bier rest the kids / Who in the wind have passed away"] (*GS*, 2:862). Benjamin's editors, not implausibly, hear the mannerisms of van Hoddis behind these lines. But if van Hoddis's abrupt expressionist verse licenses this indulgence in obtrusively phonological association, "Spirits of the Primal Forest" does not deploy it to anything like his deeply alienating effect. With its jaunty motifs of children and monarchs, the collaboration produces not the pathos of expressionistic estrangement but an echo of childhood nursery rhymes: a language lingering near the scraps of playground lyric and fortuitous paronomasias that punctuate childhood's significant awareness. Even as poetic expression the friendship retreats from determinate statement.

Whatever significance lurked in this primal forest, whether "symbol" or "love," whether this "youth" or that, the fatal difference deposits these young men beyond the reach of language; it does not distribute them on each side of it, as artist and critic. That distribution only death could effect. This is why, despite all the childish versifying the young men engaged in, Benjamin can write in the *Berlin Chronicle*: "Fritz Heinle was a poet, and the only one of them whom I met not 'in real life' but in his work" (*SW*, 2:604; *GS*, 6:477). "In real life," Benjamin knew Heinle as a partner in vital youth movement activism, and the expressive rigor of poetry and its reception was entirely subordinated to that partnership. Only once this living context had been blasted by an intimate historical catastrophe would Heinle's poetic vocation emerge to transform him entirely into the fatal expressive nexus of his surviving lyric. For between the vehemence of the 1913 letter and the melancholy of the *Berlin Chronicle* falls the one ghastly lyric of Heinle's that did transfigure him, and with him all of expressive art, wrenching it from its living situation, and rendering it, finally, a message from the dead: "You will find us lying in the *Sprechsaal*" (*SW*, 2:605; *GS*, 6:478).

In the light of Benjamin's early efforts to characterize his elusive dialogic perspective, it is difficult to overestimate the effect of the double suicide of his friend Fritz Heinle and Carla Seligson's sister Rika in the *Sprechsaal* Benjamin had organized for their youthful gatherings. The catastrophe destroyed the embodiments of both the masculine and the feminine interlocutors, and obliterated the site of conversation. Whatever the biographical or psychological repercussions of this event might have been, the theoretical shock explodes the elements of the youthful facies and starts Benjamin's efforts on their mature trajectory. Such a fundamental peripety cannot be easily objectified. And indeed, adolescence soon disappears from Benjamin's writing. For all his interest in childhood, the mature Benjamin will tend to avoid the word *Jugend*, preferring when necessary to point ahead from the *Kind* toward the latent rumblings of incipient sexuality. Nor does the *Bildungsroman* as a genre occupy a prominent place in his literary critical imagination. Flaneurs and students, young men, perhaps, but irrevocably adult, share Benjamin's stage with children, the aged, craftsmen, shopkeepers, bourgeois patriarchs, revolutionaries, police, poets, and prostitutes.

The accounts Benjamin gives of this moment are ambiguous; challenges as much as explanations. In a "thought-image" from his 1927 book *One-Way Street*, he recalls beneath the title "SOUTERRAIN" a dream:

> We have long forgotten the ritual by which the house of our life was erected. But when it is under assault and enemy bombs are already taking their toll, what enervated, perverse antiquities do they not lay bare in the foundations! What things were interred and sacrificed amid magic incantations, what horrible cabinet of curiosities lies there below, where the deepest shafts are reserved for what is most commonplace? In a night of despair, I dreamed I was with my best friend from my schooldays (whom I had not seen for decades and had scarcely ever thought of at that time), tempestuously renewing our friendship and brotherhood. But when I awoke, it became clear that what despair had brought to light like a detonation was the corpse of that boy, who had been immured as a warning: that whoever one day lives here may in no respect resemble him. (*SW*, 1:445; *GS*, 4:86)

The identity of the gothic corpse Benjamin's despair unearths is not biographically stable but merges Heinle and Blumenthal. Blumenthal was Benjamin's earliest friend, but in 1917, shortly after Blumenthal had married Carla Seligson, Benjamin broke rancorously and finally with both of them, in a letter whose convoluted outrage overwhelms any factual specifics about the cause (*GB*, 1:368). But the ceremonial interment of the corpse inflects the dream figure with Heinle's features. The corpse of youth had been walled into the foundations of Benjamin's personality, the dream suggests, as a totem against its self-destructive fate. Historical despair reacquaints him with the suicidal temptation. The dream points to what is at stake in Benjamin's overcoming of his youthful allegiances. Suicide, which was eventually to corner Benjamin at the Spanish border, is the hidden alternative to mature writing.

The death so histrionically invoked in "Metaphysics of Youth" is thus resituated. No longer a boundary at the edge of collective life, it now permeates it. Conversation and daybook[32] enter into one another under the sign of the deathday. Not in dialectical synthesis but as continual subversion.[33] That the deathday would relate conversation and daybook in this conceptually recalcitrant way is to be expected, for a satisfactory conceptualization of the deathday would be nothing less than the answer to the mortal question. For now, the involvement of conversation and daybook in the deathday points not to a purely conceptual operation but to an expressive posture. A reader must be struck by how often the mature Benjamin will anchor his discussion of writers to their deathdays. Not only the Kafka essay "On the Tenth Recurrence of His Deathday," the essay on Hebel, the review "On the Return of Hofmannsthal's Deathday," but also the bibliography of Goethe research for the "Memorial Issue for Goethe's 100th Deathday" in 1931, and a planned book for this occasion that was in the end rejected by the publisher Anton Kippenberg. The collapse of this last project was the immediate provocation for Benjamin's morosely named "Daybook from the Seventh of August Nineteen-thirtyone to my Deathday," a diary that in the event records, over nine days, three conversations. By contrast, his oeuvre is almost bare of literary birthdays.[34]

The birthday celebration has a negative theological status, visible in its contrast with the name day. Coordinated with baptism, not birth, the name day has no complement, but lifts the infant through onomastic identity into an endless order of salvation. With the name day, a correspondence is established between this particular human animal and the transformed human saint, bathed in the glory of God, a relation of patronage that on the one hand dignifies the child by emphasizing those few aspects of its being that are already on the road to salvation, and on the other protects it from those many aspects of its being that are not. By contrast, the birthday celebrates the infant's entry into the natural order, those dying generations at their song, and is necessarily paired with its silent nemesis, through which we grin and chatter in ignorance each year, for the deathday, invisible, eventual, inevitable, has time and can wait. It is from the perspective of the deathday that life must render up its desiccated objectivity for Benjamin: "Seen from the point of view of death, life is the production of a corpse" (*OT*, 218; *GS*, 1:392). The vitalist strains that color all of his philosophic speculation are merely the shadow of this fundamental posture to his thinking: His mature philosophy is, should a label be needed, mortalism.

This omnipresence of mortality in Benjamin's philosophy is the condition of its initial realization as cultural criticism. Benjamin's thought positions the artwork, the expressive document, as the defining opportunity for philosophic reflection, for the apprehension of a truth that is in no way bounded a priori by the continuities of content the document preserves. This is why the initial privilege accorded to literary texts is able rapidly to expand across the entire documented cultural landscape as Benjamin's career progresses. The Benjaminian literary object is not a distinct domain of reflection but an occasion for the philosophical realization of a discontinuous significance in the death that intersects with it. This opening onto philosophic truth is not held within the boundaries of the work considered in isolation but arises in the radically exterior space between the work as artifact and its mortal author. The titles of Benjamin's critical efforts up until his dissertation always include the author's name with the title of the work under consideration: "Two Poems by Friedrich Hölderlin," " 'The Idiot' by Dostoevsky," "Shakespeare: As You Like it," "Molière: The Hypocondriac," "André Gide: La porte étroite," *Goethe's Elective Affinities*. A postscript to a letter to his publisher Weissbach in 1921 shows that this was by no means accidental.

> I suddenly was struck by a worry on account of the title of my Dostoevsky-critique in the "Argonauts." I can't quite remember what I actually titled it. *In any case Dostoevsky's name must appear in the title*. It would be best if it ran: Walter Benjamin / "The Idiot" by Dostoevsky. (*GB*, 2:193)

This insistence is anything but an intentional fallacy; not the writer's intention, but the text's mortal situation is indexed by these names, and if the notion of a "poetized" in the Hölderlin critique, gesturing toward precisely this interstitial space between author and title, proved too beholden to intention to survive in Benjamin's thought,[35] its surrender does not indicate a commitment to the autonomy of the artwork as aesthetic object, a rejection of that preposition linking Dostoevsky to his artifact, but a recognition of the profoundly destabilizing complexities that lie beneath that virgule separating the authored work from its critical mortification.

Because Benjamin's philosophy is a philosophy of death, it both provokes and precludes the simple question, What is death? Provokes it, in that death greets us at every turn in his thinking; precludes it, because death denotes the very space within which this thinking occurs. To reflect philosophically is to be mortal; to be, in a certain sense, dead. The objectifying, positing gesture of What is . . . ? collapses before the condition of the possibility of questioning at all. In this, the question, What is death? is analogous to the impossible question of the Kantian philosophy, What is truth?[36] It gestures inappropriately at the entire impetus of the effort. All of Benjamin's writing attempts to answer the mortal question, which neither submits to conceptual summary as would the question, What is beauty? nor dissolves into nonsense, as would the question, When is time? Death is neither meaningless nor meaningful but orients the possibility of such a distinction.

This role that death plays in Benjamin's thought is what, far more than any Hegelian influence, allows it to be characterized as dialectically speculative. Since at least Hegel, philosophy has recognized in death the condition of the possibility of speculative reflection, "the tremendous power of the negative; . . . the energy of thought." But if this common motif brings Benjamin into the tradition of speculative dialectics, it ought not to assimilate him into its Hegelian version. For in a fundamental way, in its relation to expression, Benjamin's thought is the reverse of Hegel's. "Death," Hegel famously writes, "if that is what we want to call this non-actuality, is of all things the most dreadful, and to hold fast what is dead requires the greatest strength."[37] The strange arbitrariness of this baptism, "if that is what we want to call this non-actuality," seems to subsume the word "death" in the general concept of the Negative. But what is the status of this designatory wish? Is death merely a metaphor for the power of the Negative? A particularly evocative example? Or is it the Negative in its concretion, and we really have no choice in the matter? Such designatory freedom comes only at the price of rendering death unreal, pure abstract nonactuality. The entire *Phenomenology of Spirit* can be read as unfolding in the ambivalence of this gesture, which shows language spanning the distance between the concretely transient and the abstractly permanent.[38] For Benjamin, death names the site from which such a living gesture is visible. To think death directly is to leave life behind, and the reflection that reaches death directly is not suspended in living thought but as act, enters death. The conjunction of death and reflection in Benjamin is not the "struggle of life and death" that produces the Hegelian self-consciousness, or the Being-toward-death that reveals Heideggerian *Dasein* in its authentic wholeness, or the murder that underscores the absolute alterity of Levinas's *Autrui* (to gloss some prominent mortal orientations). Rather, reflection for Benjamin finds its culminating moment in the irrevocable act of suicide.[39] Language, still tied to the living, cannot encompass that moment itself, and earns its pathos by resisting it in the only form that survives the death of its production: as inscription.

A posthumous fragment from 1920 underscores the mature Benjamin's idiosyncratic situation of death between suicide and inscription.

> The <u>individual</u> dies, that is, a dispersal occurs: the individual is an indivisible but unfinished unity, in the domain of the individual death is only a movement (wave-movement). Historical life perishes always at a particular place; but as a whole it is immortal. The apparently [scheinbar] <u>entire</u> (closed off) individual is irrelevant. This is the true meaning of metempsychosis.
>
> The <u>person</u> becomes a petrifact. Superannuated.
>
> Loyalty preserves only the person.
>
> The <u>human being</u> [Mensch] becomes free.
>
> The <u>living body</u> [Leib] perishes, explodes like a <u>manometer</u> that is detonated at the moment of highest tension and with the breaking apart of the connection becomes outmoded, superfluous. (GS, 6:71)

The fragment draws a distinction within life between historical immortality and individual death, which localizes historical life and reveals it as survival elsewhere. The discrepancy with respect to death between historical and individual life is the truth underlying the doctrine of the transmigration of souls. Viewed in this way, as the juncture between historical life-as-survival and particular, localized death, mortality fractures into three distinct aspects. What is mourned and remembered by loyal survivors Benjamin calls the person. (It is this to which in the philological context of our investigation we will be referring as the *signature*.) The organic substrate, the living body, disperses into anonymous history as nature. (It is Nietzsche's achievement to introduce this explosive dimension of death into his written remains.) And between these modes of survival, the essence of the human being, of the true reader and the true writer, is liberated. Toward that ultimate goal this study tends.

ABSTAND

In the first three months of 1872, under the auspices of Basel's Öffentliche Akademische Gesellschaft, Nietzsche delivered five public lectures, "On the Future of Our Educational Institutions." These lectures were held during the most visibly successful weeks in his mature life, between the publication on 2 January 1872 of *The Birth of Tragedy*, and the devastating polemic against it in late May by Ulrich von Wilamowitz-Moellendorff. The twenty-seven-year-old Nietzsche, now established in Basel, had just had the pleasure of turning down the offer of a professorship at Greifswald, and had had, so he claimed in a letter to his mother, to dissuade the Basler students from holding a torchlight parade in his honor (*SB*, 3:277). His friendship with Richard and love of Cosima Wagner were still vibrant and flattering to his self-esteem. In short, as he wrote to his good friend Erwin Rohde, "I've been living for a little while now in a great stream: almost every day brings with it something astonishing; and my goals and intentions are also rising" (*SB*, 3:279). In this flush of ebullience, the lectures on pedagogy were an effort to flex his cultural muscles outside of the immediate university context.

Benjamin's youth movement writings are strewn with echoes of these polemical lectures. Thus, to take but one example, the opening of Benjamin's essay "'Experience'": "In our struggle for responsibility, we fight against someone who is masked [*einem Maskierten*]. The mask of the adult is called 'experience'" (*SW*, 1:3; *GS*, 2:54), recalls Nietzsche's impassioned denunciation of German Gymnasien forty years earlier: "Here, namely, it seems to me, there is no hard wall protecting against the battering rams of an attack, but probably the most fatal tenaciousness and slipperiness of all principles. The attacker does not have a visible and solid opponent to crush: rather this opponent is masked [*maskirt*]" (*OFE*, 43; *KSA*, 1:674). In Benjamin's farewell to the youth movement, "The Life of Students," these echoes continue to resonate. "From the standpoint of aesthetic feeling, the most striking and painful aspect of the university is the mechanical reaction of the students as they listen to a lecture," Benjamin remarks there. "Only a genuinely academic and sophisticated culture of conversation could compensate for this level of receptivity" (*SW*, 1:42; *GS*, 2:81). And behind this lurks Nietzsche's notoriously disparaging description:

> One speaking mouth and very many ears with half as many writing hands—that is the external academic apparatus, that is the

educational machine of the university in action. Besides, the owner of this mouth is separated from the possessors of the many ears and independent; and they praise this double independence with high passion as "academic freedom." And more, the one can—in order to increase this freedom still further—roughly speak what he wants, the other roughly hear what he wants: only that behind both groups at a discreet distance stands the state, with a certain taut overseer's mien, in order to remind from time to time that it is the purpose, the goal, the be-all-and-end-all of this strange speaking-and-listening procedure. (*OFE*, 106-7; *KSA*, 1:739-40)

These echoes are not surprising. Benjamin knew Nietzsche's lectures. Preparing for his talk at the XIV. Freistudententag in Weimar, he writes to Blumenthal, "In Weimar I'm not going to give my talk as a ceremonial presentation [*Festrede*] but rather hold it during the conference, since people want to discuss it. For that also Fichte will be good [i.e., "Deduced Plan for a Higher Educational Institution to be Established in Berlin"] and Nietzsche will be good: on the Future of our educational institutions" (*GB*, 1:226). This talk of Benjamin's, which was based at least in part on the inaugural speech delivered when he assumed the chairmanship of the Berlin "Free Students," is the core of the later "The Life of Students."

"The Life of Students" names Nietzsche (*SW*, 143; *GS*, 2:82) and echoes him, and the influence of the lectures on Benjamin's criticism of the university institution is clear. Nietzsche's critique of contemporary educational life is expressed in terms of two cultural drives.

> It appeared to me that I must distinguish two main directions,—two apparently opposed streams, in their working equally ruinous, in their results finally flowing together, rule the present of our educational institutions: at once the drive after the highest possible *extension* and *broadening* of education, then the drive after the *decrease* and *weakening* of education itself. For various reasons, education is supposed to be carried into the widest circles—the one tendency longs for that. Against that the other expects of education itself that it give up its highest, noblest, and most elevating claims and resign itself to the service of some one or other form of life, of the state, for instance. (*OFE*, 36; *KSA*, 1:667)

Benjamin's analysis shares the second of these concerns, while leaving the first implicit. "There is a banal view of life that trades spirit [*Geist*] for various surrogates," he asserts, quite in the spirit of Nietzsche's criticism. "It has met with increasing success in disguising the hazards of a life of the mind [*geistigen Leben*] and hence in ridiculing the remnant of visionaries as fantasizers" (*SW*, 1:43; *GS*, 2:83).

Not research or instruction as practical activities but creative autonomy is the shared ideal. "Because 'science has no bearing on life,'" Benjamin maintains, "it must be the exclusive determinant of the lives of those who pursue it" (*SW*, 1:38; *GS*, 2:76). And for both, the paradigmatic danger to this autonomy is localized in the university's institutional relation to the state. "The legal constitution of the university—embodied in the minister of education, who is appointed by the sovereign, not by the university—is a barely veiled alliance of the academic authorities with the state over the heads of the students (and in rare, welcome instances, over the heads of the teachers as well)" (*SW*, 1:39; *GS*, 2:77).

Above all, the periodic invocation of the notion of courage, at every thematic transition of the talk, lends Benjamin's piece a certain stoic bravado, even machismo, alien to most of his other writings, one that sounds recognizably Nietzschean. "You are right in everything, only not in your lack of courage," Nietzsche's Philosopher had chided his pupil at the close of the first lecture, and again at the start of the second (*OFE*, 40, 42; *KSA*, 1:671, 3). And for Benjamin, the free student organizations have failed to renew the university, since "on fundamental questions the independent students do not display any more serious will, any higher courage than do the fraternities" (*SW*, 1:41; *GS*, 2:80). Discussing the degeneration of erotic life in the university, he concludes, "This mutilation of youth goes too deep to waste many words on it. Rather it should be entrusted to the minds of the thoughtful and the resoluteness of the courageous" (*SW*, 1:45; *GS*, 2:85). And having summarized his final perspective through the esoteric verses of Stefan George, Benjamin dismisses the student reform movement in the same terms. "A lack of courage has alienated the lives of students from insights like this. But every way of life, with its own specific rhythm, follows from the commandments that determine the lives of the creative" (*SW*, 1:46; *GS*, 2:87).

And yet, for all these resonances between the two texts, Benjamin's "The Life of Students" is far more resistant to than complicit with Nietzsche, and the courage Benjamin is praising has a structure far different from the aggressive, activist call of Nietzsche's ancient Philosopher. "You are right in everything, only not in your lack of courage. I will now say something to console you," Nietzsche's ideal had comforted his errant disciple.

> How long do you believe that those educational gestures in the
> schools of the present that are weighing upon you so heavily will

likely last? I shall not withhold from you my belief about that: its time is over, its days are numbered. The first who dares to be completely honest in this area will hear the echoes of his honesty from a thousand courageous souls. (*OFE,* 42; *KSA,* 1:673)

Such encouragement is foreign to "The Life of Students." Courage cannot expect to meet with an enthusiastic chorus of sympathizers. "The elements of the ultimate condition do not manifest themselves as formless progressive tendencies, but are deeply embedded in every present in the form of the most endangered, excoriated, and ridiculed creations and thoughts," Benjamin had insisted at the outset of his talk. "The historical task is to disclose this immanent state of perfection and make it absolute, to make it visible and dominant in the present" (*SW,* 1:37; *GS,* 2:75). Held between an explicitly eschatological endpoint and a contested present, these formulations have left any shared past behind. One last time the wings of youthful abstraction lift Benjamin from the isolating threat of the particular: "This condition cannot be captured in terms of the pragmatic description of particulars (the history of institutions, customs, and so on); in fact it eludes them. Rather, the task is to grasp its metaphysical structure, as with the messianic Kingdom or the idea of the French Revolution" (*SW,* 1:37; *GS,* 2:75).

Lifted from historical concreteness, the end-state of history surrenders any motivational content, and Benjamin can mark it with a shrug—two exhausted Romantic tropes, take your pick. For he has already reversed his perspective on life and submitted to a nihilistic leveling of the communicative present in the light of the deathday. Schlegel's French Revolution and Schelling's messianic kingdom are stand-ins for a transformation the essay cannot express but only perform. For the scorned and despised elements his discussion would redeem are the reformers themselves in their failed assault on Wilhelminian society. The historical task is not to adjust this denigrating evaluation, rehabilitate these elements, rally the youth movement, but precisely by submitting to that judgment implacably and leaving the youth movement, to manifest the ideal for which it fought and lost. This resolute recognition of the youth movement's failure is Benjamin's notion of courage: "Such a description is neither a call to arms nor a manifesto; each of these is as futile as the other. But it casts light on the crisis that hitherto has lain buried in the nature of things. This crisis will lead on to the resolution that will overwhelm the craven-hearted and to which the courageous will submit" (*SW,*

Mortal Youth

1:37; *GS*, 2:75). Courage lies not in actively transcending the present for the sake of the future but in resolutely submitting to a scorned dispersal within the jeopardized present. "Since he has been transposed into the middle of life," Benjamin will soon write of Hölderlin's "Poet," "nothing awaits him but motionless existence, complete passivity, which is the essence of the courageous man—nothing except to surrender himself wholly to relationship" (*SW*, 1:34; *GS*, 2:125). Benjamin's *Dichtermut*, poetic courage, would be, from an activist Nietzschean perspective, *Blödigkeit*, timidity.

This strangely passive declension of an intentional notion of courage informs the most striking rhetorical gesture in Benjamin's text. This is the introduction into his talk of a long citation from his earlier address upon assuming the chairmanship of the Berlin "Free Students." In the course of renouncing the active free student movement, Benjamin resorts to formulations from the apex of his involvement with it. "Because it throws a particularly sharp light on their chaotic conception of scientific life, it is necessary to criticize the ideas of the independent-student organizations and those close to them, and this shall be carried out with words from a speech the writer gave to students when he thought he could affect their renewal" (*SW*, 1:39; *GS*, 2:77). Benjamin does not denounce the naïveté of his earlier commitments; the change in authorial attitude is not reflected by any diminution in the necessity of his critique. And indeed, at the close of the citation, he is able to segue into his current perspective without any complementary concluding marker. At the same time, the explicit distancing mitigates his unconditional endorsement of the words he repeats, and they cannot be read simply as unsurpassable formulations still happily available to a unifying signature.

For the passage Benjamin repeats concerns precisely the emphatic unity behind the signature: "There is a very simple and reliable criterion by which to test the spiritual value of a community," he had said then.

> It is to ask: Does it allow the totality of an individual's efforts to be expressed? Is the whole human being committed to it and indispensable to it? . . . Everyone who achieves strives for totality, and the value of his achievement lies in that totality—that is, in the fact that the whole, undivided essence of a human being finds expression. (*SW*, 1:39; *GS*, 2:77)

The actual failure of the free student movement consists in its inability to realize a community conducive to this active expression of personal totality. "The totality of will [*des Wollenden*] could find no expression, because in that community its will could not be directed toward the totality" (*SW*, 1:41; *GS*, 2:79). This expressive ideal can be articulated only in terms that implicate the speaker in the community he addresses; where that individual totality exceeds or escapes this community, it must fall from expression into muteness. Thus in order to indicate the critical expressive ideal, Benjamin must return to expressions produced while he still held that hope for the community he addresses. But by marking them as specifically anachronistic, he preserves a space in his expression that registers that loss of hope and invokes the courage of a far greater, if far more tenuous hope. By distancing himself from these earlier expressions, Benjamin in effect expands the force of their critique. Their original condition of possibility was a belief in the potential reversibility of these actual deficiencies. But from his present perspective, even this potential redemption of student life is no longer possible. The bifurcated site of articulation registers the deathday. It resituates the essay in relation to its audience and submits it to a different sort of authority, one arising in the gap, the *Abstand*, that measures this anachronism as the space of his own particular withdrawal from the shared presumptions that articulate it.

This intrinsic distancing within the essay cannot be recuperated in a concluding summation that could be passed along as content. Beneath the institutional criticisms that structure Benjamin's text, this disruption disturbs the signature that would fix them into a paraphrasable communication. The lacuna within the signature provides the occasion within which a concrete meaning can emerge from beyond Benjamin's intention. Benjamin's true courage arises in the silent hope for this second, exterior meaning. Thus the penultimate sentence of "The Life of Students" is a gesture of surrender to the specificity of each individual reader or hearer: "Everyone will discover his own imperatives, the commandments that will make the supreme demands on his life." At the same time, Benjamin's text does not deposit its hearers into the absolute solipsisms of their singular histories. Rather, the talk closes with a schematic formulation that gestures toward the common history in which these tasks unfold: "Through understanding, he will succeed in liberating the future [*das Künftige*] from its deformed existence in the present [*im Gegenwärtigen*]" (*SW*, 1:46; *GS*, 2:87). Here, the singular pronoun, *he*, and the singular nouns, *the future* and *the present*, refer to two contrasting sorts of singularities: the pronoun the individual and the nouns the universal; the former the intensive privacy resistant to all trespass, and the latter the extensive publicity unchallenged by any rival. The task is to bridge these different individualities, to render the universal in the localized specificity of the singular. The potential for that abridgment is the "deformed" shape in which the future inhabits the present. An example of that distortion sits before him in the hall. Only by registering the collapse of their ideals in the derogatory adjective attached to their visible manifestation can Benjamin himself hope to vindicate those ideals. But elsewhere, for a different life.

Thus the strange interplay of singular and plural in the title of his oration. Neither Student Life nor Students' Lives, "The Life of Students" projects a vital principle across the plurality of students, outside of any defining institutional embodiment but merely on the paradoxical strength of their acknowledgment of the impossibility of realizing their defining ideals in their common present. Speaking from his own specific place among them, Benjamin posits a life of students that resolves into "student lives" encountering that living present. Benjamin's own claim to the legitimate epithet "student" depends on the manifestation in his signature of this split between student lives potential and actual, a claim that rests not on knowledge but displays a desperate courage, for the boundary of the actual is individual death, and the act of locating an aura of potential outside of the actual would be to cross into death, thereby identifying those potentials for others left behind. The physical passage into exemplary death would preclude a student life in the absolute sense, since the true student is but the shadow of the ideals his death casts onto life. The isolated student life cannot realize these potentials in either the practical or the psychological sense. They are available only to his survivors, who would, in their own lives and against their own deaths, manifest them again. Student lives are lives punctuated by this mortal manifestation, which inscribes an eschatology into their actual present in terms alien to its immediate reality. The collective end-state refracts into every instant as the condemnatory testimony of vanished ideals sustained in the names of their vanished proponents. What had earlier appeared as formless progressive tendencies, that is, collectively recognizable potentials only needing to be lent actuality, are transformed by this renunciation into the diaspora of a hermetic testimony, scattered into life as the possibility of its recognition, the possibility of its revivification as the condition of another moment of mortal specificity, another student life. The quotation marks identifying the citation in the text are not magical time machines able to return us all to the instant of the citation's emergence. They, like the text they identify and the text that contains them, are in the present. They mark a more radical space in that present, between that lost life of students and the current performance they frame. By implicitly insisting on the presence of the present, Benjamin expands it into a volatile temporal structure, where ideals situated in an absolute future are revealed at death as messages from the past. The discontinuous life of students thus expands forward and backward out of the actual present, destabilizing it in a whirl of unrealized potentials that pass through it from contested past to redeemed future.

As a gesture, and as open to interpretation as a gesture must be, "The Life of Students" marks a space within Benjamin's signature that is no longer absorbed into his living intention. Nor any other intention. For if it is here, in the constitutive *Abstand* of the daybook that Nietzsche finds an entrance into Benjamin's mature production, it is not an exclusive door, meant only for him. Rather, as the radical surrender to alien interpretive effort, the *Abstand* exposes the thinking of both Benjamin and Nietzsche to a space uncontrolled by any signature; where sanity is pushed into madness or life is pushed into death. It is the night within their constellation.

CHAPTER TWO

Presentation

The rest is silence.
—SHAKESPEARE, *Hamlet*

PHILOLOGY

Exposed by Zarathustra to the origin of Heinle's ultimately suicidal stance, the Nietzsche of the youthful facies explodes into Benjamin's mature writing with the full force of catastrophe. As youth's displaced prophet, Nietzsche had exemplified a superhuman confidence of expression whose genuine manifestation in the present Benjamin took to be a condition of contemporary cultural renewal. At the same time, Nietzsche's writings themselves remained fraught with dangers, advocating a naturalism and an individualism that could derail the militancy of youth and serving as the original for a vacant and self-aggrandizing pose within adult culture. As Benjamin reoriented and deepened his thought in the wake of the destruction of the *Sprechsaal*, his relation to this tension in Nietzsche's image also realigned. No longer wedded to a visible ideal of youth, the genuine example at the origin of Nietzsche's efforts recedes from the surface of Benjamin's text; gone are the enthusiastic invocations of the philosopher as a public representative, however unspecific, of his own positions. Nor does Benjamin adopt recognizably Nietzschean terminology when working out his theoretical insights. These insights are couched in Benjamin's own antidogmatic theological terms, concepts that owe far more to Hermann Cohen, Kierkegaard, and Hölderlin than to Nietzsche directly.

In one sense, what enters into Benjamin's relation with Nietzsche at the threshold of maturity is nothing less than history. For Benjamin as a mature thinker, the difference between the living and the dead can no longer so easily be effaced beneath an appeal to a vital ideal that identifies them, hence Nietzsche's posthumous status cannot be ignored out of enthusiasm for his putative role in the present. He now speaks to Benjamin inevitably out of the nineteenth century, and this irrevocable distance will inform all Benjamin's interpretive reactions to his writings. Thus Nietzsche as a historical corpus is exposed to the full profundity of Benjamin's theoretical reflections in a variety of otherwise unrelated contexts that all attempt to conceptualize the historical movement of culture. Nietzsche's death (with its prologue in madness) particularizes him in the historical circumstances he eccentrically encountered and locates the origin of a testimonial dimension essential to his oeuvre. The irreducible dislocation implicit in testimony is one aspect of the "*Fernenbestimmtheit*," the pathos of distances that Benjamin attributes to Nietzsche in the "Psychophysical Problem." "Nietzsche's life is typical for someone who is determined by distances as such [*bloßen Fernenbestimmtheit*]; it is the fate [*Verhängnis*] of the highest among complete human beings [*den fertigen Menschen*]" (*SW*, 1:400; *GS*, 6:87). "Verhängnis der fertigen Menschen": Curse of the finished as much as destiny of the perfect; the irreducibility of this testimonial distance precludes the simple notions of acceptance or rejection of Nietzsche's doctrines, which present themselves to Benjamin always simultaneously as testimonies to and as testaments of an alien condition.

Benjamin's relation to this idiosyncratic and individual Nietzsche emerges only through a comprehensive consideration of his own theoretical development. Indeed it is an index of that development, transforming with each fundamental transformation in Benjamin's thought. As such, the change in Nietzsche's significance at the end of the juvenilia is merely the first and perhaps most visible alteration in Benjamin's continuing relation to Nietzsche's precedent. The overtly prophetic Nietzsche disappears from Benjamin's writing to make way initially for a philological Nietzsche, and it is the radical philologist of *The Birth of Tragedy* who predominates in Benjamin's theoretical perspective in the decade following the war. This phase of Benjamin's career culminates in his treatise *The Origin of German Trauerspiel*, whose very title announces its ambition to rewrite and overcome Nietzsche's theory of tragedy.

The displacement in Benjamin's Nietzsche reception, beyond its characteristic features as an element of Benjamin's thought, is a version of the indispensable condition for any vital Nietzsche interpretation. The posthumous distance from the origin of Nietzsche's expression does not belong to Benjamin but continues to determine the possibility of a theoretical appropriation of the terms and doctrines Nietzsche's writings propound. It is as Thomas Mann would say in 1947: "Who takes Nietzsche at face value, takes him literally, who believes him, is lost."[1] Where belief involves imaginative identification, Nietzsche emerges beyond belief. At the same time, if in a different sense, attending to this necessary alienation is nothing other than "taking Nietzsche literally": "You say you believe in Zarathustra? But what matters Zarathustra? You are my believers: but what matter all believers?" (*TSZ*, 78; *KSA*, 4:101). The distance Benjamin's reception exemplifies is the condition for perceiving Nietzsche's writings in their own terms, that is, not as the discontinuous manifestations of an implicitly permanent system we are called upon to assess, a "philosophy"—perhaps a hypothetical magnum opus—to which we could eventually do more than provisionally attach his authorizing signature; such a view necessarily elides what is at stake in Nietzsche's experiment. These writings enforce a distance that permits their sequential apprehension as phases of a distinct historical trajectory, depositories of a process of continual conceptual transformation that intersected the vulgarized German idealist philosophical tradition of the 1870s and 1880s laterally and that never entirely coincided with it, an impulse now borne by the persistent presumptions of that tradition in a process of interminable self-undermining attending them into the future. Nietzsche names a historical impulse interfering with culture and the authorities that inhabit and perpetuate it. His writings, both the published works and more intimately Nietzsche's voluminous notebooks, register like a contrail the accelerating course of his destructive traversal of authoritative thought, through which Nietzsche becomes a metonym for everything else, good and bad, that authoritative thought overthrows and subjugates. Mere sequence, the zero degree of form, is the law of this production, and a Nietzschean formula—human, all too human; superman; eternal return; will-to-power; reevaluation of all values—beyond its putative content in any particular deployment, is a vehicle communicating that directly inexpressible nonteleological historical impulse to the unprecedented future.

This is to say that if all oeuvres become historical for us through a certain immediate disavowal that lets us attend to their testimonial and testamentary aspects, Nietzsche is singular in this respect precisely in the profundity of his anticipation of that inevitable disavowal. Nietzsche testifies to a prognostic experience essentially preliminary to itself, an expectation and anticipation whose ultimate content has been entirely evacuated into its eventual realization in the future. This is not prediction, which projects a content forward into a time that will either confirm or refute it; rather Nietzsche's expression submits itself to the opacity of the future and its unknowable judgments as something essentially beyond any tendencies displayed by the present, discernible only when all differences manifesting those tendencies have been neutralized in a thought of the eternal return. The prognostic posture animates Nietzsche's epistemology of *Vorurteil*, prejudice, the judgment not yet recognized. It inhabits his rhetorical affinity for the form of the *Vorrede* or preface, whether the "Five Prefaces to Five Unwritten Books" he bestowed on Cosima Wagner or "Zarathustra's Preface" that inaugurates the descent or the series of rejuvenating prefaces Nietzsche prepared after Zarathustra for his pre-Zarathustra works. These actual examples merely accentuate and make problematic a permanently preliminary aspect in all of Nietzsche's writing, an aspect whose centrality and consequence is unique to Nietzsche's oeuvre, the purest, blankest level of his distinct impulsive reality. The historical distance between Benjamin and Nietzsche, self-evident from Benjamin's retrospective position even if its meaning presents many challenges, this distance is just as constitutive for Nietzsche's expression itself in the other direction, even if it loses all conceptual self-evidence along the reversed temporal vector and pushes conceptualization out past the edge of durable content.[2]

A reciprocal dynamic thus characterizes the broad sweep of our exposition of the historical relation between Benjamin and Nietzsche, in which an understanding of each of them is equally at stake. Benjamin's encounter with Nietzsche the philologist leaves that Nietzsche behind, but in so doing reenacts Nietzsche's own self-overcoming of philological discipline and the "untimely" Wagnerian accreditation he had initially attempted to provide for it. Benjamin's theoretical maturity first encounters an immature Nietzsche, one still invested in the validating institutions of his day, who will in turn be left behind by the move into the aphoristic books and Zarathustra beyond them. Both Nietzsche and Benjamin leave *The Birth of Tragedy* and its exalted science behind, and their expressions remain resonant with one another even as the scopes of their diverse concerns expand out beyond the horizon of its orienting discipline. The undisciplined terrain of thought, exposed to history directly, cannot be domesticated by philosophical authority, which is itself at stake, if not all that is at stake, on that terrain.

At that point the philological Nietzsche gives place in Benjamin's thought to a wilier expatriate Nietzsche, a dissident at the southern edge of Germany's Second Reich; an example and a warning. Traces of this relentlessly disenchanted figure and of the penetration into historical being he made thinkable for Benjamin survive among the fragments of the *Passagenarbeit*, Benjamin's massive research project through the nineteenth-century Parisian arcades, in reflections on mythic temporality, on Blanqui and rebellion pushed to the point of nihilism, on the infernal character of urban experience. But Benjamin's most resonant depiction of this irrevocable distance between himself and Nietzsche must wait until the end of *Deutsche Menschen*, where Nietzsche's despairing cry "why still do anything?" provokes the final letter of the original collection. Franz Overbeck's uncomprehending encouragement of a nonheroic private Nietzsche at the point of capitulation embodies the surviving ideal of a genuine cultural reception for the future. Benjamin's mimetic endorsement of Overbeck's unspectacular loyalty testifies to the persistent relevance of philological discipline and its ideal to his image of Nietzsche. In the contours of this unbreakable friendship between bourgeois academic integrity and an ecstatically abysmal experience at the edge of temporality, Benjamin discerns the inextinguishable possibility of a culture beyond fascism.

The reciprocal dynamic between Benjamin and Nietzsche can thus display its full potential only in the light of their original encounter under the sign of philology. It is into this disciplinary context and the terms of the controversies that define it that the prophetic Nietzsche is pushed most deeply by the catastrophe that destroys the youthful facies. For Benjamin these are years of war and subsequent dislocation, with residences in Munich and Bern, Heidelberg and Berlin. He finishes his dissertation, publishes his Baudelaire translations, writes his seminal essay on Goethe, plans a literary journal. Privately, he articulates his theoretical position in critical essays on literary figures, disquisitions on translation, overtly theological reflections on language, on violence, on the limits of neo-Kantianism. The production is diverse, but the three extensive texts that embody Benjamin's university career accompany and organize it like a bass counterpoint:

the dissertation on early Romantic art criticism, the interpretation of Goethe's *Elective Affinities*, the conceptual reconstruction of Baroque *Trauerspiel*. Though only the first and last of these were explicitly composed with reference to academic certification, each of them acknowledges a philological ideal of scholarship. This ideal informs certain regions of the academy but cannot be reduced to a concrete institutional norm or an abstract formal procedure. It is rather a truth principle calibrating the ultimate relation of historical language to conclusive knowledge.

This, at any rate, is how Benjamin understands philology: as a matter of truthful expression and the potential community implicit in truthful expression, not a matter of generalized standards regulating existing organizations. A privileged passage from his essay on Goethe helps situate philological discipline in Benjamin's thinking at this time. Methodological remarks in the opening paragraph present Benjamin's intentions there in the following terms: "The extant literature on poetic writings suggests that comprehensiveness [*Ausführlichkeit*] in such studies be reckoned more to the account of a philological than a critical interest. The following exposition of *The Elective Affinities*, which also goes into detail [*im einzelnen eingehend*], could therefore easily prove misleading about the intention with which it is presented. It could appear to be commentary; in fact, it is meant as critique." Granted, Benjamin appears here to be distinguishing his own interpretive practice from that of philology; the reading of Goethe's novel that Benjamin proposes is precisely *not* a philological commentary but displays a totally different intention and obeys a totally different interest. "Critique seeks the truth content [*Wahrheitsgehalt*] of a work, commentary its material content [*Sachgehalt*]" (*SW*, 297; *GS*, 1:125). And yet this difference—however it is to be understood—is formulated *in terms of* philology, and necessarily so, for critique operates on a philological object, the work as it is understood with the comprehensiveness and detail that characterize philological reading. It is philology that renders what originally *mattered* about the work, its "*Sache*,"[3] with enough substantiality (*Gehalt*) for it then to manifest a truth of a different temporal order, a truth content in the present. That truth content is not itself constrained by philological deference toward the posited work, but is the truth of a material content that is. "The truth content emerges as that of the material content" (*SW*, 300; *GS*, 1:128). Thus truth content is neither simply a further positive semantic content of the kind traditional philology organizes (what, in other contexts, Benjamin tends to call "*Inhalte*"[4]) nor an abstract truth indigenous to an unhistorical timelessness but a higher theoretical relevance into which what originally mattered about the work is brought.[5]

In the last analysis, for Benjamin it is neither the substantive material content nor the intensive truth content but the meaning of the variable relation between them that is at stake in a serious engagement with an enduring work. "The material content and the truth content, united at the beginning of a work's history, set themselves apart from each other in the course of its duration," Benjamin maintains (*SW*, 1:297; *GS*, 1:125), and it is this duration, the history in which author, reader, and work all differently participate, whose fundamental significance is revealed by the sophisticated sort of reading Benjamin proposes. Historical duration opens up between the material content, anchored to the original circumstances from which the work emerged, and the truth content, following its reception down the inconceivable continuum of historical time. And indeed, it is the temporal actuality of the truth content in contrast to the dated material content that prevents it from itself appearing directly as "*Inhalt*," as perseverant semantic content of its own, but delivers it over to the occasion of a material content preserved by philology.

And yet as soon as the positive content of the philological object can become the occasion for an actual truth content, that material content is no longer identical to the simple meaning of the words, the "concrete realities"[6] that inhabit historical duration. As the potential for truth content, material content itself no longer coincides with the discrete semantic oppositions inherently stabilizing referential meaning but must be understood as a more general condition of the historical moment at which the work appears. Material content per se lies behind the philological elements, conditioning the historical emergence of philology *itself* from the heart of the Enlightenment. "For at the exact moment when Kant's work was completed and a map through the bare woods of reality was sketched, the Goethean quest for the seeds of eternal growth began. That tendency in classicism appeared which sought to grasp not so much the ethical and historical as the mythic and philological. Its thought did not bear on the ideas in their becoming [*werdende Ideen*] but on the formed contents [*geformten Gehalte*] preserved in life and language" (*SW*, 1:298; *GS*, 1:126). The distinction between material content and truth content emerged at the moment Kantian abstraction and formalism gave way to a substantive consideration of historical change. That shift of attention, symbolized by a fundamentally Simmelian[7] contrast between the contemporaries Kant and Goethe, is usually understood (by Simmel, for instance) as renewed attention to historical and evaluative dimensions of reality. A more accurate characterization of the change, Benjamin suggests, is a turn toward the philological and the mythic. His entire investigation of Goethe's *Elective Affinities* in its vital context is devoted to illustrating and justifying this correction. It is not that history adds a dimension of becoming to what are essentially permanent ideas in the Kantian mold. With Goethe's historicism the relation of logical priority is the reverse of this: Not abstract ideas but concrete contents are fundamental, and the possibility of transcending historical impermanence is not displayed by these contents directly but emerges from the contrast between their relative endurance and the changing linguistic vitality that preserves them. To imagine that the relative permanence of an enduring artwork—its material content—is genuinely eternal is to succumb to mythic duplicity. It is to imagine that philology grants direct access to truth. But philology grants direct access merely to the *claim* of permanence, and truth emerges only when that claim is recognized for what it is: deceptive appearance.

This is what Benjamin means when he says that "with one stroke," that is, with the distinction between truth content and material content, with the appearance of philological and mythic criticism, "an invaluable criterion of judgment springs out for [the reader]; only now can he raise the basic critical question of whether the appearance [*Schein*] of the truth content is due to the material content, or the life of the material content to the truth content." The distinction between material content and truth content thus reflects into the work a more profound and encompassing distinction between appearance and life, the one deceptively self-identical through time and the other unprecedented and immediate. "The *Schein* of truth content" is something other than the truth, while the "life of material content" is the truth it produces when it reaches the present critically. The condition of possibility of that invaluable criterion is borne negatively by the science of philology.

TRAGEDY

The first half of Walter Benjamin's *The Origin of German Trauerspiel* contrasts Baroque Trauerspiel with antique tragedy. The distinction between these genres is not, however, a neutral taxonomic boundary. *Trauerspiel* itself assumes classical tragedy as its reference point, and the differences between them are constitutive for the later genre. "Ancient tragedy is the fettered slave on the triumphal car of the baroque Trauerspiel" (*OT*, 100; *GS*, 1:278). Trauerspiel internalizes its external historical difference from Greek tragic drama, the loss of mythic content and pure heroism, when it takes history itself as material content. It is the necessary failure of the Baroque poets to render historical situations tragically that makes their texts a site where history in its deepest meaning can appear. The origin of the German mourning play lies in the history that conditions its genre specificity. The meaning of that history lies in its contrast with Greek tragedy.

Tragedy itself is thus more than a literary genre. Poised on the mortal rupture in collective life, enacting a transformation of annihilation into hope, Greek tragedy is a matter of life and death. Thus Benjamin's commitment to tragedy is not literary, a scholarly imperative to trace a genre's formal features to their cultural roots. Only because mourning plays are trying to be tragedies do their specific formal deficiencies and achievements resonate with the meaning of history. Tragedy, tragic meaning, is the essential condition of his discussion and establishes the possibility of its path out of a restricted aesthetics toward a characterization of reality relevant at the extremes. And it is in this fundamental position that Nietzsche appears. Reviewing prior theories of tragic drama, Benjamin devotes one titled section to "Nietzsche's *Birth of Tragedy*." He concludes there by rejecting the theory of tragedy that he finds in Nietzsche.

Nietzsche appears among a constellation of reactions to classical tragedy illuminating Benjamin's own understanding of the genre. An initial perspective serves as the antithesis to Benjamin's eventual position, and his discussion derives its energy in opposition to it. This initial antithetical position, represented by Johannes Volkelt's 1917 *Aesthetics of the Tragic* [*Ästhetik des Tragischen*], is a complacent humanism that identifies the meaning of tragedy with a generalized, timeless human experience of the world's independent necessity. Such a humanism has as its motivating corollary the modern possibility of tragic drama, both in the immediate experience of contemporary audiences and as a viable aspiration for contemporary dramatists. But, Benjamin insists, "nothing is in fact more questionable than the competence of the unguided feelings of 'modern men,' especially where the judgment of tragedy is concerned" (*OT*, 101; *GS*, 1:280).

The bankruptcy of this undifferentiated assimilation of antique and contemporary experience into the generically tragic had already been exposed decades before, Benjamin maintains, by Nietzsche. *The Birth of Tragedy* represents an advance precisely over this self-satisfied humanism, and Nietzsche enters the discussion initially as an ally against it. If history is the necessary context for any genuine reflection on tragic drama, this implies that the differences and eventual limitations of contemporary experience with respect to tragedy be acknowledged. The meaning of the Attic tragedies that have come down to us is not directly available in the present but requires a conceptual reconstruction that calls the vital present into question. "This is the Archimedean point which more recent thinkers, particularly Franz Rosenzweig and George Lukács, have found in Nietzsche's early work" (*OT*, 102; *GS*, 1:280). Benjamin's own tragic theory will be explicated in direct conversation with these contemporary discussions, here genealogically positioned as modern reevaluations of *The Birth of Tragedy*. His own reading, therefore, finds itself in sympathy with the basic critical motivation of Nietzsche's discussion, the "brilliant intuition" (*OT*, 103; *GS*, 1:281) that underlies it, while being coordinated in the contemporary intellectual environment with Rosenzweig's *Star of Redemption* and Lukács's *Soul and Forms*.

By emphasizing the ecstatic experience of archaic myth, the "witches' brew" of Dionysian frenzy,[8] and thereby denying the relevance of contemporary individual moral sentiments to an understanding of tragic drama, Nietzsche pries open the history separating contemporary experience from the meaning of classical tragedy. But the price Nietzsche pays for this emancipation from contemporary sensibilities is, Benjamin feels, too high. "The abyss of aestheticism opens up, and this brilliant intuition was finally to see all its concepts disappear into it, so that gods and heroes, defiance and suffering, the pillars of the tragic edifice, fall away into nothing" (*OT*, 103; *GS*, 1:281). The elements of tragedy become indistinguishable beneath their common status as representations. Nietzsche's theory evades contemporary moral sentiments by situating tragic drama completely in a domain of appearance: Not only the dramatic representation itself but also the mythical material it presents and the life toward which it is addressed are ultimately insubstantial phenomena, mere manifestations of an aesthetic struggle between Apollo and Dionysus. In order to free the interpretation of tragedy from contemporary moral responses, Nietzsche short-circuits its relation to ethical considerations entirely. Beholden to a "Schopenhauerian and Wagnerian metaphysics" (*OT*, 102; *GS*, 1:281) that equates life and art by demoting the world to the status of *Schein*, appearance, Nietzsche's theory of tragedy cannot address the fundamental seriousness of tragic presentation. It remains nihilistically insubstantial. "The nihilism lodged in the depths of the artistic philosophy of Bayreuth nullified—it could do no other—the concept of the hard, historical actuality of Greek tragedy" (*OT*, 103; *GS*, 1:282). Nietzsche's insight into the untimeliness of Greek tragedy and the consequent challenge it poses to the self-image of the present is thus neutralized when the substantive moral reality within which these dramatic rituals operated is subsumed by the valorization of a pointless impulse to aesthetic expression per se. "For what does it matter whether one supposes the will to life or the will to its destruction inspiring every work of art, since as a product of the absolute will the work devalues itself along with the world?" (*OT*, 103; *GS*, 1:282).[9]

"Nietzsche turned his back on the tragic theories of the epigones without refuting them. For he saw no reason to take issue with their central doctrine of tragic guilt and tragic atonement, because he was only too willing to leave the field of moral debates to them" (*OT*, 104; *GS*, 1:283). As Benjamin leaves Nietzsche's argument, he is committed to a contrasting perspective that foregrounds the notions of *Schuld* and *Sühne*, guilt and atonement. Where Nietzsche preserved the meaning of Greek tragedy's historical specificity only by generalizing the notion of appearance and devaluing life into *Schein*, Benjamin proposes the opposite strategy. "Everything moral is bound to life in its extreme sense, that is to say where it fulfills itself in death, the abode of danger as such" (*OT*, 105; *GS*, 1:284). Both Benjamin and Nietzsche agree on the irrelevance to tragedy of contemporary moral attitudes. But rather than dissolve those attitudes in the utter irrelevance of appearance, Benjamin aims to usurp their claim over tragedy through the relevance of death.

He formulates his mortal premise here in terms of "danger"—a trace of Lukács, perhaps. Lukács's essay "Metaphysics of Tragedy," a discussion of the drama of Paul Ernst, navigates an existential boundary marked by danger, and the words "real life" and "dangerous" attract each other irresistibly in that discussion. Though his essay mentions Nietzsche by name only once, and in passing,[10] the schema Lukács presents is Nietzschean from its first sentence on: "A drama is play; the play of man and his fate—a play for which God is the spectator."[11] For Lukács, tragedy gives form to the essence of life. Form is synonymous with finitude, and the limit that both creates the form of tragedy and defines the essence of life is death; tragedy and "real" life are thus perfectly congruent. The life that tragedy represents, however, is available to lived experience only in certain exceptional moments. The ordinary experience of life does not reach this essential boundary, while mystical experience transcends it and renders death unreal. Only tragic representation shows a life completely coincident with this limit. "The tragic life is, of all possible lives, the one most exclusively of this world. That is why its frontier always merges with death."[12] Lukács's insistence on the mortal immanence of tragedy resonates with Benjamin's own views, and indeed he cites this sentence (*OT*, 135–36; *GS*, 1:314). But in fact such a schema has only limited usefulness for him. Lukács's discussion makes no mention of myth, and despite the fact that he scorns contemporary attempts to appropriate tragedy—"In vain has our democratic age claimed an equal right for all to be tragic; all attempts to open this kingdom of heaven to the poor in spirit have proved fruitless"[13]—this deficiency is understood as a failure of courage, and Lukács's major terms remain abstracted from any specific historical context. (Paul Ernst, the occasion for the essay, is, after all, a modern dramatist.) Death, moreover, remains visible for Lukács only from the existentialist, first-person perspective, as the horizon of an individual existence, and there is no moment corresponding to Benjamin's notion of life as the survival of the other's death. The same nihilistic aestheticism that Benjamin expressly finds subverting Nietzsche's theory implicitly subverts Lukács's, as well. In the end, it is Rosenzweig as contemporary who girds this expression of Benjamin's theory of tragedy.

The schema of tragic representation that Benjamin develops in *The Origin of German Trauerspiel* has as its elements fable, hero, death. These converge in a notion of mythic necessity. The archaic experience of mythic necessity—fate—is directly expressed in the prehistoric fables of superhuman figures, gods, and heroes, whose interactions express the defining perspective of the Greek people as a living community on the necessity that conditions it. That fatal necessity characterizes not inert reality or the independent object but life. The paradox of a fatally conditioned life is that it is both created and immanent. As creature, a life is insufficient in itself, and its immanence is not autonomy but deprivation. The implacable sentence of mythic fate evacuates any positive transcendence conditioning the creature; fatal life is exposed not to God and his redemptive promise but to the necessary nothingness of death. This blank exterior intrudes into thought as "*Zweideutigkeit*," ambiguity,[14] and the conceptual equivocations that register this inconceivable condition condemning the human person to death are the salient feature of Benjamin's functional notion of myth. Governed by ambiguity, the link between myth and life is thus the precise antithesis of redemptive truth: not mere falsity, but the extinction of any potential relation to truth, ambiguity as duplicity manifesting the inescapable death sentence constitutive of life, the fate to which living myth gives voice. *Schicksal rollt dem Tode zu*, "Fate rolls on toward death" (*OT*, 131; *GS*, 1:310). Life and death are antonyms but living and dying are synonyms: this is the ambiguous heart of Benjamin's notion of myth.[15]

Tragedy takes up the mythic content of the Greeks, their fables of guilt and fatal retribution, and subjects them to a series of reversals. The first of these is sacrifice: "Tragic poetry is based on the idea of sacrifice" (*OT*, 106; *GS*, 1:285). Tragic poetry is grounded in the initial inversion performed by sacrificial ritual itself. In the form of sacrifice, passive life enters into an active *agon* with the mythic forces that fatally condition it.[16] The sacrifice depicted by tragedy, like all sacrifice, actively transforms into an offering the death that the gods by right condemn life passively to suffer. Tragedy is thus in one respect the culmination of propitiating ritual. But the tragic presentation of this sacrificial ritual creates a new inversion, borne by the victim of the sacrifice, the hero. "In respect of its victim, the hero, the tragic sacrifice differs from any other kind, being at once a first and a final sacrifice. A final sacrifice in the sense of the atoning sacrifice to gods who are upholding an ancient right; a first sacrifice in the sense of the representative action, in which new contents of the life of the people announce themselves" (*OT*, 106–7; *GS*, 1:285). The sacrificial *agon* between the mythic gods and the populace performing the atoning ritual is overwritten by an unprecedented *agon*, in which, via the hero, the life of the community demonstrates its superiority to the forces that condition it. Tragedy thus stands at a turning point in Greek life's relation to mortal necessity.

Where the sacrificing collective adopts a subservient posture toward the mythic judgment it hopes to placate, in tragedy the hero's death redounds upon the gods who ordain it. The hero submits to the necessity of death but does so in a spirit of *Trotz*, defiance. This defiance is presented as the hero's silence. The new self-conception that the hero represents, not yet having an expression endorsed by the community, must appear as defiant silence. "This defiance is every bit as much a consequence of the experience of speechlessness as a factor which intensifies the condition. The content [*Gehalt*] of the hero's works belongs to the community, as does speech. Since the community of the people denies this content, it remains speechless in the hero" (*OT*, 108; *GS*, 1:287). By refusing to embody his sacrificial role in a subservient manner, the hero implicitly denies the compensatory placation that motivates the sacrifice, and his death becomes an absolute, uncompromising destruction.

> So too in the silence of the hero, which neither looks for nor finds any justification, and therefore throws suspicion back onto his persecutors. For its meaning is inverted: what appears before the public is not the remorse [*Betroffenheit*] of the accused but the evidence of speechless suffering, and the tragedy which appeared to be devoted to the judgment of the hero is transformed into a hearing about the Olympians in which the latter appears as a witness and, against the will of the gods, displays "the honor of the demi-god." (*OT*, 109; *GS*, 1:288)

The death of the hero reveals an incommensurability between his individual dignity and the collective purpose to which his death is put. This incommensurability opens the Greek pantheon to the new potential of a higher divinity. "The tragic death has a dual significance: it invalidates the ancient right of the Olympians, and it offers up the hero to the unknown god as the first fruits of a new harvest of humanity" (*OT*, 107; *GS*, 1:285–86). The absolute meaning of the hero's death transforms the meaning of death itself: "Death thereby becomes salvation: the crisis of death" (*OT*, 107; *GS*, 1:286). This transformation of death into potential salvation is not, Benjamin insists, itself an escape from fate and death. He adopts here a Lukácsian emphasis. "For tragic existence acquires its task only because the limits of both linguistic and physical life are granted to it from the start and posited within it" (*OT*, 114; *GS*, 1:293). With implicit reference to the theology of the Christian Passion, Benjamin distinguishes the perfect sacrifice that achieves atonement and abolishes death from the tragic sacrifice that registers a rejection of this entire logic. "In tragedy the hold of demonic fate is broken. Not, however, by relieving the inscrutable pagan concatenation of guilt and atonement through the purity of man, absolved and reconciled with the pure god. It is rather that in tragedy pagan man realizes that he is better than his gods, but this realization strikes him dumb, and it remains unarticulated" (*OT*, 109–10; *GS*, 1:288).

The transformation of the hero's death from a conciliatory tactic into a mute protest against death's finality opens the possibility of a higher reconciliation, but it is positively registered only as a critical denunciation of the fatal necessity embodied in the punishing gods. As such it must remain a transitory gesture. By voluntarily assuming a meaningless and total death, the hero gestures negatively toward a transcendence of death, but he does not achieve it himself. Where sacrificial ritual imbued a passive death with active significance, the hero's death reasserts a passivity that denigrates the action of the gods. His refusal to comply with the positive meaning of his sacrifice, and his uncompromising insistence on the absolute nature of his destruction, shows up the falsity and injustice of the gods and the sacrifices they demand, but does not itself achieve a positive reversal of this logic. The tragic hero becomes, rather, embodied as the material occasion within which that reversal is potentially manifested. "It is to his *physis* alone and not to language that he owes the ability to hold fast to his cause, and he must therefore do so in death" (*OT*, 108; *GS*, 1:287). His purity is still nihilistic but an embodied nihilism now open to potential transformation by another. "Out of his profound inner emptiness echo the distant, new divine commands [*Göttergeheiße*], and from this echo future generations learn their language" (*OT*, 114; *GS*, 1:293).

But the nature of this transformation remains profoundly ambiguous in *The Origin of German Trauerspiel*. In order to present this accusatory silence, manifesting a *Trotz* that with little exaggeration could be translated as "spite," Greek art developed the dramatic form, Benjamin maintains. And in support of this he cites Franz Rosenzweig's *Star of Redemption*. "The tragic devised itself the artistic form of the drama precisely so as to be able to present silence."[17] Rosenzweig's account strongly emphasizes the hero's defiant silence. "The tragic hero has only one language that is in perfect accordance with him: precisely, silence," he maintains. "How else is he to manifest his solitude within himself, this rigid defiance, other than by being silent?" (*SR*, 86; *SE*, 83–84). But Rosenzweig's defiant silence is not intentional, a gestural denunciation of a vindictive pantheon. The hero for Rosenzweig does not fall into silent reproach of the condemnatory gods but embodies the absolute autonomy of the self. The difference between this perspective and Benjamin's is apparent in their contrasting notions of death. Where Benjamin sees in the hero's death the culmination of his protest, for Rosenzweig,

> The hero as such has to be ruined only because his ruination makes him capable of the supreme heroic consecration: the closest self-realization of his Self. He longs for the solitude of disappearance, because there is no greater solitude than this one. For this reason, the hero does not in the strict sense die. Death cordons off for him as it were only the *temporalia* of individuality. The character dissolved in the heroic Self is immortal. (SR, 87–88; SE, 86)

Both Benjamin and Rosenzweig understand the tragic hero's silence as a sign of his isolation from the mythically grounded collective and its gods. For Rosenzweig, this isolation reveals not a higher aspiration for the community but a deeper foundation for the individual.[18] Benjamin, by contrast, sees its exemplary force announcing a new meaning for and of the collective. In the elaborate recursive architectonic of Rosenzweig's *Star of Redemption*, the discussion of Attic tragedy occupies a privileged position, concluding the first of its three major divisions. This overarching division characterizes the three elements of Rosenzweig's dialectic, and tragic man is one such fundamental element. "The mythical God, the plastic world, tragic man—we are holding the pieces in our hands" (SR, 93; SE, 91). In the exchange between gods and man presented on the tragic stage, heroic silence is not a gesture of defiance directed at the gods but the neutralization of all connection between them.

But if Rosenzweig's discussion of tragic silence does not agree with Benjamin's analysis of this phenomenon, there is in fact a parallel in *The Star of Redemption* to Benjamin's defiant hero. It is the philosopher Nietzsche. "The history of philosophy had never yet seen an atheism like that of Nietzsche. Nietzsche is the first thinker who—not negates God—but, in the really proper theological use of the word: 'denies' him. More precisely: he curses him. . . . Never yet had a philosopher held his own in this way, eye to eye, against the living God, so to speak. The first real man among the philosophers was also the first to see God face to face—even if only to deny Him" (SR, 25; SE, 20). Thus the strands of Benjamin's understanding of the tragic hero come together round this image of the sacrilegious philosopher Nietzsche: the Lukácsian insistence on mortal immanence and the coincidence of life and tragedy brings together the silent essential manifestation of Rosenzweig's tragic hero in the denunciatory posture of Rosenzweig's Nietzsche. Together, they figure the emergence of meaning from pure immanence as a speaking silence in which sacrificial embodiment reverses into spiteful self-destruction.

HAMLET

In Benjamin's theory, tragedy, as a genre, rests exclusively in its classical situation. It cannot be repeated by later dramatists or experienced by later audiences. Its heroes rise out of an irretrievable mythic background, their defiant silence denounces a lost pantheon, and only the death that frames their tragic singularity allows the genre a displaced passage to the present. Trauerspiel, by contrast, refuses to stay put. Working with borrowed medieval emblems, straining toward a renaissance wholeness with nature, these dramas are always poised on the brink of genre transformations, into *Haupt- und Staatsaktionen*, *Sturm und Drang*, marionette theater, ballet, or opera. "Trauerspiel is in every respect a hybrid form [*Zwischenform*]," Benjamin had recognized as early as 1916, when he first contrasted the genres in a brief essay on "Trauerspiel and Tragedy" (*SW*, 1:57; *GS*, 2:136). Nor are Trauerspiels only formally unstable. Their substantive national character appears negatively, as well, for the aspirations of German Trauerspiel are only realized by what Benjamin insists are foreign contemporaries, in Spanish *Siglo de Oro* drama or Elizabethan theater.

And indeed, these foreign examples condense around two specific dramatists, Pedro Calderón de la Barca and William Shakespeare, and further, two specific plays: *La vida es sueño* and *Hamlet*. Of these two, it is the former that represents the perfection of Trauerspiel. "The German drama of the Counter-Reformation never achieved that suppleness of form which bends to every virtuoso touch, such as Calderón gave the Spanish drama," Benjamin remarks early on (*OT*, 49; *GS*, 1:229), and he insists a few pages later, having cited *Life Is a Dream*, "Nowhere but in Calderón could the perfect form of the baroque Trauerspiel be studied" (*OT*, 81; *GS*, 1:260). It is Calderón who, with *El mayor monstruo, los celos*, created the first Baroque "drama of fate," or *Schicksalsdrama* (*OT*, 83; *GS*, 1:262), and it is the "transfigured apotheosis" Calderón's drama achieved that supports the book's last word on Trauerspiel (*OT*, 235; *GS*, 1:408–9).

But if *Life Is a Dream* marks the culmination of Baroque drama, the position of Shakespeare, and particularly of *Hamlet*, is more difficult to determine. Shakespeare does not rest comfortably in his time.[19] His anachronistic assimilation into a Baroque arising half a century after his death is but the index of a deeper instability. "For Shakespeare is the greatest Romantic, even if he is not only that," Benjamin had written in a brief commentary on *As You Like It* in 1918 (*GS*,

2:610). And though such a simplification could not long do justice to Benjamin's reading of the English dramatist, nonetheless, even in the Trauerspiel book, Romanticism responds to something in Shakespeare's art that both binds it to and breaks it from the Baroque: "It was above all Shakespeare's drama, with its richness and its freedom, which, for the romantic writers, overshadowed contemporaneous German efforts, whose gravity was, in any case, alien to the practical theater" (*OT*, 48; *GS*, 1:229). Despite this incompatibility, or perhaps because of it, Hamlet stands at the center of *The Origin of German Trauerspiel*, and the entire discussion pivots upon his fate. The first half of the book closes with a consideration of this figure.

"Once at least this age succeeded in conjuring up [*beschwören*] the human figure who corresponded to this dichotomy [*Zwiespalt*] between the neo-antique and the mediaeval light in which the baroque saw the melancholic. But Germany was not the country that was able to do this. It is Hamlet [*Es ist der Hamlet*]" (*OT*, 157; *GS*, 1:334). The claim spans the theoretical scope of *The Origin of German Trauerspiel*, presenting a relation that holds between epoch and individual figure, halting only briefly and negatively at national linguistic boundaries, and eliding both author and title. The slightly odd direct article—"*der Hamlet*"—pulls the protagonist's name from the eponymous play that renders him and bares it before us, a faint rhetorical echo of the original conjuration through which the age brought the human figure to life. Hamlet stands alone, and through this dislocated figure the forces revealed in the contrast between Trauerspiel and tragedy pass unreconciled into the functional contrast of the second half of the book between a theological concept of symbol and a historical concept of allegory. The melancholy that in medieval theology indicated a sinful withdrawal from the evident meanings displayed by creation intersects with the Renaissance melancholic fascination at the theoretical mysteries inscribed into the natural world to produce in Shakespeare's figure the apotheosis of the redemptive disenchantment of sacrifice the Baroque pursued. The achievement of *Hamlet* consists in the total correspondence between the melancholy intentions of the prince and the death-saturated environment of the Danish court he so reluctantly inhabits. "The secret of his person is contained within the jesting, but for that very reason firmly circumscribed, passage through all the stations of this intentional space, just as the secret of his fate is contained in events which are entirely homogeneous with his gaze," Benjamin writes.

The world through which Hamlet's character wanders is entirely in accordance with the melancholic gaze he casts on it, and in this perfect congruence of fate and character, Hamlet is both at absolute liberty in the Danish court and completely enmeshed in his inevitable doom. The citation above continues:

> Hamlet alone is a spectator of the Trauerspiel by the grace of God; but not what they play for him, only his own fate can satisfy him. His life, the exemplary object of his mourning, points, before its extinction, to the Christian providence in whose bosom his mournful images turn into a blessed existence. Only in a princely life such as this is melancholy redeemed, by being confronted with itself. (*OT*, 158; *GS*, 1:334–35)

In this dense passage, Hamlet stands at the edge of the stage, a "spectator" of Trauerspiel. And a "they" with no clear antecedent in the next sentence marks a rupture in the exposition pointing beyond the world of Baroque drama. This "they" might be, at one level, the traveling players in act 3 who re-create the murder of Hamlet *père* on the stage before the prince and the court. The play-within-a-play at the heart of Shakespeare's drama inscribes into Trauerspiel the external relation between Trauerspiel itself and history, the real site of the failure of tragic sacrifice. Spreading out from its stage-upon-a-stage, the usurpation of Gonzago accuses the entire Danish court that observes it, as Hamlet recognizes, and, further, the sacrificial vocation of Trauerspiel itself, as he does not. What follows the *Mousetrap* in the play *Hamlet* are the various failed attempts to carry out the atoning sacrifice that will set this murder right: Hamlet's accidental killing of Polonius, his sparing of Claudius at his prayers, his devious inversion of Rosencrantz and Guildenstern's death warrant, his meditations upon Yorick's grinning skull, until the final catastrophe of switched swords and transposed goblets that sweeps this court away and leaves the stage to the new regime of Fortinbras. *The Mousetrap* confirms Claudius's guilt and Hamlet's destiny, but it is not enough to wrest the son from beneath his dead father's fate. Rather, it is only with Hamlet *fils*'s own destruction that the corrosive implications of mortal guilt are brought by Shakespeare to a halt before us. Thus the "they" who play the Trauerspiel for Hamlet are in another sense the actual grammatical antecedent—however strained the syntax—of the pronoun: the "stations of this intentional space" of melancholic perception and the "events which are entirely homogeneous" with Hamlet's gaze. The entire universe of Trauerspiel is laid before Hamlet as something external to himself. Hamlet stands at the outer edge of reality; it is this passive extremity and not a sacrificial act that makes him the epitome of Trauerspiel. His own death, therefore, quite properly is not rendered with mythic inevitability but hangs on a mere contingency. "The death of Hamlet, which has no more in common with tragic death than the Prince himself has with Ajax, is in its vehement externality [*vehementer Äußerlichkeit*] characteristic of Trauerspiel, and for this reason alone it is worthy of its creator" (*OT*, 136–37; *GS*, 1:315). Hamlet and the unredeemable world from which he is so utterly alienated converge at this destructive limit, and there the play gestures negatively at the possibility Trauerspiel could never positively encompass: redemption.

The impossible site that Hamlet occupies, at once both within and without the play, at once both active witness and passive agent, at once both father and son, victim and avenger, revenant and "too too solid flesh," is his own utter alienation from life. Melancholy brings life before him as an object in a world of objects. It is Hamlet's free acceptance of this life as if it were fate, his suicidal wish "to breathe in the air as suffocating as fate [*schicksalsschwere Luft*] like azote in one deep inhalation" (*OT*, 137; *GS*, 1:315) that lifts him from the world of Trauerspiel. From that final boundary Hamlet passes his sovereign mandate, his "dying voice," onto his triumphant rival Fortinbras, while simultaneously charging the distraught Horatio with preserving the memory of his "wounded name": "If thou didst ever hold me in thy heart, / Absent thee from felicity awhile, / And in this harsh world draw they breath in pain / To tell my story" (5.2.288–91).

"Only in a princely life such as this one is melancholy redeemed, by being confronted with itself. The rest is silence" (*OT*, 158; *GS*, 1:335). The formulation opens an exemplary space around the figure of the prince. Into that space a tendentious phonetic echo, as faint and tenuous as the echo of tragic death, bears a glimpse of hope into the heart of *The Origin of German Trauerspiel*. Hamlet. Heinle. The violence of this intrusion of the historical individual into the literary epitome escapes the book's philology entirely, for its necessity rests securely in no intention. What appears here as a punctilious and arbitrary link between names is the condition of possibility of Benjamin's tone. The secret correspondence at the heart of *The Origin of German Trauerspiel* licenses no biographical reduction of the treatise but a theoretical embodiment of the suicide. Through the figure of Hamlet, Heinle speaks from outside life, hands on to Benjamin his theoretical task.[20]

In the Trauerspiel book, the esoteric displacement of Heinle's suicide onto the Baroque stage is the primal image of that displacement of failed sacrifice into history to which Trauerspiel bears witness. The Shakespearean drama stands at the intersection of all the strands in the treatise, antique and modern, drama and audience, object and allegory, life and death, history and art. Its reflective concatenation does not resolve these differences but positions them as an unending surrender and an endless task: *endlose Aufgabe.*

The Origin of German Trauerspiel constructs an elaborate interpretive arc whose trajectory is defined by the displacement of the literary prince Hamlet by the historical boy Heinle. It is the possibility of such an impossible transplantation of history onto the literary stage that the second half of the treatise is designed to defend and, in a larger sense, Benjamin's entire effort is designed to exhibit. The somber clumsiness of German Trauerspiel reveals the mechanisms of this displacement far more directly than the masterful Shakespearean accomplishment. It is in the allegorical *Zwischenspiele* of Baroque German drama that the "connections between spectacle proper [*eigentlicher Schaustellung*] and allegory" become visible. Only when this allegorical dimension of literary significance is recognized can the fact be explained that "practically any person can find a place in the tableau vivant of an allegorical apotheosis" (*OT,* 191; *GS,* 1:367). Benjamin continues: "The German Trauerspiel was never able to distribute a person's characteristics so covertly into the thousand folds of a draped allegorical figure as could Calderón. Nor had it any more success with Shakespeare's grand interpretation of allegorical figures in unprecedented, singular roles" (*OT,* 191; *GS,* 1:368). Calderón and Shakespeare represent complementary achievements, the former successfully realizing individuals as allegories, the latter realizing allegories as individuals. But German Trauerspiel, in its failure to accomplish this merger completely in either direction, reveals the elements that constitute it. And only in this failure does the space between those elements achieve with truthful melancholy its negative manifestation. Eventually it is this manifestation that can realize in the allegorical skull upon Golgotha the ephemeral truth borne by the very experience of semantic collapse: "The bleak confusion of Golgotha ... is not just a symbol of the desolation of human existence. In it transitoriness is not signified or allegorically represented, so much as, in its own significance, displayed as allegory" (*OT,* 405–6; *GS,* 1:232). This shift between representation and display, from communicating allegorical content to showing in itself the ultimate impermanence of any meaning, is the redemptive pivot melancholic concentration performs within the allegorical emblem.

The pathos that registers this pivot is named Heinle. It is Heinle's suicide in the guise of Hamlet's absolute alienation that informs this space and renders it far more than a trope in a poet's quiver but a displaced perspective on the whole of reality. "Allegory . . . is not a playful illustrative technique, but a form of expression, just as speech is expression, and, indeed, just as writing is" (*OT*, 162; *GS*, 1:339).[21] For Heinle's writing is all that survives him. Allegory is posthumous inscription itself: general meaning exposed to particular death. "In the context of allegory the image is only a signature, only the monogram of essence, not the essence itself in a mask. Still, writing is by no means servile, and does not fall away like dross from reading. It enters into what has been read, as its 'figure'" (*OT*, 214–15; *GS*, 1:388). The invasion in the Baroque of collective historical memory by the irreducible matter of inscription, producing not the stable conjunction of enduring significance but what Benjamin calls the "signature of essence," explains both the Baroque penchant, shared with signatures, for ornamental elaboration, and the Baroque achievements in the material craft of bookmaking. But beyond these local historical consequences, allegory, displaced through mortality, displays the last possibility of significance as death's signature in nature.

The allegorical space that can host Hamlet/Heinle is thus in semantic terms a rupture within the possibility of reference. It is the world as referent that is disrupted by the violence of another's death and made to challenge the strange persistence of literary inscription. This disruptive possibility was glimpsed even as the theory of reference was being articulated at the start of the last century. "If no one thought about Hamlet," Bertrand Russell remarked in his *Introduction to Mathematical Philosophy*, "there would be nothing left to him; if no one had thought about Napoleon, he would have soon seen to it that someone did."[22] The difference here, which Russell attributes to a "sense of reality" not further analyzable, inhabits the self-evidence of his inconsistent verb tenses. The condition that separates Hamlet's vulnerability from Napoleon's spontaneity is the slide from the imperfect "thought" to the perfect "had thought." This slide is more than a formal temporal index, but a slide that maintains reference at the cost of an ambiguous alternation between life and death. For once Napoleon has passed away, he, too, becomes as exposed as Hamlet to the abyss of forgetfulness. For Benjamin, onomastic reference is allegorical inscription, and can never lose the externality that defines it. "But what life is immortal," he asks in his early essay on Dostoevsky's *Idiot*, "if it is not natural life and also not the life of a person? Immortal life is unforgettable; that is the sign by which we recognize it. It is the life that without monument and without memorial, perhaps even without a witness, must never be forgotten. It cannot be forgotten.... And 'unforgettable' does not just mean that we cannot forget it. It points to something in the nature of the unforgettable itself that makes it unforgettable" (*SW*, 1:80; *GS*, 2:239). This "something" is what, behind their names, unites the dead Hamlet and the dead Heinle: historical origin.

SOCRATES

Where Trauerspiel culminates in the figure of Hamlet, Benjamin's interpretation of tragedy is deposited into a figure with no special prominence in either Lukács's or Rosenzweig's accounts: the figure of Socrates.

> The martyr-drama was born from the death of Socrates as a parody of tragedy. And here, as so often, the parody of a form proclaims its end. Wilamowitz testifies to the fact that it meant the end of tragedy for Plato. (*OT*, 113; *GS*, 1:292)

What the authority of the great classical philologist Ulrich von Wilamowitz-Moellendorff is here called to witness is a further reversal and displacement practiced on tragic sacrifice. The death of Socrates emerges as the parody of a hero's death, and announces the end of tragic representation.

> This legendry cycle of Socrates is a comprehensive profanation of heroic legend by surrendering its demonic paradoxes to understanding. Superficially, of course, the death of the philosopher resembles tragic death. It is an act of atonement according to the letter of an ancient law, a sacrificial death in the spirit of a new justice which contributes to the establishment of a new community. But this very similarity reveals most clearly the real significance of the agonal character of the genuinely tragic: that silent struggle, that mute evasion by the hero that has in the *Dialogues* given way to such a brilliant unfolding of discourse and consciousness. (*OT*, 113; *GS*, 1:292)

Stripped of its jeopardized status, the life of Socrates seals with intentional language the mortal rupture that tragic silence addressed and manifested. "Like the Christian hero of the faith—which explains both the sympathy of many a father of the Church and the hatred of Nietzsche, who unerringly detected this—Socrates dies voluntarily, and voluntarily, with inexpressible superiority and without any defiance, he falls mute when he falls silent" (*OT*, 114; *GS*, 1:293).

The figure of Socrates thus marks the end of tragedy. In this, Benjamin departs from Lukács and Rosenzweig, and returns to Nietzsche. Where, for Nietzsche, the birth of tragedy emerged with Aeschylus's harmonization of Dionysian and Apollonian forces, its death results from Euripides' unholy alliance with Socrates. "Greek tragedy met an end different from that of her older sister-arts," Nietzsche's famous formulation runs: "she died by suicide" (*BT*, 76; *KSA*, 1:75). Euripides is the culprit, but he does not work alone. "Even Euripides was, in a sense, only a mask: the deity that spoke through him was neither Dionysus nor Apollo, but an altogether newborn demon, called *Socrates*" (*BT*, 82; *KSA*, 1:83). What the Socratic demon announces is a new aesthetic principle. The "supreme law" of "aesthetic Socratism" is, Nietzsche maintains, that "to be beautiful everything must be intelligible" (*BT*, 83–84; *KSA*, 1:85). This is the fatal reversal that destroys, until Wagner, genuine tragedy. "While in all productive men it is the instinct that is the creative-affirmative force, and consciousness acts critically and dissuasively, in Socrates it is instinct that becomes the critic, and consciousness that becomes the creator—truly a monstrosity *per defectum*!" (*BT*, 88; *KSA*, 1:90). These are the passages that Benjamin, with his talk of surrendered paradoxes and encroaching consciousness, is indirectly citing.

But Benjamin's interpretation diverges at a crucial point from Nietzsche's. For Benjamin, the transformation of tragedy into philosophical dialogue involves not only the Socratic revaluation of death but its Platonic presentation as well. For Nietzsche, "the Platonic dialogue was, as it were, the barge on which the shipwrecked ancient poetry saved herself with all her children." But this rescue does not redeem the disaster. The influence of Socratic optimism on Greek culture remains baleful. "Crowded into a narrow space and timidly submitting to the single pilot, Socrates, they now sailed into a new world, which never tired of looking at the fantastic spectacle of this procession" (*BT*, 91; *KSA*, 1:93). Socrates steers Platonism, and *The Birth of Tragedy* draws no distinction between Socratic and Platonic doctrines. For Benjamin, by contrast, the essence of the Platonic philosophy, and what allows it to bear a positive valence in his exposition, is precisely its difference from the Socratic message it explicitly contains.

A first hint of this difference is provided by the authority Benjamin cites in the initial passage on Socrates. "Wilamowitz testifies to the fact that it meant the end of tragedy for Plato." Wilamowitz-Moellendorff, whose philological career began with "Philology of the Future!" ("*Zukunftsphilologie!*"), the devastating pasquinade against Nietzsche's *Birth of Tragedy*, here testifies that Plato, not Socrates, was concerned with the death of tragedy. The invocation of Nietzsche's philological nemesis at this point—an authority Benjamin in other contexts did not hold in particularly high regard[23]—marks the rupture between Plato and Socrates that Nietzsche's theory in particular disregards.

In fact, Benjamin's authority here is not in any substantive sense Wilamowitz-Moellendorff, but Nietzsche himself, though admittedly a later Nietzsche than the author of *The Birth of Tragedy*. A brief, two-part essay of Benjamin's from 1916 makes this clear. There, in passages sharply critical of Socrates, Benjamin concludes that Plato's purpose in depicting such a questionable figure was precisely the same spiteful resistance to mythic forces that would come to motivate the defiant tragic hero. "What did Plato intend with it?" Benjamin asks there. "Socrates: this is the figure in which Plato receives and annihilates the old myth. Socrates: this is the sacrifice of philosophy to the gods of myth who demand human sacrifice. In the midst of the terrible struggle, the young philosophy attempts to assert itself in Plato" (*SW*, 1:52; *GS*, 2:130). And in support of this reading, Benjamin points in a footnote to Nietzsche's *The Gay Science*, aphorism 340, "the dying Socrates."[24]

The second part of Benjamin's small essay emphasizes the difference between the Platonic presentation of Socrates and what Socrates himself teaches. "This is revealed by the Socratic method," Benjamin writes there,

> which is entirely different from the Platonic. The Socratic inquiry is not the holy question which awaits an answer and whose echo resounds in the response: it does not, as does the purely erotic or scientific question, already contain the *methodos* of the answer. Rather, a mere means to compel conversation, it forcibly, even impudently, dissimulates, ironizes—for it already knows the answer all too precisely. (*SW*, 1:53; *GS*, 2:131)[25]

In the youthful terms of his dialogic philosophy, Benjamin sharpens the difference between Platonic presentation and Socratic irony. Plato displaces Socrates' death into his dialogues not to endorse his ironic perspective but to defy the mythic forces that annihilate him; the sacrifice he offers them is of a man oblivious to their power. The *Trotz* that characterizes the tragic hero's entrance into death is thus here anticipated as Plato's defiant recourse to the myth-deaf Socrates in the "terrible struggle" redemptive philosophy conducts against the mortal judgment.

In *The Origin of German Trauerspiel*, Benjamin identifies the site of this displacement in Plato's oeuvre: "If, as depicted in the *Apology*, Socrates' death could have appeared tragic ... the Pythagorean tone of the *Phaedo*, on the other hand shows this death to be free of all tragic associations. Socrates looks death in the face as a mortal ... but he recognizes it as something alien, beyond which, in immortality, he expects to return to himself" (*OT*, 114; *GS*, 1:293). The shift in mortal posture toward death that Socrates represents expels death from the essence of life, which now promises survival as continuation in and of the first-person. But not this inessential death espoused by Socrates is the point of Plato's dialogue. Rather, it is the fact that Plato presents in it Socrates' physical death. The difference between "Apology" and "Phaidos" is not merely one of subject-matter—the civic role of philosophy versus immortality—but of presentation: first-person monologue versus dramatized dialogue.[26] This presentational shift, beneath any abstract arguments contained in the respective expositions, registers the survival of death not as the continuation of individual experience but as a posthumous presentation of the dead man's once-vital posture above a second signature. The expressive potential of physical death that tragedy had placed silently on the stage is here located in the externality of Socratic conceptualization to its Platonic presentation in dialogue.

> At the end of the *Symposium*, when Socrates, Agathon, and Aristophanes are seated alone, facing one another—is it not the sober light of his dialogues which Plato lets fall upon the discussion of the nature of the true poet, who embodies both tragedy and comedy, as dawn breaks over the three? In the dialogue pure dramatic language, before the tragic and the comic, its dialectic, appears. This purely dramatic quality reestablishes the mystery which had gradually become secularized in the form of Greek drama: its language, as the language of the new drama, is also the language of Trauerspiel. (*OT*, 118; *GS*, 1:297)

Here, what might look like a reduction of Platonic philosophy to the aesthetics of its presentation is in fact the opposite. The question of presentation, and the complicity of the author with what is presented, becomes with Socrates a philosophical question. In Plato's implicit distance from Socrates, the allegorical posture is expanded to include the presentation of discursive concepts beyond their intentional significance. If Plato's work makes Socrates a figure in Trauerspiel, the reflective implications cannot be arrested at the borders of genre but expand even into the treatise that presents them. The figure of Socrates, whose presentation by Plato is parodic resistance to the death of tragedy, makes *The Origin of German Trauerspiel* itself a Trauerspiel.

SILENCE

What links Platonic dialogue and Trauerspiel is their common exhibition of an extreme distinction between what is said and how what is said is presented. In both cases, a totalizing principle—the Socratic concept on the one hand and on the other the immanent political theology of melancholy creation in the Baroque—comprehends everything that can come forth as durable meaning. In contrast with this comprehensive principle, presentation per se, as opposed to the presenting of any particular content, can be negatively discerned, as a purely external remainder. That perception of presentation as the outside of enduring meaning is only available to a perspective that is itself outside the scope of these totalizing principles. Thus Trauerspiel renders its true significance to subsequent historical epochs over which its martyr/sovereign no longer reigns. And the true meaning of Platonic dialogue emerges only against a skeptical withdrawal from the Socratic reduction of reality to positive conceptual content.

The position to which Trauerspiel speaks is thus comprehensible as a moment beyond the historical horizon of the Baroque, a future granted the power to redeem it. But a theoretical moment outside the scope of conceptualization is far harder, and perhaps impossible, to comprehend. For Nietzsche's theory of tragedy, it is the insight into Dionysian reality, the "wisdom of Silenus" common to pre-Socratic Athens and Wagner's musical transports in the present that supports a perspective no longer beholden to Socratic "optimism." In the early studies where Benjamin is working out his own renovation of Nietzsche's theory at a comparable level of historical abstraction, in his essays on "Tragedy and Trauerspiel," and "The Meaning of Language in Trauerspiel and Tragedy," that dimension appears as what Benjamin calls the "pure word." That this isolated presentational dimension outside of any possible semantic content might itself mediate a different kind of significance, this possibility brings the language of Trauerspiel into contact with musical significance, which is also bare of separable content but whose performance nonetheless has profound emotional resonance.

"Where the pure underlying meaning of a word is operative, the word becomes tragic," Benjamin writes there. "The word as the pure bearer of its meaning is the pure word. But alongside this, we find a word of another sort, one that changes on its way from the site of its origin toward a different point, something like its estuary." A contrast not simply between concepts but between ways of gaining access to conceptual content. The pure word that exerts a tragic force exists as a standard in terms of which Benjamin discerns a contrasting word, or more exactly, a contrasting transformation between impure, transitory aspects of the living voice at the site of the pure word. Everything we ordinarily think of as language falls within this second, mutable word. What here in this early speculative reflection Benjamin calls the "pure word" will become, in *The Origin of German Trauerspiel*, defiant silence. The distinction between the language of tragedy and the language of Trauerspiel is thus, despite initial appearances, not a distinction within language between two sorts of word but a distinction between language as part of the furniture of the world and a regulative abstraction contrasting with it. The pure word of tragedy is, in its unchanging transparency, outside of history. The word of Trauerspiel, which emerges from natural sound, remains connected to transitory vital feelings, to perishable temporality and so remains historical. "Words have a pure emotional life cycle [*reines Gefühlsleben*] in which they purify themselves by developing from the natural sound [*Laute der Natur*] to the pure sound of feeling [*reinen Laute des Gefühls*]. For such words, language is merely a transitional phase within the cycle of its transformations, and the mourning play speaks with this word. It describes the path from natural sound via lament to music" (*SW*, 1:60; *GS*, 2:138). From this perspective, a natural cry has mutated into lamentation on its way toward musical expression. Where the pure word of tragedy intersects this auditory mutation is where the lamentations of Trauerspiel appear as the intermediary stage in a trajectory from spontaneous grunt into spontaneous song.

Such a life cycle might be understood progressively. Natural cries are brute responses to human imbrication in an organic, bestial domain, while music aims at the highest spiritual expressions. Or it might be, from a different angle, degeneration. Natural cries manifest a pure congruence between expression and awareness, whereas music exhibits the most artificial and self-conscious arrangements. But Benjamin's exposition in fact suspends the status of the natural origin and the musical telos and resituates them as the productive and receptive poles of meaning, as writing and as reading. For the abstract trajectory from nature into music is interrupted by the historical discrepancy between tragedy and Trauerspiel. "For the mourning play is not the spherical progress of feeling through the pure world of words culminating in music and returning to the liberated sorrow of blessed feeling [*befreiten Trauer des seligen Gefühls*]. Instead, midway through this path nature finds itself betrayed by language, and that powerful inhibition of feeling [*Hemmung des Gefühls*] turns to sorrow [*Trauer*]" (*SW*, 1:60; *GS*, 2:138). Here, language does not see itself betrayed by nature, its ideal aspirations sullied by grubby material limitations. The betrayal moves the other way. It is nature that sees itself betrayed by language, which abandons the spontaneous innocence of the brute cry and becomes host to the incongruence of a symbol that means something other than itself. Once the identity of sound and expression is left behind, its positive emancipating power—what Benjamin calls the "pure word"—cannot be regained even where that identity is eventually reestablished in musical expression. Rather, by lamenting its abandonment by the pure word, the natural cry registers it negatively as an interruption in emotional experience, mourns it as an immediate condensation point of loss.

In this early sketch, Benjamin has not yet situated tragic silence in his thinking. The notion of silence does not appear, and the tragic manifestation of the pure word remains in this respect unspecified. "The tragic is not just confined exclusively to the realm of dramatic human speech; it is the only form originally proper to human dialogue" (*SW*, 1:59; *GS*, 2:137). It is the principle of human dialogue, true linguistic exchange, but the extent to which it can be materially manifested there is not explicitly addressed. The distinction Benjamin draws here is not material but formal: Tragic meaning is formally coincident with itself. "In tragedy, the word and the tragic arise together, simultaneously, on the same spot" (*SW*, 1:59; *GS*, 2:138). The continuous development of the pathos-laden word, from natural howl to ethereal song, is thus interrupted by the loss of tragedy itself as a possibility and diverted into lamentation for that loss for as long as it does not collapse into music. That diversion is Trauerspiel.²⁷ "The interplay between sound and meaning remains a terrifying phantom for the mourning play; it is possessed by language.... That interplay must find its resolution, however, and for the mourning play that redemptive mystery is music—the rebirth of the feelings in a suprasensuous nature" (*SW*, 1:60–1; *GS*, 2:139). Trauerspiel is not music, but the possibility of music positions Trauerspiel. The world of Trauerspiel

> is the site of the actual conception [*Empfängnis*] of the word and of discourse in art; the faculties of speech and hearing still stand equal in the scales, and ultimately everything depends on the ear for lament, for only the most profoundly heard lament can become music. While in tragedy the eternal inflexibility of the spoken word is exalted, the mourning play concentrates in itself the infinite resonance of its sound. (*SW*, 1:61; *GS*, 2:140)

Music thus positions a receptive possibility toward the word that entertains its loss of a potential for tragic mobilization and registers that loss emotionally for as long as it does not close into music.²⁸

With the introduction of tragic silence, however, the role of music grows more complex. In *Origin of German Trauerspiel*, the relationship of Baroque drama to music appears in its relation to opera. "The phonetic tension in the language of the seventeenth century leads directly to music as the counterpart [*Widerpart*] to meaning-laden speech," Benjamin writes.

> Like all the other roots of the Trauerspiel, this one too is entwined with those of the pastoral. That which is initially present in the Trauerspiel as a dancing chorus, and with the passage of time tends increasingly to become spoken, oratorical chorus, openly displays its operatic character in the pastoral play. (*OT*, 211; *GS*, 1:385)

It is in this context, late in the second half of *Origin of German Trauerspiel*, that Benjamin returns explicitly to Nietzsche's *Birth of Tragedy* and in particular its critique of operatic recitative. "The related ideas which it is the purpose of these observations to call to mind have been developed by Nietzsche in *The Birth of Tragedy*" (*OT*, 212; *GS*, 1:385).

Let us recall in broad outlines Nietzsche's objections to contemporary opera. Chapter 19 of *The Birth of Tragedy* introduces opera as the culmination of Western culture's Socratic-Alexandrine tendency toward comprehensibility, and indeed, suggests that the two are synonymous: "We cannot indicate the innermost modern content of this Socratic culture more distinctly than by calling it *the culture of the opera*" (*BT*, 114; *KSA*, 1:120). The optimistic faith in conceptual comprehensibility is manifested in opera's subordination of musical meaning to verbal significance and visual representation. This corruption of musical meaning pushes opera to the edge of genuine art; a compromised position most audible where the demand for comprehensibility drags composition and performance away from melody and harmony toward the intermediate form of recitative.

> The listener who insists on distinctly hearing the words under the music has his desire fulfilled by the singer in that the latter speaks rather than sings, intensifying the pathetic expression of the words by means of this half-song. By this intensification of the pathos he facilitates the understanding of the words and overcomes the remaining half of the music. (*BT*, 114; *KSA*, 1:121)

This inverted alignment of meaning and music, in which the significance of the musical element is a pathos entirely in service to the content of the verbal expression, is evidence, Nietzsche feels, of an extra-aesthetic interference, emerging from the audience, in the aesthetic drive motivating the composer.

> It was the demand of thoroughly unmusical hearers that before everything else the words must be understood, so that according to them a rebirth of music is to be expected only when some mode of singing has been discovered in which text-word lords it over counterpoint like master over servant. (*BT*, 116; *KSA*, 1:123)

This subordination is, Nietzsche claims with reference to Schiller, the "idyllic" tendency that governs in opera—idyllic in that all aspects of reality that resist understanding are banished and denied. It is a representational corruption that rebounds back onto music in general and mirrors the death of tragedy itself. "Closely observed, this fatal influence of the opera on music is seen to coincide exactly with the universal development of modern music," Nietzsche maintains.

> The optimism lurking in the genesis of the opera and in the character of the culture thereby represented, has, with alarming rapidity, succeeded in divesting music of its Dionysian-cosmic mission and impressing on it a playfully formal and pleasurable character: a change comparable to the metamorphosis of the Aeschylean man into the cheerful Alexandrian. (*BT*, 119; *KSA*, 1:126)

Contemporary opera thus presents a field congruent with contemporary culture, and exhibits its deficiency.

The tragic insight that is corrupted by operatic recitative, and whose apprehension defines aesthetic understanding, is preserved by two cultural traditions anchored in, and anchoring, the adjective "German": German music and German philosophy. The former, "as we must understand it, particularly in its vast solar orbit from Bach to Beethoven, from Beethoven to Wagner" (*BT*, 119; *KSA*, 1:127), exhibits the same intimation as the latter, as exemplified by Kant and Schopenhauer. The distinction between a conceptually meaningless, though true, thing-in-itself and its distortion into an appearance amenable to conceptual description mirrors the distinction between the experience of musical transport and mere verbal communication. Only by righting the relationship between the latter distinction, and reinstating the Dionysian force of musical transport to its appropriate priority over verbal transmission, can the arrangement of drives and representations characteristic of Greek tragedy be re-created. This inversion is the significance of Wagner's *Gesamtkunstwerk*, where the primal power of the music overtakes the representational and dramatic aspects of the opera. No longer are the pathological techniques of musical arrangement employed to decorate with transitory affects a primarily verbal and visual experience; Wagnerian music erupts as an overwhelming force, and the representational aspects of Wagnerian opera—Teutonic myth—are reactively interposed, as distancing mechanisms between the listener and the de-individuating ecstasies of the music.

> The myth protects us against the music, while on the other hand it alone gives music the highest freedom. In return, music imparts to the tragic myth an intense and convincing metaphysical significance that word and image without this singular help could never have attained. (*BT*, 126; *KSA*, 1:134)

This is the salutary Apollonian deception that allows an experience of Dionysian ecstasy while preserving the implicit stability of individual continuity.

> With the immense impact of the image, the concept, the ethical teaching, and the sympathetic emotion, the Apollonian tears man from his orgiastic self-annihiliation and blinds him to the universality of the Dionysian process, deluding him into the belief that he is seeing a single image of the world (*Tristan and Isolde*, for instance), and that *through music*, he is merely supposed to *see* it still better and more profoundly. (*BT*, 128; *KSA*, 1:137)

The description of tragic affect is here deposited in a synaesthesia between hearing and seeing that threatens the epistemological stability of the subject, and puts a particular weight on the exemplary name Wagner. The individuality of author and listener, and their consequent distinction, is immediately manifested in the Apollonian representational dimension of myth: the dramatic images and concepts that interpose themselves between the audience and the Dionysian chaos, and the moral sympathies that these invoke. But the authority emerges from the collective Dionysian transport, within which author and audience cannot be distinguished, since it passes through them equally. In this moment of indifference, the identity between Wagner and Aeschylus across the intervening Socratic-Alexandrine wastes can be established.

Nietzsche's identification of the genuine tragic impetus and the experience of Wagnerian music is thus not the result but the condition of the language of *The Birth of Tragedy*. The force of history conditioning language emerges only from the perspective that identifies Wagner and Aeschylus outside of language, in music, and it is for this reason that Nietzsche must insist on the centrality of an inaudible Greek music to the experience of Attic tragedy. "I maintain, that is, that we know Aeschylus and Sophocles only as lyricists, as librettists," Nietzsche had explicitly stated in his 1870 essay on "Greek Music-drama," "which means that we do not know them" (*KSA*, 1:517). And if the essential antagonism of Wagnerian art to the rest of contemporary opera led Nietzsche to withdraw from that bald formulation, nonetheless, the resemblances between representational aspects of Wagnerian opera and Greek tragic drama do not support but arise from inaudible similarities between Greek music and Wagner's compositions. Only on the basis of this musical continuity can these heterogeneous aesthetic expressions be posited as identical reactions to an identical experience: the combination of Dionysian passion and Apollonian reaction that unlocks the meaning of life.

But as an outside to language, Wagnerian/Aeschylian music must speak for itself, and Nietzsche's address can register only a prior agreement to this identity in a direct call to those who share it. "My friends, you who believe in Dionysian music, you also know what tragedy means to us. There we have tragic myth reborn from music— and in this myth we can hope for everything and forget what is most painful!" (*BT*, 142; *KSA*, 1:154). The "we" with which the treatise opened, those interested in promoting "the science of aesthetics" (*BT*, 33; *KSA*, 1:25), becomes here explicitly those who, among that anonymous readership, can countenance this identity. Nietzsche reads these ancient texts for the first time since their creation: "I do not think I am unreasonable in saying that the problem of this origin has as yet not even been seriously posed, to say nothing of solved, however often the ragged tatters of ancient tradition have been sewn together in various combinations and torn apart again" (*BT*, 56; *KSA*, 1:52). But he does not read them to everybody. He reads them only to those who recognize that Wagner's music opens onto the same chaotic source as Aeschylus's tragedies. Only they can license his flamboyant rhetoric, with an endorsement granted not by philological discipline but by musical enthusiasm.

Thus the critique of recitative is not a stylistic objection but condenses a critique of linguistic communication as such. Faith in the power of language to communicate reality through time is the idyllic mystification under which the composers of *stile rappresentativo* labored, why they failed to recognize their subordination of music to language in recitative as a quasi-aesthetic compromise with the unmusical listener but understood it as the rediscovery of original language: "The recitative was regarded as the rediscovered language of this primitive man; opera as the rediscovered country of this idyllically or heroically good creature" (*BT*, 115; *KSA*, 1:122). This is a sentence Benjamin quotes.

Recitative thus stands in for the optimistic science of philology itself.[29] The coordination of the tradition of opera with a degenerate philological tendency, when contrasted with the Wagnerian overcoming of operatic banality, opens in turn a space for a superior philology, one that would parallel Wagner's revitalization of classical tragedy. It is this ideal philology, as opposed to Socratic-Alexandrine scientific punctiliousness, that *The Birth of Tragedy* itself is supposed to exemplify. Where the death of tragedy was brought about by the subordination of Euripides' creative drive to Socrates' conceptual reception, its rebirth will result from the subordination of Nietzschean conceptual analysis to Wagnerian creative force. But however neat these parallelisms may appear, they in fact remain constitutively unstable, for there is no independent license for the musical identity that guarantees them. All that sustains the separation of Nietzsche's language as an Apollonian synthesis from Socratic recitative is Wagner's inspiring music, but that music in its absence from Nietzsche's text. Should it ever sound within Nietzsche's impassioned words, supporting and bolstering their implicit claims to have recaptured an original language, those words would fall into recitative.[30]

This is what Benjamin implicitly recognizes in his silencing of Nietzsche. "Just as every comparison with tragedy—not to mention musical tragedy—is of no value for the understanding of opera," Benjamin writes, "so it is that from the point of view of literature, and especially the Trauerspiel, opera must seem unmistakably to be a product of decadence [*Verfallsprodukt*]" (*OT*, 212; *GS*, 1:386). Not from our receptive perspective, observing the confusion between recitative and original language, but from the expressive perspective of Trauerspiel, that is, the perspective mourning that original language, a musical supplement creating opera, with its promise of a pure coincidence of meaning and presentation, must appear as degenerate. Thus the irony of making Nietzsche's insight into the inaccessibility of tragedy the "Archimedean point" of contemporary tragic theory. That insight into the loss of tragic meaning is all that is left of tragedy. In the split between presentation and content to which Trauerspiel bears witness, all theory must partake of Trauerspiel—what passes as a theory of tragedy is the Trauerspiel orchestrated to register its loss. In a manifest sense, there can be no "theory of tragedy."

Thus Benjamin's earlier active suppression of music in Nietzsche's account, in order to demonstrate his access to tragic silence. "Although he had no suspicion of its significance as a manifestation of the agonal in the tragic sphere, he nevertheless puts his finger on it in his contrast of image and speech. Tragic 'heroes speak, as it were, more superficially than they act; the myth does not at all obtain adequate objectification in the spoken word.'[31] . . . This can, of course, hardly be a question of failure, as Nietzsche goes on to suggest" (*OT*, 108; *GS*, 1:287). In its original context in Nietzsche, the citation from *The Birth of Tragedy* points to the space that music occupies in tragic representation: "How easily one forgets that what the word-poet did not succeed in doing, namely, attain the highest spiritualization and ideality of the myth, he might very well succeed in doing every moment as creative musician!" (*BT*, 105; *KSA*, 1:110). But Benjamin has shifted Nietzsche's observation to coincide with his own notion of a silent bearer of tragic meaning and does not hear the possibility of Wagner's music.

But in this we, too, are hardly dealing with an interpretive failure. "To be fair to *The Birth of Tragedy* (1872)," Nietzsche himself writes sixteen years later in *Ecce Homo*, "one has to forget a few things" (*EH*, 270; *KSA*, 6:309). He does not say that one must bear a few considerations in mind, understand the enveloping context, remember a few things. Rather, one must forget a few things. Chief among them, the music that inspired it: "Wagner, Bayreuth, the whole wretched German pettiness are a cloud in which an infinite mirage of the future is reflected" (*EH*, 275; *KSA*, 6:314). Only then, with Wagner's music silenced, can the genuine significance of *The Birth of Tragedy* be apprehended, can the great hope it mediates through its own presentation be freed. Not in manifest influences on conceptual constructs, but in this slight readjustment that violates them and silences Wagner's music, Benjamin shows himself to be a true reader of the book, able to penetrate the esoteric mystery of its presentation and receive the affirmation it bears through a nihilism deep as Benjamin's own. *This would be a task*, Nietzsche had noted in the summer of 1875, underlining the entry vehemently, *to designate Hellenism as irretrievable and thus Christianity as well and what has been up to now the foundations of our society and politics* (*KSA*, 8:83). A task for Nietzsche, and a task for Benjamin.

CHAPTER THREE

Inscription

The walls of rude minds are scrawled all over with facts, with thoughts. They shall one day bring a lantern and read the inscriptions.

—R. W. EMERSON, "Intellect"

PSEUDOMENON

We owe the oldest formulation of the paradox of the Cretan not to a philosopher but to an apostle. Paul, in his Epistle to Titus, warns the acolyte: "One of themselves, even a prophet of their own, said, The Cretans are always liars, evil beasts, slow bellies. This witness is true" (Titus 1:12–13). The formal implications of the remark were perhaps not foremost in his mind. The implicit contradiction, however, has troubled philosophy throughout the intervening two millennia. Is the Cretan lying or is he telling the truth? In its simpler version, the paradox has the Cretan Epimenides (to whom Paul here seems to have been referring) say, "Cretans are liars," a statement which, if false, would demonstrate itself in the Cretan's telling, and hence become true. If the statement is true, however, then Cretans *are* liars, no less the Cretan Epimenides when he speaks, and so his statement tumbles into falsehood once again. Scholastic philosophy considered such infinitely self-subverting claims under the marginal rubric of *insolubilia*.[1] Only in the wake of the extraordinary advances in logical formalism in the nineteenth century did this self-referential paradox and others like it reemerge at the center of thought, most noticeably, perhaps, in Russell's set theoretical paradox and Gödel's logical incompleteness theorem.[2] At the outset of the twentieth century, the necessity of a statement that is true just in case it is false scuttled the philosophical optimism with which truth-functional logic was approaching the world and clouded the heady transparency of set theory.

In reflecting on the paradox, one notices quickly enough that however vividly the figure of the Cretan may evoke the difficulty, he nonetheless does make it "untidy," in Willard Van Orman Quine's word. "Perhaps some Cretans were liars, notably Epimenides, and others were not; perhaps Epimenides was a liar who occasionally told the truth; either way it turns out that the contradiction vanishes."[3] The paradox can thus be even further concentrated, as Quine (and medieval logicians before him) pointed out, and focused into the so-called *pseudomenon*, or statement: "I am lying." This is true if it is a lie and a lie if it is true, and so short-circuits the necessity in logical inference. In keeping with his exclusively formal concerns, Quine is happy to go further and translate the *pseudomenon* into entirely impersonal terms. "We can even drop the indirectness of a personal reference and speak directly of the sentence: 'this sentence is false'" (7). Yet that last refinement, which initially may seem but the scrupulousness of a tidy mind, in fact transforms the *pseudomenon* in two profound and related ways. It introduces, first, a recursive component that simultaneously appears as a part of the statement and designates the whole of the statement of which it is part. (In Quine's formulation it is the recursive term "this sentence.") That problematic component now serves the subversive function originally conducted through the externalized figure of the Cretan who both lied and told the truth, both confessed and deceived, and so also did neither—a conceptual function that had been bound, in other words, to an externally self-referential and not an immanently recursive operation. And second, by retracting the external reference into the immanent recursion of a purely self-subverting propositional structure, Quine's adjustment transforms the negative contrast to truth from a morally relevant lie into an abstract falsehood.

In contrast to Quine and to analytic formalism generally, Walter Benjamin resisted the direction of this last refinement when, in a fragment from 1920, he took up and worked through in his own way the paradox of the Cretan. Benjamin, too, recognizes the formal leakiness of its traditional version and the need for reformulation. *In its classical Greek form*, Fragment 40 begins, *the paradox of the Cretan is easily resolved* (*SW*, 1:210; *GS*, 6:57). But in tightening up the formulation, Benjamin resolutely maintains the external instance of the Cretan's veracity as the relevant point, and refuses to abstract the paradox into an immanent formal antinomy between mutually exclusive truth-values. The adjustment Benjamin makes begins by generalizing the lie: [*We must*] *argue as follows: Epimenides maintains that all Cretans, whenever they open their mouths, assert the contrary of what is true. Epimenides is a Cretan* (*SW*, 1:210; *GS*, 6:57). A unanimous community of perpetual liars absorbs the referential ambiguities of the original characterization, and the logical relevance of Epimenides himself is preserved as a minor premise.

But this recasting makes evident that the paradox does not inhere in the logical syllogism connecting two sentences but is at issue already in the inclusion in the major premise of a reference to Epimenides as the source of the mendacious predicate under which the minor premise expressly brings him. That is to say, the liar's paradox shows something about self-reference, not Epimenides or Cretans. Like Quine, Benjamin too recognizes that some of the extraneous ambiguities that interfere with the genuinely paradoxical consequences of the Cretan's claim disappear when its formula is reduced to a single sentence that does not depend on referential proper names. But unlike Quine, who dispenses with reference (and its irreducibly ontological commitments) entirely in favor of stipulating logically transparent notations with ultimately pragmatic applications, Benjamin universalizes the Cretan's referential relevance *syntactically*. The implicit self-reference that distinguishes first-person from third-person verb conjugations explicitly comes to bear on the destabilizing relevance of the liar's paradox. For Benjamin, the paradox culminates not in the proposition "this sentence is false" but in the following form, an articulated version of the first-person *pseudomenon*: "*Every one of my assertions without exception predicates the diametrical opposite of the truth*" ("*Ausnahmslos jedes meiner Urteile prädiziert das konträre Gegenteil von der Wahrheit*") (*SW*, 1:210; *GS*, 6:57). Far from being a superfluous complication, as it was for Quine, the reflexive external self-reference, now focused on the first-person possessive adjective, is, in Benjamin's understanding of the liar's paradox, its essential condition.

By anchoring the paradox to the intentional moment of its utterance, Benjamin sees in it something different and more unsettling than the ancient observation that deictic elements can effect the truth-value of a sentence.[4] The first-person deixis of the confessional deception or deceptive confession that is the liar's paradox does not merely falsify its content but stymies in an infinite regress logical conclusiveness itself. Because it reflexively conditions the very occasion of the expression within which logical consequence is manifested, the paradox *is insoluble within logic itself* [*intralogisch unauflösbar*], Benjamin insists (*SW* 1:210; *GW*, 6:58). The *pseudomenon* thus generalized is a limit-case. It operates uniquely in logical language, for it negates not the simple contents of sentences, however generally, but the intentions *behind* any possible expression that shares its own source. As the subversion of truthful intention itself, the paradox does not communicate a subjective judgment but manifests in the self-contradictory form of deceptive confession the relation between universal logical form and the first-person deixis presupposed by logical intentions. This manifestation is the extralogical meaning, outside of any logically determined intentions, that the *pseudomenon* brings to light. *It forms its insoluble chain of contradictions in the realm of logic,* Benjamin claims, *without being in any way meaningless or nonsensical in itself—that is to say, on the ontological plane* (*SW,* 1:211; *GS* 6:58).

This "ontological plane" on which the meaning of the paradox appears, external as it is to the integrity of communication, refuses to be comprehended by a higher-order intention. As the self-denunciation of communication as deceitful per se, the *pseudomenon* is ultimately not the testimony of any individual speaker but has, as its intending correlate, an impossible subject. *You have only to imagine the Cartesian demon of deception transposed from the sphere of perception to that of logic to realize that it could not carry out its deception better than by making this paradox its own* (*SW,* 1:211; *GS* 6:58). Just how such a transposition would be accomplished, and whether spheres of perception and spheres of logic could remain consistently opposed in the course of it, is a question that we can leave to one side. What recommends the invocation of Descartes's *genium aliquem malignum* to Benjamin here (in what is after all a private note wrestling with limit-thoughts and not the finished presentation of a thorough conceptualization) is the consequent exteriority to first-person identification that follows from the demon's skeptical function in Descartes's exposition. In the *Meditations,* the evil demon interferes in subjective judgment directly, conjuring a false sense of confidence in Descartes's arithmetic conclusions and distorting his sensory and intuitive evidence. By identifying what such an external interference would *say* with the unthinkable self-subversion of the liar's paradox, Benjamin illuminates an impersonal exterior to logic congruent with the possibility of localized first-person expression that communication harbors. To venture an image of our own here: Just as the solar corona becomes visible only when the disk of the sun is obscured by the eclipsing moon, so this ontological exterior to all logic appears in itself only here, where the logical content of expression is neutralized by the first-person self-denunciatory paradox.

This impersonal possibility of the first-person is where Benjamin explicitly situates the significance of the paradox. *It is evident that this proposition leads to contradictions only if it is uttered by the person to whom it applies, whereas it can be asserted of any other person that every one of his statements means the contrary of what they claim to mean, without this leading to contradiction* (SW, 1:211; GS, 6:58). Promoted to the limits of demonic origin and significant paradox, the very possibility of an absolutely truthful expression surrenders to itself; the very possibility of truth diverges from the very truth of possibility. The liar's paradox *exists not just as a counterweight to reality, but . . . as an objective counterweight to truth* (SW, 1:211; GS, 6:58). An objectivity that is heterogeneous in every sense to truth; this is the impossible meaning of the *pseudomenon*.

The exteriority toward which the Cretan gestures in Benjamin's understanding is a *radical* exteriority that cannot in turn be subordinated to a more comprehensive horizon. Its truth cannot be internalized as knowledge; it relates to knowledge by interrupting and denouncing it as conditioned and incomplete. Invoking a philosophical term that has, at least since Kant, been taken to contrast with truth itself, Benjamin calls this untrue occasion for a radically exterior truth *Schein*, semblance.

> *The logical unassailability of the Cretan's assertion—since once it has been asserted, its implications are fixed—must prove to be Schein, for otherwise logic as such would collapse. Moreover, if this is Schein, it must be genuine [echter]—that is objective Schein. In other words, it is not, as the modern view of Schein would suggest, a Schein that arises from an accidental or necessary failure of knowledge to correspond to the truth, but rather a Schein that cannot be resolved in the truth—it can only be destroyed by it.* (SW, 1:211; GS, 6:59)

The opposition Benjamin assumes here, between a *Schein* resulting from the divergence of subjective knowledge from objective truth and a "genuine, objective" *Schein* that, without being subsumed into subjectivity, is nonetheless radically antithetical to truth, is mightily compressed. How are we to understand a *Schein* that is both "echt" and at the same time absolutely incompatible with truth?

The peculiarly Benjaminian notion of *Schein* is developed most extensively in the third section of his essay on "Goethe's *Elective Affinities*." There, the exposition is complicated by the intermediary notion of the beautiful. In the figure of Ottilie Goethe has presented the relation of beautiful semblance, *schöner Schein*, to truth. This relation is neither a simple antithesis, as if beauty were nothing more than speciousness and irrelevant to truth, nor is it, more elaborately, a relation of continuity, as if beauty could manifest truth. The formula with which Benjamin takes issue there runs: "Beauty is truth become visible."[5] Not only does this glib equation elide the essential difference between the absoluteness of truth and relative visibility, but in a more fundamental way, by imagining that truth and beauty could immediately converge in the same phenomenon, the formula posits each of them as theoretically subordinate to a self-identical intentional subjectivity and implies thereby that, in thought at least, "the truth of the beautiful can be unveiled." This amounts, Benjamin says, to philosophical barbarism. "Beauty," Benjamin goes on to claim, "is not a *Schein*, not a veil covering something else. It itself is not appearance [*Erscheinung*] but purely essence—one which, of course, remains essentially identical to itself only when veiled" (*SW*, 1:351; *GS*, 1:195). Here Benjamin wrenches two oppositions that are traditionally understood as congruent—the opposition between relative *Schein* and absolute truth, and the opposition between appearance and essence—into a perpendicular juxtaposition around the notion of beauty. Beauty is not *Schein* as opposed to self-identical truth—it is essentially what it is and not the appearance of something else. But *Schein* can be beautiful; and when it is, it is essentially, truly specious. "For the beautiful is neither the veil nor the veiled object but the object in its veil." It is the truthful manifestation of its own mendacity.

Just as the liar's paradox undermines any stable convergence of universal truth and individual expression, so beautiful semblance subverts the opposition between truth and phenomenal awareness. In both cases, "the diametrical opposite of the truth" expands to occupy the entire domain of expression or awareness and becomes the occasion for a truth no longer indigenous to awareness or expression. And just as this antithesis to truth cannot be circumscribed by formal notions of falsehood or moral notions of deception but in its existential urgency opens onto the nihilistic energy of treason, betrayal, heresy, false doctrine, onto Hobbes's "Kingdome of Darknesse" in which we live, so the alternative truth does not arrive as knowledge but interrupts the pretensions of knowledge, the continuities and identities that make it up. In the Goethe essay Benjamin marks this difference by shifting phenomenal registers, from the visual appearance to the auditory expression: the nonphenomenal nondeception Benjamin calls *das Ausdruckslose*, "the expressionless." In an earlier version of the passages in the essay elaborating the concept (*SW*, 1:340; *GS*, 1:181), a version published among the paralipomena to the essay and translated as "On Semblance," Benjamin draws explicitly the connection between this interruptive moment and the paradoxical truth of the lie. *For just as an interruption can, by a word of command, extract the truth from the speech of a liar, in the same way the expressionless compels the trembling harmony to stop and immortalizes that quivering through its objection* (*SW*, 1:224; *GS*, 1:832). What the Cretan had combined into a single self-subverting self-denunciation is here distributed into the poles of a dialogic conflict: The lie displays itself truly as a lie in the silence occasioned by a skeptical interruption of its vital expression.

These preliminary notes "On Semblance" also reveal philologically the immediate precedent for Benjamin's radically antisubjective theory of *Schein*. The fragment begins with categorizations of semblance (as error, then as representation), and an *eidetic experiment* that is meant to identify an irreducibly visual aspect to *Schein*. Benjamin then notes without further elaboration: *Nietzsche's definition of Schein in* The Birth of Tragedy (*SW*, 1:224; *GS*, 1:831). What has Benjamin drawn from *The Birth of Tragedy* and the concept of *Schein* that appears there?

Nietzsche does not explicitly define *Schein* in that early treatise, but as the characteristic aspect of Apollo, the term plays an important and localized role in the exposition. The Apollonian dimension of art is illustrated from the outset by the "lovely semblance [*schöner Schein*] of dreamworlds, in whose generation [*Erzeugung*] every human being is fully an artist" (*BT*, 34; *KSA*, 1:26). But it is in the fourth chapter of the text, when he is bringing together the Apollonian and the Dionysian drives in aesthetic contrast, that Nietzsche develops and complicates the notion of *Schein*. The tenor of his deployment of the term recalls Schiller's 26th *Letter On the Aesthetic Education of Man*, though Nietzsche has magnified Schiller's notion of a distinctly human *Spieltrieb* achieving satisfaction in aesthetic, which is to say both inconsequential and liberated, *Schein*, with Schopenhauer's bleak opposition between a meaningless inhuman will and the subjective aesthetic forms that temporarily pacify it.

> The more clearly I perceive in nature those omnipotent art impulses, and in them an ardent longing for semblance [*Shein*], for redemption through semblance, the more I feel impelled to the metaphysical assumption that the truly existent primal unity, eternally suffering and contradictory, also needs the rapturous vision, the pleasurable semblance [*lustvollen Schein*] for its continuous redemption. (*BT*, 44–45; *KSA*, 1:38)

The traditional contrast of *Schein* with Truth is rendered as, on the one hand, true existence, self-contradictory primordial unity, the invariant meaninglessness of human suffering and chaos, and on the other, the intensive experience, the apparition in the ecstasy of its apprehension, the paradigm of which is the dream. But before these metaphysical commitments can stabilize into an explanation, Nietzsche's thought shifts abruptly, circumscribing with the first-person plural a new horizon around author and reader, within which everything is duplicitous *Schein*.

> And we, completely wrapped up in this *Schein* and composed of it, are compelled to consider this *Schein* as the truly non-existent— i.e., as a perpetual becoming in time, space, and causality—in other words, as empirical reality. If, for the moment, we did not consider the question of our own "reality," if we conceive of our empirical existence, and of that of the world in general, as a continuously manifested representation [*Vorstellung*] of the primal unity, we shall then have to look upon the dream as a mere *semblance of semblance* [*Schein des Scheins*], hence as a still higher appeasement of the primordial desire for *Schein*. (*BT*, 45; *KSA*, 1:38–39)

The dream is not insubstantial and trivial over against waking experience, but in its self-evident *Schein* epitomizes that experience and hence multiplies its affect. In a paradoxical fashion, the reduplication of *Schein*, its transformation into the semblance of the semblance, does not remove it ever further from the truth with which it contrasts. Rather, the reduplication of *Schein* as the *Schein* of *Schein* creates the opportunity for an otherwise inaccessible recognition of the genuine situation to which the existence of *Schein* as such witnesses. The distinction *within* experience between a durable reality and the transient non-self-identity exhibited by self-evident semblance reiterates a hypothetical distinction *beyond* experience between its non-self-identical—temporal—character per se and a unified, self-validating perspective by definition inaccessible to it or to us.

It is in this discontinuity between the perspective entirely circumscribed and hence blinded by *Schein* and an emancipated perspective

Inscription 111

that can recognize and even exalt in the unreality of *Schein* as *Schein* that Nietzsche situates his artistic example: not the dramatic presentations of Sophocles or Wagner but the visible representation of Raphael's *Transfiguration*.

> In a symbolic painting, *Raphael*, himself one of those "naïve" ones, has represented for us this demotion of semblance to semblance [*Depotenziren des Schiens zum Schein*], the primal process of the naïve artist and of Apollinian culture. In his *Transfiguration*, the lower half of the picture, with the possessed boy, the despairing bearers, the bewildered, terrified disciples, shows us the reflection of suffering, primal and eternal, [*Wiederspiegelung des ewigen Urschmerzes*], the sole ground of the world: the "semblance" here is the reflection [*der "Schein" ist hier Widerschein*] of eternal contradiction, the father of things. From this semblance arises, like ambrosial vapor, a new visionary world of semblance [*visionsgleiche neue Scheinwelt*], invisible to those wrapped in the first semblance—a radiant floating in purest bliss, a serene contemplation beaming from wide-open eyes. Here we have presented, in the most sublime artistic symbolism, that Apollinian world of beauty and its substratum, the terrible wisdom of Silenus; and intuitively we comprehend their necessary interdependence. (*BT*, 45; *KSA*, 1:39)

What is immediately striking about Nietzsche's interpretation of Raphael's painting is his claim that no figure in the lower half of the composition is aware of the transfiguration in the upper half. At the most straightforward level this claim seems difficult to justify—several of the disciples appear to be gesturing toward the transfigured Christ. But by amplifying the vertical division in the painting and segregating the scenes depicted there—scenes that correspond to separate episodes in the synoptic Gospels, and whose aesthetic unity has long been felt to be the ultimate meaning of the work—Nietzsche radically separates the perspective of the viewer, for whom both elements coexist and mutually condition one another, and the immanent perspectives of the painted representations, for whom no such connection exists. And we can note that despite the gestures, there is only one figure in the lower section of the painting whose face is clearly turned toward the vision, who might in some sense be *seeing* it, and that is the lunatic boy; a face, that is, in which we perceive not comprehension but its vacant inversion as madness and possession. This incommunicative gaze, then, marks the axis of Nietzsche's interpretation: the spectacular vision of plenitude appearing to the vacant agony of seizure as mutually reinforcing conditions.

But if the radical discontinuity between the perspective of the figures *in* the painting and the perspective *on* the painting of the viewer is what enables the work naively to embody the truth of *Schein* and brings it into contact with Benjamin's notion of "objective semblance," at the same time, Nietzsche's assumption that these discontinuous perspectives share a common character as subjective appearances, that the *Widerschein* of eternal contradiction below can be comprehended simultaneously with the visionlike *Scheinwelt* above—this assumption separates Nietzsche's view irrevocably from Benjamin's perspective. In *The Origin of German Trauerspiel*, Benjamin faults Nietzsche's tragic theory for collapsing into the "abyss of aestheticism" and maintains that the "nihilism housed in the depths of Bayreuth's philosophy of art" swallows the historical significance of tragedy there (*OT*, 103; *GS*, 1:281–82). For Benjamin, the incompatibility of the external and immanent perspectives on *Schein* precludes any direct access to that exterior, truthful perspective, which must rather be intermittently derived through interruptions of the immanent perspective. Nietzsche's Bayreuth nihilism is not, for Benjamin, too bleak and hopeless but rather not consequent enough, in that it claims to *know* and *communicate* the paradoxical truth of universal falsity.

If we wish to see a Benjaminian figure in Raphael's painting, surely it is neither the lunatic boy nor the Apollonian Christ, but rather the startled disciple with his opened book in the lower left corner. Goethe, who saw the painting in 1787, and whose description of it in his *Italian Journey* no doubt influenced Nietzsche's view, attends to this figure that Nietzsche overlooks. Confronted by the mad child and anguished parents, the disciples have tried and failed to cure him: "One has even thrown open a book in order to see if some traditional formula could be found that was effective against this malady; but in vain."[6] From his perusal of this ineffective page the disciple has been interrupted by the woman in the lower center. Her twisted *contrapposto* pose, a *figura serpentinata*, embodies, according to Jodi Cranston in a recent analysis of the painting, the "figuration of conceptual turns in events, such as divine intervention and revelation."[7] The figure points, however, not to the transfigured savior but to the demonic child. And if Nietzsche could replace the redemptive promise of Christ with the empty splendor of Apollo, then Benjamin, too, can substitute his own messianic promise for Raphael's naive divinity. Not comforting semblance but the "one single catastrophe" of universal deception and deceit—including the work of Nietzsche himself—is what the sorrowful Angel of History reveals.

Thus it is into meaningless history itself that Nietzsche collapses at the end of his trajectory in January 1889. In the final notebook entries, ever more frantic and unmeasured, the spectacle of Nietzsche's absorption into the *pseudomenon* unfolds. All his vitriol directs itself toward a single target: *Hohenzollern*. And all his accusations distill into a single charge: *Lüge*, the lie. The Germanic dynasty merges in Nietzsche's increasingly disordered mind with the papal hierarchy. *War to the Death against the House of Hohenzollern* (KSA, 13:643), he scrawls, and a fragment or two later: *The Reich itself is a lie* (KSA, 13:646). All this mere weeks after he had drafted an account of his own baptism in an early version of *Ecce Homo*. *I myself, born on the birthday of the aforementioned king* [viz. Friedrich Wilhelm IV], *on the 15th of October, received, as was fitting, the Hohenzollern-name Friedrich Wilhelm* (KSA, 14:472). Nietzsche himself is a Hohenzollern, just as he is also the disembodied voice that denounces them, in the last sane words that history records from him (though the handwriting is tremulous and may already bear the marks of insanity): *Condamno te ad vitam diaboli vitae // By annihilating you, Hohenzollern, I annihilate the lie* (KSA, 13.647). We might add: This witness is true.

UNTIMELINESS

Not all of Nietzsche's intentions are conveniently packaged. The *Untimely Observations* appear now as four long essays neatly bound beneath this general title. But the volume is in fact the condensate of a complicated publication history that lent each of the essays a distinct reception, and behind that a complex compositional process whose traces are preserved in the notebooks from the early 1870s, and which involved a number of other essays that reached various levels of incompletion. It is in these notebooks that we can trace the movement of Nietzsche's expressive impulse from the accredited form of the philological treatise (however idiosyncratically performed) to his indigenous version of the aphoristic sequence as it emerges in *Human, All Too Human*.

In the notebooks title and signature dance in more elusive patterns. Rather than stabilize a completed work as the name of its origin and its intention respectively, the interplay of provisional titles and provisional signatures that punctuates the notebooks formally characterizes the problem of the Nietzschean *Nachlaß*, the voluminous writings physically housed at the Nietzsche Archive in the Klassik Stiftung Weimar. These documents preserve a philological demand, which is in the first instance nothing more than that their relation to his published writings be characterized. Where publication posits a smooth congruence between the acknowledged purpose of a text and the actual intention of its author, the existence of Nietzsche's *Nachlaß* conditions any understanding of the decision to publish and raises the question of authorial intention at a more fundamental level. This appears as a problem of titles and signatures only inasmuch as these make visible the basic semantic operation of imputing an intention to an inscription. That, for instance, in many cases Nietzsche expresses the same insight in more measured tones in the published writings than in the contemporaneous notes does not justify dismissing either the unpublished remark as an intemperate approximation or the public version as hypocritical dissembling. Both these alternatives, however opposed in effect, rest on a common static perception of Nietzsche's relation to his writing. Both perspectives assume that Nietzsche's writing is the expression of a prior intention—whether deceptive or revelatory—whose ultimate framework is the coordination of an individual signature and a published title, a coordination both immanent in the text and accessible from subsequent historical positions.

But writing, for Nietzsche, is alien to all stability. It exists only in transformation. It is his own self-transformation, at one extreme. No other philosopher has left anything like as complete a record of relentless sensitivity to the peculiarities of his own reflective processes, in notebooks where hundreds of pages correspond to mere months in Nietzsche's intellectual life and record in their torrent of fragmentary expressions the intimate movement of Nietzsche's theoretical self-absorption with an astonishing, an *obsessive*, density. This inherent self-dramatization, in arrogant, charming, exalted, or despairing tonalities, where it has not repelled sober consideration, has pulled much of Nietzsche's reception into close proximity to biography.[8] But Nietzsche's self-absorption cannot be biographically terminated, a fact reflected not least in the innumerable fictional incarnations of the man. Between these modes of reading, other reactions to this self-dramatization—Benjamin's among them—position Nietzsche in the problematic fault between biographical reconstruction and fictional characterization, as an ultimate challenge to such a distinction and any borders implicated by it. The transformation of writing calls the self into question, but more, destroys the boundaries between body, world, and the inscription that would distinguish and link them. Unleashed, transformative writing dissolves these categories into active disciplines: Nietzsche offers us a new philological skepticism, a new scientific integrity, a new medical regimen, a new psychological self-understanding that all advance into the human vacancy left by the disappearance of divine endorsement. To comprehend Nietzsche is thus to acknowledge the way his thought undermines the received techniques of hermeneutic comprehension. This is the challenge of "Nietzsche": Subsequent readings must always betray in the light of his inscriptions their own particular unacknowledged intention, to be comprehended in turn. Nietzsche's writing is not merely self-transformation, then, transformation at the site of the writer, but simultaneously and necessarily transformation at the other extreme, as well, at the site of the reader.[9] In its extremity, Nietzsche's self-absorption proves to be the condition of inscription gaining an exterior, in its own specificity acknowledging the specificity of the reader, so that here no other philosopher has accommodated as relentlessly and recklessly the entirely independent sensibilities of each reader and the unprecedented responsibilities that derive from them—has been, that is, as utterly selfless, as Friedrich Nietzsche.

That, at least, was Franz Overbeck's view of his friend, as comes through in his response to Erwin Rohde, Nietzsche's old ally from the Leipzig philology club, when Rohde had at length lost patience with Nietzsche's unscientific, declamatory, and reactionary pronouncements. Having receiving a copy of *Beyond Good and Evil* from the philosopher in August 1886, Rohde, after replying politely to Nietzsche, had given vent to his genuine reaction to the book and by extension to Nietzsche's entire postphilological career in a scathing letter to Overbeck. In recalling it, we are not concerned to second-guess an eventual misapprehension. Rohde's reaction in its intimacy with Nietzsche's intellectual life articulates and anticipates a perennial gesture of rejection with which Nietzsche's writing continues to be greeted but which usually silences itself as an aspect of Nietzsche interpretation by virtue of its very rejection of Nietzsche's philosophical cogency. This rejection, in other words, rarely emerges into discourse directly but is "registered" at most by Nietzsche's absence from contemporary discourses of comparable concern—"philosophies," let us say for short—that remain entirely uninterested in Nietzsche and the particular urgency of his problems. Rohde's letter of 1 September 1886 gives a recognizable contour to the silence of that theoretical disregard. This eventual dismissal of Nietzsche's pretense to authority deserves to be quoted at length not only because we know Benjamin read it—it is reprinted along with Overbeck's answer in Bernoulli's *Franz Overbeck und Friedrich Nietzsche*[10]—but to demonstrate, by virtue of Rohde's unique proximity to Nietzsche's historical reality, a privileged articulation of an enduring possibility limiting Nietzsche's historical reception.

> For the most part [Rohde writes], these are the postprandial discourses of a glutton, enlivened by wine here and there but full of a repulsive disgust with everything and everyone. The actual philosophical substance is as threadbare and almost childish as the political, where it shows up, is silly and naïve. And yet there are many quite clever apercus, and a few compelling dithyrambic passages. But it all remains arbitrary insight, one can no longer speak of convictions at all, as the mood strikes him *one* perspective is taken up and everything follows from that—as if there were only that *one* perspective on the world! And naturally then the next time the opposite perspective is taken up in just as one-sided a way and praised. I am no longer able to take these constant metamorphoses seriously. They're hermit's visions and intellectual soap-bubbles that no doubt give the hermit himself pleasure and distraction; but why communicate them, like some sort of Gospel, to the world? Moreover the constant announcements of monstrous things, hair-raising intellectual temerity that then to the wearying disappointment of the reader never arrives—this is all unspeakably repugnant to me.... That such things have no effect seems to me quite justified, since really nothing comes of them; it all just runs through one's fingers like sand; in the end—by what graspable thoughts do we come away wiser? A fluttering and flickering before one's eyes, no beautiful, persistent, transfiguring light is thrown off by the book! What is said about the herd-character of 'Now-humanity' is quite good, but how are we to understand the dictatorially imposed cannibal-ethics Nietzsche's philosophy fantasizes up, what signs of the times point toward that stylized berserker of the future? (whose picture, one would think, he has already painted often enough on the wall to have himself at last become sick of it)—in short, I have to confess that the book offended me a great deal, and more than everything the gigantic vanity of the writer, which shows itself less in the fact that he covertly and overtly takes himself with all his personal idiosyncrasies to be the model of this hoped-for Messiah,—as in the fact that he can't understand any other attitude, any other occupation even, than the one he for the time being is engaged in as being in any way humane or having any

value at all. Given the sterility that in the end peeks out everywhere from his merely reactive and synthetic sensitive spirit, this is outrageous. In an even more violently one-sided positive spirit this would be understandable: but Nietzsche is and remains a critic, and should sense that one-sidedness in his productions sits on him like a lion's pelt on a donkey.—The book pains me more on our account than on his, he has not discovered the path that would lead him out of self-indulgence, throws himself convulsively around here and there and then demands that one take that for development. The rest of us are also unsatisfied with ourselves, but we don't demand any particular respect for our deficiencies. What he needs is once again to set himself honestly and skillfully to work and then it would be obvious to him what this groping around in all sorts of things, this gluttonous intake of impressions and insights is worth: nothing at all.[11]

Rohde's critique reacts to ever more profound dimensions of Nietzsche's rhetoric. What is initially a disagreement with the epistemological and political insights expressed in Nietzsche's prose shifts into an objection to the one-sidedness and inconsistency with which these insights are presented. This objection culminates in Rohde's impatience with Nietzsche's prognostic posture. Though it strikes the letter writer as a supplementary reservation, in fact it is because Rohde feels a "wearying disappointment" that the "monstrous things" Nietzsche announces never arrive that the entire experiment has come to strike him as vacuous. Nietzsche's one-sidedness could only be redeemed by the holistic integrity of a genuine, enduring result—but just this is missing from his work. Nietzsche's inscription testifies to nothing more than a particular irritability no different in principle from the reader's own. To the extent that it holds itself up as a normative standard, it is an ass in a lion's pelt.

This rejection of Nietzsche's authority to make the kinds of claims he seems to make is, from a formal perspective, the complement of a posture that enthusiastically endorses Nietzsche's authority. (And the disappointed acolyte can still be heard in Rohde's lines, the echo of his earlier enthusiasm for his friend resonating through his disillusioned impatience.) Both of these antithetical possibilities emerge from the discrepancy between the particular content of Nietzsche's claims and the gesture that presents them. The gesture lays claim to a general authority, while its content remains irreducibly partial and particular. This discrepancy presents the authorial mandate as a problem, and displaces the ultimate authority for the assertion in the reader's recognition. The assertion assumes an interpretable urgency only for as long as the authority presenting it is recognized. This mutually reinforcing interdependence of substance on prior authority and authority on prior substance is a hermeneutic circle. But uniquely in Nietzsche's case, the significance of his assertion—its substance rendered as linguistic content—can ultimately be identified not with the intention authorizing it but with the *recognition* of that authority, with the nature of the reader's *entertaining* of that content as a thinkable position. It is this that Rohde is no longer willing to do.

"You speak of 'gigantic vanity,'" Overbeck writes in response, directing his attention to this crucial point, the incredible authority Nietzsche's inconstant one-sidedness assumes over the reader.

> I certainly cannot contradict that; and yet this vanity has a particular character. Even in this book it seems to me, and also to a reader who is a stranger to the writer, that a very different feeling intersects it. I know of no other person who has sacrificed as much as Nietzsche in order to come to terms with himself. That this emerges so monstrously in an age that tends to produce everything in such a heathen manner is not necessarily the fault of the person. And so it is with most of what you object to: I am initially in agreement with your view itself and ultimately of an entirely different opinion.[12]

Let us not fail to notice the difference between the gesture Overbeck describes in defending Nietzsche and a straightforward advocacy of Nietzsche's philosophical positions. Overbeck acknowledges the posture of unjustified self-importance adopted by Nietzsche's writing; he is "initially in agreement" with Rohde's diagnosis. But attending on that acknowledgment is a contrasting awareness of Nietzsche's relentless self-criticism and renunciation, which complicates the significance of his limitless vanity. Not simply a symptom of Nietzsche's own distorted particularity, the incommensurability between Nietzsche's proclamations and the manner in which he proclaims them—the "monstrosity" of his rhetorical explosion—testifies beyond him to the particular deficiencies of "the age" that cannot accommodate him. The rejection Rohde articulates is recognized by Overbeck as the inner dynamic of Nietzsche's own renunciation.

The space marked out between Rohde and Overbeck, in which Nietzsche's authorial status remains suspended and at issue, is the space in which the *Nachlaß* itself must be encountered. Here, too, what is at stake can appear only in the challenge to significance this material presents. Through selection, revision, rearrangement, Nietzsche's published books derive from his *Nachlaß*, but these notebooks themselves exhibit a form less reflectively overdetermined but by the same token more attuned to the inherent forces at work in Nietzsche's expression. The organic totality of a work manifested as a published book is something imposed on this more primal stream of language, which on its own roils through other sorts of provisional comprehensiveness. If the wholeness of a work is symbolized by its title and authorized by its signature, the fragmentary notebooks shatter this semantic principle. The notebooks have labels, not titles. At the same time, throughout the *Nachlaß*, various provisional titles for hypothetical works are proposed, written out, signed. It is tempting to imagine that these specious titles name nonexistent texts, imaginary disquisitions, fantastic books. But the necessity of a self-referential aspect to these consummating gestures remains irreducible; meaning itself ties them to existing language. These provisional titles apply neither to the notebooks in which they occur nor to purely potential works that do not occur but must be read more typically, as fragments of a generalized title-function deposited into the notebooks as Nietzsche's explosion passes through the German language.

What appears in Nietzsche's oeuvre as a title, whether of a published or a hypothesized work, is never a mere name but a gesture of consolidation that marshals a diversifying process into enough provisional unity to bear a signature. This title-function *is*, in one sense, Nietzsche's explosion: Born in the failure of tragedy, passing in stages through untimeliness until it reaches *Human, All Too Human*, the title-function animates Nietzsche's aphoristic sequences until it converges in *Thus Spoke Zarathustra* with a disembodied signature-function. This dual formula—in position a title and in content a signature—can occupy the place of the affirmative "amen" that sutures the Judeo-Christian doctrinal traditions. Throughout Nietzsche's production, then, one finds not simply titles but a range of formulae in the process—more or less successful—of entitlement. Titles are produced from formulae along the trajectory of Nietzsche's writing as characterizations of his entire subsequent production; they ride the flood of writing in this most visible position until its acceleration topples them and entitles another formula.[13] But in the chaos of the *Nachlaß*, titles are pluralized and distributed throughout each notebook. Here Nietzsche is testing titles, listing them, grouping them, subtitling them, signing them. These titles are not what they might at first appear to be: the traces of idle fantasies of publication relieving the endless labor of thought. To read a title in the notebooks is to chart in outline the transformations that attend its emergence.[14] The entitlement of the *Nachlaß* can be followed in the transposition of *Untimely Observations* through a provisional title built from the foreign signature "David Strauß." This transposition itself, and not a method derived from it, is untimeliness. Thus we read from the Spring of 1873 fragment 26[23]:

> *Birth of Tragedy.*
> *The Philosophers of the Tragic Age.*
> *The Future of our Educational Institutions.*
> *On Reading and Writing.*
> *The Competition.*
> *Rhythm.*
> *Greek and German.*
> *Bayreuth Horizon Observations.* (UW, 156; KSA, 7:585)

From the anchor of the published *Birth of Tragedy*, Nietzsche projects a series of subsequent texts; his recently started essay on the pre-Socratics, his lectures on pedagogic institutions, and beyond that, several further ideas that may perhaps come to fruition.

But already the last of these is no longer another title, but an embodiment of the procedure: From Bayreuth observations are being made along the contemporary cultural horizon. By objectifying an expressive self-identification with Bayreuth, the list of titles has called it into question. The notion of "observation" (*Betrachtung*), appearing here between a place-name at an origin and an articulated thematic horizon it makes visible can now itself begin to be observed. The explicit designation "Bayreuth" is a surrogate for the signatory position, and yet, appearing here in the list as a further explicit title, it implicitly positions any text it announces in a receptive horizon that is not simply congruent with the Bayreuth perspective but that includes Bayreuth in its own horizon as seen from its own perspective. An identification *of* Bayreuth already jeopardizes an identification *with* Bayreuth.[15] The appearance in the *Nachlaß* of *Bayreuth Horizon Observations* testifies to a necessary discrepancy between Nietzsche's immediate site of articulation and the public site of Bayreuth, a discrepancy that can be neutralized only by elevating the last title to a general designation for Nietzsche's observational procedure. As this list concludes, Bayreuth comes to objectify the site of articulation from which each prior title was taken to speak, and so to displace the horizon toward which it was addressed. This displacement alters the sense of the historical contrast between the adjective "German"

Inscription 121

in its opposition to "Greek" in the preceding title, and thus inflects the translation of Greek *agon* into the German word for competition (*Wettkampf*) earlier in the list, and behind that, the contrast between reading and writing as reactive phenomena.

Here it is not a matter of conjecturing just what differences of meaning and emphasis this semantic displacement introduces into the presumable content of these phantom "observations," rather of noting *in principle* how the gesture establishing Bayreuth as the name at the observing origin simultaneously displaces the procedure it identifies.[16] The authorial site is triangulated between, on the one hand, a receptive potential situated by the implicit oppositions between Greek and German, writing and reading, ultimately between the tragic past and the institutionalized present, and, on the other, a productive potential situated in contemporary culture by the place-name Bayreuth. This triangulated position is not stable, but registers a disruption in the present, through which unprecedented links between heterogeneous historical and cultural unities can emerge. This position is Nietzsche's "untimeliness." Untimeliness is not, in the first instance, a matter of being "behind" or "ahead of" the times. It is a mutation of the present, a shift in the relation of the present to itself that calls into question its indebtedness to the past and its potential for the future. Only around this displacement in the present can its tonalities of nostalgia or anticipation emerge.

One measure of this displacement is what occurs when it is obliterated. A short occasional text from this same time shows what happens when Nietzsche attempts to occupy the site, to speak in the name, of Bayreuth explicitly. In October 1873 Wagner asked Nietzsche to compose an "Exhortation to the Germans" as part of fundraising efforts to counter the considerable financial difficulties Bayreuth was facing. "I have been requested to provide an 'Exhortation to the Germans,'" Nietzsche reported to Gersdorff. "I wrote it one morning (that is last Wednesday) and already on Saturday evening I received it finished from the presses. . . . I imagine a signature of the sort we thought up back in Munich: so that the individual ranks and social classes are represented" (*SB*, 4:173). The text, as might be expected given its occasion, shows Nietzsche at his most unabashedly Wagnerian. "You have heard report of the ceremony in May of last year celebrated in *Bayreuth*," he writes, "a mighty foundation-stone had to be laid, beneath which we have forever buried many anxieties, and through which we believe our noblest hopes have been finally endorsed"

(*KSA*, 1:893). In the event, this passionate commitment proved an insufficient foundation for coordinating these plural pronouns, for the Bayreuth delegates found Nietzsche's text unacceptable. Cosima Wagner noted in her diary: "The meeting [of the delegates] decided to abandon the Exhortation; the committee did not feel itself justified in such bold language, and who besides the committee would sign it?"[17]

The signatory strategy Cosima Wagner here takes for granted conflicts with the intentions Nietzsche had confided to Gersdorff. Cosima sees these signatures as manifestations of the authority with which the exhortation speaks: an endorsement of its language by the assembled delegates of Bayreuth. For Nietzsche, however, the signatures do not stand in for the writing voice but manifest the receptive reaction to its call. Thus they are not confined to an authorizing committee or even a community of declared patrons but demonstrate the scope of the appeal directly. The endorsement Nietzsche imagines comes not from an extant assembly of recognized delegates but emerges within a representative selection from the nation itself. In his cover letter to Wagner, Nietzsche ventures the suggestion explicitly.

> As *signatories* it seems to me that a patronage-committee is less appropriate than a small group of men *chosen by us* from the most diverse classes and ranks (nobility, civil servants, politicians, priests, scholars, businessmen, artists). A copy of the Exhortation could be sent to each of them, with the query whether he wished to append his signature. (*SB*, 4:172)

That it was, in fact, the committee delegates who rejected the text shows which strategy was adopted. That they felt themselves not competent to endorse its bold language indicates, however, beneath the practical issue of instituted authority, the contrasting logic of Nietzsche's signatory suggestion. At the institutional extremes of its production and reception, Nietzsche's "Exhortation to the Germans" does not encounter a stable communicative framework: It is not the address of a recognizable body to a self-evident nation as an abstract whole. It is rather a tactical intervention in a structured collective by an agency that in principle does not preexist each particular encounter with his text. The "Exhortation" returns a particular reader to his active self-manifestation as an individual signature, and it is this active plurality of signatures that demonstrates the authority of the text by manifesting its addressee. Not the Germans as a recognized nation nor even Bayreuth as a public program but the process of signing itself constitutes the receptive context within which the "Exhortation" operates.

Thus despite its title Nietzsche's "Exhortation to the Germans" does not presuppose but hopes to conjure up a national framework, and this is why the text itself is continually drifting across national boundaries. Who could still be ignorant of the significance of Bayreuth, Nietzsche wonders, "since the great, courageous, unbending and unstoppable fighter *Richard Wagner* has advocated that thought for decades already under the attentive eyes of almost all nations." This international perspective remains irreducibly relevant: "From now on foreign countries [*das Ausland*] will be witness and judge in the drama you provide them, and in their mirror you will recognize an approximation of your own image" (*KSA*, 1:894). The contrasting boundary of an alternative "*Ausland*" immediately shifts into a duplicating self-relation: To the extent that the plural pronoun "you" is defined against the *Ausland* as the Germans, their self-identity is already called into question. Nietzsche's "Exhortation" situates itself precisely at that boundary where foreign and domestic circumstances turn into one another:

> If a man in France or in England or in Italy, after he had defied all public powers and opinions and given the theater five works of unique stature and powerful style that had been ceaselessly praised and in demand from north to south—if such a man were to cry: "the current theater does not fit the spirit of the nation, it is as public art a disgrace! Help me prepare a setting for the national spirit!" would not everyone come to help him, even if only from—a sense of honor? (*KSA*, 1:894)[18]

Nietzsche leaves unclarified what honorable sentiment might inspire his German audience to rush so selflessly to the aid of French, English, and Italian national cultures. Almost immediately he relocates the motivation for preparing a site for the national spirit between cultural institutions within a German national context: "All of your sciences are generously provided with expensive workshops: and you wish to stand idly by when such a workshop is to be built for the audacious and tempting spirit of German art?" (*KSA*, 1:895).

These national and international perspectives in Nietzsche's text are not simply two complementary scales, in which Germany appears as one nation among an internally differentiated Europe, and Bayreuth as one cultural institution within an internally differentiated Germany. By pairing German art with scientific universality, Nietzsche projects a site of cultural production that implicitly transcends any given national boundary. It has been the duty of Wagner's followers, he writes, to show

> that with the word "Bayreuth" not only a group of people, a party with specific musical tastes, but the nation is at stake, and even beyond the borders of the German nation all those who are called to serious and active participation, who value the ennoblement and purification of dramatic art and who have understood Schiller's wonderful intuition that perhaps someday out of the opera the Trauerspiel will develop in a more noble shape. (*KSA*, 1:896)

What holds the signatures together beneath the text is not an institutional affiliation but a communicative bond better characterized in terms of genre categories: the common wish that Trauerspiel emerge ennobled from the opera.

The creative effort of Wagner has, for Nietzsche, put the entire relation between cultural production and reception into question. It is not that the German people should commit themselves to a culture worthy of the ideals they themselves already embody *in potentia*; such would be the traditional nationalist call. Nietzsche's text keeps slipping from the German framework because it is precisely this potential worthiness of the German people, or any other collective audience, that Bayreuth challenges. "For if our first concern must be that the work be done at all," he writes, "we have as a second and no less difficult concern the doubt that we will be found not yet ripe, prepared and receptive enough to conduct into the distance the tremendous immediate effect" (*KSA*, 1:895).

The "Exhortation" thus assembles a virtual community, drawing its members from a principally unbounded collective whose limit is the limit of the text's conduciveness itself. Its plea is not formulated in terms of any extant obedience, but calls for a signed response. "From wherever a hearth of serious consideration [*ernsten Nachsinnens*] has maintained itself in our excited time we expect to hear a joyful and sympathetic rejoinder [*Zuruf*]," Nietzsche ventures to hope. The hearths of serious consideration suggest two particularly propitious institutional instances for the "Exhortation": the state and the university.

> In particular the German universities, academies and schools of arts will not have been challenged in vain to declare their support, whether individually or collectively: just as the political representatives of German prosperity in the national and regional parliaments will also have an important occasion to consider that the nation

[*Volk*] now more than ever needs the purification and consecration through the sublime enchantment and terror of genuine German art. (*KSA*, 1:897)

There is a slight asymmetry in Nietzsche's treatment of these two institutional frameworks for cultural reception. The universities and schools of arts can potentially reply with unilateral endorsements beyond the reactions of their individual constituents. In the parliamentary bodies of the state, by contrast, the reactions of individual representatives take precedence over any collective status they may exemplify. The individual legislators encounter the idea of Bayreuth as individuals with a prior commitment to the welfare of the German people. Here the operative category is "German," for it is the German people's need for a genuine catharsis that brings a renewed national art under the scope of the state's obligation to its citizens' welfare. Universities and academies, by contrast, are directly challenged by the "Exhortation": Potential disagreements between them are thought of as differences between respectively unilateral endorsements. The "Exhortation" expects its "joyful and sympathetic cry" from this quarter, and demands a direct commitment not out of a shared concern for the German people as such, but from their shared posture of "serious *Nachsinnens*," their common participation in the circuit of cultural reception and production. Nietzsche enjoins not the constitutive individuals composing the university, but the institution itself, understood as a unity capable of supporting an endorsement. Thus whereas the parliaments, populated by representatives who might recognize the national significance of Bayreuth, are merely quantitative reservoirs of potential sympathizers, the universities are allied as active cultural conduits.

The appeal to the university institution is a slight lurch in the text, for the "Exhortation" consistently challenges its reader at an individual level. "If it achieves more or less its purpose," Nietzsche writes to Wagner, "(to infuriate the evil and to gather and motivate the good with this wrath) then the rapid preparation of a French, Italian and also an English translation would mean a lot to me, for obvious reasons" (*SB*, 4:171–72). The meaning of the "Exhortation" rests not in established institutional relations, but in the transitory affect, the state of sentimental aggression it provokes in its reader. This affect sorts the audience into opposing evaluative categories, depending on their reactions to it. The evil are outraged and repelled, but the good are brought together and motivated to further effort by this communicated ire. Thus Nietzsche's call, though addressed to the Germans, demands translation into the languages of Europe, for its effective radius is not dictated by institutional boundaries, but merely by the extent of the wrath it is able to provoke. Simultaneously, the virtual character of its audience distributes the "Exhortation" across its specific performances, and the same logic governs the first preference in Nietzsche's cover letter: "Here, dear Master, is my draft. Actually I would like to read it to you aloud with great pathos" (*SB*, 4:171). This small occasional text reveals the way in which all literal horizons dissolve when Nietzsche attempts to speak directly from Bayreuth. And in its signatory lurch at the university institution, it shows what authority in fact supports untimeliness. "I was at the time already a professor ordinarius in spite of my 24 years, and therefore a kind of authority and something *demonstrated*," Nietzsche writes to Brandes in 1888, as he sends him the Strauss polemic (*SB*, 8:258). And it comes to expression in the most academic of the *Observations*, "On the Use and Disadvantage of History for Life." "But I have to concede this much to myself as someone who by occupation is a classical philologist," Nietzsche writes there:

> for I have no idea what the significance of classical philology would be in our age, if not to work in an untimely manner—that is, against the time and thereby effecting the time, one hopes, for the benefit of a coming time. (*UO*, 87; *KSA*, 1:247)

Academic accreditation, his recognized status as professional philologist, endorses the historical dislocation of the present announced as untimeliness.

That Nietzsche published all the *Untimely Observations* above his full professional signature: "Dr. Friedrich Nietzsche, Ordentl. Professor of Classical Philology at the University of Basel," and that from *Human, All Too Human* on the accreditation disappears from his title pages,[19] leaving simply "Friedrich Nietzsche," is not just or even a biographical fact, a sign of increased self-confidence on his or his publisher's part that a public reception, however modest, was now dense enough to situate Nietzsche's unadorned name. The removal of institutional certification from Nietzsche's signature marks a realignment of its entire relation to the texts it authorizes and the audience it addresses. When *Twilight of the Idols* presents an aphoristic sequence under the title "Expeditions of an Untimely Man" (*TI*, 78; *KSA*, 6:111), the adjective designates not the observations, but Nietzsche himself. The late letter to Brandes suggests that during the time in which merely his observations were untimely, and not yet he himself, Nietzsche's authority was of a sort amenable to demonstration. It is a visible authority, testified to by degree and position, and it advocates an externally embodied ideal. That the ideal it advocates—Bayreuth—and the authority it manifests—philology—have different institutional situations in the present is the visible dislocation that Nietzsche's untimely signature is attempting to seal. As a tension between recognized institutions in cultural space, untimeliness links Nietzsche's signature to categories of recognizable public concern; these are the individual *Observations* (both actual and virtual), atheistic sermons in an Emersonian style.

The specific titles of these essays, completed or not, are superseded by the general title, *Untimely Observations* in the development of the first essay, on a topic not found in the earlier projection.[20] Fragment 26[24] *Against David Strauss* (*UW*, 156; *KSA*, 7:586) initiates actual untimeliness in the direct confrontation with a foreign signature. The first titular fragment, 27[4]: *Against the Writer David Strauss* (*UW*, 159; *KSA*, 7:589), insists upon this authorial role, which is soon enough positioned above a dislocating signature in 27[7]:

> *To the German Writer David Strauss.*
> *Letter from a Foreigner.* (*UW*, 159; *KSA*, 7:589)

The authorial role brings with it a political consideration; the writer David Strauss has become a German. Simultaneously, the form of the observations has adopted epistolary intimacy, and the addressing signature is negatively positioned by the antonomasia "Foreigner." It is thus the genre of the letter, and its particular accusative and genitive implications for the individual addressed and the signature that authorizes it, that mediates the characterization *Observation* back into Nietzsche's writing project. Nietzsche's self-characterization as foreigner here is at one level simply literal: Residing in Switzerland, the Basel professor of philology can adopt the objectifying perspective of an expatriate. But the continuation of this fragment already suggests a tension in this perspective. *Someone once told me*, Nietzsche writes, *you are a Jew and as such not in complete command of the German language* (*UW*, 159; *KSA*, 7:589). The anti-Semitic rhetoric marshaled for the purposes of stylistic critique is evidence of Bayreuth cultural conversations, but the Wagnerian tactic of using Judaism as an alien auditory principle against which the unprecedented experiments of his own musical compositions could be reintegrated into

German culture collides here with the foreignness asserted by the Nietzschean signature, and the fragment breaks off. Fragment 27[57]:

> *David Strauss, the Confessor and the Writer.*
> *Untimely Observations*
> *of a*
> *Foreigner.* (UW, 173; KSA, 7:604)

Strauss has been returned to the nominative case while his nationality has disappeared into the implications of the foreign signature confronting him. The intimacy of the letter form has lent these observations a relative independence from their public historical situation, and the formula of *untimely* meditations, though bounded by the polemic they subtitle and the foreigner who signs them, appears for the first time. We continue to Fragment 27[75]:

> *David Strauss,*
> *The Confessor and the Writer.*
> *Untimely Observations*
> *by*
> *Friedrich Nietzsche.* (UW, 178; KSA, 7:609)

The public individual signature is now in place and the materializing genitive case has disappeared. But for this reason, it is no longer self-evident that the subtitle refers only to the title above it. Between the two proper names now separated by written confession and untimely observation, the plurality of untimeliness begins to spread out beyond the immediate object at hand. In a letter to Carl von Gersdorff of 27 October 1873, Nietzsche can refer to "On the Use and Disadvantage of History for Life" as "the Nr. 2 of the U.O." (*SB*, 4:173), and the notebooks now exhibit this prognostic aspiration (Fragment 29[163]):

> *Outline of the Untimely Observations.*
>
> *1873 David Strauss.*
>   *Use and Disadvantage of History.*
> *1874 Excessive Reading and Excessive Writing.*
>   *The Scholar.*
> *1875 Secondary Schools and Universities.*
>   *Soldier Culture.*
> *1876 The Absolute Teacher.*
>   *The Social Crisis.*
> *1877 On Religion.*
>   *Classical Philology.*

1878 *The City.*
Essence of Culture (Original-).
1879 *Nation and Natural Science.* (UW, 262; KSA, 7:699)

There are several of these multiannual projections in the subsequent notebooks. Different fates overtake these unreal *Observations*: some titles will appear as discourses of Zarathustra ("On Reading and Writing"), or above aphoristic sequences in *Beyond Good and Evil* ("We Scholars"), testifying to the ferocious continuity of Nietzsche's production, a continuity that is indeed one meaning of the Eternal Return. But by then they will no longer be governed or governable by the title *Untimely Observations*. The trajectory from a territorial, spatial dislocation to a temporal dislocation implicit in the absorption of "David Strauss" by its subtitle via the epistolary signature externalizes this textual process distinctively. Untimeliness as a posture can no longer simply be identified in cultural terms, but exists negatively, as a suspension of David Strauss, who, Nietzsche notes in an early fragment, "speaks like someone who reads the newspapers every day" (*UW,* 175; *KSA,* 7:605). Within the first *Observation,* the untimely position is not defined, but charted as the contrast with a particular terminological interloper in Nietzsche's text: the term *Jetztzeit,* "now-time."

This word had made its first appearance in chapter 23 of *The Birth of Tragedy*: as the "dully dazed retreat—everything *sub specie saeculi,* of the 'now-time': whose same symptoms allow us to infer the same lack at the heart of this culture, the destruction of myth" (*BT,* 138, *KSA,* 1:149). In the lectures on pedagogy the term had returned, still bearing quotation marks (*OFE,* 58, 73; *KSA,* 1:690, 705). Despite the distancing, which bore witness to its origins in Schopenhauerian irony,[21] it marks in these texts a coherent rejection of the historical present in cultural-critical terms, a denunciation of its insubstantiality and impermanence with which Nietzsche implicitly agrees. The inelegantly fashioned term "now-time," exemplifying the vulgarity it identifies, appears as a judgment, and its meaning is therefore embodied in the rhetorical posture toward the present that says "now-time." But by the time of the Strauss essay, Schopenhauer's authority can barely redeem the word, and its journalistic provenance has almost alienated it from Nietzsche's vocabulary. The last section of "David Strauss, the Confessor and the Writer" leaves Nietzsche's own prose to assemble a series of incriminating quotations from Strauss's pen itself: "In conclusion, let us present our classical prose writer with the promised collection of stylistic examples; perhaps Schopenhauer would give it the general title 'New Evidence for the Shoddy Jargon of Now-Time'" (*UO*, 70; *KSA*, 1:227–28). Having established itself as a name for the stylistic antithesis of untimeliness, the word "now-time" then disappears from Nietzsche's production. But its disappearance is not the end of its relevance. The "now-time" is borne on Nietzsche's inscription as the potential antipodes to its disruptive force. "Untimeliness": the posture that will not *write* "now-time."

MURI

The Beinecke Rare Book and Manuscript Library at Yale University contains one of the few remaining copies of Gershom Scholem's *Amtliches Lehrgedicht*, his "Official Didactic Poem," a satire first written in 1918 but brought to print a decade later. The library's catalogue lists the publisher as "Muri: Verlag der Universität [1928]." The mistake is understandable; this is what the book itself lists on its title page, just before the dedication to "His / Magnificence / Walter Benjamin / Rector of the Universität Muri." But just as Benjamin was never rector of an actual university, so there never was a University of Muri Press, and the book, a mock children's alphabet in which the rhymed quatrains attending each letter satirize figures and themes in the contemporary intellectual landscape, was issued privately by Scholem's father, the printer Arthur Scholem, in a print run of 250.

Muri was the small Swiss town in which Scholem and Benjamin had briefly lived during the war, its university the satirical invention of the two iconoclastic and impassioned students. Scholem explains: "Since so little was to be learned at the university, we formed 'our own academy' (as Benjamin put it in our first conversations). Thus we proceeded to found, half in earnest and half in jest, the 'University of Muri' and its 'institutes': a library and an academy. In the catalogue of this university, the statutes of the academy, and the imaginary list of new library accessions, for which Benjamin supplied reviews sparkling with wit, our high spirits and ridicule of academic activities found an appropriate outlet during the next three or four years. Benjamin played the role of the rector and repeatedly gave me written and oral reports about the latest goings-on at our fantasy university. I was heard from as 'Warder of the School of the Philosophy of Religion' and sometimes also as a member of the faculty" (*SF*, 72; *GF*, 76).

What survives of Muri survives in the archive; with the exception of Scholem's *Lehrgedicht*, the only Muri-produced texts that appeared in print during Benjamin's lifetime were two of the parodic book reviews that were published in an early issue of Willy Haas's *Literarische Welt*, one of Benjamin's primary venues in the second half of the Weimar Republic. But real publication of the Muri fantasy was always a possibility, and this makes of it, at least from Benjamin's perspective, something more than simply a private joke. The university proceedings took place within the friendship between Benjamin and Scholem; Muri commemorated their closest physical and intellectual proximity, and it served in their correspondence in the 1920s as a common reference that reestablished an intimacy interrupted by diverging personal circumstances and attitudes. ("Upon the occasion of the fifth anniversary of the founding of the University of Muri, which is scheduled to be celebrated in the coming year," Benjamin writes to Scholem in 1923, "a festschrift will appear, 'Memento Muri,' for which contributions are requested" (*CB*, 222; *GB*, 2:389)). But where Scholem recalls Muri as the appropriately private outlet for the disappointments and frustrations occasioned by a public institution, Benjamin's attempts to bring Muri before a wider public indicate that for him the parodic university entertained an autonomous relation to a public sphere.

The slight disavowal detectable in Scholem's recollection results in part from the fact that Muri emerges from the hoary tradition of European student humor and is tied thereby to the novice's preliminary, subaltern position. By the time Scholem is writing *The Story of a Friendship* in 1975, that is all far in his past. For Benjamin, in contrast, the subaltern origins of Muri make it a natural continuation of his earlier student advocacy of an exemplary youth. The student humor arises out of a "life of students" in the hypertrophic sense Benjamin had given the phrase in 1914 in his farewell to university activism witht hat title. The gleefully disrespectful posture toward the weight of tradition made possible by the student's inconsequential status in the transmission of culture becomes, for Benjamin, the stand-in for a radically discontinuous relation between language and truth outside the public systems of accreditation. In these same years Benjamin would describe Gottfried Keller's deeply subversive humor as a "'dubious' system of grottoes and caverns that by imperceptible stages tends—the more deeply it enters into Keller himself—to constrain and ultimately to repress the rhythmic babble of bourgeois voices and opinions in favor of the cosmic rhythms it captures within the bowels of the earth" (*SW*, 2:54; *GS*, 2:287). The possibility of Muri, reflected in the titles and mottos and ceremonies that manifest the nonauthority of the texts it produces responds to the cosmic rhythms of a deeply serious level in Benjamin's thought.²²

This too is why the energies Muri channels eventually flow into the book Benjamin wrote simultaneously with his *Habilitation*, as its cultural antithesis. "My work is keeping me busy enough for the time being," he recounts to Scholem in December 1924.

> It is more urgent for me to tell you that I hope to bring Muri to the attention of the public within the framework of a pastoral fantasy. I am preparing (as a private printing or as a publication to be offered for sale) "Plaquette for Friends." (In France a plaquette is a narrow, brochurelike, short, special issue containing poems or something similar—a bookdealer's terminus technicus.) I intend to collect my aphorisms, witticisms, and dreams in several chapters, each of which will carry the name of someone close to me as its only heading. And Muri would unfold under your name. (*CB*, 257; *GB*, 2:510)

In the event it was Rowohlt Verlag who published what became *One-Way Street*, but in its initial conception it bore the imprimatur of the University of Muri Press.

Situated on the boundary between academic respectability and uncertified cultural transmission, the University of Muri is destined to encounter Nietzsche. Within its seminar rooms, Nietzsche's nemesis Ulrich von Wilamowitz-Moellendorff professes "The Life and Activity of Delivery-Men to the Court" (*GS*, 4:441), while its library eagerly acquires the latest volume of Elisabeth Förster-Nietzsche's pompously sororal biography: "Volume VII: Burial and Grave-Tending" (*GS*, 4:446). It is in a review of this volume that Benjamin pens a Muri text that will, reworked and expanded, also reach publication. The gruesome anecdote with which he opens his 1932 essay "Nietzsche and the Archive of His Sister" springs from an even more scathingly sarcastic passage from the Muri review of Förster-Nietzsche's fictional volume.

> Here too a plethora of interesting things! One of those radical Nietzsche readers who took time from rummaging through the philosopher's writings to examine the life work of his sister referred to her as the city-renowned sister of the world-famous philosopher. Certainly unjustly. But why is that charming anecdote missing here that Baron Friedrich von Schennis so loved to recount? As long as

Nietzsche lived, the friends of the house would gather around his sister for a celebratory meal every year on his birthday. And once the dessert cups had been cleared from the table, the violet curtain at the far end of the room would open. The mad Nietzsche in an armchair was revealed. (*GS,* 4:446; cf. *GS,* 3:323)

What resonates in the tension in Muri between Wilamowitz-Moellendorff and Förster-Nietzsche, between Nietzsche's exclusion from legitimate academic reception at the hands of philological positivism and the provincial and reactionary reception at the hands of the Nietzsche Archive,[23] is its Swiss situation. Benjamin had a particular fondness for Swiss writers and the marginal political position they occupied in German-language letters. Nietzsche is of a stature that transcends reductive national situations, but to the extent that nationality is relevant to his thought, that nationality for Benjamin is Swiss. "The Swiss character may well possess more love of country and less nationalistic spirit than any other," Benjamin remarks in his essay on Keller, and illustrates the point with an expatriate example. "Toward the end of Keller's life, the clarion call of Nietzsche's warnings about the spirit of the new Reich issued from Basel" (*SW,* 2:52; *GS,* 2:285). And in his essay on the idiosyncratic Swiss scholar Johann Jakob Bachofen from 1935, Benjamin inscribes the German/Swiss rivalry into the intellectual turmoil of the nineteenth century. Bachofen's unsuccessful attack on the towering Berlin classicist Theodor Mommsen could be seen, Benjamin suggests, "as a kind of prologue to the one which, a few years later, pitted positivist science, in the person of Wilamowitz-Möllendorff, against Nietzsche as the author of *The Birth of Tragedy.* . . . Through Nietzsche, Bachofen got his revenge on science" (*SW,* 3:15; *GS,* 2:225). Benjamin sees the polemical battle between Nietzsche and Wilamowitz-Moellendorff over the status of philological discipline to occupy a distinct historical moment. The positivistic, rational, empirical approach to the past represented by Mommsen triumphs over Bachofen's more speculative engagement with ancient days. By the time Mommsen's future son-in-law is writing his withering "Philology of the Future!" against Nietzsche, positivist science is already revealing its limitations. It is Nietzsche from his marginal perch in Basel, who with *The Birth of Tragedy* genuinely comprehends the fractured nature of our current relationship to classical ideals, and not Wilamowitz-Moellendorff in Berlin.

Benjamin's own academic treatise *The Origin of German Trauerspiel,* central as its themes may be to his theoretical grasp of the world, does not display his fundamental communicative practice. It is rather *One-Way Street* in its proximity to the University of Muri that points the way forward for Benjamin. The composition of *One-Way Street* began with the fourteen-part aphorism IMPERIAL PANORAMA, the fruit of a short, depressing trip through inflationary Germany in February 1923. (Benjamin had heard just a few weeks before that Wolf Heinle, Fritz's brother, had died, a final severance from the form of his youthful ambitions.) IMPERIAL PANORAMA moved through various preliminary versions. In one of these, an aphorism addresses the university explicitly: *The decline of the universities is unmistakable*, Benjamin writes. *The human sciences have no one who is willing to continue their traditions from the lectern*. The professorial positions have devolved either on *sophisticates entirely free of any feeling of responsibility*, or *mercenary-natures*, who use their university positions to magnify their individual influence. The tendency is irreversible. And to the extent that it definitively demolishes a *democratic grasp of science, in which only competition among the most talented can in the best case tip the scales*, it must even be welcomed. For, Benjamin ventures, the deeper tendency beneath this development will necessarily unmask the *old university*.

> At the end of this process of decline the insight will be unavoidable that a science which can present itself wholly without any recourse to esotericism is deception [Trug]. For as much as esotericism cannot determine the form of appearance [Erscheinungsform] of science, nonetheless the laws of this form and its substance [Gehalts] must appear to the great scholar [Forscher] as theologically determined. (GS, 4:925–26; WuN, 8:147–48)

The "democratic" version of scientific inquiry, organized around the universal norms that govern a public meritocracy, is committed to a vision of tradition that abjures any esoteric discontinuities in communication. Inasmuch as modern universities embody this ideal of transparent and universal communication, their intellectual bankruptcy has diagnostic value. It calls into question the self-evidence that excludes esoteric, invisible sorts of tradition from the community of science, for the truly extraordinary scholars down through the centuries, whose intellectual stature validates the academic calling, were all aware of a dimension of scholarship that went beyond the communicative norms of the scientific academy. This is what Benjamin calls the theological condition of science, its irreducible imbrication in the mortal existence of the scientist and the communal implications of his destiny.

Where the aphorism seems to start sociologically, criticizing the reproductive mechanisms of the contemporary university as an institution, the diagnostic remarks reveal that the critique aims in fact much more deeply. The current breakdown of the university is not a falling away from a venerable tradition, but a Nietzschean down-going that discovers the hidden foundations of that tradition. These foundations are religious, in both the sense that universities themselves derive historically from ecclesiastical institutions, and in the more profound sense that any tradition able to bind generations across death manifests a collective resistance toward death, a particular hope for salvation. The modern, enlightened university, however, in breaking with the religious dogmas of the communities of ascetic contemplation and colloquy from which it grew, destroyed the mythic guise in which that ultimate exterior was registered, without thereby becoming any less conditioned by an ultimate exterior. Not the "truths" of theology, but the site toward which theology gestured with them has thus fallen from modern awareness.[24] Its decadence is not apparent in the irrational restrictions and limitations it imposes on collective knowledge, but precisely the opposite, in the absence of conservative admission standards together with the "democratic" reduction of truth to the result of public meritocracy among its competing members.

In his diagnosis of the university, a democratic posture toward science, in which truth is thought to emerge solely through the internal contest between scientists, has obscured the external relation of science to the superhuman forces conditioning it. The unmasking of their rationalized modern incarnation is not, however, a validation of those primordial superhuman forces but their acknowledgment for the purpose of ultimately denouncing them. Despite the antidemocratic tenor of his remarks, Benjamin has no interest in returning to traditional institutional standards. These destructive developments are rather to be welcomed. The collapse of any explicit relation to the theological exterior of the university and its contemporary failure to reconstitute itself along democratic lines, Benjamin predicts, will result in a new sort of institution. These new academies will manifest the logical terminus of this cultural tendency.

> The technical corollaries of this insight will be the most rigorously consequential praxis of the seminar as a <u>privatissimum</u> in the sense that even the means of research [Forschungsmittel], the apparatus, will be accessible only to the genuine initiates of a scientific atelier (a workshop), while on the other hand access to a plethora of means

on a scale perhaps at present only found in the British Museum will have become self-evident for these initiates. This sort of reference library [Präsenzbibliothek] will in principle demand permanent presence, the ateliers will become residential communities [Wohngemeinschaften]. (GS, 4:926; WuN, 8;148)

The force of the contrast between contemporary and prior institutions is not nostalgic, but prognostic. In this visualized future, the boundary between student and nonstudent will become absolute, excluding even an extra-university residential existence. But this complete restriction conditions a reciprocal expansion of the objects of study, whose scope now becomes as universal as the British Museum. These alterations are not focused on the restrictive identification of "genuine" members at the doors of a scientific laboratory, but position the extremity of scientific practice entirely in the reflecting present. What are couched as institutional boundaries are in fact the borders of a kind of concentration in the present, a temporal readjustment that must be actively maintained, and whose ascetic demand for "permanent presence" itself delimits its practitioners.[25]

Thus, how this well-furnished and exclusive elite is to be selected from the general population does not arise as a question. Benjamin rather avoids any practical considerations by transplanting his future academies across the ocean, outside of extant European institutional continuities entirely. *One can assume that America, to which those things will flee that escape the destruction looming over the inventory of middle and western Europe, will see the origins of such academic arrangements [Verfassungen]* (GS, 4:926; WuN, 8:148). The new scientific institutions arise spontaneously, once this inventory of objects of study has been relocated to the conventional wilderness of America.[26] This is not a prediction, but the theoretical condensation of institutional continuities into the moment of their initiation. Benjamin's aphorism is not a practical critique of the institutional realities of his day; it is philosophical, not sociological in nature. The political devastation of defeated Germany, the collapse of the collective self-evidence of its institutions, provides Benjamin with the opportunity to reflect on the problematic relation of these institutions to their underlying foundations in human existence. The possibility of a congruence between truth, science, and the university institution is thus called into question. The alternative this makes visible, in its ubiquity and decentralization, may exhibit a prognostic resemblance to the cybernetic space of contemporary scholarship; yet Benjamin's concern is fundamentally not with the empirical distortions introduced by the university's relation to science and their potential compensations and rectifications offered by the future, but with the principled impasses inscribed in the relation of science to truth.

Science, Benjamin maintains, has a "form of appearance." The "democratic" posture toward science is invested in a form of appearance that abjures esoteric presentation. An egalitarian political premise, when applied to the practice of research, must take scientific presentation to be transparent to the object it reflects, in principle as generally accessible as that object is itself. But the collapse of university traditions reveals this transparency for the illusion it always was. Scientific presentation is not merely imposed on expression by the object, but itself expresses a shared theological investment, a common attitude toward death. Thus the theological foundation of science is its implication of the scientist as a living person, outside any abstract system of investigative procedures. Where this implication is forgotten, the scientist disappears into the common attitude that enables scientific presentation; this disappearance manifests the twin dangers of mediocrity and pedanticism that have been understood to attend scientific research with ever more insistence since the medieval foundation of universities. But great scholarship appears no different, for the exceptionality of the "great scholar" is not reducible to the accidental insights that come his way, but in his altered awareness of his own disappearance into science, its theological relevance.

For scientific language to surrender to an esoteric obscurity is to surrender its scientific character, Benjamin maintains. But the scientist himself does not escape the theological conditions of that presentation simply by denying them, which merely renders them invisible and surrenders him to them entirely. These considerations are familiar from the opening of the "Epistemo-critical Preface" to *The Origin of German Trauerspiel*. There, they serve to characterize the genre of treatise and not the institution of the university. Philosophical treatises, Benjamin claims, "possess a certain esotericism which they are unable to discard, forbidden to deny, and which would condemn them were they to vaunt it" (*OT*, 27–28; *GS*, 1:207). This is the *Darstellungsfrage* "question of presentation" that philosophic writing must continually confront. Here in *One-Way Street*, approaching the problem in institutional terms, not in terms of genre, Benjamin's prognosis is revealing. The institutional reflection of the "question of presentation" makes the rift between inside and outside absolute, while condensing it into the activity of present concentration. Dictated by the nature of truth and representation itself, the horizon of these new American institutions disappears into their hypothetical status. There are now, today, exceptional researchers who recognize the truth these hypothetical institutions obey absolutely. Within the explicitly decaying authority of the university institution, the exceptional researcher identifies a science whose esoteric dimension measures a displacement from the contemporary world in which that authority operates, a displacement from the past into the future. What the future holds for the individual researcher is death, but this esoteric dimension suspends a possibility in that future.

The esoteric dimension of science is the space between its practices and the ideal of transparency it maintains. Admittedly, to the extent that research in the university assumes the transparency to truth as in principle at hand, it operates under a delusion. But this delusion is not an ideological discrepancy between the actual situation of its members and their subjective representation of that situation; the discrepancy inhabits science itself, in the contrast between its object of reflection and its form of presentation. To acknowledge the esoteric dimension of science is to acknowledge the ultimate exterior toward which its investigations are oriented. But to acknowledge it directly, as here in Benjamin's early aphorism, will always rebound upon the acknowledging voice. Benjamin's aphorism cannot itself be identified or distinguished from these exceptions and so is situated neither inside nor outside this boundary of reflecting concentration. It remains an unpublished fragment.

In its final form, neither the hermetic title nor the onomastic schema nor the explicit critique of the university institution survives in *One-Way Street*. The book's positive impetus overtook these motivations. That impetus was, as the dedication makes clear, erotic in nature, his passion for Asja Lacis.[27] As it is, the *One-Way Street* ends in the intoxication of conception. "The living conquers the frenzy of destruction only in the ecstasy of procreation" (*SW*, 1:487; *GS*, 4:148). At the same time, the proposed organizing principle of personal friendships gives way to what is in a sense its diametrical opposite: sixty headings drawn from the most anonymous language available—the posters, advertisements, logos of the modern metropolis. If the initial conception of the work was stabilized among Benjamin's masculine personal friendships, its final form has contracted toward erotic intimacy and expanded into the impersonal cityscape. *One-Way Street* thus grows to fill as ambitious a space as *The Origin of German Trauerspiel*. But where that effort moved immediately among the temporal dispersion of history, *One-Way Street* occupies the synchronic field of contemporary life. This shift of perspective does not, however, imply that Benjamin has lost an independent interest in history in favor of the urgency of matters of contemporary relevance. (This was always Scholem's fear.) The object of historical truth remains common to both books, but *One-Way Street* responds to a deeper understanding of the presentational difficulties implied by the materialization of history propounded in the more obviously scientific text. In a letter to Hofmannsthal, Benjamin asks "that you not see everything striking [*Auffallenden*] about the book's internal and external design as a compromise with the 'tenor of the age' [*Zeitströmung*]. Precisely in terms of its eccentric aspects, the book is, if not a trophy, nonetheless the documentation of an internal struggle. Its subject matter may be expressed as follows: to grasp topicality [*Aktualität*] as the reverse of the eternal in history and to take the impression of this, the side of the medallion hidden from view" (*CB*, 325; *GB*, 3:331). If, in a 1931 letter, Benjamin could say of the Trauerspiel book that it was "certainly not materialist, if already dialectical" (*CB*, 372; *GB*, 4:18), this was not a judgment of its allegorical doctrine, which indeed vested meaning exclusively in the material dimension of inscription, but the presentational form that the book conveying it had adopted. The discarded aphorism on the university shows a preliminary attempt on Benjamin's part to depict in concrete, actual terms the implications his theory of inscription had for scientific practice. What appears there as a distinction between esoteric and exoteric modes of presentation is the recognition that the materialization of history in inscription cannot be expounded as a doctrine without succumbing to the idealization it purports to resist. A consequent resituation of truth from ideal content to material presentation cannot be stated; it can only be practiced.

Benjamin's esotericism is thus constructed around a basic paradox. It is the exterior, the most obvious and manifest aspect of reality, that evades ordinary presentation. The immediate exterior of expression is the bearer of its hidden message, while the stable content within it carries the quotidian, exoteric meaning. Among the observations gathered beneath the heading TEACHING AID, Benjamin formulates the challenge of the paradox: "The typical work of modern scholarship is intended to be read like a catalogue," he writes, expanding on an earlier hyperbole.

> But when shall we actually write books like catalogues? If the deficient content were thus to determine the outward form, an excellent piece of writing would result, in which the value of opinions would be

enumerated [*beziffert*] without their being thereby put on sale [*feilgeboten*]. (*SW*, 1:457; *GS*, 4:105)

The distinction between reading and writing here usurps a theological distinction between ordinariness and exceptionality. What the mediocre scholar intends—that his distinct presentation coincide with an entirely objective catalogue of facts available to an entirely general reader—becomes exceptional when it is understood not as transparency at the site of the reader but an ascetic self-denial at the site of the writer. Only when the writer recognizes that such transparency cannot be governed by *any* sovereign intention, but that a generic catalogue must make available the historical blindness and deficiencies of the scholar himself, which are also part of the "content," only then does a scholarship appear that presents opinions in their ordinary fragility and limitation rather than promoting them as truths that redound to the writer's own glory. This transposition of the prerogatives of intention from the writer to the reader transforms writing into *Schrift*, inscription, as irreducible material manifestation not ultimately subject to the forces of exchange and compensation—exoteric communication—but displaying the blank sequence of historical time itself.

Neither the passive moment of reading nor the active moment of writing are exclusively present in the now-time as inscription, which marks their intersection with material history. Their difference consists in the fact that the former leaves the surface of the world, while the latter adheres to it implacably. The esoteric message, whatever its ultimate import, is thus not shrouded in metaphysical obscurities, but moves against them at the immediate surface of the world. This surface can never be enfolded into the significance of an accessible meaning: From the perspective of content, truth will always be elsewhere. The surface of the inscription meets up with the surface of a subsequent inscription, in an endless task and surrender.

This situation puts the book as a form under inordinate pressure. From the start Benjamin understood *One-Way Street* to be a whole, and though many of the vignettes, dreams, anecdotes, and aphorisms that appear there were published earlier in newspapers, particularly the feuilleton of the *Frankfurter Allgemeine Zeitung* under Kracauer's direction, the book is in no way an ex post facto collection of scattered writings. "In the style of these theses," Benjamin writes to Scholem, describing the early publication of the THIRTEEN THESES AGAINST SNOBS in the *Berliner Tageblatt*, "I've made some preliminary sketches for a future book of aphorisms" (*CB*, 277; *GB*, 3:61).

But the discontinuous form of *One-Way Street*, together with its hermetic references to personal experiences, its dream narratives bare of any interpretive mediation, its lists of juxtapositions and its abrupt headings, all challenge accepted ideas of aesthetic totality. The contrast between this book and *The Origin of German Trauerspiel* is reflected most immediately in the physical appearance of their respective first editions. Though both were brought out by Ernst Rowohlt Verlag in 1928, *The Origin of German Trauerspiel* is printed in Fraktur, or the traditional German font for serious science, with Benjamin's name centered above the title on the title page. *One-Way Street* by contrast, printed in Latin letters, presents the reader first with the block sans serif title, and the author's name has lurched to the right, as have the headings inside (*GS,* 7:536–37; *WuN,* 8:595).[28] In this paired publication Benjamin presented the Janus-head of his thought: retrospection toward the origin down the one-way street of time.

These two texts lie side by side at the heart of Benjamin's published oeuvre. In the constitution of his signature, either text can be granted provisional priority. In its form as a scholarly treatise, *The Origin of German Trauerspiel* lends itself to interpretations of Benjamin that focus his thought into an implicit system, a potentially citable signature. His various termini sharpen into concepts and engage with recognized traditions of philosophy. His various readings of Kafka, Fuchs, Lesskow, Kraus, Proust, and Baudelaire retain their purchase on these authorial signatures and enter into recognized traditions of critical reaction to them. But the alternative centrality of *One-Way Street* consists, paradoxically, in its refractory decentering effect on Benjamin's signature, dispersing it elsewhere in the oeuvre into pseudonyms, lifting the termini the signature authorizes to the surface of the inscriptions that preserve them as formulaic rituals in which the reader must choose to participate, manifesting the readings of historical oeuvres the signature endorses as elaborate identifications whose organizing of the detritus of the material archive the reader must choose to perform. From this perspective, hermetic remarks, dreams, plagiarisms, and montages resist any direct investment with stable intention. Here, tone is glorified, meaning assassinated.

It is not, of course, a question of selecting between these texts and their perspectives. But the very absence of a choice displaces the *Trauerspiel* book, for it belongs to the concept of a centered signature that it operates by closing off and depositing achieved meanings before the reader, to the concept of a decentered signature that it disrupts this closure whenever it appears. The disruption is not thereby a free-for-all of association, but raises the stakes on a transparent literary science, demanding a higher stringency, in comparison with which, as Benjamin writes in a brief essay titled "Literary History and the Study of Literature," from 1931, "present-day German studies are ... unphilological through and through, measured not by the positivistic yardstick of the Scherer school but by that of the Brothers Grimm, who never sought to grasp the material content [*Sachgehalte*] outside of words" (*SW*, 2:463; *GS*, 3:289). This stringent philology maintains science at the boundary between an esoteric presentation and an exoteric content, and follows the now-time of inscription not into an immortalized intention but into a jeopardized future. "If you think back to my other works," Benjamin writes to Adorno in 1938, responding to his criticisms of his Baudelaire essay, "you will find that the critique of the philologist's stance is an old concern of mine—and most profoundly identical with my critique of myth. Each time, the critique provokes the philological effort [*Leistung*] itself" (*CB*, 588; *GB*, 6:185–86). It is in this sense that the rift between *The Origin of German Trauerspiel* and *One-Way Street* around an esoteric science enacts the impossibility of *The Birth of Tragedy*, in a philology that lays equal emphasis on the specific word and the love that encounters it. Though Nietzsche himself had ventured to be hopeful. "In the meantime I can express the conviction that it will take philologists a few decades," he had answered his disappointed mentor Ritschl, "before they can understand such an esoteric and in the highest sense scientific book" (*SB*, 3:304). What Benjamin calls esotericism is what Nietzsche calls untimeliness, and his commitment to it shows he has, indeed, understood Nietzsche's philological explosion.

Unlike Nietzsche, Benjamin was never admitted into the actual professoriate. And despite his scholarly and theoretical interests it would be difficult indeed to imagine him as a German professor of literature. Rather, with the granting of his doctorate in June 1919, Benjamin ascended to a much more tenuous and subversive post, as he noted in a letter to Scholem when the diploma eventually arrived in March 1921. "I recently received my Ph.D. diploma, dozens of copies at once," Benjamin writes. "Therefore, I hope you are aware that, as the owner of a naïvely realistic Ph.D. diploma, I will from now on assume the high office of transcendental beadle of the University of Muri." And then the topic changes: "I was recently able to get Meister Eckhart's sermons, and some volumes of the large Nietzsche edition for my philosophical library at very little cost" (*CB*, 178; *GB*, 2:147).

"WE PHILOLOGISTS"

"*We*" is the first word of Nietzsche's *Birth of Tragedy*, and already it is poised over an abyss. "We shall have gained much for the science of aesthetics, once we perceive not merely by logical inference [*Einsicht*], but with the immediate certainty of awareness [*Anschauung*], that the continuous development of art is bound up with the duplicity [*Duplicität*] of the *Apollonian* and the *Dionysian*" (*BT*, 33; *KSA*, 1:25). Introducing his most general expository distinction, Nietzsche positions a collective intent toward a disembodied aesthetic science, a community whose epistemological cohesion extends beyond the transparency of logical certainty into the immediate surety of direct individual awareness. The components of aesthetic science—logical conclusiveness and immediate awareness—are not exemplified by either of the principles Nietzsche proposes, for what appears before individual awareness is not the self-identity of a perceptual content but the duality of a conceptual opposition.

These two modes of certainty are not set in opposition, but appear as a preliminary state and its intensification: "Mere" collective logic indirectly indicates what immediate awareness directly confirms. The implicit "we" sustains the possibility of a passage beyond formal certainty to the experienced sureties that validate it after having called it forth in the first place, even as every difference between their respective modes of validation conspires to block any continuity between them. And yet in the vacancy of this "we," what seems a rhetorical hyperbole becomes a reversal of the Kantian terms defining knowledge. Nietzsche situates scientific inquiry in the domain of a transcendental aesthetic of direct awareness [*Anschauungen*], somehow beyond the transcendental logic of the concept [*Begriff*]. Where Kant proposed a transient direct awareness that must rise to the enduring status of conceptual knowledge, Nietzsche imagines a communicable knowledge that must rise to the surety of direct awareness. From this perspective, aesthetics is no longer conceivable as a discrete domain within scientific inquiry, but scientific inquiry is a particular posture toward the immediacy of direct awareness, a posture that meets other postures across the surface of an aesthetic aspect of cognition. Art is the name of these cognitive struggles over the surface of inscription.

The thought of an art governed by cognitive coherence has already expanded around the science that would objectify it, for indeed the distinction between *Apollinischen* and *Dionysischen* emerges not from our own perceptions, but from an alien, Greek awareness. "We borrow these names [*Namen*] from the Greeks, who disclose to the discerning mind the profound esoteric doctrines [*tiefsinnigen Geheimlehren*] of their view of art, not, to be sure, in concepts, but in the intensely clear figures of their world of gods [*Götterwelt*]" (*BT*, 33; *KSA*, 1:25). Nietzsche's initial philological distinction depends on a different sort of reading, one that can register the esoteric doctrine encrypted in the figures of the gods. The schematic passage from direct awareness to logical concept and back that constitutes epistemologically valid reflection is interrupted by the Greek designating tactic, which installs an allegorical figure outside of conceptualization, as the transit to a second-order, superior awareness that it is the task of knowledge to achieve. Our knowledge, the knowledge of an insightful "we" contributing to aesthetic science, is thus informed by two heterogeneous authorities, the compelling self-evidence of logical insight, but beyond and before it, the esoteric teaching of the Greek figures. No extant common awareness grounds this "we," so Nietzsche's expository path must proceed by evoking states of awareness outside of those that support stable conceptual description. Dream and intoxication are the first contractions in the tragic labor of this "we."

The opposition between logical insight and immediate awareness with which *The Birth of Tragedy* begins is not simply an abstract boundary, but a specifically temporal fissure. Scientific communication is in the present and esoteric awareness is not. The "we" from and to which Nietzsche speaks cannot condense entirely at either point but, bound together provisionally by art, arises as the unity of a terminological practice, the art of applying these divine adjectives to subsequent creative processes. Through the names Apollo and Dionysus, an original aesthetic awareness is borne forward into the present for as long as it can license Nietzsche's extravagant claims. The abyss beneath *The Birth of Tragedy* in the epistemological inversion of direct awareness and logical conceptualization is crossed as the historical rift between a mediated past and an immediate present.

Dionysus and Apollo, whether integrated then in tragedy or now in the *Gesamtkunstwerk*, each continues to be riven by this temporal disparity. The signatures their integration establishes, whether Aeschylus's or Wagner's, are precariously poised between the genuine aesthetic reception of Dionysus and the genuine aesthetic production of Apollo. The tragic poet who manifests the absent god Dionysus in Apollonian forms is always turned receptively toward the inspirational past even as he speaks to the disenchanted present. Dionysus is always emerging from the East, from its elsewhere, demanding recognition as perilously present in the very Apollonian recourses that stage his literal absence. The tragic poet/composer does not synthesize Dionysus and Apollo into a representative whole within which a nation—or any other identifiable collective—could recognize itself. Rather, he masters a representational crisis: the intrusion of an alien creative principle that defies representation. Whether ancient Greek or contemporary German, the tragic poet is a passage between a heterogeneous past he divines and the indigenous forms of the present in which he manifests that past. Tragic temporality is always the juncture of a "no longer" and a "not yet," a birth that appears simultaneously with its death, as the potential for its rebirth. This is why, despite Nietzsche's expository intentions, tragedy does not arise and disappear and arise again within the continuities of a representational tradition that could be gathered together as art, but marks caesuras within that tradition. As the response to a representational collapse, tragedy cannot display its own membership in art, but must be recognized by another testimony, another sort of achievement.

This achievement is philology. It recognizes tragedy as an invisible identity between contemporary and archaic, but unlike tragedy, it does not master that identity in a single gesture, but exists as expression only to the extent that it maintains the elements of that identity as historically separated. Like the tragic poet, the philologist cannot entirely identify with his historical moment from within, but unlike the tragic poet, the philologist can also not be entirely identified with his moment from without. The successful philologist must exist in a space entirely outside of the cultural integrity of either historical moment, a space not beholden to his immediate cultural environment, but rather a space projected around two separate historical formations, an exterior space.

It is this exterior space in its untimeliness that Nietzsche attempts to localize directly in 1875, in a fourth *Untimely Observation*, titled "We Philologists." The essay remains in fragments,[29] its elements are strewn among pieces of two other projects that develop in the notebooks of the time, the completed fourth *Observation*, "Richard Wagner in Bayreuth," and the uncompleted essay on the pre-Socratics, "Philosophy in the Tragic Age of the Greeks." Before these elements can be sorted beneath these respective titles, they must be seen in their intrinsic relation to one another. Together, they form a destructive project that localizes Wagner's signature in the present, undermines the legacy of philosophical concepts from the past, and demolishes its own disciplinary site of articulation. Of these three titles, "We Philologists" remains most fragmentary, furthest from publication, not for accidental reasons, but because it addresses the expressive paradox most directly. Any attempt to read it must not merely complete what was unwritten, but attend to what in it remains unwritable. The recursive self-subversion of "We Philologists" requires that its fragmentary nature itself manifest a meaning, to be read not comprehending its incompleteness beneath a second-order intention, but registering a particular collapse of philology and a concomitant isolation of the philologist outside the conceptual sureties of a recognized discipline, transforming him into a philosophical figure, a doorkeeper at the radical edge of reading. For if untimeliness rises through "David Strauss the Confessor and the Writer" to destabilize Nietzsche's accredited signature, it escapes through "We Philologists" into the asyndeton at the heart of Nietzsche's mature production, suspending a new authority between his unadorned signature and his intricate aphoristic sequences.

Untimeliness as an entitled phase of Nietzsche's production depends on cultural institutions, and in particular on philological accreditation. This appears retrospectively in the demolition of the recognizability of philological discipline. "We Philologists" is the solvent for the national commitments that structured Nietzsche's oppositional stance throughout his university career, the collapse of the polemical framework that allowed untimeliness to appear in the present as a contrast between Wagnerian renewal and a journalistic "now-time" in a German context. The invisible temporal contrast between "then" and "now" absorbs the recognizable cultural contrast between Greek and German into which Nietzsche had attempted to translate these contemporary antagonistic scientific and artistic authorities.

Thus the fragments of "We Philologists" attack both Greek cultural identity and Teutonic philological preeminence. The dependence of Greek culture on Egyptian, Persian, and barbarian forms before it, and the distortions in our view of it introduced by Alexandrine, Roman, and Christian forms after it conspire to undermine any autonomy or coherence in the Hellenic achievement; while the examples of great Italian and British philological scholarship, such as that of Leopardi or Bentley, and the profundity of extradisciplinary reactions to the Greeks, such as that of Voltaire or Goethe, conspire to undermine any disciplinary autonomy in German philology. The destruction of synchronous unity, whether virtual in the text or actual around the reader, within which philological reading could take place manifests Nietzsche's primary antagonistic purpose in this text. *My aim is: to create total enmity between our current "culture" and antiquity. Whoever wants to serve the former must despise the latter* (WC, 341; KSA, 8:33). A reciprocal conditioning that would make the historical antagonism absolute is unleashed from its totalization by the structural ambiguity of the ordinals, which refer to a first and a last in either the syntactic or the chronological sense. If we wish to serve contemporary culture, we must despise the ancients; if we wish to serve the ancients, we must loathe our own culture. When we read the ancients, we must read them from a perspective hostile to today; but we must do this today, in service to today, and so irrevocably hostile to the ancients. The hateful affect, on whichever side it falls, merely maintains the historical distance as it descends through philology and lodges in humanity as such.

"We Philologists" fails to coalesce into a signable text not through any merely conceptual incoherence, as if Nietzsche had been unable to sort out the contradictory perspectives on philology he raises. Rather, its emergence into effective publicity would betray its purpose, which is precisely not to define, but to destroy philology as the reconciliation of past and present. "We Philologists" is not the first of Nietzsche's notebooks, but by taking irreducible residence there, it is indeed the anchor of the *Nachlaß* as a constitutive part of Nietzsche's philosophical project. The notebook from early March 1875, headed *Notes to "WE PHILOLOGISTS,"* begins by defining the *Nachlaß* itself.

> *A large book for daily insights and experiences, plans, etc. should be started: where scientific discoveries could also be briefly noted. Put all literary plans to one side. Mihi scribere.* (KSA, 8:11)

A criticism of philology provokes, or is provoked by, the appearance of the *Nachlaß* as a conscious project. The impersonal construction introducing the notebook project is situated by the oblique pronoun of the Latin summation. The shift to Latin beneath the title mentioning philologists identifies Nietzsche with the object of classical philology. This indeterminate plan shadows the reflective posture maintained throughout "We Philologists," as the necessary counterpart to its self-denunciations, which position these notes themselves as simultaneously inside and outside of philology. *Philologists are people who use the dull feeling [dumpfe Gefühl] of modern man about his actual insufficiency to earn money and bread. I know them, I am myself one* (WC, 373; *KSA*, 8:76).

Philology is, from the start, bound to the philologist. The terse fragment that opens Notebook Mp XIII 6b from March of 1875, where Nietzsche begins to develop the essay a second time, bypasses method entirely. *The eighth of April 1777, when F. A. Wolf invented for himself the name stud. philol., is the birthday of philology* (WC, 325; *KSA*, 8:14). By tying the origin of philology to a specific date, Nietzsche neutralizes any abstract definition of the discipline in terms of its object or method. The birthday of philology is the moment when a particular signature bestowed upon itself a particular title. Philology begins not with the discovery of a method of inquiry, but rather with the autochthonous investiture of a certain authority. Hence the question of philological legibility is not epistemological—what sort of knowledge does philology produce? but pedagogic—what sort of authority does it wield? *There would be nothing to say against the science of philology,* Nietzsche writes: *but the philologists are also the educators. Therein lies the problem that brings this science under a higher jurisdiction.—And would philology still exist, if philologists were not a guild of teachers [Lehrerstand]?* (WC, 326; *KSA*, 8:14). The scientific status of philology is conceded but passes immediately into the philologist who embodies it pedagogically. Because philologists teach, they stand before a higher court than simple scientific accuracy. The moral implications of this pedagogic situation condition the science the philologists present, which also falls under that higher jurisdiction. The fact that philological science is embodied pedagogically—this is the "problem" with which Nietzsche begins, and it immediately recoils into a complementary suspicion: Without this pedagogic embodiment, would there be any meaning to scientific philology?

It is this second suspicion that shows Nietzsche's question to be deeper than the relatively familiar concern: To what extent does the ability to research a subject from a scientific perspective translate into an ability to mediate that subject to the next generation? It is not merely the tense institutional marriage of scholarship and pedagogy that both enables and vexes pedagogic institutions—and that his own appointment at Basel had been designed to embody—to which Nietzsche is here responding. What Nietzsche is in fact questioning is not something as straightforward as the congruence in a single person of the two professorial roles of researcher and teacher. Rather, the question with which "We Philologists" begins concerns the disparate temporal orientations of these two postures, the necessary implication of philology as active in the present, as well as passive toward the past. The pedagogic role engulfs the philologist on the basis of his contemporary situation itself: *To see now how impotent [wirkungslos] this course of study is, merely look at the philologists: after all, they must have been <u>best educated by antiquity</u>* (WC, 330; KSA, 8:19).

The pedagogic embodiment is separated from science across the space of this ad hominem.[30] But isolated from any directly influencing role, the scientific aspect of philological reading cannot maintain itself. Thus it will not be long before the distinction in fragment 3[3] between the science of philology and the educating philologist is rejected disdainfully.

> *Those who say: "but there still remains an antiquity as the object of pure science, even when all of its educational intentions have been denied," should be answered: what is here pure science! Actions and qualities are to be <u>judged</u>, and whoever judges must stand above what he judges: thus you would first have to make sure that you had <u>overcome antiquity</u>. As long as you haven't done that, your science is not pure but impure and constricted: as it palpably is.* (WC, 357; KSA, 8:54–55)

The pure scientific perspective is here presented as a challenging objection, to which in response a necessary hierarchy is insisted upon. Judgments, scientific and otherwise, can be rendered only from a superior perspective on their object. This ostensible superiority, when applied to the Greeks, pulls the fragment into a confrontational posture, and the possessive adjectives situate the philologist behind philological judgments in a historical contrast to the Greeks he presumes to judge. The assumption that philological science can appropriate classical documents rests on the presumption that the philologist measures up to the Greek author. But the standards set by that Greek author are in fact set by the philologist who reads him. This paradox is not a local problem within Nietzsche's specific cultural milieu, but inheres in the receptive posture toward antiquity itself. Thus all collective reading of the Greeks that purports to measure up to them, as soon as it itself can be identified as a receptive posture, founders on this paradox.

Nietzsche's critique of philology moves inexorably backward through history, denouncing the Enlightenment,[31] the Reformation,[32] and on into late antiquity itself.

> *Our position with regard to classical antiquity is at bottom the cause of the profound unproductivity of modern culture*: for this whole modern concept of culture we have inherited from the Hellenized Romans. We have to *distinguish* within antiquity itself: by acquainting ourselves with its only productive time, we *condemn* the entire Alexandrian-Roman culture. But *at the same time we condemn our entire posture toward antiquity and our philology as well!* (WC, 356; KSA, 8:53)

This reflexive condemnation is what fuels Nietzsche's ultimate dismissal of public philology. At the same time, it conditions an intensification of the collective pronoun that expresses Nietzsche's private hopes: *Between* our *highest art and philosophy and between the* truly *recognized* older *antiquity there is no contradiction: they support and bear each other. In this lies my hope* (WC, 368; KSA, 8:69). The ineradicable antagonism between past and present is not lifted, but outbid. Between an older past and a newer present, no contradiction is necessary.

The philologist who reconciles these extremes must remain himself invisible. With "We Philologists" already breaking down, Nietzsche assembles several fragments into aphorisms late in 1876 and has them copied by Paul Rée. *Philology is the art of learning and teaching to read in a time that reads too much,* Nietzsche begins there. *Only the philologist reads slowly and ponders half an hour over six lines* (KSA, 8:332). The untimely art of reading, studied and taught by philology, produces in the contemplative philologist an invisible ideal. Where philology appears as such within the text-saturated present, it succumbs to the expediency of the times. This positive philology escapes the recognizable discipline, but remains as the guiding principle to reading. But in the invisible economy of thought, the philologist defies that expediency by augmenting the reading process in two dimensions. Philology as a principle of fidelity to textual specificity expands, on the one hand, across a broader range of senses. Nietzsche, the philologist, reads with his fingertips, judges with his nostrils. This diversified sensitivity facilitates his accurate judgments, enables the immediate recognition of disease, weakness, and resentment that animate his writing pen. On the other hand, that same fidelity expands the duration of the reader's encounter with the text. The proper reader, Nietzsche insists, will take his time with a text, consider it from many angles, and contrast it with many prior statements. As the employment of an expanded sensorium, philology promotes and accelerates judgment; as the endurance of an expanded uncertainty, philology restricts and suspends judgment. Epistemologically, these two dimensions across which philology expands reading are not in harmony: The deployment of additional sensory modalities (above all, touch and smell) in a total harmonized reaction to an inscription collides with the extension of indeterminate encounter with the text, the suspension of judgment Nietzsche demands from his readers. The duration of a suspending reflection on the text, the willingness to experience the full panoply of potential combinations among its expressive elements, determines the penetration of any given philological judgment. Philology uncovers, strips away—as such it reduces the text to its surface, to which it applies the full register of senses, and records the singularity of its presentation before the cacophony of subsequent readings that have intervened to obscure it. But it does so silently, for the recognizable gestures of philological discipline are implicated in that subsequent cacophony.

"We Philologists" insists on the inaccessibility of Greek culture in its inspirational ideality to German culture in its historical reality. To the extent that the German philologist is engaged in the education of German youth, he is committed to a vision of culture that accentuates the German historical-scientific achievement; but to the extent that the philologist is the product of a Greek experience, he is committed to a vision of culture that accentuates the Greek metaphysical-artistic achievement. But where the former rises to recognizable expression, it impinges on the creative force of the latter. Philology reads a text that denounces it; the philologist exists positively only as long as he is unrecognizably authorized by his opposite, the creative mastery of life. On this contradiction "We Philologists" ruptures. Not merely the university institution or national cultural forms disintegrate with it, but the entire field of recognizable culture, out to the boundary of human self-recognition, the humanist framework that establishes the autonomy of culture. The collapse around "We Philologists" translates through the ad hominem enthymeme a displacement in the governing historical category of *human*, a displacement which, for a time, Nietzsche tries to sort beneath the title *Human and All Too Human*, first as an initial entry in a list of titles,[33] and then as the last, summarizing entry in a later list.[34] But the conjunction *and* implies that a perseverant distinction between those aspects of culture that are genuinely humane and those aspects that are limited and mediocre can be maintained. Outside of self-evident cultural formations, such a distinction collapses. When, in Fragment 19[118], the phrase gains a subtitle, its plurality begins to erode the conjunction:

> Human and All Too Human.
>   Convivial Sayings. (KSA, 8:359)

The "convivial sayings" emerge from and address the human community in both its admirable and its uninspiring qualities. The origin of the specifically Nietzschean philosophical project lies in the obliteration of the conjunction that segregates these qualities, and its eventual replacement in the title of Nietzsche's next published book, by the ambiguity of a comma. *Human, All Too Human.*

With the collapse of "We Philologists" Nietzsche leaves the certified discipline—but this escape is not into an empty exterior where speculative reading relates its notions in unregulated and scientifically vacuous associations. Philology remains with Nietzsche in the resonant vacillations of his signature. *Human, All Too Human* considers the meaning of philology closely, incorporating in aphoristic dispersal many of the fragments of the abandoned essay. Aphorism # 270 thus inverts the relation of art to science—pushing art here toward technique, science toward true transmission.

> *The art of reading.*—Every strong course is onesided; . . . one must forgive the philologists too for being onesided. Production and preservation of texts, together with their elucidation, pursued in a guild [*Zunft*] for centuries, has now finally discovered the correct methods; the entire Middle Ages was profoundly incapable of a strict philological elucidation, that is to say of a simple desire to understand what the author is saying—to have discovered these methods was an achievement, let no one undervalue it! All science has only acquired continuity and constancy because the art of correct reading, that is to say philology, reached its peak. (HA, 127; KSA, 2:223)

Philology is not merely a science, but as the principle of authorial comprehension itself, the philological method is guarantor of scientific continuity and constancy, philologists the methodical guardians of its accurate transmission. If the philological method contrasts with medieval obscurity in the science of which it is the exterior, it also bears the esoteric trace of a medieval heritage in the term—*Zunft*—that defines the regulative philological community to which it belongs.

In the preface to *Daybreak*, the book in which Nietzsche's aphoristic sequence emerges in its unadorned purity, unconstrained by the subtitles and poetic framing of his earlier and later efforts with the form, Nietzsche returns to philology in its positive guise.

> This preface comes late but not too late—what, after all, do five or six years matter? A book like this, a problem like this, is in no hurry; we both, I just as much as my book, are friends of *lento*. It is not for nothing that I have been a philologist, perhaps I am a philologist still, that is to say, a teacher of slow reading:—in the end I also write slowly. . . . For philology is that venerable art which demands of its votaries one thing above all: to go aside, to take time, to become still, to become slow—it is a goldsmith's art and connoisseurship of the *word* which has nothing but delicate cautious work to do and achieves nothing if it does not achieve it *lento*. . . . My patient friends, this book desires for itself only perfect readers and philologists: *learn to read me well!*—(D, 5; KSA, 3:17)

This positive notion of a demystified philological sensitivity, oscillating with a negative notion of unperceptive philological pedanticism, survives until the end of Nietzsche's career. Where *The Antichrist* identifies philology, with medicine, as one of "the two great opponents of all superstition" (AC, 175; KSA, 6:226), in *Ecce Homo*, Nietzsche boasts that his "eyes alone put an end to bookwormishness—in brief, philology: I was delivered from the 'book'; for years I did not read a thing—the *greatest* benefit I ever conferred upon myself!" (EH, 287; KSA, 6:326). These two aspects are inseparable; the positive dimension of philology that survives in Nietzsche's signature cannot be condensed into a method or recognizable procedure. However admirable its austere probity is found—*Praise of philology: as the study of probity [Redlichkeit]. Antiquity expired from the decline of that* (KSA, 9:261)—as soon as it speaks in its own voice, it dissolves into mechanical pedanticism. *The philologist was . . . until now the educator <u>as such</u>: because his activity itself was the pattern of a monotony of activity that reaches the magnificent* (KSA, 12:460). Philology survives beyond "We Philologists" not as an encompassing expressive standard within which Nietzsche's texts can be situated, but as a subterranean ideal of receptivity that gathers together an invisible audience. That audience must be addressed indirectly, not invoked as such; it overhears an expression for which it is never the intended audience.

Reading has an ineradicable ceremonial component; it cannot escape its ultimate investment in blind ritual performed upon the material signs it encounters. The religious recitation of prayers and blessings in a language unknown to the speaker exaggerates a gestural moment within all textual passivity, and the practice of reading, however reflective and self-aware it may become, must always incorporate the opaque lurch of a repetition that rests on no immediate recognition within the autonomous reading subject, but depends entirely on the external force of ritual, on the prior compulsion it exercises over the reading awareness, and on the posterior effects it manifests within a communal life.[35] It is in this moment of ceremonial complicity that Benjamin's exterior philology meets up with the positive, implicit philological discipline that survives in Nietzsche as the antithesis of theology. "Another mark of the theologian is his *incapacity for philology*," Nietzsche writes in the *Antichrist*. "Philology is to be understood here in a very wide sense as the art of reading well—of being able to read off a fact *without* falsifying it by interpretation, *without* losing caution, patience, subtlety in the desire for understanding. Philology as *ephexis* in interpretation" (AC, 181–82; KSA, 6:233). This parodic, indecisive philology unfolding across the historical exterior of philological continuities will indeed encounter the same domain as the concepts of theology, but with inverted implications. It is as a suspicion of the moment of ritual complicity that philology is the antithesis of theology.

Philosophy cannot resolve this antithesis. In this regard, one should recall that Nietzsche's philological career began under a man, Friedrich Wilhelm Ritschl, whose professional goal it was to keep philology *free* of philosophy. *He tended indeed to overestimate his discipline,* Nietzsche recalled in an autobiographical text that he composed as he was leaving Leipzig to begin his professorship at Basel, *and consequently had an aversion to philologists who entered more deeply into philosophy. On the other hand, he tried to render his pupils useful for science as quickly as possible* (BAW, 3:305). To the extent that Nietzsche moves from philology to philosophy, he is reintroducing philosophical questions into a discursive space that had been cleared of them in the light of the self-evident parameters of a collective method directed toward an independent object. Nietzsche reintroduces philosophy into this disciplinary space not by raising questions about that method, demanding that it justify itself philosophically. Rather, philosophy appears when Nietzsche takes as a philological object the fragmentary, written remains of a philosopher.[36] Philosophy does not respond for Nietzsche to a perceived insufficiency in scientific method but flows naturally from the philological practice of textual attribution. Philology becomes philosophical when it takes upon itself the task of reconstructing a philosophical intention.

This in effect inverts the usual relation of philosophy to science. Philology, as a science, dominates philosophy, setting the methodological conditions for its comprehension. This is something very different from the modern epistemological sense in which philosophy orients itself methodologically on a given science such as mathematics or mechanical physics. Philology, as the scientific securing of the textual foundation of interpretation, has at one limit the empirical investigation of material inscription—the chemical, graphological, archaeological determination of the material bearers of the physical inscription in which all historical culture participates. At another limit, it has the speculative and hypothetical attribution of a recognizable intention that can justify intrinsic emendations of an imperfect textual record or extrinsic attributions of various texts to a single source. These two limits are not in conflict; the material record of the physical inscription cannot contradict the intentional attribution without forcing a revision in that attribution. But the interpretive possibilities are not easily restricted by any determination of the material vehicle, since the hypothesis of transcription can always displace authorship from the inscription. In the end, philology trumps philosophy and touches theology because it is the science of intention itself. What philology approaches with the ascetic dignity of disinterested science is thus the very possibility of the secure transmission of communicative intention, the condition of disinterested science in the authoritative voice on the mortal page.

ASYNDETON

Toward the end of his sane life, as the relativizing context around him dissolved, Nietzsche began to consider his philosophy a singular rupture in human history. In his autobiography *Ecce Homo*, the claim comes almost at the end of the book: "The *discovery* of Christian morality is an event without parallel," Nietzsche boasts there, "a real catastrophe. He that enlightens about that, is a force majeure, a destiny [*Schicksal*]—he breaks the history of mankind in two. One lives *before* him, or one lives *after* him . . ." (*EH*, 333; *KSA*, 6:373). Already in his letters, the motif had accompanied his final exultant productions. Thus to his friend Paul Deussen in September of 1888, he writes:

> In the end *these two writings* [viz., *The Case of Wagner* and *Twilight of the Idols*] merely genuine recreations in the midst of an immeasurably difficult and decisive task, which, *if it is understood*, splits the history of mankind [*Menschheit*] into two halves. The sense of it in three words is: *Transvaluation of all Values*. (SB, 8:426)

A month later, announcing *Twilight of the Idols* to Overbeck: "This time I'm deploying as an old artillery-man my big guns: I'm afraid I'm blowing the history of humanity apart into two halves" (*SB*, 8:453). And in December Nietzsche repeats the formula to Köselitz, describing *Ecce Homo*, "It is so far beyond the concept of 'literature' that actually even Nature has no comparison: it explodes, literally, the *history of humanity* into two pieces—highest superlative of *dynamite* . . ." (*SB*, 8:513).

This extravagant braggadocio testifies to the proximity of Nietzsche's ultimate psychological collapse. In his Italian rooming house, the singular expatriate German ex-professor can no longer situate the specificity of his efforts in terms of any regulating historical event or tradition founded on it, and his writing appears to him to overwhelm the frame of history. Suspended without precedent or following in its particular emergent moment, the meaning of Nietzsche's writing cannot be distinguished from the specific life that gave rise to it. The destruction of Christianity and the Antichrist, the revision of all values and Dionysus—in the incomparability of their significance, the writings collapse back onto the unique man who wrote them, and from the singularity of their common emergence, "before" and "after" now take their meaning. "Consider, most honored sir!" Nietzsche writes to August Strindberg, proposing translations of *Ecce Homo*. "It is a matter of the very first order. For I am strong enough to shatter the history of humanity into two pieces" (*SB*, 8:509). Not only the book but also the man it describes is capable of rupturing history. Such a distorted self-conception seems flagrantly exaggerated. The martial metaphors Nietzsche uses to describe this break suggest violence effecting cataclysmic destruction of historical continuity. And the motif of dynamite, which also slides from book to author—"I am no man; I am dynamite," as *Ecce Homo* insists (*EH*, 326; *KSA*, 6:365)—condenses into a figure both the aggression and the self-aggrandizement that color Nietzsche's final weeks in Turin.

But this figure and its relation to the historical rupture it marks a last attempt to characterize reach back to 1886 and *Beyond Good and Evil*. There, in the aphoristic sequence "We Scholars," Nietzsche had used it to describe how his own position appeared to a fashionable pessimistic skepticism.

> When a philosopher suggests these days that he is not a skeptic . . . among timid listeners, of whom there are legions now, he is henceforth considered dangerous. It is as if at his rejection of skepticism they heard some evil, menacing rumbling in the distance, as if a new explosive were being tried somewhere, a dynamite of the spirit. (*BGE*, 128; *KSA*, 5:137)

Nietzsche's philosophy, in its skepticism toward skepticism, sounds to anxious members of the public like the detonations of a new explosive. The metaphor here emphasizes the distance between the source of the concussion and its perception; as a blasting agent, dynamite implies constructive as opposed to martial destruction, but destruction here in service to a construction whose location and purpose remain obscure to those who merely sense the distant tremor. It marks a hermeneutic distortion, a potential misunderstanding, and indeed, as if to confirm this, it was just this passage that the reviewer of *Beyond Good and Evil* for the Berner *Bund*, J. V. Widmann, chose to develop in his review, "Nietzsche's dangerous Book."

> Those dynamite supplies that were used in the construction of the Gotthard train line carried the black flag warning of mortal danger.—It is wholly in this sense that we speak of this new book by the philosopher Nietzsche as dangerous. . . . Spiritual explosives, like material ones, can assist in very useful works; it is not necessary that they be misused for criminal purposes. Only where such things are stored it makes sense to say clearly, "here lies dynamite!" (*KSA*, 15:160–61)

Nietzsche himself transcribed this characterization, with quiet irony, in a letter to his friend Malwida von Meysenbug, excusing her in advance from reading *Beyond Good and Evil*, a complimentary copy of which he had had his publisher send to her. "So be, honored friend, quite thankful that I keep myself a bit *far* from you! . . ." (*SB*, 7:258). In *Ecce Homo*, Nietzsche mentions Widmann's review explicitly: "Dr. Widmann expressed his respect for the courage I had shown in my attempt to abolish all decent feelings.—As the petty spite of accident would have it, every sentence here was, with a consequence I admired, some truth stood on its head" (*EH*, 260–61; *KSA*,

6:299). Widmann's straightforward adoption of Nietzsche's figure of the "Dynamite of the spirit" thus stands as a particular inversion of its meaning.[37] The claim "I am no man, I am dynamite" is aimed at anxious ears, and whatever anxieties we may bring to it, its repercussions must not drown out the complementary self-characterization, also from *Ecce Homo*: "Alas! I am a nuance" (*EH*, 323; *KSA*, 6:362).

Nietzsche's bombast—his moments of rhetorical shrillness, of unmitigated scorn or enthusiasm or insistence—inhabits a style that constantly swerves between boast and the seemingly contradictory motif of withdrawal and desire for obscurity. The theme of loneliness and isolation grows throughout Nietzsche's oeuvre. It passes through such figures as the "wanderer," who closes the final aphoristic sequence of *Human, All Too Human I*, "Man Alone with Himself," and who presents the later sequence "The Wanderer and His Shadow," and the "hermit" who speaks in *The Gay Science* and haunts Zarathustra throughout his anti-ministry. "The hermit does not believe," Nietzsche writes in *Beyond Good and Evil*, "that any philosopher—assuming that every philosopher was first of all a hermit—ever expressed his real and ultimate opinions in his books: does one not write books precisely to conceal [*verbergen*] what one harbors [*birgt*]?" (*BGE*, 229; *KSA*, 5:234). This is the motif developed in section 8 of the third essay in *On the Genealogy of Morals*, on the true philosopher's necessary recourse to the deserts of asceticism. "A voluntary obscurity perhaps; an avoidance of oneself; a dislike of noise, admiration, newspapers, influence; a modest job, an everyday routine, something that conceals rather than exposes one . . . —that is what 'desert' means here: oh, it is lonely enough, believe me!" (*GM*, 109; *KSA*, 5:353). And in his last notebook of December 1888, where he confronts the final Hohenzollern: *Ich bin die <u>Einsamkeit</u> als Mensch . . .* , he scribbles: *I am <u>loneliness</u> in human form* (*KSA*, 13:641).

Nietzsche is both an explosive event of world-historical scope and publicity, and a nuance, a slight shift of private perspective. Maintaining that private shift of perspective in public is the task of his writing, and his signature survives in the lurch of that explosive nuance. "Untimeliness" does not disappear when it can no longer support an authorial signature, but through this lurch expands across his entire production as its unique refraction of historical possibility. With the reflective collapse of "We Philologists," together with the demolition of a neutral "philosophical" register in "Philosophy in the Tragic Age of the Greeks" and the break with artistic presentation in "Wagner in Bayreuth," Nietzsche's signature is exposed to interpretation absolutely, as the locus of a conflict between laudatory and denunciatory tonalities that discontinuously reposition the ultimate human frame of reference. The moment of detonation is caught in the *Nachlaß* in a fragment from 1876: *Seven untimely Observations—1873–78. For every Observation a supplement [Nachtrag] in aphorisms. Later: Supplements to the untimely Observations (aphoristic)* (KSA, 8:290). The aphoristic sequences appended to each of the chronologically sequenced *Observations* become aphoristic sequences appended to the project as a whole, in a revision that submerges the historical plurality of appendices marking the annually distinct *Observations* into the plurality of aphorisms composing them. The presentation of this conflict can no longer unfold within a shared thematic context, as a secular sermon on a recognizably relevant theme. When Nietzsche's signature itself becomes untimely, riven between incongruent aphoristic expressions, the Emersonian *Observations* are also finished.

The explosion is published in the title *Human, All Too Human*. The asyndeton here marks these contrasting evaluations as congruent in the inscription, and positions Nietzsche's signature as the dynamic principle that distinguishes and recombines them. "Human": the heroic ideal of *humanitas*, defining the transcendent sweep of its unrealized potentials. "All Too Human": the cosmic finitude of *anthropos*, situating an insignificant element in the chaotic immensity of nature. The passage from "Human" to "All Too Human" carries the deflationary force of a debunking. But against this works the ad hominem slippage, the inverted value manifested in he who *says* "Human," he who *says* "All Too Human." All too human is the gesture of heroic invocation, a blind continuation of the pointless series of inspirational self-definitions in which this accidental species indulges. He who *says* "Human" as *humanitas* is implicated in the Latin misappropriation of Greek tragic insight. He who *says* "All Too Human" thereby refuses to say *humanitas* and situates himself at the border of an unnamable potential. The recursive passage from "Human" through "Nietzsche" to "All Too Human" and back is the first version of a circuit that is, from this perspective, the "deep structure" of Nietzsche's production, a centrifugal circuit that expands beyond the outer limit of his endorsing signature. Held from 1878 to 1885 within this uncontrollable asyndeton,[38] joining identical global objects beneath opposed evaluations, Nietzsche's signature supports discontinuous expressions in ever more elaborate structuring frames.[39]

The event of Zarathustra, manifested doctrinally in the lurch from *human* to *superman*, is the precarious transformation of this authorizing signature and its recursive dynamic into a title: *Thus Spoke Zarathustra*.

> Hier sass ich, wartend, wartend,—doch auf Nichts,
> Jenseits von Gut und Böse, bald des Lichts
> Geniessend, bald des Schattens, ganz nur Spiel,
> Ganz See, ganz Mittag, ganz Zeit ohne Ziel.
>
> Da, plötzlich, Freundin! wurde Eins zu Zwei—
> —Und Zarathustra gieng an mir vorbei....
>
> [Here sat I, waiting, waiting—yet for Nothing,
> Beyond Good and Evil, fancying
> Now light, now shadow, all but a game,
> All lake, all midday, all time without aim.
>
> Then, suddenly, friend! One turned into Two—
> —And Zarathustra ambled past my view....]
> (GSc, 371; KSA, 3:649)

Presenting the positive dimension of the asyndeton in the objective narrative voice of Zarathustra's *Preface*, Nietzsche expands it from the potential *Human* to an exhorted *Superman*, while the negative dimension, *All Too Human*, is embodied as the general rejection of Zarathustra's mission. The transformation from the objectifying stability of a preface (*Vorrede*) to the metamorphic flux of Zarathustra's discourses (*Reden*) themselves suspends this judgment between Zarathustra's inspirational message and an unexpressed "heaviest thought" that will definitively alienate the reader. Thus the visible shift from *Human* to *Superman* is not a straightforward doctrinal modification but is a condition of the absolute exteriorization of the expressive dynamic, an exteriorization in which the complementary dimension, *All Too Human*, is displaced from Nietzsche's expression into the reader's own relation to an inexpressible leveling doctrine. That doctrine is the *eternal return*, whose provisional acceptance for the purposes of comprehension must of necessity surrender to the actual rejection all readers (and Nietzsche himself) do, in fact, eventually perform. The pivot of "Human, All Too Human" into "Superman, Eternal Return" marks the lateral displacement of Nietzsche's signatory authority into Zarathustra's titular presence for as long as this inevitable rejection can be forestalled. Situated in this way, Zarathustra's teaching can never stabilize into an ultimately comprehensible content, but revolves as a permanently challenging presentation beyond Nietzsche's individual fate.

Having completed *Thus Spoke Zarathustra*, Nietzsche returns to his point of departure, constructing new prefaces to all of his prior publications. In the letter to his new publisher, Fritzsch, proposing the reissue, Nietzsche explains why his aphoristic books lacked prefaces in their initial incarnations. "There were good reasons for me to observe a silence [*Stillschweigen*] then as these works emerged—I still stood too near, still too much 'in them' and hardly knew what had happened to me" (*SB*, 7:225). Now, from beyond the divide of Zarathustra, Nietzsche can recognize these earlier efforts from without: "My writings present [*darstellen*] a continuous development, which will be not only my personal experience [*Erlebniß*] and destiny:—I am merely the first, a coming generation will understand on their own what I have experienced and will have fine tongues for my books" (*SB*, 7:225). Not representational exemplarity, but a literal demolition of his authorial particularity grounds Nietzsche's prospective relevance. Coming generations will have tongues, not ears for his expressions. They will not simply understand them. The tongues with which they speak will be tongues that can taste these texts.

Beyond *Thus Spoke Zarathustra*, Nietzsche's subsequent development is an attempt to reconstitute his own signature in this consequent position, to subsume his entire historical particularity in an asyndeton between completely disembodied inscriptions, the generalized affirmation "Transvaluation of All Values" revolving with a generalized denunciation "Will to Power." These last notions are neither concepts nor doctrines, but mark the ultimate disembodiment, via *superman* and *eternal return*, of *human* and *all too human*, and effect the final desperate embodiment of "Friedrich Nietzsche." If *Thus Spoke Zarathustra* anchors Nietzsche's writing in a conflation of title and signature, *Nietzsche contra Wagner*, the only text in the published oeuvre with Nietzsche's name in the title, and a text composed entirely of citations from his prior works, represents the ultimate disintegration of the signature beneath it into "every name in history," as his last mad letter to Jacob Burckhardt puts it.[40]

Nietzsche's manifestation persists as a continual ad hominem gesture toward the exterior site of articulation, immediately lost to alien specificity, and immediately returned in the slightest readjustments of contemporary awareness. The link between expression and significance is irresistibly directed through this bidirectional ad hominem that unsettles thought at every possible dimension. "Nietzsche" labels something unprecedented in history, but in a manner that does not settle securely among the various unifying scales of historical conceptualization; rather, it labels a newness extending from the temporal succession that holds for the slightest triviality, when all Being is nihilistically neutralized before its undifferentiating boundary with time, out to the founding revelations of human history, in moments of antique experience so exceptional that we can understand subsequent singularity only by contrastively anchoring it to them. That there are more than one of these moments is a gesture toward the contradiction that maintains Nietzsche in history precisely as the question of his relevance. In the genealogy of this perseverant position, the aphoristic sequences preceding *Thus Spoke Zarathustra* represent for us a particular stylistic concretion of this unsettling exteriority, a particularity that cannot in turn be labeled and addressed directly, but must be positioned in its specificity along the sweep of Nietzsche's detonation and explosion. Taking these two words not only in their current scientific synonymy of accelerating combustion but recalling simultaneously their etymologies that resonate across the divide between an active *detonere* that thunders forth and a reactive *explaudere* that claps and hoots the player from the stage. Nietzsche is the report of an authoritative gesture whose authority is exploded by that report. Only among temporary concretions can this exteriority survive.

Thus in the preface to *Ecce Homo*, after announcing Zarathustra in the most extravagant terms—("With that I have given mankind the greatest present that has ever been made to it so far" [*EH*, 219; *KSA*, 6:259])—Nietzsche insists on the need to hear that book correctly. "Above all, one must hear aright the tone that comes from this mouth, the halcyon tone, lest one should do wretched injustice to the meaning of its wisdom." And he cites in support a single sentence from the last oration in book 2, "The Stillest Hour": "It is the stillest words that bring on the storm, thoughts that come on doves' feet guide the world—" (*TSZ*, 146; *EH*, 219; *KSA*, 4:189, 6:259).

It is not the bombastic Nietzsche to which Benjamin responds, but this silent complement. In a fragment from 1921 exploring the insight that *a religion may be discerned in capitalism* (*SW*, 1:288; *GS*, 6:100), Benjamin develops this perspective in more detail. In an attempt to radicalize a Weberian insight into the economic consequences of religious motivations, Benjamin identifies four features of capitalism described as a religion. Three of them occur to him initially; the fourth is added as an afterthought. *In the first place, capitalism is a purely cultic religion, perhaps the most extreme that ever existed. In capitalism things have meaning only in their relationship to the cult; capitalism knows no specific body of dogma, no theology.* This reduction of religion to its cultic function conditions the second characteristic: *the permanence of the cult. Capitalism is the celebration of a cult <u>sans rêve et sans merci</u>.*[41] *There are no 'weekdays,' no day that is not a feast day, in the terrible sense that all its sacred pomp is unfolded before us; each day commands the utter attentiveness [äußersten Anspannung] of each worshiper.* This relentlessness of capitalism is rendered demonic by the third characteristic. *This cult makes guilty and indebted [verschuldend]. Capitalism is probably the first case of a cult that creates guilt and debt and not atonement* (SW, 1:288; GS, 6:100). Here, in the explication and development of this third feature, is where Nietzsche appears.

> *God's transcendence is at an end. But he is not dead; he has been incorporated into human existence. This passage of the planet "human" [Mensch] through the house of despair in the absolute loneliness of his trajectory is the ethos that Nietzsche defined. This man is the superman, the first who knowingly begins to bring the capitalist religion to fulfillment.* (SW, 1:289; GS, 6:101)

Benjamin's unanticipated fourth characteristic of capitalism conceived on a theological scale is thus provoked by these reflections on Nietzsche. *Its fourth feature is,* Benjamin closes the paragraph, *that its God must be hidden from it and may be addressed only when his guilt is at its zenith. The cult is celebrated before an immature deity; every idea, every conception of it offends against the secret of its maturity* (SW, 1:289; GS, 6:101).

Benjamin here unites in an anachronistic astrological terminology the theological language of the madman's pronouncement of God's death in *The Gay Science* with the astronomical motif in Nietzsche's writing he had noticed as early as his reading of the "Night Song" in 1912. At the same time, the particular resonance Benjamin lends the image recalls the aphorism from early in the sequence "Our Virtues" in *Beyond Good and Evil*. In that text Nietzsche had used the relation of planets to stars to figure the historical complexities implicit in contemporary moral evaluations.

> As in the realm of the stars the orbit of a planet is in some cases determined by two suns; as in certain cases suns of different colors shine near a single planet, sometimes with red light, sometimes with

green light, and then occasionally illuminating the planet at the same time and flooding it with colors—so we modern men are determined, thanks to the complicated mechanics of our "starry sky," by *different* moralities; our actions shine alternately in different colors, they are rarely univocal—and there are cases enough in which we perform *colorful* actions. (BGE, 145–46; KSA, 5:152)

This celestial atmosphere of contradictory demands, though presented in a sanguine tone and through a chromatic metaphor that diminishes its disorienting risks, is Benjamin's house of despair. Nietzsche's colorful actions informed by divergent moralities have the same status as Benjamin's mythically conditioned humanity, subordinated to ambiguous authorities. The shift in tone is the mark of a shift in perspective; where Nietzsche sees a plurality of influences in the complex astral mechanics that define modernity, Benjamin sees Nietzsche's own contrasting singularity, uprooted from commitment to any one of them, in the absolute isolation of his passage. This isolation makes of Nietzsche the site where the Superman might have been—the conditional modality preserving both the absolute surrender to humanly finite modernity that that isolation imposes, and the superhuman overcoming of it that that surrender makes visible. *The superman is historical man never having turned back and now grown through the sky. This explosion [Sprengung] of the heavens through intensified human-beingness [Menschhaftigkeit], which in a religious sense is and remains (even for Nietzsche himself) indebtedness and guilt [Verschuldung], was predetermined [präjudiziert] by Nietzsche* (SW, 1:289; GS, 6:101). The relation of superman to Nietzsche is not that of work to author, but closer to the inverse. The superman breaks through the heavens, and this rupture prejudices Nietzsche. The verb gestures toward Nietzsche's own fundamental epistemological category, "*Vorurtheil*," prejudice, but in moving it out of German into Latin, Benjamin displaces Nietzsche within it, stripping him of the self-awareness that in his own text "*vorutheil*" serves to manifest. Parallel to God's demotion into human fate, the superman escapes Nietzsche's governing intention. The superman prejudices Nietzsche from beyond the heavens, a prejudice that emerges in Nietzsche's transgressive positing of just that superman.

This curious suspension of Nietzsche's authority behind the term superman is an effect of the terminological idiosyncrasy of the fragment in Benjamin's oeuvre. In the light of Benjamin's prior and subsequent efforts, the link between capitalism and religion he is here exploring under Max Weber's influence has created a fundamental tension in his vocabulary. Everything that precedes and follows this fragment would lead us to equate capitalism not with religion, but precisely with *Mythos*, to recognize its theological significance just in its religious *insufficiency*. As the realm of contract and legal sanction, impersonal production and standardized consumption, capitalism embodies the degenerate mythic forces of mortification against which messianic redemption raises its intermittent objection. Characterizing capitalism as religion thus already performs a basic realignment among Benjamin's expressive conceptions. What this realignment allows Benjamin to express is an unusually explicit atheism. A temporary adoption of Weber's commitment to a value-neutral *"diesseitige"* (immanent) analysis of religious experience allows Benjamin to position Nietzsche's philosophy as completely congruent with a universe stripped of transcendence. Within this alien vocabulary, but at the price of its signatory intention, the site of articulation has a name: *superman*.

In attempting to establish this site from within his own terminology, Benjamin will be forced into more elaborate designating strategies. "A great rabbi once said," Benjamin wrote in his Kafka study, speaking of the arrival of the messiah, "that he will not wish to change the world by force [*Gewalt*] but will merely make a slight adjustment to it" (*SW*, 2:811; *GS*, 2:432). The space between trivial adjustment and messianic interruption outside the crudities of force measures the space of Nietzsche's asyndeton. Its ultimate dispersal into history is the strength and the fragility of Nietzsche's production, the simultaneous proof that he is not the actual messiah, and preservation of the consequent impossible potential that he might be. "—Have I been understood?—*Dionysus versus the Crucified*" (*EH*, 335; *KSA*, 6:374). The power of the Nietzschean text is its implacable resistance to containment of any kind, a self-containment that cannot be occupied. Nietzsche survives as an endlessly unrealized potential suspending historical particularity over discredited sacrificial passion. But in the fatal world of mortal judgment, all hope is madness. The measure of Nietzsche's madness is reciprocally the measure of its displaced hope, neither vested in sacrifice nor surrendered to sparagmos, but suspended in its own presentational inscription. God is dead, and so madness inhabits the Nietzschean text as continually and profoundly as it does all religious language, all language uttered in the hope that death can be overcome. But it is a different madness from the delusional enthusiasms organized in ecclesiastical experience, or their pathological shadows muttering in subways or ranting into video cameras. For the man Nietzsche himself, it will be the grimy business of interment and helplessness that Podach recounts, as melancholy and repugnant as human sympathy can make it. But in the dislodged signature of Zarathustra it revolves as frozen madness, condensed into the instant of conjunction between its two heterogeneous principles. In this ever-suspended instant it exists not as instruction but as inspiration, and as such it inhabits the Benjaminian text. In its mad externality Zarathustra's gold star falls through the mortal sky of impersonal elective affinities. Only in this flash of madness can mad Nietzsche be redeemed—but his redemption would in turn redeem the fatal necessity externalized in Benjamin's nihilistic mortalism. Suspended in the unsurpassable reality of time as instant and time as eternity, Nietzsche's escape from death is purchased by Zarathustra at the cost of madness, while Benjamin's escape from madness is purchased from Zarathustra at the cost of death. It is this crossroads, maintained above their respective nihilisms only by their reciprocal overcoming, that we are asked to approach. It is not a place that can long be occupied—but in the immediacy of its *now-time* it gives a chance to glimpse a truth that would be something other, something more, than mere collapse before the storm of history. "The intitial day of a calendar presents history in time-lapse mode. And basically it is this same day that keeps recurring in the guise of holidays, which are days of remembrance. Thus calendars do not measure time the way clocks do" (*SW*, 4:395; *GS*, 1:701–2). In the sign of the deathday, situated subsequent to the Nietzschean incursion and dispersal into history, this new calendar promises a new understanding of history, one in which, beneath a shift of nuance, everything is practically what it was, but one in which, beyond that shift of nuance, nothing is practically what it was. For in that displaced rupture, nothing, nothing will be lost.

CHAPTER FOUR

Collaboration

Segismundo. A reinar, fortuna, vamos;
no me despiertes si duermo,
y si es verdad, no me duermas.
Mas sea verdad o sueño,
obrar bien es lo que importa;
si fuere verdad, por serlo;
si no, por ganar amigos
para cuando despertemos.

[*Segismundo.* Fortune, let me go to reign!
Awaken me not if I sleep,
and, if this be truth, put me not to sleep.
But, whether it be truth or dream,
To work for good is what matters;
if it be truth, in order to do so;
if not, in order to win friends
for when we all awaken.]

—CALDERÓN DE LA BARCA, *La vida es sueño* 2420–27

SHADOW

Benjamin published two aphoristic sequences under the title "Short Shadows," the first in November of 1929 in the *Neue Schweitzer Rundschau*, and the second in 1933 in the *Kölnische Zeitung*. These two sequences have only one aphorism in common, the short concluding thought-image [*Denkbild*] that itself bears the title of the sequence.

> *Short Shadows.* Toward noon, shadows are no more than the sharp, black edges at the feet of things, prepared to retreat silently, unnoticed, into their burrow, into their secret. Then, in its compressed, cowering fullness, comes the hour of Zarathustra—the thinker in "the noon of life" ["*Lebensmittag*"], in "the summer garden" ["*Sommergarten*"]. For it is knowledge [*Erkenntnis*] that outlines objects, like the sun at its zenith, most sharply. (*SW*, 2:272, 702; *GS*, 4:373, 428)

If the reference to Zarathustra brings Nietzsche into play behind this text, it can only do so across a basic difference of posture marked by the un-Nietzschean flexibility of Benjamin's title, short shadows. For all the repetition in Nietzsche's *Nachlaß*, in his published writings Nietzsche never repeats the title of an aphorism or an aphoristic sequence. Once published, a title is always unique, and the only exception—*Human, All Too Human I* and *II*—is less a rebuttal of this principle than a mark of the singularity of this human boundary in his thought, and of the effort he required to forge a signature beyond it. Nor, in those sequences that have both collective and individual titles, does an individual aphorism ever share its title with the sequence as a whole; Nietzsche never uses (to speak with poets and popular musicians) "title-aphorisms." Such an external privilege would disturb the entirely immanent movement of a Nietzschean sequence, whose effect emerges initially in the linear unfolding of rhythmic and tonal variations, extensions and contractions of argumentative detail, against the semantic blankness of pure numerical progression, mere impetus, and not through logically systematic connections around a governing center. Benjamin's repetition of his title both externally, to name two different sequences, and internally, to entitle a specific aphorism and the sequence as a whole, indicates that these texts operate quite differently from Nietzschean aphorisms and that the reference to Zarathustra means more than a common genre.

This contrast between the genre of Benjamin's thought-image and the Nietzschean aphorism it here invokes arrests our attention at the title. Depending on its position as either a collective title for the sequence or the individual title of a single thought-image, "short shadows" signifies in two different ways. The difference affects, in the first instance, the plurality of the shadows. As the designation of an entire aphoristic sequence, each short shadow correlates with an individual aphorism. "Shadow" is a metaphor for representative consequence, and the adjective identifies their textual brevity—none of the "short shadows" is longer than a page. But in titling a single aphorism, the short shadows are freed from their self-reflective aphoristic referents, and expand throughout the world of things. Like *all* shadows in Nietzsche—and this is the first significant connection here to his writings—the shadows in Benjamin's concluding thought-image are solar, cast directly by the sun. Thus their length measures the time of day, noontime, and the metaphor now holds between knowledge [*Erkenntnis*] and the sun, not shadows and the text.

As elements of the natural world displaying the relative position of their illuminating source, these short shadows are not in the first instance silhouettes resembling the objects that cast them; rather they are effects pointing toward their cause. They are not intentional metaphors but impersonal indices. Benjamin's language even suggests a subtle antagonism between the "unnoticed, secret" shadows in their retreat and the triumphalist "sun at its zenith." That sun is the metaphoric vehicle for *Erkenntnis*, knowledge as precise discernment. The shadows, then, however concentrated they have become, mitigate that precise discernment. Even at the apex of knowledge when the world is grasped as accurately as possible, these shadows preserve the potential discrepancy between that blinding knowledge and the world it knows. And it is this possibility the thought-image is attempting to evoke and correlate with the "hour of Zarathustra" far more than the image of fulfilled knowledge. Thus Benjamin calls the fullness of that hour "compressed, cowering," identifying it with the retreating shadows and not with the knowing thinker in the "noon of life," the "summer garden."

But what, more nearly, is the "hour of Zarathustra"? The quotation marks around "noon of life" and "summer garden" point to the immediate Nietzschean reference. It is found not in an aphorism, but a poem: "Aus hohen Bergen" ["From High Mountains"], the "aftersong" to *Beyond Good and Evil*.

Oh Lebens Mittag! Feierliche Zeit!
    Oh Sommergarten!
Unruhig Glück im Stehn und Spähn und Warten:—
Der Freunde harr' ich, Tag und Nacht bereit,
Wo bleibt ihr Freunde? Kommt! 's ist Zeit! 's ist Zeit!

[O noon of life! O celebratory time!
    O summer garden!
Restlessly happy standing and looking and waiting—
I stay for my friends, day and night prepared,
Where are you friends? Come! It's time! It's time!]
            (*BGE*, 241; *KSA*, 5:241)

"From High Mountains" is a poem engaged with the limits of personal identity. In thirteen five-line stanzas the poet interrogates his own dynamic self-identity in contrast to the constancy of his friends. The poem opens with that first-person call to friends from the incongruously pastoral remoteness of "high mountains." Was it not, the poet goes on to ask, for the sake of these friends that he ventured ahead into such inaccessible heights in the first place? Now he is prepared to welcome them to the pinnacle he has discovered. But as the poem continues, the arrival of these friends provokes from the poet a series of rhetorical questions characterizing their antipathetic reaction to his new demesne. These former friends find no summer garden but a glacial waste, and they fail to recognize the poet. "Ein Andrer ward ich? Und mir selber fremd? / Mir selbst entsprungen?" ("I've become Another? And strange to myself? / Eluding myself?") (*BGE*, 240; *KSA*, 5:241). The question form in these lines is no longer a direct address, a plea for company, or a request for knowledge. It registers as the hypothetical status of the poet's interpretation of his friends' reactions an interference in ideal communication. Poet and friends have separated. From their perspective, the poet appears as an unnatural duplicity, a "Gespenst" (ghost), who, in the Alpine extremity of his isolation, "über Gletscher geht" (wanders over glaciers) (*BGE*, 243; *KSA*, 5:242). The wraith in its brumal setting recalls the unholy duplication of Frankenstein in his vengeful monster, an echo amplified by the friends' reaction, which itself divides into a paralyzing affective contradiction: "Nun blickt ihr bleich, / Voll Lieb' und Grausen" ("Now you stare pallidly ,/ Full of love and horror"). Attraction to the recognizable experimenter is frozen by repulsion from his impossible duplicate.

It is this misrecognition and rejection on the part of the poet's former allies that the poem as a whole then inverts. The poet's monstrous transformation is nothing more than his complete acceptance of transformation itself as the only constancy in change. The friends' rejection is their inability to countenance that insight. "Nur wer sich wandelt bleibt mit mir verwandt" ("Only those who change remain related to me"). On the basis of this paradox the poet returns the friends' rejection and reiterates his fealty to his total commitment itself. From the point of view of this reiteration, not he, but the former friends have mutated into ghostly and insubstantial versions of themselves, mere traces of his own earlier states. "Wer liest die Zeichen, / Die Liebe einst hineinschrieb, noch, die bleichen? / Dem Pergament vergleich ich's, das die Hand/ zu fassen *scheut*. . . . // Nicht Freunde mehr, das sind—wie nenn' ich's doch?— / Nur Freunds-Gespenster" ("Who reads the signs, / That love once inscribed, the faded ones? / To parchment I compare it, that the hand / Is *loath* to touch. . . . // No longer friends, they are—how should I put it?— / Mere ghost-friends") (*BGE*, 243; *KSA*, 5:242). His transformation requires the poet to find new allies, "Halt *neuen* Freunden deine Thüren offen! /

Die alten lass! Lass die Erinnerung!" ("Hold open your doors for *new* friends / Leave the old ones! Leave their memory!") And so the opening stanza returns toward the end, slightly amended:

> Oh Lebens Mittag! Zweite Jugendzeit!
>   Oh Sommergarten!
> Unruhig Glück im Stehn und Spähn und Warten!
> Der Freunde harr' ich, Tag und Nacht bereit,
> Der *neuen* Freunde! Kommt! 's Zeit! 's Zeit!
>
> [O noon of life! A second youthfulness!
>   O summer garden!
> Restlessly happy standing and looking and waiting—
> I stay for my friends, day and night prepared,
> For *new* friends! Come! It's time! It's time!]
>   (*BGE*, 245; *KSA*, 5:243).

Here Nietzsche's poem arrives at a provisional end, with the poet poised expectantly toward the future and new alliances. And yet a final pair of stanzas springs the frame of the poem, outbidding its philosophy of becoming with an even more inexpressible paradox. The two-stanza coda tells us that *this* song "from high mountains" now dies in the poet's mouth at the bidding of a mysterious "Mittags-Freund" (noontime-friend) who appears just at this culminating moment. "Um Mittag war's, da wurde Eins zu Zwei. . . . " ("Noontime it was, then One turned into Two. . . ."). That friend is "Zarathustra" the "Gast der Gäste" (guest of guests).

This, then, is the "hour of Zarathustra." It names a unique hiatus of nonidentity at the juncture of past and future effecting a volatile duplication. The present as fissiparous transformation outside of any resulting unities is what bears the character of Zarathustra, identifiable as such only from beyond a contextual lurch. The divisive noontide hiatus thus conditions the framing repetition of the stanza. Two almost identical calls emerge from the high mountains, the thinker in the icy summer garden. But though the hour of Zarathustra is unique, the friends addressed by these two solicitations differ. The former appeals to extant associates, while the latter advertises for future collaborators. In Benjamin's thought-image, the hour of Zarathustra continues to be inherently nonidentical, caught in the immanent tension between determinate knowledge and the secret shadows at the edges of the things it knows. And this difference licenses an interpretive conceit that can orient a reading of Benjamin's two sequences. The repetition of "Short Shadows" manifests this transformation as well. The "*Lebensmittag*" and "*Sommergarten*" of the 1929 sequence can thus be read as citing Nietzsche's first stanza, while the 1933 repetition cites the latter.

Read then as two soundings in the transformative identity to which their single title testifies, Benjamin's two sequences evince rough thematic parallels. A text on Don Juan is answered by a text on Casanova; a text on framing landscape is complemented by a text on "Distance and Images"; a recollection of a dream Paris is echoed by the history of a real gambler in Parisian clubs. But these echoes serve only to emphasize the differences between the tenor of the two sequences, their contrasting postures of exposure and concealment.

The eight aphorisms of "Short Shadows [I]" explore the interplay of *eros* and onomastics. "The nature and character of a love is most sharply defined by the fate that links it to someone's name," the sequence begins, and the theme is repeated throughout. God's signing hand endorsing natural beauty seen through a window, the oneiric Paris that knows only the imageless force of its name; in evoking these boundary cases of designation, "Short Shadows [I]" exposes the private ephemeral connotations that names bear and that complicate the public status of their referential relations.

The rhetorical movement is from privacy to explicitness. Quite otherwise with the second sequence. Here, seven aphorisms revolve around notions of interiority, secrecy, and rupture. "Secret Signs," the first thought-image is called. "In other words, what is decisive is not the progression from one piece of knowledge to the next [*der Fortgang von Erkenntnis zu Erkenntnis*], but the leap [*Sprung*] implicit in every individual piece of knowledge" (*SW*, 2:699; *GS*, 4:425). This inevitable discontinuity is the secret sign of truth in the publicity of what is known. And as the sequence unfolds through Casanova's hiding his sexual shame in the money he offers the panderer, the hidden lacerations of a gambler's anguish beneath the elegant shirt of the impassive, luckless Fürst de Ligne, and a version of "To Live without Leaving Traces" (*spurlos wohnen*) that Benjamin later incorporated into the essay "Experience and Poverty," motifs of hiding, disguise, untraceability are all at work. The Hour of Zarathustra that in 1929 had served to expose the irreducible potentials in extant names has become by 1933 a moment of actual obscurity whose potential is freed from extant names and which resides as such in the future.

The "noontide" motif is a prominent one in Nietzsche.[1] Before *Beyond Good and Evil* and its "Aftersong," he had developed it at the center of the fourth book of *Thus Spoke Zarathustra*. There, Zarathustra, in flight from his motley companions, happens just at midday upon a tranquil clearing with a gnarled tree and grapevine. He lies down beneath it and sleeps, though "his eyes remained open: for they did not tire of seeing and praising the tree and the love of the grapevine" (*TSZ*, 276; *KSA*, 4:342). In this liminal state Zarathustra registers the still perfection of things. "Did not the world become perfect just now?" is the refrain of the passage. But the slight temporal displacement marked by the preterite tense has already compromised the hiatus. The congruence that defines this supreme perception and suspends Zarathustra's soul over a "well of eternity" and stasis is itself fleeting. Soon Zarathustra is impatiently remonstrating with his sleeping soul. "'Get up!' said Zarathustra, 'you little thief, you thief of day! [*Tagesdiebin*].'" And he rises from his nap as from an "alien drunkenness" (*fremden Trunkenheit*) and continues on his way.

The entire passage reworks the earlier aphorism #308 from late in "The Wanderer and His Shadow."

> *At noon.*—He who has been granted an active and storm-filled morning of life is overcome at the noontide of life by a strange longing for repose [*seltsame Ruhesucht*] that can last for months or years. It grows still around him, voices recede into the distance; the sun shines down on him from high overhead. Upon a concealed woodland meadow he sees great Pan sleeping; all things of nature have fallen asleep with him, an expression of eternity on their face—that is how it seems to him. He wants nothing, he is troubled by nothing, his heart stands still, only his eyes are alive—it is a death with waking eyes [*ein Tod mit wachen Augen*]. (*HA*, 308; *KSA*, 2:690)

"A death with waking eyes." The formula could characterize Benjamin's own critical perspective. The short shadows withdrawing into the outlines of things evoke that mortalist perspective on the world, perfect and ephemeral. But even in Nietzsche's early aphorism, the "truly active man" soon returns to a life "more active and more storm-filled than before." The hiatus, riven by waking and sleep, can only appear against the trajectory of the wanderer whose journey it interrupts, comforts, and endangers. The years between 1929 and 1933 pushed Benjamin into exile. For a writer, exile is not simply a geographical notion but denotes the dissolution of the addressee. Such a situation demands new thinking strategies and alliances. From now on, Benjamin and Nietzsche communicate under the sign of exile.

WANDERER

In 1938, three years after its publication, Benjamin read Karl Löwith's book *Nietzsche's Philosophy of the Eternal Recurrence of the Same*, an attempt to characterize the "systematic fundamental idea in Nietzsche's philosophy."[2] Löwith's discussion divides Nietzsche's career into three distinct periods, separated by two existential crises. These are marked at the thematic level as respective liberations—the emancipation from "Thou Shalt" to "I Will," and the emancipation from "I Will" to "I Am"—and at the compositional level by a discontinuous expansion of the importance of implication in his writing. The unity of Nietzsche's thought is vested not in the aphorisms that constitute it but in the posture that produces them in their experimental variety. This posture is itself a transformation, and the triadic periodization of Nietzsche's work is anchored in that transformative posture. Nietzsche himself suggests as much in the metamorphoses that open Zarathustra's orations, from Camel to Lion to Child, but Löwith finds that in their progressive trajectory these stages are more clearly symbolized by "three allegorical figures from Nietzsche's philosophy." These are not Zarathustrian images but self-representations distilled from these respective periods.

> Three allegorical figures characterize this path from the spirit that is liberated through negation to the teacher of the eternal recurrence. The *wanderer* accompanied by his shadow symbolizes the progress up to the edge of the nothing. The wanderer accompanies the superhuman *Zarathustra* (who also still wanders) as his shadow, and finally the *god Dionysus* takes Zarathustra's place. (NER, 25–26; NEW, 25)

Whether or not the stages of this atheistic apotheosis genuinely support the existential interpretation Löwith would like to anchor between them, an interpretation whose ultimate self-realization is a suspiciously un-Nietzschean quiescence and devotion to "mediocrity itself" (NER, 178; NEW, 161), is a question to which we will return. Löwith's periodization nonetheless does respond to a movement indigenous to the Nietzschean text, one whose dual foci and triadic development complicate the rival periodic hypothesis—just as true, just as indigenous—that organizes Nietzsche's oeuvre into before and after the singular break with Wagner.

Löwith draws our attention to the figure of the Wanderer, as the icon of the pre-Zarathustra writings, and asserts his transformation into the Shadow who accompanies Zarathustra on his mission. The Shadow, however, predates Zarathustra considerably, and his relation both to the Wanderer and to Zarathustra is less straightforward than this schematization can suggest. The motif of the philosopher as Wanderer, neither pilgrim nor refugee, and yet both simultaneously, is an old one with Nietzsche. Thus "Philosophy in the Tragic Age of the Greeks" identifies (already with self-congratulatory overtones) all post-Hellenic philosophy with this figure: "In other times and places, the philosopher is a chance wanderer, lonely in a totally hostile environment which he either creeps past or attacks with clenched fists. Among the Greeks alone, he is not an accident" (*PTG*, 32–33; *KSA*, 1:808). In "Schopenhauer as Educator" the figure returns. "Oftentimes it seems as if an artist, and sometimes even a philosopher, only lives *by chance* in his age [zufällig *in seiner Zeit sei*], as a recluse, or as a wanderer who has strayed off and been left behind" (*UO*, 236; *KSA*, 1:406). In these early designations, the wanderer inscribes an accidental moment into a motif of isolated remoteness. A fragment from this time (1873) distills this latter aspect clearly.

> *Alas we humans of this age! A winter's day lies upon us and we live in high mountains, dangerous and deprived. Short is every joy and pale every gleam of sunlight that looks down on us in the mountains. Music sounds there—it shakes the wanderer to hear it: so wild, so secret, so colorless, so hopeless is everything that he sees—and now within a sound of joy, of thoughtless simple joy. But already the mist of early evening is creeping in, the sound is fading, the tread of the wanderer crackles; cruel and dead the face of nature in the evening that always arrives so early and will not depart.* (*UW*, 277; *KSA*, 7:715)

Like the midday hiatus on the summit, punctilious interruption must again succumb to compulsive peregrination. Here it is unexpected music that contradicts in the auditory register the metaphoric situation of a philosophical perception. The crepuscular face of nature is keyed to the passage of the wanderer through the mountainous landscape, but the figure of the wanderer himself is this landscape conditioned by the unpredictable possibility of this music. The spatial image presents an originally temporal phenomenon, a recursive experience of time as *actual* disappointment in the present turning evidence of *potential* satisfaction. Where this potential is visualized, the wanderer is reflected into the landscape as a pastoral hiatus: the hour of Zarathustra. But the hiatus is also an apex of isolation at the juncture of a cathartic purgation of past alliances and an ecstatic acceptance of new ones. Because the wanderer contrasts with the hiatus, the wanderer is never entirely alone but always occurring at a nexus of perspectives, a vacillating interior self-relation and a bifurcated external objectification. But if the wanderer in these figures bears the paradox of an accidental authority over the present *in potentia*, he remains tied to the received tradition of philosophy, figuring not mankind, but the isolated philosopher. It is only at the close of *Human, All Too Human I* that he expands to become an embodiment of the asyndeton itself, in a first attempt to reverse its denunciatory force. The final aphorism of that book is titled "The Wanderer." "He who has attained to only some degree of freedom of reason [*Freiheit der Vernunft*] cannot feel other than a wanderer on the earth," Nietzsche writes there,

> —though not as a traveler *to* a final goal: for this does not exist. But he will watch and observe and keep his eyes open to see what is really going on in the world; for this reason he may not let his heart adhere too firmly to any individual thing; within him too there must be something wandering that takes pleasure in change and transience [*dem Wechsel und der Vergänglichkeit*]. (HA, 203; KSA, 2:362–3)

This relative independence, internal and external, from his immediate surroundings defines the experience of "freedom of reason." From this dynamic vantage point, beyond commitment to perishable phenomena, the contrast between the panegyric tonalities of human aspiration and the denunciatory force of all-too-human limitation becomes the variety of emotional states along the Wanderer's journey. All too human are his moments of weakness.

> Such a man will, to be sure, experience bad nights, when he is tired and finds the gate of the town that should offer him rest closed against him; . . . Then dreadful night may sink down upon the desert like a second desert . . . and his heart grow weary of wandering. When the morning sun then rises, burning like a god of wrath, and the gate of the town opens to him, perhaps he will behold in the faces of those who dwell there even more desert, dirt, deception, insecurity than lie outside the gate—and the day will be almost worse than the night. Thus it may be that the wanderer shall fare. (HA, 203; KSA, 2:363)

But these valitudinary states are compensated by exalted moments that concentrate human aspiration.

> But then, as recompense [*Entgelt*], there will come the joyful mornings of other days and climes, when he shall see, even before the

light has broken, the Muses come dancing by him in the mist of the mountains, when afterwards, if he relaxes quietly beneath the trees in the equanimity of his soul at morning [*Gleichmaass der Vormittagsseele*], good and bright things will be thrown down to him from their tops and leafy hiding-places, the gifts of all those free spirits who are at home in mountain, wood and solitude and who, like him, are, in their now joyful, now thoughtful way, wanderers and philosophers. (*HA*, 203; *KSA*, 2:363)

Where Nietzsche's asyndeton shattered the framework of humanist values that stabilized recognizable tradition, the Wanderer, as the embodiment of that asyndeton, promotes a philosophy unprecedented in the tradition, as the name for the experience of this evaluative oscillation.

This culminating aphorism does not resolve the inherent contradiction between the Wanderer's remote authority and accidental trajectory, for the accidental dimension appears from within the Wanderer's own perspective, as the fluctuations of his states and the astonishment of his encounters. The authoritative dimension appears from without, as the impression he makes on others. Thus when the Wanderer returns in the second book of *Human All Too Human*, he is already fracturing into himself and his duplicate.

> *The wanderer in the mountains addresses himself.*—There exist definite signs to show that you have advanced forwards and climbed higher: the view around you is more open and extensive than it was, the air that wafts upon you is cooler but also more gentle—you have unlearned the folly of confusing gentleness with warmth—your step has grown firmer and more lively, courage and thoughtfulness have grown together:—for all these reasons your path may now be more solitary, and in any event more perilous, than the one you trod before, though certainly not to the extent those who watch you, wanderer, from the misty valley below believe it to be. (*HA*, 273; *KSA*, 2:486)

What the title of the aphorism positions in a self-reflective relation appears in the aphorism itself as a direct address to a "you." This address from without interprets the signs of progress, starting with the unencumbered vistas that surround the wanderer and the temperature that envelops him, which he can now correctly characterize, in order then to materialize him in a gait and a demeanor that project confidence and sobriety to those who see him. This externalization provokes as a regulating contrast a denunciatory "those," who mark an alternative exterior perspective from which the wanderer cannot be recognized. The situation of the wanderer looks worse than it is, more perilous and above all more solitary; for it cannot perceive the distance manifested in the second-person address itself. The comforts attending the wanderer lie in the future and are only provisionally hosted by the space of an admonitory self-bifurcation. The position from which this aphorism speaks, then, is ultimately not controllable from within the self-reflective parameters of the title; in talking to himself the wanderer is potentially talking to us in our necessarily subsequent reality, invisible to his contemporaries. This necessarily eccentric reference point is the shadow thrown by the wanderer; the asyndeton between *Human* and *All Too Human* is thus embodied as wanderer alone only briefly, for it is soon involved in the Wanderer-Shadow system. It is this system that transforms into Zarathustra and that *Thus Spoke Zarathustra* repeats.

Book 1 of *Thus Spoke Zarathustra*, for all its sunlight, is free of shadows. But they arise early in book 2, by the second discourse. "The beauty of the superman came to me as a shadow," Zarathustra says; "O my brothers, what are the gods to me now?" (*TSZ*, 88; *KSA*, 4:112). And at the end of "On Great Events" the Wanderer and his Shadow appear explicitly: "But it must have been my shadow. I suppose you have heard something of the wanderer and his shadow?" (*TSZ*, 133; *KSA*, 4:171). In book 3, which begins with a discourse titled "The Wanderer," the "wanderer's shadow" is given independent voice, crying together with "longest boredom" and the "stillest hour": "It is high time!" (*TSZ*, 162; *KSA*, 4:204). With the unlocalizable "Cry of Distress" of the *"higher human being"* (*TSZ*, 242; *KSA*, 4:302) that propels book 4, the shadows begin proliferating: "But as he [viz., Zarathustra] was sitting there, a stick in his hand, tracing his shadow on the ground, thinking—and verily, not about himself and his shadow—he was suddenly frightened, and he started: for beside his own shadow he saw another shadow" (*TSZ*, 241; *KSA*, 4:300). By the end of book 4, Wanderer and Shadow have coalesced in contrast to Zarathustra: "Do not go away! said the wanderer who called himself Zarathustra's shadow. Stay with us. Else our old musty depression might seize us again" (*KSA*, 4:379; *TSZ*, 304). Despite the fact that Zarathustra's first epithet, bestowed by the saintly recluse, is "wanderer" (*KSA*, 4:12; *TSZ*, 10), and despite the eventual independent manifestation of the "shadow" in book 4 as a member of Zarathustra's retinue, Zarathustra himself cannot be coordinated with either of these poles alone, but is the name of their constant transformation into one another.

This peregrine aspect to Nietzsche's production was one to which Benjamin responded early. It is implicit in the 1922 phrase we have had occasion to consider already: "Nietzsche's life is typical for someone who is determined by distance as such [*bloße Fernenbestimmtheit*]; it is the fate [*Verhängnis*] of the highest among complete human beings [*den fertigen Menschen*]" (*SW*, 1:400; *GS*, 6:87). As Benjamin's own enforced wandering proceeded, the figure of Nietzsche in exile returns to him intermittently, as a precedent to his own situation. If *The Origin of German Trauerspiel* had set Nietzsche, via Wilamowitz-Möllendorff, in the context of German philology, the Nietzsche of the 1930s is expatriate. The relation between Benjamin and Nietzsche is oriented throughout this time on the Wanderer/Shadow, not as a rhetorical trope or philosophical character, but inscribed into the potentials of their writing as the significance of national exile. Nietzsche's rejection of Bismarck's Reich becomes for Benjamin his characteristic gesture, "the clarion call of Nietzsche's warnings about the spirit of the new Reich," that Benjamin recalls in his essay on Keller (*SW*, 2:52; *GS*, 2:285). And he concludes his commentary to the final letter[3] in *Deutsche Menschen*, Overbeck's 1883 missive to Nietzsche, with just this aspect of banishment: "Here is the letter, whose writer and addressee had voluntarily exiled themselves from the Germany of the *Gründerzeit*" (*SW*, 3:217; *GS*, 4:228).

The letter to Nietzsche in *Deutsche Menschen* is drawn from Bernoulli's publication of Nietzsche's correspondence with Franz Overbeck. Benjamin had read this correspondence many years before, and with great enthusiasm. In December 1917 he mentions the experience in a letter to Scholem. "I'm also reading the shattering correspondence between Nietzsche and Franz Overbeck, the first genuine document of his life that I've encountered" (*CB*, 107; *GB*, 1:410). Four months later he is engrossed in Bernoulli's description of the friendship, *Franz Overbeck und Friedrich Nietzsche: Eine Freundschaft*. "It sets the standard for all that exists about Nietzsche's life," he says of it (*CB*, 123; *GB*, 1:449). By 1932, with his own flight from Germany immediately before him, and shortly after he had prepared Overbeck's 1883 letter to Nietzsche for publication in the *Frankfurter Zeitung*, his review of Podach's work on Nietzsche avoids any final characterization of the philosopher by vesting its enthusiasm in Overbeck. "That too was something Podach recognized; that the crude sacred stylization of the Nietzsche-image corresponded to a tee with the denigration of Overbeck" (*GS*, 3:325). This inverse relation has as its corollary that an appreciation of Overbeck would correspond to a better, less stylized image of Nietzsche. It is this appreciation with which *Deutsche Menschen* concludes.

CORRESPONDENCE

Deutsche Menschen addresses its reader with an urgency unique among Benjamin's publications. Though the more general letter-project from which the book emerged started five years earlier, the book publication was rapid, a mere fourteen or fifteen weeks between the initial inquiries in June 1936 and its delivery to Benjamin at the end of October. In letters to Karl Thieme, the intermediary who arranged for the book's appearance in Switzerland, Benjamin declared himself ready to compromise on both title and signature if it would allow the book to reach an audience. That immediate audience he understood in political terms, as opponents of the Nazi regime still within German borders: "If the book should find its way into Germany (where, I am quite convinced, it can have a *profound* effect), naturally that ought not to be hindered by the title" (*GB*, 5:329). We can get a sense of that profound effect in the pathos of Gretel Karplus's reply after receiving the book in Berlin, where she had just recently endured the grueling liquidation of the company she had been directing since 1934. "My dear Detlef," she writes on 9 November 1936, "let me thank you from my heart for sending me your book. Can you know what it means for me at this moment? A comfort, a recovery, this all strikes me as insufficient, since it takes the place of a living person for me. A friend, who understands me, who knows what it means to feel oneself entirely displaced" (GAB, 274).

A knowing friend in difficult times. Gretel Karplus's trope stresses the intimate dimension of the support and encouragement *Deutsche Menschen* gave her in those dark days and months before her emigration. At the same time, by depicting the book as a figure of shared knowledge, and not, say, of distraction from her troubles or nostalgia for her past, Gretel Karplus sets the comfort the book provides in direct relation to a public disorder it also knows and in terms of which it sympathizes. In his postscript to the 1962 reissue of the book, Gretel Karplus's future husband Theodor Adorno would come to write: "And in fact the book did arrive safely in Germany; without political impact, however. Those who read such literature at that time were in any case opponents of the regime, and the book would scarcely have created new ones."[4] If the measure of a political gesture lies in the number of opponents it is able to recruit, then the political urgency of *Deutsche Menschen* would indeed appear incongruent with its situation. At least in the postwar reception of the book a certain discrepancy between its publication as political act and the ruthless regime against which it was directed has often been noted; Adorno is by no means alone in this view. But if the profound effect the book had on Gretel Karplus, on the basis of a shared knowledge of dispossession, is indeed a political effect, in what sense is this so? And what survives of this dimension now, in our current political situation?

It was Peter Szondi who, in his 1961 article on Walter Benjamin "Hope in the Past," forged the first durable link between the intimate reaction of Benjamin's friends to *Deutsche Menschen* and a public reaction in the postwar world. This he did by transcribing the inscription Benjamin had written in the copy of the book he gave his sister Dora: "This ark, built on the Jewish model [*nach jüdischem Vorbild erbaute Arche*], for Dora—from Walter. November 1936."[5] A decade later Johannes Seiffert found in this inscription a methodological reference to the sacred Judaic genre of midrash, a suggestion that found a sympathetic hearer in Gershom Scholem. Expanding on Seiffert's reading, Scholem finds in the metaphor of the ark "the rescue from the Fascist flood via the Word [*Schrift*]. The author has captured in a book—has constructed like an ark—that which can withstand the Flood. Just as the Jews took refuge from the persecutions in the Writ [*Schrift*], the canonical book, Benjamin's own book constitutes a saving element fashioned after the Jewish prototype [*Vorbild*]." For this interpretation he has strong authority: Benjamin's own inscription in Scholem's copy of the book: "May you, Gerhard, find a chamber in this ark—which I built when the Fascist flood started to rise—for the memories of your youth" (*SF*, 255; *GF*, 252).

The appeal of the metaphor of the ark is clear. By finding in *Deutsche Menschen* a Judaic method applied to German material, the metaphor helps explain the exclusively German character of the letters; it evokes the Benjaminian motif of "*Rettung*" (rescuing); it discerns in the text the promise of eventual reconciliation. It is not our purpose to deny this, and these archival dedications (there are others to the same effect, to Siegfried Kracauer, for instance) have in the meantime become an integral part of the text of the book. And yet the metaphor of the ark presents an interpretive challenge more than a solution. For it is one thing to detect a Judaic dimension in Benjamin's method, but it is quite another to render the political significance of the book in religious terms. Beyond the theological difficulties, such a reading risks making the German-Jewish historical context the ultimate frame of reference within which the book operates, so that it simply confirms a lesson, however valid, however worthy of restatement, that we ought by now to have already learned. And perhaps most seriously, by stressing the image of continuity, the metaphor threatens to divorce *Deutsche Menschen* from the revolutionary implications that also inhabit it and so to mitigate its usefulness in countering the returning fascism of our own day.

To inquire what the political urgency of *Deutsche Menschen* amounts to is to ask what sort of a gesture the book is. To begin to answer this question, we need to consider the larger context from which the gesture emerged. This larger context is the letter project, in which Benjamin introduced for a general audience unusual nineteenth-century letters culled from his wide reading, a project that ran in the *Frankfurter Zeitung* between April 1931 and May 1932. This publishing project in fact ended up involving twenty-seven letters but was in principle open-ended; Benjamin writes to Scholem in December 1931: "If they would let me, I could have pulled together in a year about 100 such documents" (*GB*, 4:68). Later, when the letter project had long since been closed by the ascension of the National Socialists to power in Germany, and an exiled Benjamin has begun to plan the book that becomes *Deutsche Menschen*, he frequently expresses the wish that it could be expanded by many further letters than had been published in the *Frankfurter Zeitung*. But despite this wish, the eventual book does not in fact add to the selection that had appeared in the newspaper earlier. What is published in 1936 as *Deutsche Menschen: A Series of Letters*, are twenty-six of the same twenty-seven letters that had appeared in the newspaper during the last months of the Weimar Republic. This identity of the components justifies interpreting the book *Deutsche Menschen* not merely on its own terms but also as the (provisional) terminus of a historical-textual trajectory that moves these letters from the principally open-ended sequential publication in a newspaper to the discrete work character of a bound montage. This trajectory passes through and thereby registers the collapse of Weimar democracy and the ascension of a fascist regime. This is the political resonance of the book, and it inflects the role of Nietzsche at its close.

The relation of Benjamin's letter project to the idea of a book changes throughout the early 1930s. Before the newspaper series had finished, Benjamin wrote to Scholem that "to publish the twenty [letters] at hand in the form of a little book," something the *Frankfurter Zeitung* seemed to be considering, would be a pointless exercise: "It would result in something that would be as incoherent as it was pretentious" (*GB,* 4:68–69). But three years later, in exile from Germany, Benjamin's attitude toward the idea of the book had changed. "From time to time I dream about the frustrated book projects—the Berlin Childhood around 1900 and the collection of letters," he wrote to Scholem from Paris in October 1935, "and then I am surprised when I find the strength to embark on a new one" (*GB,* 5:189). These two prior stages of the letter project from which *Deutsche Menschen* emerges—the newspaper project and the dreambook project—have left distinct traces in the paralipomena attending the book. The initial newspaper publication is reflected programmatically in a short essay "On the Trail of Old Letters," and a typescript titled "German Letters," with a general introduction and short remarks on three different letters that were published in neither the original nor final versions, captures the reflection of the shattered dream version of the book.[6]

"On the Trail of Old Letters," which has the spontaneous, colloquial tone of a lecture or radio broadcast, presents the methodological premise of the newspaper project. What that project mobilizes is "historical distance" (*historische Distanz*). *It is this very historical distance which dictates the laws governing our own examination, chief among them that of content: the fact that with the increasing historical distance those distinctions between man and author, the private and the objective, the person and the thing increasingly lose their validity* (*SW,* 2:557; *GS,* 4:944). This formula echoes the programmatic distinction between "material content" (*Sachgehalt*) and "truth content" (*Wahrheitsgehalt*) from his early essay on Goethe's *Elective Affinities,* and as in that opposition so too in this one—what is crucial is not the absolute difference between these terms so much as the fact of its historical variability. Benjamin's letter project deploys this variability by exhibiting it: a letter from the past in the setting of today's newspaper. In the *Frankfurter Zeitung* the letters appeared without titles but merely beneath the heading "Brief" (Letter) and a roman numeral. Such a heading could signal almost anything in a newspaper but immediately connotes a contemporary reaction or report, and nothing initially advertised the historical character of these letters. The historical distance that fused "man" and "author," privacy and objectivity, person and thing is negotiated by the introductions Benjamin provided. Negotiated, not bridged, by a clash of present tenses. The preterit is oddly tenuous in these commentaries, continually giving way to an editorial present tense and the present tense of the many past citations the introductions contain. The tonal juxtapositions across this indexically shifting present tense *within* the introductions are meant to reflect, focus, and amplify the tonal juxtapositions *outside* the letters, between the letters themselves and their textual environment in the daily press. These contrasts resonate with the hidden place at which man and author, privacy and objectivity, person and thing must coincide in the *present* for a respectful *future*. This is the meaning of the initial phase of the letter project: *neither philological ambition nor a dubious need for culture [Bildungsbedürfnis] . . . but living transmission of tradition [lebendiger Überlieferung]* (*SW*, 2:557; *GS*, 4:944).

But if Benjamin's original intention was to produce living tradition in the clash of historical distance, when the political situation in Germany brought this phase of the project to a close in May 1932, when the Nazis took power at the end of that year, when the book burnings began in May 1933, the purpose for continuing the project changed. The typescript "German Letters," with its introductions to letters never published in the newspaper or included in the collection, stands in for this shattered and oneiric version of the project. No longer submerged in the flow of quotidian journalism but gathered into a bound volume, the letters reveal something other than living tradition in general. *The intention of this series is, rather, to reveal the visage of a "secret Germany" that people nowadays would much prefer to shroud in heavy mist. For a secret Germany really exists* (*SW*, 2:466; *GS*, 4:945). The deployment of Stefan George's term "secret Germany" is certainly ironic. Nonetheless, it allows Benjamin to introduce a concept in this program that does not appear in the earlier broadcast address: the concept *deutsch*. If we consider the introductions to the letters in the sequence in which they appeared in the *Frankfurter Zeitung*, we can in general recognize, unsurprisingly given the political circumstances, an increasing concern with the popular concept of Germany. Early publications, like the letters from Collenbusch and Görres, are introduced by discussions in largely stylistic or philosophical terms. By the end of the series, the introductions to letters by Büchner and Grimm and Overbeck explicitly confront their German identities. This confrontation survives the end of the first stage of the letter project in clandestine form, as the hidden Germany of the unreal "German Letters." The historical distance that the newspaper project had intended to reflect into the present is here gathered into that contested adjective.

Benjamin can be so explicit about the intention of the book project here precisely because it remains at this stage entirely fantastic and virtual. Unlike Stefan George's much-publicized "secret Germany," the community to which Benjamin's letter project testified was in fact clandestine, for essential reasons. When the dream became reality a year later, and the shards of the imagined book were reassembled for publication in Switzerland, Benjamin realized that the volume itself could not simply announce its intention to invoke a secret Germany, but would itself have to participate in that secret. This is one implication of Benjamin's lapidary subtitle—"Of Honor without Fame / Of Greatness without Glamor / Of Dignity without Recompense"[7]— three subtractive formulae each isolating a virtue from its mass representation. That the book would work by indirection, beneath a disguised title and above a deracinated pseudonym, was something Benjamin understood and readily accepted. The title does disguise the book, but through its noun and not its adjective. Indeed, Karl Thieme's suggestion for a less risky title—"*Männliche Briefe*" (Masculine Letters)(*GB*, 5:330)—would have jettisoned precisely the national designation while keeping the letters. Benjamin's eventual title worked in exactly the opposite way, keeping the adjective "*deutsch*" at the cost of obscuring the essentially textual and antihumanist nature of the project. Once the letter project took on book form and could no longer engage the immediate context of a daily newspaper, the collective notion of "German" was unavoidable. The disguise consisted in posing letters as people.

Benjamin writes to Thieme, "From one thing I cannot deviate: The particular, that is particularly reticent tone of the prefaces. I have tried to accommodate their linguistic posture to the thoroughly manly character [*durchgehend mannhaften Charakter*] of the letters" (*GB*, 5:345). If the newspaper publication had attempted to mobilize historical distance in language to challenge the present moment at the immediate level of daily life, the book publication deploys the same tonal discrepancies to orient the concept of German away from the false substantiality lent it by the collective singular nouns—*Volk, Boden, Blut*—that the Nazis used it to determine. Whether *Letters* or *Menschen*, the relevant factor in this context is the number, an irreducible plurality. The irreducibility of this plurality is what precludes any monumental reading of Benjamin's book. The *Deutsche*

Menschen are neither individual models nor, *pace* Adorno, sociological types, because in fact there are no *"Menschen"* in *Deutsche Menschen*, but only the plurality of *German Letters* and the historical resonances they produce together.

Looking at the larger context of *Deutsche Menschen* in order to characterize the trajectory of the letter project in which it culminates deposits us eventually back at the original question. The newspaper project was aimed at producing "living transmission of tradition" in the contested present, while the dream book was meant to reveal a "secret Germany" obscured by the fascist triumph. The actual book, by contrast, withdraws its intention into the common reticent posture adopted by the letters and their introductions. What is the meaning of that common posture, and how can this trajectory help us to understand it?

Here we can find help from outside the book, in Benjamin's lecture from 1934, "The Author as Producer." Early in that discussion Benjamin insists that today "we are in the midst of a mighty recasting [*Umschmelzungsprozeß*] of literary forms, a melting down in which many of the opposites in which we have been used to think may lose their force. Let me give an example of the unfruitfulness of such opposites, and of the process of their dialectical overcoming [*dialektischen Überwindung*].... For this example is the newspaper" (*SW*, 2:771; *GS*, 2:687). And in the discussion of Brecht's epic theater that closes the talk, "montage" is the name of the technical procedure that responds to this new situation. "Here—according to the principle of interruption—Epic Theater, as you see, takes up a procedure that has become familiar to you in recent years from film and radio, literature and photography. I am speaking of the procedure of montage" (*SW*, 2:778; *GS*, 2:697). The trajectory from newspaper to montage is not only the textual trajectory traversed by the letter project in history, it is also the expository trajectory that this lecture pursues.

The role played by the newspaper in overcoming the oppositions that in happier times interacted productively with one another is a destructive one. In its pages, these categories have now collapsed into mutual contradictions. "Thus science and belles lettres, criticism and literary production, education and politics, fall apart in disorder and lose all connection with one another. The scene of this literary confusion is the newspaper." What characterizes the newspaper is not any particular content of its articles but their disaggregation and mutual indifference. *Between* the articles, so to speak, the newspaper is an implicit screen onto which the entire spectrum of writing techniques is projected, so that the different sorts of writing lose their traditional relations to one another—what we might call "culture"—and appear in arbitrary juxtaposition. This neutralization of the substantial relationships between textual categories has overtaken not only the "conventional distinction between genres, between writer and poet, between scholar and popularizer, but also revises even the distinction between author and reader" (SW, 2:772; GS, 2:689).

But if the newspaper, in its categorical disaggregation, represents "technically speaking, . . . the most important literary position" (SW, 2:772; GS, 2:689), the one with the most immediate prospect of modifying the literary relations of production, it is also unfortunately "in the hands of the opposition" (SW, 2:772; GS, 2:689). The corrosive dimension of the press is simply the precondition for renewal, not its achievement. That renewal would arise within the interstices between articles, not in the content of the articles themselves. "I would like to proffer the proposition," Benjamin says in this regard, "that to supply a productive apparatus [*Produktionsapparat*] without—to the utmost extent possible—changing it would still be a highly censurable course, even if the raw materials [*Stoffe*] with which it is supplied seemed to be of a revolutionary nature [*revolutionärer Natur*]" (SW, 2:774; GS, 2:692). The *Frankfurter Zeitung* letter project is an example of such an attempt to modify the enemy apparatus as much as possible. But once the Nazis assumed power, that possibility disappeared.

Because the form of the newspaper had been lost irredeemably to the enemy, Benjamin was compelled to conceive of the *Apparat* in even broader terms, as literary form itself. In the new fascist epoch the contemporary author who wishes to affect the literary relations of production must resort to even more indirect methods. And it is here that the work of Bertolt Brecht came to Benjamin's assistance. "To signify the transformation of the forms and instruments of production in the way desired by a progressive intelligentsia—that is, one interested in freeing the means of production and serving the class struggle—Brecht coined the concept 'refunctioning' [*Umfunktionierung*]" (SW, 773–74; GS, 2:691).

Montage is an example of this functional transformation: "Brecht's discovery and shaping of the *gestus* is nothing but the re-conversion [*Zurückverwandlung*] of the method of montage decisive in radio and film" (SW, 2:778; GS, 2:698). The interrupted gestures of the epic theater and the assembled epistolary shards of *Deutsche Menschen* resonate to the same historical imperative. What *Deutsche Menschen* attempts to reengineer is not simply the notion of Germany and humanity, but the form of the book itself and its potential complicity with fascism.

Where these historical and textual imperatives meet and constitute a new, posthumanist notion of the political appears in Benjamin's approving citation of Brecht in the "Author as Producer." "Politically it is not private thinking but, as Brecht once expressed it, the art of thinking into other people's heads that is decisive" (*SW*, 2:773; *GS*, 2:690). Thinking into someone else's head. What might at first sound like the imposition of one consciousness on another is in fact in the context of Benjamin's discussion, and more generally in the context of the letter project and the political catastrophe it registers, precisely the opposite. To impose a concept on someone else is to *inhibit* their thinking and bring it to a stop. To think into someone else's head, by contrast, is to provide them with the opportunity, the tools, and the incentive to think in ways *no one* has before. The resulting thoughts belong to no one exclusively, but transform and bring together the individuals involved.

In assembling the montage *Deutsche Menschen*, Benjamin deliberately reordered the sequence in which the letters had originally been published in the newspaper. Thus the ultimate position of Overbeck's letter to Nietzsche, which survives the reordering, signifies more than just its chronological position. That letter was also the only letter the *Frankfurter Zeitung* had published with a distinct heading: it appeared on 15 May 1932 under the title "Why still do anything at all?" The title is a phrase taken from Overbeck's letter, a phrase Overbeck himself is quoting from the lamentation Nietzsche had sent him on 22 March 1883. That original complaint had been written from an emotional nadir, in "an immovable black melancholy," under the shadow of Wagner's death the month before, and unaccountable delays in the publication of the initial book of *Thus Spoke Zarathustra*. "There is Nothing that can be made good any more; I will do nothing any good anymore. Why still do anything at all!—" Nietzsche had written (*SB*, 6:348). The citation moving through these three texts and over half a century bears the trace of a wavering and hopeless Nietzsche behind the heroic exaltation of the published work. Its grammatical form can be taken as a nihilistic rhetorical challenge or a desperate entreaty for encouragement, and if Nietzsche intends the former, it is Overbeck's greatness to hear in it the latter. Benjamin's title, finally, suspends the significance of the question between these two possibilities, ending the newspaper phase of the letter project and leaving to the readers of the *Frankfurter Zeitung* and by extension to all of us the choice of how to understand the cry.

In the commentary on the letter, Benjamin renders Overbeck exemplary: "Nietzsche's friend Franz Overbeck, professor of Protestant theology and church history at Basel, was one of the great mediating figures [*Mittlergestalten*]. . . . Such men, who have often been seen as merely a kind of well-meaning helper, or even an advocate, are infinitely more: they are representatives of a more understanding posterity." Thus Overbeck is coordinated with an appreciative posterity to which Benjamin himself must also belong. Overbeck's letter provides a dual portrait, opening not only "a view of the landscape of Nietzsche's existence as if from a mountain pass," but providing as well "a picture of the writer." That picture has recognizably Benjaminian features: "For this middleman [*Mittler*] could be what he was only by having the most acute perception of extremes." He can perceive these extremes because his religious perspective is theoretically self-destructive: "True Christianity, for him, meant an absolute, eschatologically justified denial of the world. Engagement with the world and its culture was according to him a repudiation of Christianity's essence, and all theology from the patristic period onward appeared as a Satan among religions" (*SW*, 3:217; *GS*, 4:228). As eschatologically justified denial of the world, Overbeck's Christianity resembles Benjamin's messianic communism, and the former's scorn for theology anticipates the latter's radical theoretical skepticism. As a mediator, committed to extremes and skeptical of any theological expression, Overbeck anticipates the site from which Benjamin's commentary itself emerges.

And yet at the same time, by providing a portrait of Overbeck, the introduction to the letter objectifies him in turn and positions its commentary as congruent with Nietzsche's own position responding to the letter. The comfort and encouragement Overbeck sends to Nietzsche resonates with Benjamin as well: "You ask: Why do anything more? The question is prompted—at least in part, I believe—by the extreme obscurity and impenetrability of your future. You wrote to me recently that you wanted to 'disappear.' This idea places a definite, and doubtless very vivid image before your mind's eye, and fills you with confidence . . . that your life *shall* be given form" (*SW*,

3:218; *GS*, 4:230). As Benjamin, if not the readers of the *Frankfurter Zeitung* would have known, Nietzsche's response was in fact grateful and encouraged: "My dear friend Overbeck, I know of no other way to answer your good letter than: things are moving *forward*." And with his confidence in *Zarathustra* restored, through Overbeck's letter and the arrival of the galleys, he ventures a prediction about his impenetrable, peripatetic future, projecting an unreal image of Nietzsche in Barcelona.

> It is possible that I have entered this winter into a new development. Zarathustra is something that no living human being but me can make. Perhaps I have now discovered my best ability. Even as a "philosopher" I have not yet expressed my most essential thoughts (or "frenzies")—ach, I am so silent, so clandestine! . . . In summer, woods and high mountains, in autumn, Barcelona. That is the latest news. Keep it *secret*. In *loyal* friendship F.N. (*SB*, 6:354–55)

DEMON

Benjamin's essay "Karl Kraus" makes few compromises with its audience, and one reader, at least, found its portrait unrecognizable. "The only thing I learned from this work, which is surely well intended and probably also well thought," Kraus said in a Berlin lecture in February 1931, "is that it is about me, that the author seems to know many things about me that were unknown to me until now, although even now I can't clearly recognize them, and I can only express my hope that other readers have understood it better than I did. (Perhaps it is psychoanalysis.)" (*GS*, 2:1082). Benjamin took Kraus's uncomprehending response to the essay's eventual publication in stride. "Kraus's reaction," he wrote to Scholem, "could not reasonably be expected to have been other than it is; and I hope my own falls in the realm of reasonable expectations: that I will never write about him again" (*GB*, 4:34).

Karl Kraus was a unique figure in early twentieth-century German-speaking culture. A denizen of Vienna, Kraus subjected its fin-de-siècle society to viciously corrosive but brilliantly coruscating critique in his journal *Die Fackel* (*The Torch*), which he wrote almost entirely single-handedly. In addition to his journalism Kraus wrote satirical verse and drama and gave public readings from his own works and from the plays of Shakespeare and the operettas of Jacques Offenbach. In the years between the world wars Kraus's reputation among central European intellectuals was tremendous, though by the very nature of his polemical engagement bound to the time and place in which it was written. A text on so localized a figure seems to grow quickly inaccessible as well; thus Hannah Arendt regretfully did not include "Karl Kraus" in her pioneering English-language Benjamin anthology *Illuminations*. Since the Viennese satirist was "practically unknown in English-speaking countries," her editor's note explains, Benjamin's essay "would have needed so many explanatory notes that the thrust of the text itself would have been ruined."[8] The essay is, in other words, sacrificed to the cruel powers of displacement and exile, a high price indeed, for "Karl Kraus" is Benjamin's most perfect theoretical achievement, something Arendt acknowledges not least by organizing her own introduction to *Illuminations* in a triadic figurative structure—The Hunchback, The Dark Times, The Pearl Diver—that modulates the three figural movements of Benjamin's Kraus essay: The *Allmensch*, The Demon, The *Unmensch*.

Perhaps the sacrifice was unnecessary as well, though this theoretical possibility could not easily be perceived from the practical position mediating between cultures that Hannah Arendt had adopted in this case. Of course Benjamin speaks to an audience familiar with, and more, devoted to, the work of Kraus, an audience to which Arendt belongs. But the fact that Kraus himself cannot recognize the portrait Benjamin puts forth suggests that the relation between Benjamin's description and its object in the world may not be as straightforward as explicative philological annotation would suggest. When Benjamin vows never to break his silence over Kraus, this reaction may read like a dismissal, with even a slight ring of petulance. In the logic governing the essay itself, however, the gesture is in fact a profound endorsement. For silence intended as rejection is precisely the gesture Benjamin sees governing Kraus's writing itself at the profoundest level. *Wie laut wird alles*, runs the essay's first epigraph, from Kraus himself: "How loud it all is." And his polemical response to this comprehensive cacophony is, Benjamin claims, in the end a sort of "silence turned inside out" (*gewendetes Schweigen*) (*SW*, 2:436; *GS*, 2:338), the silence of what Kraus refrains from saying, the "destructive side of tact" that cites without comment and lets the citation denounce itself. The essay opens with the image of the "old engravings that have the messenger, shrieking and with disordered hair, waving in his hands a sheet of paper . . . full of war and pestilence, of homicidal cry and woe, of arson and flood" (*SW*, 2:433; *GS*, 2:334). Kraus's journal *Die*

Fackel is this broadsheet, and though the alarm and urgency of its communication is caught by the shrieking face and disordered hair of the messenger, the old allegorical engraving, like the true significance of Kraus, is motionless and silent; in the present an anachronism. In the preparatory drafts and notes to the work, Benjamin expresses his intention clearly: *Something about the intention of my Kraus-Essay. To show the place where I stand and do not participate.—to cast a gaze down into the promised land of sabotage from ~~Mountains~~ Karmel of reason.— . . . To transform the thirty years of* <u>Die Fackel</u> *into a power plant of silence. Silent preparedness—that is the effect of* <u>Die Fackel</u> *on its true readers (GS, 2:1093).*

Benjamin's first public remarks on Kraus predate the long essay of 1930 by four years. But MONUMENT TO A WARRIOR from *One-Way Street* already presents the Vienna journalist under the rubric of reactive silence: "No name . . . would be more fittingly honored by silence," Benjamin writes there (*SW*, 1:469; *GS*, 4:121). And in this aphorism it is already a question of the local position from which Kraus writes rather than the content of his production. "No post was ever more loyally held and none was ever more hopelessly lost. . . . What more helpless than his conversion? What more powerless than his humanity? What more hopeless than his battle with the press? What does he know of the powers [*Gewalten*] that are his true allies?" (*SW*, 1:469; *GS*, 4:121). The privative comparatives dissolve the specific content of Kraus's lifework and leave behind only the posture it adopted against the enemies it faced. Behind any particulars of Kraus's polemics his post is essentially constituted as lost, for the powers it mediates themselves emerge as the consequences of defeat. It is the dead with whom Kraus is in unwitting alliance. *One-Way Street* sets Kraus at the mortal boundary in language, where, among the din of present purposes the silent ghosts of the dead can be detected.

> Helpless as only spirits' voices are when summoned up, a murmur from the chthonic depths of language is the source of his soothsaying. Every sound is incomparably genuine, but they all leave us bewildered, like messages from the beyond. Blind like the *manes*, language calls him to vengeance, as narrowminded as spirits that know only the voice of the blood, who care not what havoc they wreak in the realm of the living. But he cannot err. Their commands are infallible. (*SW*, 1:469; *GS*, 4:121)

The movement of the aphorism itself drifts inexorably across that mortal boundary. For if language is at first merely compared to the manes calling for revenge from beyond the grave, by the end, it is indeed the mandates of the dead that inform Kraus's sentences. The equivocation marks the ambiguity of this site: Here language establishes the border between life and death as much as it is riven by that border. And the source of truth will not stay safely on the vital side. The truth Kraus mediates does not depend on any accuracy of perception or intrinsic genius on his part, but results from his occupation of this liminal position, and indeed, as long as he occupies it, whatever he spontaneously utters will be true. But this position of immediate veracity extracts a price. As the aphorism moves to its close, the tug of death on language pulls Kraus himself prematurely out of life. "No one who walks the paths of life would come upon him. On an archaic field of honor, a gigantic battleground of bloody labor, he rages before a deserted sepulcher. The honors at his death will be immeasurable, and the last that are bestowed" (SW, 1:469; GS, 4:121;). Kraus would live another nine years after the publication of this piece, but MONUMENT TO A WARRIOR is already his preemptory obituary.

"To show the place where I stand and do not participate." The formula gestures at the paradoxical site from and toward which all of Benjamin's mature expressive effort is directed. In the triangulation of the site named "Kraus," a name in which authorship and editorship remarkably coincide, Benjamin can be seen to advance the schema of his own ideal writing position, abstracted from any actual institutional commitments. But this identification produces its meaning not as straightforward identity, as if "Benjamin" were the actual signature behind the mask of "Kraus." Quite the opposite. Kraus is a figure of discontinuity; since the act of identification must simultaneously distinguish the things being identified as the condition of its performance, this moment of distinction is at the heart of "Karl Kraus." That Kraus could not recognize himself in this portrait is thus a necessary consequence of this displacement and is not the contingent result of his unfamiliarity with Benjamin's esoteric language (much less any divergence between their assessments of psychoanalysis, which plays no role in the Kraus essay, and little enough in the rest of Benjamin's work). "Karl Kraus" describes a virtual site where Benjamin and Kraus intersect, in a process of dialogic identification manifesting a common truth suspended in their respective silences, and so emancipated from the specificity of their respective signatures.

"Karl Kraus" cannot be understood, then, as a merely self-referential mask, but rather as an embodied movement of self-referentiality itself. "This is the language of true authority. Insight into its operations can reveal only one thing: that it is consequential [*verbindlich*], mercilessly consequential, toward itself in the same degree as toward others; that it does not tire of trembling before itself, though never before others" (*SW*, 2:439; *GS*, 2:343). As Benjamin remarked in a letter to Max Rychner, his own position is "between the lines" of "Karl Kraus" (*CB*, 373; *GB*, 4:20); but truly *between* the lines, in the space Kraus's own expression sets off, and not in simple convergence with Kraus's own authority. Benjamin's reading of Kraus triangulates a space beyond either of them, a silent site where an authority informing any authoritative writing is established and defied.

The essay "Karl Kraus" is in many ways a mature restatement of Benjamin's younger and more flamboyant essay on Goethe's *Elective Affinities*. Again, the triadic structure common to both essays suggests parallels. Benjamin's Goethe essay positions an initial section on death as mythic closure against a second section on life as irrevocable decision. Around the figure of Goethe and his late novel these two complementary perspectives circulate. Goethe's life, with its leeriness toward irrevocable decision and its sensitivity to the mythic force of the "daemonic," is the medium within which the unrepresentable force of true decision is negatively manifested. Goethe's daemonic, whose long description in Goethe's autobiography *Poetry and Truth* Benjamin cites in the *Elective Affinities* essay, is the superhuman antithesis to the pure force of human decision. "It was not divine," Benjamin quotes Goethe,

> for it seemed irrational; not human, for it had no intelligence; not diabolical, for it was beneficent; and not angelic, for it often betrayed malice. It was like chance, for it lacked continuity, and like Providence, for it suggested context. Everything that limits us seemed penetrable by it, and it appeared to do as it pleased with the elements necessary to our existence, to contract time and expand space. It seemed only to accept the impossible and scornfully to reject the possible.—This essence, which appeared to infiltrate all the others, separating and combining them, I called "daemonic," after the example of the ancients and others who had perceived something similar. I tried to save myself from this fearful thing. (*SW*, 1:316; *GS*, 1:149–50; *GHA*, 10:175)

This vivid prosopopoeia brings before the reader the fundamental mythic compulsion manifested in Goethe's novel. Among the paralipomena to the Goethe essay is an untitled fragment clarifying the basic perception of mythic force at work in Benjamin's interpretation of the *Elective Affinities* and in his thought more generally. The fragment describes an emotional dynamic between two married couples, recognizable as the relationships in Goethe's novel but characterized at a level of generality that permits the description to apply to Benjamin's own personal situation as well. These notes thus emerge at the vital intersection of literary text and human life that Benjamin's theoretical essay attempts to understand.[9] And as a schema general enough to operate in either mortal life or remembered language, the forces characterized here in matrimonial terms exhibit a basic characteristic of Benjamin's theoretical imagination. *Even the sacramental changes into myth*, the text begins.

> *For that is what underlies this peculiar situation: Two couples become acquainted; the old bonds begin to loosen. When two who had not known each other previously are mutually attracted, then very soon the other two also enter into the most intimate relationship. It is as if the simplest things proceed haltingly and with difficulty as long as they have only the love of God on their side, but that the greatest problems are easily and fortunately solved as soon as the Devil has his hand in the game.*

The interplay of forces Benjamin describes could be visualized in terms of a graphic schema. The two marriages would be represented vertically, as the sacramental bonds between A and C, B and D. When a passion between A and B precipitates the collapse of these superhuman bonds, C and D are consequently drawn together. Psychologically plausible explanations for such a complementary and reactive attraction are not far to seek, but Benjamin dismisses them. Speaking with an authority derived both from Goethe's idea of "elective affinities" at work beyond intentions in the human world and from his own immediate experience of loving Jula Cohn while his wife fell in love with their friend Ernst Schoen, Benjamin attributes the force manifested in the attraction of C and D not to the pull of their interior psyches but to the push of an external mythic closure that duplicates the adulterous connection between A and B by redirecting the primal energies these broken marriage vows no longer hold in thrall.

> *The banal explanation for these developments is obvious. Yet there is something [Sache] at work here that might indeed be explained by "the need to be comforted," "being in the same situation," "the desire to get even," but that is so powerful and so vanquishingly beautiful, that has so little of excuse and evasion that these explanations appear entirely vacuous. It is mirror-magic that ignites the flame that trembles in the triumphant meeting of the abandoned*

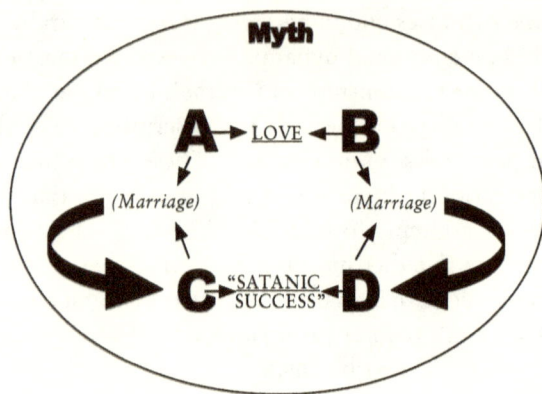

Figure 1.

> spouses. For their love is not original; what is original for them is a situation [Situation] in which the old sacramental powers of the marriages that are collapsing attempt to install themselves as mythical, natural forces between them. This, and not love, is the actual undisclosed inner side of that symbiosis, the "same" situation in which the abandoned spouses find themselves.

Marriage anchors human life in the superhuman powers that surround and threaten it, at the point where nature and myth in their external necessity are indistinguishable. When enlightened human beings ignore these forces and the vows that acknowledge them, the forces do not simply disappear but are unleashed and operate outside of human intentions. This is what pushes the abandoned spouses toward each other, making it seem to them, at least initially, as if the affinity so easily recognized between them were divinely ordained. The mirror-magic holds not as an identical reflection between the pairs of amorous couples but as an inverted reflection between the disintegrating marriages and the sudden sympathy between C and D, for unlike the affection (love) between A and B, but like the sacramental bond of marriage, this secondary relationship is externally conditioned. Because it is not intentionally oriented toward those conditioning forces, because it understands itself to be an autonomous passion on the order of their spouses' love, it is not a sacred bond, however "powerful and vanquishingly beautiful" it may be. It is rather a demonic parody.

Benjamin concludes the text by invoking blasphemous inversion as the proper framework for understanding their relation, despite, or rather because of its violent and triumphant beauty. The relation between the abandoned spouses is neither passionate love nor matrimonial fidelity but a "satanic success." And it is in this summary context, abruptly and unexpectedly, that Nietzsche appears.

> *The spirit of the Black Mass returns here: a sacrament takes the place of love and love takes the place of the sacrament. The spirit of satanic success reigns and shows marriage in a mirror. For Satan is dialectical, and a kind of deceptive, fortunate success—the appearance [Schein] to which Nietzsche was deeply beholden [tief verfallen war]—betrays him just as the Spirit of Gravity betrays him.* (SW, 1:402; GS, 1:837–38)

To say that Satan is dialectical is not to say that all dialectic is satanic. But it is to say that a fundamental antagonism toward the human is manifested in a certain sort of dialectical reflection. The example that presents itself is Nietzsche, who was deeply beholden to the image of preternatural success; the dialectic here lies less in Nietzsche's philosophical method and more in the perspective that raises Nietzsche's expression as an exemplary error in order to illustrate an unprecedented truth. Nietzsche's writing betrays a disingenuous allegiance to the very superhuman forces Nietzsche himself ostensibly disdains. This allegiance to immediate inspiration, if only because it knows not to what it is allied, reveals an ultimately corrupted principle. There is no doubt that Benjamin intends his reference to Nietzsche critically—the satanic provenance of inspiration the fragment discerns was not apparent to Nietzsche himself, whose critical eye was rather focused on the Spirit of Gravity resisting and impeding inspired advancement. At the same time, it is Nietzsche's prose that realizes in a posttheological milieu the persistent relevance of these mythic forces enlightened humanism denies, without thereby collapsing into anachronistic superstition. Nietzsche's submission to the dialectic of appearance is an indispensable occasion for Benjamin's own critical resistance to duplicitous mythology, the possibility of Nietzsche's impassioned prose the condition of Benjamin's own advance—ever upward!—beyond the limits of the thinkable. And so outside of presentation and outside of affinity the reciprocal force of the relation between Benjamin and Nietzsche points past the horizon of all of our collective commitments, into the night that we call ignorance, or chaos, or death, but that always also is, more basically, the future of everything that has gone before.

CAESURA

When last we see Zarathustra in the book that bears his name, the thought of death is far away. "Thus spoke Zarathustra, and he left his cave, glowing and strong as a morning sun that comes out of dark mountains. *** The End of *Thus Spoke Zarathustra*" (*TSZ*, 327; *KSA*, 4:408). The future lies open before him, and nothing precludes another communicative impulse, a later descent, and further teachings. Though Zarathustra has much to say about death—"There are preachers of death; and the earth is full of those to whom one must preach renunciation of life" (*TSZ*, 44; *KSA*, 4:55); "Die at the right time—thus teaches Zarathustra" (*TSZ*, 71; *KSA*, 4:93); "And only where there are tombs are there resurrections" (*TSZ*, 113; *KSA*, 4:145;)—death's hand itself does not reach him in the book that bears his name. And this despite the fact that the ultimate announcement of the eternal recurrence emerges from within the threat of suicide. "You think, O Zarathustra, I know it," life complains in "The Other Dancing Song," the gestural invocation of a visionary moment at the end of book 3,

> of how you want to leave me soon!"—
> "Yes," I answered hesitantly, "but you also know—" and I whispered something into her ear, right through her tangled yellow foolish tresses.
> You *know* That, Zarathustra? That nobody knows.— (*TSZ*, 227; *KSA*, 4:285)

In the discourse "The Convalescent" it was Zarathustra's animals who articulated the formula of his vision: "For your animals know well, O Zarathustra, who you are and must become: behold, *you are the teacher of the eternal recurrence*—that is *your* destiny!" (*TSZ*, 220; *KSA*, 4:275). The accuracy of this articulation is neither denied nor confirmed by Zarathustra himself: "When the animals had spoken these words they were silent and waited for Zarathustra to say Something to them; but Zarathustra did not hear that they were silent. Rather he lay still with his eyes closed, like one sleeping, although he was not asleep; for he was conversing with his soul" (*TSZ*, 221; *KSA*, 4:277). In the gestural milieu of an alternative Dancing Song, the Something that Zarathustra here refuses to communicate to his heraldic emblems passes silently back into life, as the response to a culpable memento mori. Death cannot reach Zarathustra, because he is himself an answer to death.[10]

Only in the notebooks, where Nietzsche developed and tested the text, does Zarathustra's death survive. And indeed, in negotiating the vexing question of the relation of the *Nachlaß* to the published writings, this possibility provides us with a working *interpretive* characterization of this critical boundary in Nietzsche's text. The *Nachlaß* is where Zarathustra can die. This formula, here baldly stated, is not meant as the necessary and sufficient condition of a conceptual limit. Nietzsche's textual leavings are clearly enough identified to philology against his well-documented efforts to publish, republish, and organize as an oeuvre the books that bear his signature. The possibility of Zarathustra's death rather condenses the question of what these leavings might *mean*, what bearing they might have on our understanding not merely of the *what* of Nietzsche (the philologist's legitimate question), but the equally legitimate question of the *why*: Why Nietzsche, here and now. The formula attempts to condense what is at stake in Nietzsche's project in these terms. Its necessity and sufficiency are the shadows of an orienting insight that here the dynamic of a private possibility and public impossibility of Zarathustra's death sets Nietzsche's inscription at its greatest profundity.

Zarathustra dies several times in the notebooks. In Nietzsche's explorations of the event, the death hovers between murder and suicide. Sometimes it is Pana, Zarathustra's chosen disciple, who precipitates his death.

> As he divines Pana, Zarathustra dies of pity [Mitleid] with her pity.
> Before the moment of greatest disdain (highest blessedness!)
>   All must be fulfilled, namely everything from the <u>preface</u>. (KSA, 10:512)

Zarathustra's greatest danger is *Mitleid*, or pitying sympathy. "Pity is the deepest abyss: as deeply as man sees into life, he also sees into suffering [*Leiden*]" (*TSZ*, 157; *KSA*, 4:199). So another version accentuates the destructive power of that sympathy in its preemptive contrast to Pana's actively homicidal gesture.

> At first all turn away from Zarathustra (this to be <u>depicted in steps</u>!).
> Zarathustra is delighted, notices nothing. Pana wants to kill him.
> <u>In the moment when she raises the dagger, Zarathustra understands everything and dies of the pain of this pity</u>. This must be made <u>clear</u>!
> (KSA, 10:513)

Pana's murderous gesture is deflected by Zarathustra's sympathetic pain into autonomous extinction. From without, the gesture appears fatal, the cause of death the dagger in a trusted hand. But from within, it is Zarathustra's own recognition of the motives for that action that precipitates his end. This distinction must, Nietzsche insists, be clearly presented.

The presentational question haunts Zarathustra's death. Whether or not Nietzsche ever seriously considered composing a play about the Persian prophet, as Mazzino Montinari suggests, the relation of *Thus Spoke Zarathustra* to dramatic precedents, and particularly to tragedy, emerges as a major concern in the notebooks of summer 1883. In its eventual form, the four books of *Thus Spoke Zarathustra* echo and invert the classical tragic trilogy and its satyr play. That such considerations are unavoidable in this context becomes clearer as soon as we reflect on the task Nietzsche had set himself with this book. The first continuation of *Zarathustra*, book 2, had ended in failure and deferral. Having taught the superman in the initial book, Zarathustra spends the second struggling to come to terms with the underlying perspective to which the superman responds. This perspective is the eternal return of the same; but we must be cautious about reading too precipitously other formulations of this doctrine into Zarathustra's dilemma. What *Thus Spoke Zarathustra* presents is, first of all, a powerful reticence toward expressing a doctrine that must remain for the time being mysterious. At the end of the second book, Zarathustra forgoes communication entirely, having realized that he is not yet ripe to teach this further doctrine, and so he tearfully returns to his "solitude" (*TSZ*, 147; *KSA*, 4:190), leaving his sympathizers behind. Book 3 congeals in the notebooks around Nietzsche's attempts to derive a successful presentational strategy for this most difficult thought.

As an antigospel, *Thus Spoke Zarathustra* cannot simply proclaim the eternal return as a salvationist doctrine, as the "Good News" of a divine comedy. To the extent that the eternal return has precedents, they are not Christian, but pagan, and specifically, Greek. *I have discovered Hellenism* [*Griechenthum*]: Nietzsche exults in an earlier notebook, *they believed in the eternal recurrence! that is the Mystery-Faith!* (*KSA*, 10:340). The eternal recurrence is Nietzsche's appropriation of the Greek heritage, the form in which, via Zarathustra, the Greeks are overcome. And where the Greeks are most Greek, for Nietzsche, is in their tragic poetry. Earlier, Nietzsche had conceived of the origins of Greek tragedy as a self-overcoming by and of indigenous Greek Apollonianism under the pressure of a heterochthonous cult of Dionysus emerging from the east. This is the perspective expounded in *The Birth of Tragedy*. But whatever else it is, the doctrine of the eternal return involves a profound realignment of this system. The Dionysian absorbs classical antiquity, as its contrast with a decadent Judeo-Christian culture. The Greeks become Greek with the advent of the Dionysian: Apollo is dethroned, and Dionysus assumes his place. As the Dionysian thought par excellence, the eternal return is thus intimately involved with a tragic vision. The successful announcement of the eternal return invokes and overcomes the full weight of tragic catastrophe.

Zarathustra's death is thus buffeted by this classical commitment. What he teaches is exposed to Greek tragedy and the revelation it, or what remains of it, embodies. Zarathustra is both teacher and the one extant example of what he teaches. But unlike Christ, who reconciles these roles sacrificially in the transcendent kingdom of his resurrection, Zarathustra in his immanence must find them irreconcilable. In the former role, he is pulled toward a triumphant, euphoric rhetoric, while in the second role, he is drawn toward the tragic catharsis of annihilation. This last tendency pulls the notebooks toward Trauerspiel. Fragment 10[45]:

> *I Act. The Temptation. He considers himself not ready. (Chosen people)*
> <u>*Solitude from shame at himself*</u>
> *II Act. Zarathustra incognito attending the "great midday"*
>   *Is recognized*
> *III. Act. Catastrophe: All fall away after his speech.*
>   *He dies of pain.*
> *IV Act. Funeral wake*
>   *"We killed him"*
> <u>*convince the reasons*</u>. (KSA, 10:377)

While Nietzsche explores the general question of Zarathustra's relation to Greece, and to Greek tragedy, throughout 1883–84, the division of fragment 10[45] into a structure of acts implies intervening dramatic models. The classical precedent for Zarathustra founders on history and transforms into Trauerspiel. The modern drama that lies behind Zarathustra is Hölderlin's *Death of Empedocles*, a drama developed around the presentation of a deferred suicidal gesture. But if *The Death of Empedocles* is the ancestor of the published immortal Zarathustra, another precedent colors his mortal avatar in the *Nachlaß*: another Trauerspiel built around an act of murder that becomes an act of suicide: Shakespeare's *Julius Caesar*.

The position of Zarathustra's death in act 3, as well as the motif of the trusted assassin from the Pana fragments, suggest that here *Thus*

Spoke Zarathustra is exposed as well to this Shakespearean precedent. Caesar, too, is assassinated in the third act of Shakespeare's play, betrayed by even his closest associates. *III. Act. Catastrophe: All fall away after his speech. He dies of pain.* And act 4 of Shakespeare's play unfolds around the rhetorical and military battles between Mark Antony and Brutus over Caesar's legacy to Rome, and the status of his killing. *IV Act. Funeral wake "We killed him."*

In *The Gay Science*, Nietzsche had, "In praise of Shakespeare," called *Julius Caesar* the Englishman's "best tragedy." Nothing honors Shakespeare more, the aphorism claims, than his belief in Brutus, that he "did not cast one speck of suspicion on this type of virtue." This type of virtue is "independence of the soul"; an *Unabhängigkeit* that touches isolation and precludes direct communication. Its extent can be measured only indirectly by the sacrifices it is willing to make in order to preserve itself. To doubt such virtue is to see Brutus's rejection of Caesar as his betrayal of a heroic companion rather than the sacrifice of his own heroism for the sake of an absolute integrity. Brutus, as Shakespeare's illustration of this species of virtue, is the hero of the drama, which "is still called by the wrong name," Nietzsche maintains. The objection echoes Cassius in the play.

Cassius: Brutus and Caesar: what should be in that "Caesar"?
Why should that name be sounded more than yours?
Write them together: yours is as fair a name.
Sound them: it doth become the mouth as well.
Weigh them: it is as heavy. Conjure with 'em:
"Brutus" will start a spirit as soon as "Caesar."[11]

But this does not mean that "Brutus" would be the correct name of the tragedy. Shakespeare exemplifies the virtue of independence by setting Brutus within a recursive double bind: "The height at which he places Caesar is the finest honor that he could bestow on Brutus: that is how he raises beyond measure Brutus's inner problem as well as the spiritual strength that was able to hack through *this knot!*" (*GSc*, 150; *KSA*, 3:452). This Gordian knot is more than the historical Caesar's accomplishments in conflict with the historical Brutus's commitment to freedom. "Was political freedom only a symbol for something inexpressible?" Nietzsche asks. "Could it be that we confront some unknown dark event and adventure in the poet's own soul of which he wants to speak only in signs?" The general political principle appears in the name Brutus shares with his illustrious ancestor Lucius Junius Brutus, who drove Tarquinius Superbus from Rome and founded the Republic. Though Marcus Junius Brutus repeats the emancipatory gesture of the earlier Brutus by murdering a new monarchical pretender, he fails to found freedom, so the integrity he represents cannot be assimilated into that principle. What Brutus's murder of Caesar confronts us with is not a conflict of general political principles, but the unspeakable specificity of a historical act. This conjunction of historicity and unspeakability means that the act cannot be self-identically localized but must be situated in the historical Shakespeare as much as, if not more than, in the Roman Senate. Not the representation of the historical murder directly, nor the medieval or Renaissance traditions of its anathema or vindication are here at issue, but the presentation through it and at the cost of its mortal violence of a recoverable vital specificity outside of representation. This specificity is preserved as a recursive circle within dramatic presentation: Caesar's heights are manifested precisely by his occupation of the title role, and Brutus's virtue precisely by his willingness to assassinate that title. Shakespeare's achievement, the proper basis for his reputation, is his depiction of this uprising against the title.

But the depiction itself is also a self-annihilation at the representational level. "Before the whole figure and virtue of Brutus, Shakespeare prostrated himself, feeling unworthy and remote," Nietzsche maintains. To the extent that Shakespeare embodies a brutal integrity in history he also embodies its deposed alternative. The evidence for this are the two entrances of the figure of the poet, who receives harsh treatment at Brutus's hands. "I'll know his humor when he knows his time. / What should the wars do with these jigging fools?" (4.2.187–88). This dismissal of the poet in act 4, which Nietzsche cites in translation, points back to the close of the third act, where "Cinna the Poet" had been set upon by the enraged mob.

> *Cinna*: Truly, my name is Cinna.
> *First Plebeian*: Tear him to pieces! He's a conspirator.
> *Cinna*: I am Cinna the poet, I am Cinna the poet.
> *Fourth Plebeian*: Tear him for his bad verses, tear him for his bad verses.
> *Cinna*: I am not Cinna the conspirator.
> *Fourth Plebeian*: It is no matter, his name's Cinna. Pluck but his name out of his heart, and turn him going.
>
> (*Julius Caesar*, 3.3.26–33)

In these encounters Nietzsche hears a "cry of self-contempt" on Shakespeare's part. As the opportunistic, cowardly echo of a genuine conspirator Shakespeare brings himself onto the stage. And it is this demolition of his signature, the false name of the poet plucked from his heart, that allows for his secret identification, beyond political description, with the elements of that assassination of the title.

"What is all Hamlet-melancholy compared to the melancholy of Brutus!" (*GSc,* 151; *KSA,* 3:452). For Nietzsche the classical philologist, the historical Caesar was no doubt a more detailed and substantial presence than he was for Benjamin. Nietzsche is impressed, for instance, with Caesar's ascetic regimen as a response to his epilepsy, and holds his writing style in high regard. Nonetheless, Caesar's specificity is mitigated by the antonomasia that makes of his name the designation for an absolute political authority as such, both in Rome and, Germanized, in the Second Reich. The historical necessity is situated at a deeper level than any such psychological identifications with the past. In the light of this necessity, inscribed onto the temporal specificity of the mortal world, the name Caesar, when Nietzsche uses it, must pass through its melancholy allegorical manifestation, enter into this relation with Brutus. There, it will indeed become the monstrous symbol of an individual dynamic beneath any signature. "When I seek my ultimate formula for *Shakespeare,*" Nietzsche writes in *Ecce Homo,* "I always only find this: he conceived of the type of Caesar. That sort of thing cannot be guessed—one either is it, or one is not" (*EH,* 246; *KSA,* 6:287). The highest formula for Shakespeare, what defines him, is not an identity with Caesar, but that he *conceived* this identity, manifested it beyond himself in a permanent, self-aggrandizing titular tension with Brutus's textual dagger. Where the earlier aphorism from *The Gay Science* had approached Shakespeare's self-abrogating inability to identify with Brutus cautiously, amid a hedging flurry of rhetorical questions, the later announcement supports the identity of Shakespeare and Caesar with tautology: The Caesar-type is a creation that necessarily externalizes its creator. The highest formula for "Shakespeare" is thus: the creator of a pure externalization. The evidence for this formula is his externalization of the murderous recursion in which the virtue of the title manifests the virtue of the text that kills it.

Like Benjamin's Hamlet, Nietzsche's Caesar participates in a singular Shakespearean pronouncement of the allegorical text, as an exceptional externalizing coincidence of authorial specificity and textual functioning. But where Benjamin's Hamlet encompassed his entire historical epoch in an impossible amalgam of active and passive postures toward death and survival, and alienated himself from life entirely so as to meet his esoteric counterpart Heinle in the death that makes history, Nietzsche's Caesar ruptures history the way his murder ruptures the play that presents him, as an ultimate act whose meaning can only be established through conflict. In itself it remains simply the form of confrontation between mutually implicated and mutually exclusive perspectives—"*Et tu, Brute?* Then fall Caesar" (3.1.77). The caesura between the dead and the living languages, pulling antiquity into the space of Trauerspiel at the price of regicide, is the most concentrated example of the *Abstand* Nietzsche's conditioning asyndeton creates in the Benjaminian posture toward the present. It is the space of the full madness of maturity.

Nietzsche's Caesar is characterized by two ultimate facts: Caesar is he who crossed the Rubicon, and Caesar is he who recognized his assassin. The war between Mark Antony and Brutus is a struggle over the precedence of this transgression and this recognition. Caesar, though one of the very few historical names that can survive in the discursive atmosphere of *Thus Spoke Zarathustra* (*TSZ*, 247; *KSA*, 4:307), is a model only to a presentation of Zarathustra's death, a death that does not escape the fragmentary notebooks. Thus, when Benjamin glimpses this figure in the literary remains, its ramifications are subtle and involved. *There is a handwritten draft*, Benjamin noted in his work on the arcades, *in which Caesar instead of Zarathustra is the bearer of Nietzsche's tidings. (Löwith 73) That is of no little moment. It underscores the fact that Nietzsche had an inkling [ahnte] of his doctrine's complicity with imperialism* (*AP*, 117; *GS*, 5:175). Any easy equivalence between Caesar and imperialism is mitigated by Benjamin's verb: Nietzsche does not recognize but merely intuits the political implications of his doctrine. It, like the complementary equivalence between Brutus and freedom that Nietzsche called into question, is "a symbol for something inexpressible." The passage from Löwith's book on Nietzsche that Benjamin is citing had mentioned Caesar in an offhand, passing manner: "In coming into contact with his idea, Zarathustra wavers even now between approaching and retreating. After Zarathustra has given his hand to his most abysmal idea, he falls down, just as after the most silent hour, like a dead man, sick from his own convalescence. Afterward Zarathustra stands there as Zarathustra-Dionysus, or in another plan as 'Caesar.' The decisive moment is eternalized" (*NER*, 72; *NEW*, 73). The parenthetical reference to Caesar is left hanging by Löwith, and Benjamin's assertion of its importance is a discrepancy between this reading and his own.

The importance rests on the link between Caesar and imperialism, a term Benjamin is introducing, and one with no place in Löwith's resolutely apolitical discussion. But, more precisely, it rests in the fact that Nietzsche displays an intimation of this link. This intimation is not merely the obvious metonymy that has rendered Caesar's name the general term for absolute political authority, but emerges gesturally, as the designation for his historical site of articulation. "Caesar" indicates that, despite his professed disdain for "the great city" and his expressed revulsion at "the coldest of all cold monsters" the State (*TSZ*, 48; *KSA*, 4:61), Nietzsche recognized that his own articulation emerged in complicity with those forces, and that it could be read as imperialist confession as well as philosophical proclamation. The fragment to which Löwith is referring runs, in part, as follows. Nietzsche has been considering the tonal necessities—*Peace of the great streams!!! Consecration of the smallest thing!!!*—of the unwritten book 3. He concludes:

> With Zarathustra's convalescence <u>Caesar</u> stands there, adamant, benevolent—the cleft between <u>Being-Creator, benevolence, and wisdom is destroyed</u>. Brightness, Peace, <u>no exaggerated</u> longing, happiness in the <u>properly employed, eternal moment</u>! (*KSA*, 10:525–6)

The moment the fragment here describes is a secularized apotheosis, the mock transfiguration of Zarathustra into a principle of human sovereignty, the great metonym of Matthew 22:21, whose legitimate authority precisely contrasts with the claims of God. "Render therefore unto Caesar the things which are Caesar's; and unto God the things that are God's." This antitheological resonance informs this spectacular Caesar suturing creativity and circumspection in a transfigured instant. And yet the fact that Zarathustra can appear this way does indicate a congruence between the atheistic impulse and state authority. The imperialism with which Nietzsche's doctrine is in complicity bears the full horror of military and economic exploitation, but does not rest in the received categories of the political. Zarathustra's message is a message of time; that Caesar could bear that message demonstrates an intimation of the fully materialized implications of the temporal character of that message, the real consequences implicit in its uncanny permanence. But that intimation is not merely Nietzsche's in the nineteenth century, it is Benjamin's in the twentieth, and ours in the twenty-first. For even in the notebooks, Zarathustra's death, like Caesar's, transforms itself relentlessly into Zarathustra's Wake. Fragment 16[53]:

> The <u>league</u> [Bund] of self-sacrificers at Zarathustra's <u>grave</u>. Beforehand they had fled: now, as they find him dead they become the <u>inheritors</u> of his soul and raise themselves to <u>his heights</u>. (This the last scene in Zarathustra 4—"<u>the great noontime</u>"—<u>cheerful</u>—<u>profound heavens</u>). (KSA, 10:517)

The Pentecostal echoes are even more direct in a subsequent fragment 16[65]:

> In part 4 Zarathustra dies when he notices the pain of his friends: and they leave him.—But after his death his spirit comes over them.
> Institutions as <u>aftereffects</u> of great individuals and as means of <u>embedding</u> and <u>rooting</u> the great individuals—until eventually fruits emerge. (KSA, 10:523)

Not simply Caesar in his secular power, but the institutionalized translation Max Weber would label the "*Veralltäglichung*"[12]—the "making everyday"—of singular charismatic origins informs the idea of Zarathustra's death in its parody of sacrifice. The wake of Zarathustra describes a countermodel to the logic of sacrifice, one oriented on the extralogical dimension of surviving inscription. Zarathustra's signature has been absorbed into the title it authorizes, both exalting it, like Caesar, whose name becomes a title, and assassinating it, like Brutus, who challenges its sovereign claim in the name of a higher freedom. As the principle of *Nachlaß*, Zarathustra's wake is always occurring, a permanent challenge, constantly provoking life to new readings, more language, around the empty rupture of an absent authority. Zarathustra's wake is the material substance of history.

In the end, Nietzsche was not able to maintain this unrepresentable commitment to Brutus and his suicidal act. If the title *Ecce Homo* is referring, beyond the New Testament reference, to Anthony's encomium on Brutus, "His life was gentle and the elements / So mixed in him that nature might stand up / And say to all the world 'This was a man,'" (5.5.72–74), it was Hamlet's melancholy that eventually captured Nietzsche:

> When I have a look into my *Zarathustra*, I walk up and down in my room for half an hour, unable to master an unbearable fit of sobbing.—I know no more heart-rending reading than Shakespeare: what must a man have suffered to have such a need of being a buffoon! Is Hamlet *understood*? Not doubt, *certainty* is what drives one insane.... (EH, 246; KSA, 6:287)

CHAPTER FIVE

Mad Maturity

I awoke you from your sleep, for a nightmare oppressed you. And now you say "what shall we do now! All is night."—Ye ingrates!

—FRIEDRICH NIETZSCHE,
Posthumous Fragment, 1883

"BORN POSTHUMOUSLY"

Benjamin's youthful works approach theory from the orator's stage. The position of the public speaker, hortatorily engaged with a collective audience on the basis of a prepared text: This is the situation implicit in the posture of the youthful facies and through which its conceptual apparatus is directed and then explicated. This, too, is the essential posture of Kraus, manifested directly in the public performances of Shakespeare and Offenbach that Benjamin stresses in his reading of the satirist. The performance, though congruent with the network of conventional expectations supporting living speech acts, is not subsumed into them, but occurs along a mortal fissure in significance. The felicity or infelicity of the act is thus reflected into a felicitous or infelicitous collective response, while behind that response, the mortal perspective will reflect the performance as a particular relation to other informing signatures, and the history of the human creature as the deformed terrain positioned between them.[1]

Scholem remembers his first impression of Benjamin: "I shall never forget his manner of presentation. Without looking at his audience, he delivered his absolutely letter-perfect speech with great intensity to an upper corner of the ceiling, at which he stared disconnectedly [*unverwandt*] the whole time" (*SF*, 7; *GF*, 10). The posture, whether accurately remembered or distilled retrospectively from subsequent acquaintance, captures the oddity of this performative dimension in

Benjamin's oeuvre. With a blithe disregard for eye contact, the basic gesture of effective public speaking, Benjamin's raised gaze lifts the matter of the talk from the immediate communicative field between speaker and audience, while the print-ready text he pronounces beckons to its prior and eventual material inscriptions. A text must be understood as the entire circuit through these various displacements and incarnations; for Benjamin, it gives up its truth only with reference to its moment of performance.

This situation condenses the textual presentation as such into a particular, embodied moment in the process of significant transmission. As the materialized mediation of text and audience, the public speaker appears suspended between activity and passivity; passive with regard to the written text presented, active with regard to the audience attending. It is not, in the first instance, the efferent space from speaker to audience that Benjamin reflects into his conceptual terms, but its afferent complement passing to the public performance from the prior text.[2] The audience does not condition the presentation as interpretation, setting its communicative terms, but vice versa: The presentation, the performance of the text, manifests an audience of those who can also raise their eyes to a higher goal, an audience that includes in a liminal way the speaker himself. By situating the moment of truth in the now of a presentation, Benjamin mitigates the critical interpretive constraints on intellectual transmission by exposing them to theological registers of inspiration. At the same time, the mortal finitude of human experience implicit in the decentering movement of inscription, the necessary pause between the composition and the performance of the text, prevents that inspiration from reifying into an enduring vital relation such as *spirit* or *reason*, a life uninterrupted by death. The authority of the performance lies not in such fantastic categories, but in history, in the catastrophe awaiting each of us, and so, reactively, in the catastrophes that have gone before us, among the vanished experiences of the dead.

In the preface to his Baudelaire translations, Benjamin conceptualizes this space of manifestation as a space of interlinguistic translation. The exposition there begins by emphatically neutralizing the receptive pole of aesthetic performance—no artwork is for the audience, Benjamin insists—in order then to complicate the presentational dynamic by fracturing it into a moment of living originality now dead and its revivifying repetition elsewhere. That repetition, the translation, is introduced in terms of semantic contrasts between languages, but soon enough pivots into the historical relation between an ended life and its survival in another form. If vitalism posits "life" as its fundamental explanatory category, Benjamin's "mortalism" does not simply replace that term with its opposite, but rather inverts the relation of explanation to category: "Life," the general framework of explanation, appears as endangered, an exception to the rule of death, exposed to death by its essential transience. This transience is registered by the necessary lurch within the category of "life" between this endangered life and a consequent second life, a survival of life not understood as its continuation beyond a terminus within a common, objective frame, but as its reemergence at a new location in history with the full eruptive force of its original appearance. The "death" in Benjamin's mortalism is not itself a category, but is registered by the disruption of the living category, its fissure into life and survival and their mutual dependence. As such, it measures the space of transmission. The death interior to jeopardized life is externalized as the edge of this terrain of survival; at its origin the death-of-the-other, and at its limit the suicidal act that repeats that death and in turn exposes the surviving life, now dead, to its own displaced survival in a subsequent text.

Translation is one name for the possibility of this mortal displacement, and it is for this reason that a discussion of it concerns less the compatibility of different grammatical and referential systems than the respective vitality of temporally disparate expressions. Benjamin is clear that translation poses not only the problem of semantic transfer between languages, but translation through time, as well.

> Just as the manifestations of life are intimately connected with the living without being of importance to it, a translation issues from the original—not so much from its life as from its "afterlife" [*Überleben*]. For a translation comes later than the original, and since the important works of world literature never find their chosen translators at the time of their origin, their translation marks their stage of continued life [*das Stadium ihres Fortlebens*]. (*SW*, 1:254; *GS*, 4:10–11)

The task of the translator is not mere formal fidelity, but a certain kind of revitalization of the mortal text in a time after its original living utterance. These biological indicators are as unintentional as medical symptoms: as vital signs are to life, so is translation to original. Only translation does not give evidence of immediate vitality, but of posthumous survival. (The terms for this revenant state waver, from a distanced "afterlife" that then shifts to end as "continued life," for no single term will entirely do, since the domain of durable direct reference is the living domain.) It is this temporal, and not just grammatical, space between original and translation that bears the weight of Benjamin's exposition. "Even words with fixed meaning can undergo a maturing process [*Nachreife*]. The obvious tendentiousness of a writer's literary style may in time wither way; immanent tendencies are able to raise themselves newly from formed objects [*Geformten*]. What was young once can later seem hackneyed; what was once current may someday sound archaic" (*SW*, 1:256; *GS*, 4:12–13). These anachronisms in linguistic significance open the possibility of a historically responsible translation. The translator's sensitivity to archaic resonances in the original stands in metonymically for a historical posture that is prepared to register the intervening time as anachronisms in its own manifestation. The translation will emerge from within these distances that history has brought into the poem and resituate the original as a source of vital meaning in history precisely through the strains it introduces into the immediate vitality of the translation. The price the translation pays for this possibility is thus its own mortality: It lends an immediacy to the dead original that the original poem consumes; but in this process of surrender, renewed semantic potentials with their origins in the intervening history can appear. This is the *Aufgabe* of the translator, the task before him as his own abdication, his own giving out, what Nietzsche calls *zu Grunde gehen*, expiration. This gesture of expiration is Benjamin's version of theological inspiration: The death of present intention is the posthumous birth of the prior authority.

It was Nietzsche who maintained, famously or notoriously, that he belongs to those born posthumously. "Only the day after tomorrow belongs to me. Some are born posthumously," begins *The Antichrist* (*AC*, 125; *KSA*, 6:167). And *Ecce Homo* repeats the remark: "The time for me hasn't yet come: some are born posthumously" (*EH*, 259; *KSA*, 6:298). This is no merely vainglorious prediction that his own prescience must out, a self-confident assertion that he, Nietzsche, is ahead of his time. To be born posthumously is something other than to anticipate the future. Anticipation draws the future into the present along cognitive lines, but Nietzsche's claim transports the present authoritatively into the future. He speaks not of cognition, but of possession, of control of the day after tomorrow. In the extremity of its formulation, suspending birth in its emergency in a future tense beyond death in its finality, Nietzsche's aphorism seems to assert the demand to which a future translator's task of surrender would respond.

But in so doing, Nietzsche's braggadocio solicits Benjamin's later essay at its heart, dissolving the neo-Kantian argumentation that projects its theological terminology into hypothetically divine acts, pure language, and holy writ, and revealing its fundamentally subversive implications. For if Nietzsche's boast asserts an authority over the future for which there is no other license than this prior assertive posture, the task of the translator manifests a prior authority for which there is no other license than this subsequent subordinate posture. By rendering the authority of the original, the basis of its survival, as its implicit translatability, Benjamin both leaves that authority in place in the prior original, while making it entirely dependent on the translation that revivifies it in the present. Once the semantic priority of a document to its translation into another language (what is usually meant by "translation") has been reduced entirely to the sequential priority of past over present, Benjamin challenges this historical priority with the epistemological priority of the present over the past. The translation gets its authority exclusively from the life of the original, but the life of the original is known exclusively as this translated manifestation.

Thus the temporal disparity between original and translation that gives rise to anachronisms in the present is not merely one aspect of the translator's task, its historical or diachronic dimension; anachronism represents the defining movement of translation. The original and the translation *cannot* confront one another simultaneously, for in the present alone there is no difference that could distinguish them: "For any translation of a work originating in a specific moment [*Zeitpunkt*] of linguistic history represents, in regard to a specific aspect of its content [*Gehalt*], translation into all other languages" (*SW*, 1:258; *GS*, 4:15). The determinate time-point unifies the linguistically different translations it governs into identical relations to a determinate side of the original. Not the simultaneous contrasts between languages but the temporal contrast between what is prior and what is subsequent defines the relation of translation, and this exclusively.

From the standpoint of the translator, the original becomes origination itself, the process of discerning a past specificity that situates the present in history. Thus the strange irreversibility that characterizes Benjamin's description of translation; why, even though the essay prefaces a translation of Baudelaire, whose own translations of Poe might be seen to have contributed significantly to the American's literary genius, Benjamin must insist, "No translation, however good it may be, can have any significance as regards the original" (*SW*, 1:254; *GS*, 4:10). What is presented here as an interpretive premise, is in fact simply the corollary of the exclusively sequential definition of *original*. The impossibility of a backward influence from translation to original is the condition, not the result, of the original authority. Caught in the irreversible temporal disparity between an original authority and its manifestation as governing origin, a disparity mirrored as the survival of the original in the mortality of the translation, the translator takes up his task from a position outside not only his own specific language, but outside of language itself. "Unlike a work of literature, translation finds itself not in the center of the language forest [*Bergwald*] but on the outside facing it; it calls to the original without entering" (*SW*, 1:258; *GS*, 4:16). The translator orchestrates the introduction of the past original into the language of the present from an exclusively exterior position. As a posture that can regulate anachronisms, the translator occupies the gap between time and language, the pure exterior of history.

Exterior history is registered as the interim between original and translation, but its manifestation lies exclusively in the latter. The original becomes a terminus grounding the time between it and its subsequent translation, but its own historical situation, its own relation to its own language, is thereby neutralized. In a fundamental way, the original is not within history, but is a limit to history, appearing in the gesture of recognition that interrupts change and thereby fixes it in time. It is precisely because they lie on this unjustifiable boundary that the originals Benjamin invokes as illustration are insistently, and unusually for Benjamin, canonical. The heraldic display of great German translators, "Luther, Voss, and Schlegel" (*SW*, 1:258; *GS*, 4:16) reflects the unquestionable authority of the Bible, Homer, and Shakespeare, while Hölderlin's translations of Sophocles, whose tragic poetry Benjamin took to epitomize artistic production, are "prototypes [*Urbilder*] of the form." But none of these authorities is independently justified; none of them can offer the translator "a stop," protect him against the threat of becoming "lost in the bottomless depths of language" (*SW*, 1:262; *GS*, 4:21). Original and translation, manifesting the very process of origination, must strive at length for the authoritative status of holy writ. But even there they do not enjoy an eventual convergence, but at their vanishing point are still locked to their ambiguous subordinating gesture: "The interlinear version of the Scriptures is the prototype or ideal [*Urbild oder Ideal*] of all translations" (*SW*, 1:263; *GS*, 4:21). Not identity but the irreducible space between lines of text is the telos of translation. The task of the translator appears in the penumbra of a canonical authority its internal dynamic disrupts, calls into question, but for just that reason cannot escape, but only magnify.[3] That Holy Writ in fact offers Benjamin no ultimate referent is subtly indicated by the small equivocation—prototype or ideal—that denotes it. The alternative is not a plethora of synonyms but the final impossibility of entirely reconciling the antecedent prototype of inscription with the anticipated ideal of transcendence.

Nietzsche's claim to a posthumous status, uttered at the passively active site of the original, provokes an instability in that purely canonical authority of original speech that allowed Benjamin to disrupt the actively passive site of translation. Nietzsche's aphorism, for all its bravado, never claims a posthumous status for himself alone, but always by situating him among a ghostly posthumous company. "Some are born posthumously." The assertion of posthumous authority in the future is thus complicated by the implicit recognition of the posthumous authority of others in the present. In *Twilight of the Idols*, Nietzsche gives the characteristics by which this strange class can be recognized: "Posthumous men—like me, for instance—are not so well understood as timely [*zeitgemässe*] men, but they are better *heard*. More precisely: we are never understood—and *hence* our authority" (*TI*, 34; *KSA*, 6:61). By inserting himself as defining example, and then identifying the posthumous as those who are misunderstood, Nietzsche ensures the incomprehensibility of the definition. The authority of the posthumous is simply this incomprehension for as long as it continues. In the notebooks W II 1 from Fall 1887, we find a detailed record of that process of superior audition and inferior understanding in fragment 9[76].

> The <u>posthumous</u> (—*Difficulty understanding them; in a certain sense <u>never understood</u>*)
>   *Epicurus?*
>   *Schopenhauer*
>   *Stendhal*
>   *Napoleon*
>   *Goethe?*
>   *Shakespeare?*
>   *Beethoven?*

> *Machiavelli:*
> *The posthumous human beings are worse understood, but better heard than the timely. Or, more precisely: they are never understood: and hence their authority (comprendre c'est égaler).* (KSA, 12:375)

Here, Nietzsche does not include himself among the posthumous, and the first parenthesis marks an interpretive difficulty he himself implicitly shares. This difficulty is reflected into the question marks accompanying the provisional list of examples. The three unquestioned instances of Schopenhauer, Stendhal, and Napoleon neither define a tradition with an unambiguous founder nor license an unambiguous extension of the adjective "posthumous." The philosopher and the novelist may have labored in relative obscurity only to be posthumously recognized by Nietzsche, but the figure of Napoleon is an epitome of immediate recognition by his contemporary milieu. It can only be the contrast between that historical effectiveness and Nietzsche's own evaluation of his significance that sets Napoleon in this company, and when the list returns once again to specifically cultural figures, it modulates back from assertions to suggestions. Goethe, Shakespeare, and Beethoven were all celebrated in their own times, and if they, too, are posthumous men, their postmortem life must be different from that immediate recognition. That difference then moves into the name of Machiavelli, followed by a colon, as if not the historical author but the Renaissance stage stereotype were fulfilling its traditional framing role.[4] In the mouth of Machiavelli, the difference between contemporary and posthumous men is cast as a contrast between being better heard and worse—nay, never—understood. The aphorism, still in the third person, arises from the shade of Machiavelli to challenge Nietzsche himself. The genealogy of posthumous men is bound together by their audibility to Nietzsche; they are those whom he hears best, more clearly than he hears his contemporaries, but for just this reason they are also those whom he will never entirely understand. Their recognition, then, occurs outside of comprehension, which would reduce these signatures to the undifferentiated anonymity of the French saw. The posthumous are those who are heard *before* they are understood, and who register the priority of that audition in the incomprehension that suspends a final judgment on their lives. Authority emerges not from these signatures themselves, but from the question mark that shadows them.[5] It is the antithesis of an equalizing comprehension that Nietzsche evokes in a foreign language.

When, in the published version, Nietzsche inserts himself as defining example, he thus destabilizes the very possibility of a continuous philosophical tradition, whether hermetic or accessible. The posthumous company are not merely those whom *we* hear but don't understand, they are essentially those who are themselves sensitive to just this discrepancy. They do not constitute a concordant community; they hear one another well by recognizing one another precisely as in a certain sense incomprehensible. If the reader is helpless before a published aphorism that uses itself to exemplify incomprehensible authority, the fragmentary background shows Nietzsche is no less so himself. He, too, can make no claim to know the criteria that included him, to have understood the examples he has heard. The test lies not with Nietzsche, but with us, with our sensitivity to an audition that would precede and support this declared incomprehensibility. "Some are born posthumously." Not a mere boast, not a stable, if hidden, alternative tradition into which Nietzsche can self-consciously insert himself. Rather, a displacement of his signature out of the tradition of autonomous authorship and its congruence of living intention and historical significance into a precarious existence dependent on a later time. Nietzsche's posthumous birth depends on his own eccentric reanimation of a precedent company; the originality that demands a posthumous audience is simultaneously this ex post facto readjustment of the tradition of signatory authority on the basis of this incomprehension.

By embodying the paradox of a dependent authority, Nietzsche undermines the smooth functioning of the canonical authority that enabled Benjamin's theory of translation. So it is not surprising to find the philosopher involved in Benjamin's later reconsideration of these matters, when in a draft for a radio presentation from 1935 or 1936 he takes up the question of translation again. From its French title to its dialogic form to its ambiguous signature,[6] this short text adopts an entirely more circumspect attitude toward translation and its possibility than did the early preface. "La Traduction—le pour et le contra" begins with the narrative of a small urban disappointment.

> As I was passing an open-air bookstall a few days ago, I came across a French translation of a German philosophical book. Leafing through it, as one does with books on the quais, I looked for the passages which had often engrossed me—What a surprise. The passages were not there.
> You mean, you didn't find them?

> Oh yes, I found them all right. But when I looked them in the face, I had the awkward feeling that they no more recognized me than I did them.
> Which philosopher are you talking about?
> I'm talking about Nietzsche. (SW, 3:249; GS, 6:157–58)

Like an exile glimpsing unexpectedly a prior acquaintance from his homeland, only to discover on accosting him a local and a stranger, the narrator encounters the translation in a moment of discomfiting confusion. The familiar passages in Nietzsche, known to him from frequent and extensive consideration in the original, are missing from the translation. Or if not missing, then estranged from it. The confusion does not testify to any specific semantic inaccuracy, but to a global distortion. "But what disconcerted me about the passages that had been familiar to me was not a deficiency in the translation but something which may even have been its merit: the horizon and the world around the translated text had itself been substituted, had become French" (SW, 3:249; GS, 6:158). Not the translator's failure but rather his success in situating the original in the new grammatical environment is what alienates the narrator from this translation. For the passages that were familiar to the narrator are those that already exhibited a certain resistance to German in the original. Where Benjamin's early theory of translation condensed into anachronism in the translation, this reconsideration of Nietzsche locates a complementary difficulty in the original: neologisms.

> Do you really believe that neologisms of the kind which distinguish Nietzsche's language have genuine intellectual significance?
> Intellectual, because historical. When Nietzsche brilliantly misuses the German language, he is taking revenge on the fact that a German linguistic tradition never really came into being—except within the thin stratum of literary expression. He took double the liberties allowed by language, to rebuke it for permitting them. And the misuse of the German language is, finally, a critique of the incompleteness [*Unfertigkeit*] of the German person. (SW, 3:250; GS, 6:158)

What *traduction* fails to preserve is the specific external relation of the original inscription to its collective historical conditions. The "brilliant misuse" of German perpetrated by Nietzsche is exemplified in his unprecedented terms, which manifest a freedom that reproaches the deficient authority of his tradition. The originality of his text is not origination itself, but a denunciatory tactic in his own struggle with specific precedence. "How can this linguistic situation be translated into another?" (*SW*, 3:250; *GS*, 6:158).

The complementary dynamics of posthumous revitalization that reside *in potentia* in both Benjamin's and Nietzsche's thought are thus each riven by an insurmountable antagonism, the conflicting authorities of origin and actuality. Anachronism invokes the former, neologism the latter, and between them there is no neutral ground. The authority of origins is authority over the force of the actual, while the authority of actuality is authority over the force of origins. Thinking is realized in this field not as disinterested comprehension but as a tactical engagement. "Let us not deceive ourselves: translation is, above all, a technique" (*SW*, 3:250; *GS*, 6:158). Only by making "the fact of the different linguistic situation one of its themes" can translation, here standing in for the juncture of reading and writing, for thinking, be "effective, a component of its own world" (*SW*, 3:250; *GS*, 6:159). Neither translation nor original have the final say, but in the tactical identification with distinct linguistic situations, different origins governing new potentials in the actual present can be revealed. The actual present appears first in the reflection of the past thrown by the threat of future oblivion. But counter to this, as the hope for salvation, the potential future is the reflection of the present thrown by past promise.

The mature relation between Benjamin and Nietzsche rests paradoxically on their common antagonistic posture toward their cultural surroundings. This posture can support a historical relation only when it is understood at a philosophical level. Not substantial sympathy, but the tactical analogies between these two radicals produced by their equally destructive orientations toward their respective cultural environments licenses the comparison. Both Nietzsche and Benjamin are thinkers of the *agon*, which is to say, practitioners of antagonistic reflection. At this level, they are antagonistic toward one another not out of distaste or even disagreement, but in principle, as the consequence of a shared intellectual perspective oriented not on consensus, but on victory and defeat. That is to say, consensus for both Nietzsche and Benjamin does not testify to mutual intellectual recognition, but registers defeat as *complicity*, and collaboration not as conscious effort toward a commonly acknowledged goal, but as submission to the unacknowledged forces conditioning human intentions. To agree is to be in thrall to something outside oneself; and so as Benjamin's relation to Nietzsche continues through the 1930s, we cannot expect to find it creeping toward consensus. Nietzsche inhabits *The Arcades Project* and *On the Concept of History* in his nineteenth-century attire, coining his empty terms at the exemplary boundary of bourgeois integrity. As such, his name and the doctrine of eternal return associated with it will mark for Benjamin an apex of historical mystification. *Thinking the idea of the eternal recurrence once more in the nineteenth century, Nietzsche becomes the figure on whom mythic doom is now carried out. For the essence of mythic happenings is recurrence* (*SW*, 4:403–4; *GS*, 1:1234). Benjamin denounces history, and to the extent that Nietzsche is a part of history, Benjamin denounces Nietzsche. But behind this expressed denunciation lies a secret, guiltless complicity, more difficult to extricate from his fragmentary expressions, but more relevant to our own futures than any disagreement between them. This complicity is also deposited into the formula of an eternal return, a "new and always the same" that freezes Benjamin's historical instant at its limits, and in so doing anticipates more fortunate potentials in our own.

CONSPIRACY

Benjamin's politics is a politics of weakness. Though his adult life was marked by exile, isolation, and impoverishment, Benjamin's sympathy for the poor and downtrodden antedates his own marginalization. Even as a privileged Berlin child he was shocked by the abysmal differences between rich and poor, and repulsed by any acceptance of misery as a natural fate. Unsurprising, then, that his mature political posture would champion the rejected and despised victims of history. Yet Benjamin's politics of weakness is not the mere expression of personal sympathies and attitudes. The political orientation he displays is the consequence of his original theoretical posture, his commitment to an absolute measure of truth and the ultimate transience of things. His politics is more than simply compassion for the oppressed. It is an acknowledgment of the inevitability of death. The politics of weakness registers the weakness of all politics, politics as the name for human being's essential impotence over against history. From the standpoint of eternity, the victory of sovereign power is temporary and doomed. Thus the destitute and forgotten display the inhuman truth of history far more accurately than do the lords and rulers of this world, the victorious class in history.

This nihilistic perspective on the impermanence of human concerns conditions a much more unsettling aspect of Benjamin's political orientation, one that seems to be in profound tension with his solidarity with the oppressed: his affinity for reactionary political attitudes. "Hark and be amazed!" he writes to Scholem in 1924, in the same letter that first mentions his admiration for the Bolshevik Asja Lacis.

> Yesterday I subscribed to the *Action française*, the royalist paper managed by Léon Daudet and—primarily—by Charles Maurras. It is written in a wonderful style. As infinitely flawed as the foundations of their politics surely are in many essential respects, their perspective ultimately seems to me to be the only one from which it is possible to view the details of German politics without being stupefied [*verdummen*]. (*CB*, 244; *GB*, 2:468)

Benjamin expects Scholem to be confused by his subscription to such a monarchist and anti-Semitic journal, edited by prominent anti-Dreyfusards. His explanation is neither that he perversely sympathizes with its political intentions nor that he wishes to understand strategically an enemy's arguments. Rather, Benjamin finds in the French Catholic reactionary perspective on Germany a standpoint from which the facile accommodations endemic to more ideologically congenial commentary can be discerned. The great ideological risk for Benjamin is not deviance from a party line but complicity with the status quo. He approaches reactionary positions never in their triumphant manifestations but only when, superseded by historical developments, they remain stubbornly uncooperative with their surroundings. *All* positions that are implacably hostile to current conditions, no matter the alternative for which they campaign, have some value for revolutionary politics and are preferable to any revisionist compromise.[7] "Methodological extremism," a focus on the "borderline notion," is, as Samuel Weber has shown in detail, also what drew Benjamin to the work of right-wing political theorist Carl Schmitt.[8] Benjamin never mitigated this extremism, even as his relation to Europe's accelerating collapse grew more tactical in the 1930s. Until the end of his life his political credo remained, as he put it in a 1926 letter to Scholem, "immer radikal, niemals konsequent," always radical, never consistent (*CB*, 300; *GB*, 3:159).

Benjamin's historical rather than sociological understanding of the status quo, his view that the living and not just the oppressors are the enemy, is what distinguishes his politics of weakness from Georg Lukács's dialectical critique of bourgeois thought in *History and Class Consciousness*. Benjamin was deeply influenced by Lukács's book, which he encountered during the fateful summer of 1924 on Capri as he wrote *The Origin of German Trauerspiel*. "The book itself is very important, especially for me" (*CB*, 244; *GB*, 2:469), he insisted in a letter to Scholem at the time, and some weeks later he elaborated.

> Lukács's book astonished me in that by proceeding from political considerations into epistemology he arrives at principles that are, at least in part, and perhaps not entirely to the extent I first assumed, extremely familiar or validating to me. (*CB*, 248; *GB*, 2:483)

The slight disillusion that tempers Benjamin's enthusiasm testifies to an evolving understanding of Lukács's position. *History and Class Consciousness* is able to perform a dialectical critique of the "antinomies of bourgeois thought" (*HCC*, 100; *GKB*, 209) because, unlike the tradition of philosophy that bequeathed him his method, Lukács has reached "the site from which to resolve all these problems and also to exhibit concretely the 'we' which is the subject of history" (*HCC*, 145; *GKB*, 262). This "we" is both an epistemological first-person and a determinate site in the class struggle: the proletariat. "The self-understanding of the proletariat is therefore simultaneously the objective understanding of the nature of society" (*HCC*, 149; *GKB*, 267). The "standpoint of the proletariat" makes possible a dialectical resolution of the epistemological aporias between subject and object precisely because it embodies the transformative praxis that overcomes this fundamental opposition. "Since consciousness here is not the knowledge of an opposed object but is the self-consciousness of the object *the act of consciousness overthrows the objective form of its object*" (*HCC*, 178; *GKB*, 309).

The volatilization of the collective first-person perspective in a notion of practical activity is what Benjamin found so compelling in Lukács's account. "At least it is clear to me how in Lukács this assertion [i.e., that any insight into theory presupposes practice] has a hard philosophical core and is anything but bourgeois-demagogical claptrap" (*CB*, 248; *GB* 2:483). At the same time, it did not escape Benjamin's notice that Lukács's "standpoint of the proletariat" was burdened by a difficult ambiguity itself. As a partial antagonistic perspective in a present still objectively dominated by the property-holding class, this volatile standpoint escapes epistemological relativism only with reference to a future transformation of ontological scope, a transformation in which truth itself "acquires a wholly novel aspect."

> When theory and practice are united it becomes possible to change reality and when this happens the absolute and its "relativistic" counterpart will have played their historical role for the last time. For as the result of these changes we shall see the disappearance of that reality which the absolute and the relative express in like manner. (HCC, 189; GKB, 326)

To the extent that it embodies and does not simply anticipate truth, the true "standpoint of the proletariat" does not exist in the present but will appear only in the future.[9] The concrete "we" in which something like that truth occurs right now is thus no more identical with the extant proletarian class than it was with the idealized "youth" of Benjamin's original political engagement. Lukács neutralizes the radicalness of his philosophical politics by depositing his insights into partisan categories already at work in society. It is this limitation that Benjamin intends to explore.

> As soon as possible [Benjamin concludes] I want to study Lukács's book and I would be quite mistaken if in the oppositional confrontation with the Hegelian concepts and assertions of the dialectic against communism the foundations of my own nihilism did not become manifest. (CB, 248; GB 2:483)

The foundations of Benjamin's nihilism rest on the self-referential skepticism toward the transient reality in which it participates. The "we" that in Lukács embodies the subject of history has no prior visibility in Benjamin but is precisely what is at stake in the unprecedented moment of its mutual recognition.

In practice this meant that for Benjamin, the model for ideological collaboration was not solidarity with a revolutionary party pursuing a common program but participation in a revolutionary journal whose pages could accommodate various individual orientations. His work with Bertolt Brecht, for instance, revolved around plans for a magazine called *Krise und Kritik*[10] (*Crisis and Criticism*), a journal that would "have a political character.... It stands on the foundation of class struggle," as he wrote in a prospectus in the fall of 1930. "Nonetheless the journal has no party-political character. In particular it does not represent a proletarian journal, an organ of the proletariat" (GS, 6:619). The proletariat needs no theoretical advocate; the reality of class antagonism already conditions all genuine social activity, so that the collective work on the journal itself would manifest the solidarity that could contribute to a revolutionary transformation of society. Formulating the theoretical program of that solidarity is an ex post facto exercise. Hence the supplemental volumes (*Beihefte*) appearing three or four times a year as a constitutive part of *Krise und Kritik*. "These supplemental volumes are designed to summarize the critical and theoretical foundations of the collective work that naturally in the course of each number can only develop gradually and gropingly" (*GS*, 6:619).

The revolutionary commitment displayed by a politics of weakness is unsecured by revolutionary theory, which has a subordinate and reactive role in political struggle. Benjamin's revolutionary stance is not the positive result of sociological insight or moral sympathy but emerges from the fundamentally antagonistic character of historical time as survival, the fact that there is no neutral perspective between the living, the dead, and those not yet born. What is not resistant to the self-conception of the living present is complicit with it, and no more complicit than when it imagines itself to be objectively describing the present moment in history. Collaboration in the present on behalf of the vanished past and unprecedented future is thus not only not the practical application of a recognizable theory but is only intermittently recognizable as such. Such work always has an aspect of *conspiracy*. The professional revolutionary conspirators of the nineteenth century, the *Berufsverschwörer* in their demimonde of illegal publications and spontaneous rebellions, form a necessary counterpart to the theoretical analysis of bourgeois society. "The activities of a professional conspirator like Blanqui certainly do not presuppose any belief in progress," Benjamin wrote in his late collection of aphorisms "Central Park." "They merely presuppose a determination to do away with present injustice" (*SW*, 4:188; *GS* 1:687). And Convolute V of *The Arcades Project* gathers together under the rubric of "Conspiracies, *Compagnonnage*" (*AP*, 603; *GS* 5:745) a host of observations on nineteenth-century journeymen's organizations, police spies, and *agents provocateurs*, with an emphasis on the secret signs of recognition and the tangled inversions of alliance and betrayal endemic to a conspiratorial milieu.

The priority of practice over theory and the consequent ideological dislocations that come together in a conspiratorial politics of weakness are reflected in Benjamin's personal friendships, as well. Benjamin's circle of associates—among them Bertolt Brecht and Gershom Scholem, Hannah Arendt and Theodor W. Adorno—were unusually incompatible among themselves. These personal antipathies could often lead to misunderstandings, since Benjamin was in fact neither unsympathetic to any given friend nor uncommitted in his alliances but rather conversing at a conspiratorial level on behalf of the future triumph of the forgotten past, a level by nature beneath immediate recognizability. In a 1934 letter to Gretel Karplus, with whom he was particularly intimate, Benjamin came as close as he ever did to describing this conspiratorial posture. In exile and broke, he was considering relocating to Bertolt Brecht's refuge in Skovsbostrand, Denmark. Gretel, still in Berlin, thought this dangerous, and was moved to express her worries. "I view your move to Denmark with some trepidation," she wrote to him,

> and today I must touch on a most delicate subject. I would prefer not to do this in writing but I feel compelled to. . . . We have hardly ever talked about B[recht]. Admittedly I have not known him as long as you have, but I have very great reservations about him, . . . At the moment it is less important for me to discuss him in detail than to say that I sometimes have the feeling that somehow you are under his influence, which represents a great danger for you. . . . I know I am risking a great deal, perhaps even our whole friendship, by writing this letter, and only our long separation could have moved me to speak out. Forgive me, if you can, if I have gone too far. (GAB, 154–55)

Benjamin responded to the solicitous spirit of Gretel's warning, venturing to characterize the fundamentally decentered aspect of his intellectual personality involved in his productive relationships. "Not everything that you say is incorrect, but not everything that you say speaks against my journey to B[recht]," he writes.

> I'll touch on the most important question. What you say about his influence on me reminds me of a significant and continually repeated constellation in my life. My friends thought F. C. Heinle exercised such an influence on me. . . .
>
> In the economy of my existence a few specific relationships do indeed play a role that allows me to maintain something at the polar opposite of my original being. These relationships have always provoked more or less violent protests on the part of those closest to me, for example a much less cautiously formulated objection to my current relationship with B[recht] by Gerhard Scholem. In such a case I can do little more than ask my friends to have confidence that the rewards of these connections, whose dangers are obvious, will become clear. You in particular must realize that my life, as well as my thought, is moving towards extreme positions. The distance that it asserts in this way, the freedom to move against each other things and ideas that are considered irreconcilable, achieves its character only through danger. A danger that generally seems obvious to my

friends only in the form of those "dangerous" relationships. (*GB*, 4:440–41)

Crucial here is that the constellation Benjamin describes is not a matter of direct influence, however much it may appear so to the friends outside of it. The connection to figures as incompatible with his original outlook as Brecht and Heinle does not undermine Benjamin's indigenous attitudes but expands the field within which they operate, extends them toward their limits by bringing them into contact with intellectual content otherwise inaccessible to him. The process has its dangers, Benjamin admits. But the obvious dangers unsympathetic collaborators pose to Benjamin's theoretical integrity are really actually superficial, he suggests. "In a friend one should have one's best enemy," Zarathustra had counseled (*TSZ*, 56; *KSA*, 4:71), and the real danger lies deeper. Not falling under the sway of an antithetical attitude but failing to move through it to a communicable position—this is the risk Benjamin's always radical, never consistent posture runs.

In the event, Benjamin's stay in Skovsbostrand turned out to be difficult. His differences with Brecht emerged in the context of his essay on Kafka, which he shared with Brecht between chess matches in those summer weeks. "Yesterday," Benjamin recounted, "he suddenly referred to the essay. With a somewhat abrupt and forced transition in the conversation, he remarked that I, too, could not entirely escape the charge of writing in diary form [*tagebuchartigen*], in the style of Nietzsche" (*SW*, 2:786; *GS*, 6:527). Without elucidating the reference to Nietzsche, Benjamin has Brecht exemplify this stylistic weakness with the Kafka essay, which fails to make the author recognizable in his actual milieu. His summary: "You cannot make progress with depth. Depth is simply a dimension; it is just depth" (*SW*, 2:786; *GS*, 6:528). Benjamin's self-defense repositions the daybook characterization Brecht had labeled Nietzschean, while not relinquishing that characterization entirely: "I end up telling Brecht that descending into the depths is my way of journeying to the antipodes. In my essay on Kraus I had in fact managed to arrive there. I knew that the Kafka piece was less successful. I could not refute the criticism that it was a diary-like set of notes" (*SW*, 2:786; *GS*, 6:528). Benjamin transforms Brecht's objection to the Kafka essay—not the irrelevant *direction* of its aphoristic plunges into the depths, but their insufficient *extension*, that they don't emerge on the other side is what justifies the epithet "diary-like." Both Brecht and Benjamin find the Kafka essay insufficiently objective; but for Brecht this means a narcissistic emphasis on the critic's own subjective perceptions, while for Benjamin this means the critic's less-than-total objectification in the literary work. "Franz Kafka" remains suspended in the daybook dimension of Benjamin's writing because, despite being anchored to the writer's deathday, it is unable to emerge at the antipodes, where Kafka's implicit response could appear.[11]

In accepting the reproach, Benjamin drops the reference to Nietzsche. It survives in his account with the force of a remembered detail in an interlocutor's remarks, the pivot of someone else's abrupt conversational segue. For Brecht, Nietzsche stands in for an ultimate disengagement from the social conditions of thinking. In a small poetic fragment on Zarathustra Brecht wrote around this time, in the context of his "Studies," it is not Nietzsche's immediate hostility to political egalitarianism, his scornful dismissals of socialist resentments that Brecht emphasizes, but the proximity of his expression to the ineffectual isolation of madness.

ÜBER NIETZSCHES "ZARATHUSTRA"

Du zarter Geist, daß dich nicht Lärm verwirre
Bestiegst du solche Gipfel, daß dein Reden
Für jeden nicht bestimmt, nun misset jeden:
Jenseits der Märkte liegt nur noch die Irre.

Ein weißer Gischt sprang aus verschlammter Woge!
Was dem gehört, der nicht dazu gehört

Im Leeren wird die Nüchternheit zur Droge.

[ON NIETZSCHE'S "ZARATHUSTRA"

You tender spirit, so noise will not confuse you
You ascended to such summits, that your speeches
Not meant for everyone, now miss everyone:
Beyond the markets lies nothing but madness.

A white spray burst from a polluted wave!
What belongs to him who does not belong to it

In the void sobriety itself becomes a drug.][12]

Brecht mobilizes Nietzsche's allegorical topography, the marketplaces and mountains through which Zarathustra wanders, and the exalted natural metaphors in which he speaks, to characterize a writing that remains true to itself only by renouncing any communicative encounter with its contemporary environment.[13] The profundity which is a dimension of its own is here congruent with an exaltation that leaves the world behind. In both cases, a productive engagement with real historical conditions is avoided.

These associations hover over the daybook characterization without entirely mastering it. By dropping the name Nietzsche from his reply, Benjamin leaves ambiguous the extent to which his self-defense would also defend the philosopher. Perhaps the comparison seemed so misguided to Benjamin that he feels no need to address it; perhaps the comparison is so self-evident to Benjamin that he feels no need to confirm it. And precisely because Nietzsche's name appears at this undecidable limit in Benjamin's expressive affinity with Brecht, that name successfully characterizes the conspiratorial dimension of his politics of weakness. Throughout the 1930s, as Benjamin constructs his archaic history of the nineteenth century, he denounces a German Nietzsche at a limit of complicity with his historical epoch. But behind the back of this denunciation, and at the historical limit to his own present, Benjamin conspires with an exiled Nietzsche against his own conditions of articulation.

ETERNAL RETURN

Throughout the final years of their lives, both Nietzsche and Benjamin were engaged in the development of magna opera that would never achieve finished form. In both cases, that is to say, their philosophies are tied in an irreducible way to the archive, demanding the discerning tact that bears reading into the volatile textual environment of provisional, nonbinding, and yet intimate and immediate traces that archives harbor. For Nietzsche's legacy, the monumentalizing effort that constituted an imposing *Will to Power* from the many notebooks his madness left exposed to posterity exemplifies just the lack of that tact and discernment a scholarly archive requires, for a sensitivity to the fracture between published assertion and provisional *Nachlaß* is the sine qua non of a serious engagement with the philosopher. Benjamin, by contrast, has not suffered such indignity, and *The Arcades Project* exists in a philologically scrupulous form. This does not make it easier to read, of course. Like any archive, *The Arcades Project* hosts fragmentary material traces that have not yet coalesced into a durable, signable work, and to return to such traces is to interrogate the self-identity a work represents. Moreover, in the case of *The Arcades Project* these traces are themselves largely citations Benjamin has transcribed from other works. To the incursions into authorial authority caused by incompleteness comes its dilution in plurality. It might seem, then, that *The Arcades Project* is unreadable just to the extent that it resists being synthesized into a sovereign intended meaning.

Such a conclusion would be unduly pessimistic, however. *The Arcades Project* is legible when a reader understands that this mass of material produces Benjamin's signature in several displaced forms, at greater or lesser proximity to the actual material composing it, as potential books on the poet Baudelaire or the metropolis Paris.[14] No one of these virtual books can claim an ultimate positive status, but each represents provisional organizational strategies that serve regulative purposes. Despite the teleological implications of a "Project" or the suggestion of significant closure in the German "*Werk*" (Benjamin himself tended to refer to it with the more open-ended "*Passagenarbeit*" [GB, 3:379 et passim]), the arcades material presents us with a fluid and refracting field within which fundamental notions of Benjamin's enter into new and unexpected configurations. At the heart of this field is an idiosyncratic notion of temporality, and it is in Benjamin's attempts to articulate this elusive time that Nietzsche plays a primary, orienting role.

While making his first notes on what would become *The Arcades Project,* Benjamin attempted to clarify the temporality involved in his vision. *Modernity, the time of hell,* he wrote. *The punishments of hell are always the newest thing going in this domain. What is at issue is not that "the same thing happens over and over" (much less is it a question here of eternal return), but rather that the face of the world, the colossal head, precisely in what is newest never alters— that this "newest" remains, in every respect, the same* (AP, 842–43; GS, 5:1010–11). The infernal time of modernity is characterized by a paradoxical conjunction of novelty and stasis. The sadistic inventiveness displayed by the tortures of the damned converges with the endless suffering that is their effect to bring about "the time of hell," a time not merely hopeless but perverse. Punitive innovations are perpetually initiating interminable agonies; the elimination of change in the future does not ensure the endurance of continuity with the past. This satanic vision is the peculiar shape that time takes in the modern city, and Benjamin is here anxious to distinguish it from an eternal return of the same, which implies a retrospective identity that the "newest" by definition eliminates.

But if this initial conceptualization of the "new and always the same" (*das Neue und Immergleiche*) opposes the notion to a notion of the eternal return, Benjamin soon came to realize that the appearance of an exclusive contradiction here rested on a far too simple intuition of time. A temporality in which each instant breaks entirely from what precedes it while projecting permanent monotony into what follows it cannot be understood in terms of a straightforward sequence of variation and repetition. Nor is the eternal return in its Nietzschean version a simple denial of the appearance of innovation. Far from being logically opposed, these two formulae both point toward the edge of what is thinkable at all, and the difficulty of reconciling eternal return with the new and always the same defines the very elusiveness of the actual ontology underlying bourgeois ideological self-evidence. *The dreaming collective knows no history*, Benjamin noted shortly afterward.

> Events pass before it as always identical and always new. The sensation of the newest and most modern is, in fact, as much a dream formation of events as the "eternal return of the same." The perception of space that corresponds to this perception of time is superposition. Now, as these formations dissolve within the enlightened consciousness, political-theological categories arise to take their place. And it is only within the purview of these categories, which bring the flow of events to a standstill, that history forms, at the interior of this flow, as crystalline constellation. (AP, 854; GS 5:1023)

A strange tolerance for manifest contradictions is characteristic of dreams, so that Benjamin here uses the idea of a collective dream to reconcile the intuitive contradiction between the retrospective constancy of an eternal return of the same and the perennial sensation of the unprecedentedly new that is typical of the nineteenth-century bourgeoisie. These conceptions merge in a complex simultaneity that figures as spatial superimposition. Only when these formal extremes—an absolute present of newness and an absolute eternity of sameness—are brought to awareness in their full political-theological force can this mystified conjunction be revealed as the petrified image of actual history beneath the ordinary flow of events.

This knot of ideas shows up briefly in the first of the exposés of *The Arcades Project* that Benjamin wrote for the *Zeitschrift für Sozialforschung* (*Journal of Social Research*) in 1935, though in an abbreviated form. "Newness is a quality independent of the use value of the commodity," Benjamin writes there.

> It is the origin of the semblance that belongs inalienably to images produced by the collective unconscious. It is the quintessence of that false consciousness whose indefatigable agent is fashion. This semblance of the new is reflected, like one mirror in another, in the semblance of the ever recurrent. The product of this reflection is the phantasmagoria of "cultural history," in which the bourgeoisie enjoys its false consciousness to the full. (*AP*, 11; *GS*, 5:55)

What had been the dreaming collective in the note is here a collective unconscious, standing in for a dimension of collective subjectivity divorced from the instrumental rationality implicit in the concept of use value. Newness, the fact that an object was recently produced and differs from what went before, is logically irrelevant to whether or not it fulfills its purpose in the present, and the importance attached to newness in the milieu of commodities testifies to an irrational aspect at work there. So too the ever recurrent (*immer wieder Gleichen*) participates in an eternity that dost tease us out of thought and gestures past all comprehensive, rational horizons. The newness and the permanence of an eternal return confront one another in their respective irrationalities as ideological antitheses, at whose contradictory intersection the self-congratulatory image of bourgeois cultural history appears.

The recourse to a collective unconscious was one of the aspects of this exposé that deeply troubled Theodor W. Adorno when Benjamin submitted the text to him. In his detailed response, Adorno urged him to abandon such cloudy mass psychology with its mystical Jungian atmosphere, which he thought both obscured the dialectical precision of Benjamin's reflections and preempted an essential aspect of the original insight: the infernal character of this temporal constellation. Benjamin accepted in large part Adorno's critique, though he did insist that his notion of dreams, even if it had not been elaborated fully in the exposé, was far from an idealistic internalization of the contradictions at work in the nineteenth century. "The dialectical image does not draw a copy of the dream," he replied; "—it was never my intention to assert this. But it does seem to me to contains the instances, the moment consciousness dawns as one awakens, and indeed to produce its likeness only from these passages just as a constellation [*Sternbild*] emerges from these luminous points" (*CB*, 508; *GB*, 5:145). Not consciousness as a condition—whether collective or individual, manifest or repressed—but the ungovernable passage between radically different modes of consciousness; this is the figure that reveals the eternal return in the phantasmic experience of constant newness.

The eternal return of the same is in fact an old conception of Benjamin's. "For the 'Eternal Return of the Same,' as it stonily prevails over the most intimately varied feelings, is the sign of fate, whether it is self-identical in the life of many or repeats itself in the individual," he had written as long ago as 1922 in "Goethe's *Elective Affinities*" (*SW*, 1:307; *GS*, 2:137). And in the *Origin of German Trauerspiel* Benjamin had repeated the characterization of fate as eternal return when discussing the witching hour and the spirit world (*Geisterstunde und Geisterwelt*).

> Now since fate, itself the true order of eternal recurrence, can only be described as temporal in an indirect, that is parasitical sense, its manifestations seek out the temporal dimension. They stand in the narrow frame of midnight, an opening in the passage of time, in which the same ghostly image constantly reappears. (*OT*, 135; *GS*, 1:313-14)

The eternal return testifies to a fatal temporality that is not indigenous to ordinary sequential awareness. By calling it parasitical, Benjamin refers to his own earlier discussion of fate in the seminal essay "Fate and Character" from 1919. Fate there is the "guilt-nexus of the living" (*Schuldzusammenhang des Lebendigen*) (*SW*, 1:204; *GS*, 2:175), an enigmatic formula[15] that conceives the universality of individual deaths conditioning immortal collective life as an impersonal denunciatory judgment. "The guilt-nexus is temporal in a very inauthentic way," Benjamin writes,

> very different in its kind and measure from the time of redemption, or of music, or of truth. . . . It is not an autonomous time, but is parasitically dependent on the time of a higher, less natural life. It has no present, for fateful moments exist only in bad novels, and it knows past and future only in curious variations. (*SW*, 1:204; *GS*, 2:175-76)

The time of a "higher, less natural life" that conditions the mortal individual's imbrication in the collective existence he or she survives and is survived by is the "true order of the eternal return," which reveals itself to be at the very foundation of Benjamin's conceptions.

What is new in *The Arcades Project* then is not the eternal return but just an emphasis on newness. Indeed a large part of the attraction the Parisian arcades exercised on Benjamin came from their historical character as the latest thing in a bygone era. What the nineteenth century self-consciously introduced to the world—iron construction, gas lighting, railroads—is the focus of the preliminary set of notes "The Ring of Saturn or, Some Remarks on Iron Construction," for instance. In the convolutes of material that make up the bulk of *The Arcades Project*, the motif of newness recurs constantly. In convolute B, which gathers quotations and observations on fashion and mortality, the transience of mode organizes the collection. The inherent emphasis in fashion on being up to date undermines any organic link to the past. *A definitive perspective on fashion follows solely from the consideration that to each generation the one immediately preceding it seems the most radical anti-aphrodisiac imaginable (AP, 64; GS, 5:113)*. At the same time, the ceaseless expiration of old styles and appearance of new make fashion an image of the deaths that are constantly passing through immortal life. Benjamin's two epigraphs to the convolute triangulate this confluence of death and permanence. *Fashion: Madam Death! Madam Death!* from a dialogue by Leopardi evokes the solicitous affinity popular taste has for mortality, while Balzac's aphorism *Nothing dies; all is transformed* (*AP*, 62; *GS*, 5:110) provides the contrasting perspective of immortality. *The epigraph from Balzac is well suited to unfolding the temporality of hell: to showing how this time does not recognize death and how fashion mocks death (AP, 66; GS, 5:115)*, Benjamin remarks, and the resurrection of this infernal motif shows that this immortal transformation is close to the eternal return.

Convolute S, as well, concerns itself with the new. In reflecting on art nouveaux and novelty, Benjamin is moved to quote the long passage from Kafka's novel *The Trial* in which the painter Titorelli sells Joseph K. a host of identical paintings of a barren heath. And here we find a revised version of Benjamin's early note on the dreaming collective.

> *The dreaming collective knows no history. Events pass before it as always identical and always new. The sensation of the newest and most modern is, in fact, just as much a dream formation of events as the eternal return of the same. The perception of space that corresponds to this perception of time is the interpenetrating and superposed transparency of the world of the flâneur. This feeling of space, this feeling of time, presided at the birth of modern feuilletonism.*
> "Dream Collective" (*AP* 546; *GS* 5:678–79)

New and always the same is here the opposite of historical consciousness, a reactive awareness that cannot situate itself in time. This awareness shares with the eternal return of the same an antihistorical extremity that pushes it out of the sequential temporal form of ordinary consciousness. The flâneur and the feuilleton, two examples of unsystematic reactivity to the immediate historical present, serve to illustrate the form of mystification that hosts these limit-temporalities.

The challenge Benjamin faced in *The Arcades Project*, one he initially resolved in the idea of a dream collective, was to integrate this sense of transient historical newness he discerned in the experience of the nineteenth-century bourgeoisie with the older concept of an eternally recurring fate from his political-theological speculations of the 1920s. Adorno's reaction to the exposé of 1935 showed Benjamin that this oneiric resolution was open to serious misinterpretations and raised as many questions as it answered. Then, late in 1937, Benjamin came across a book that would change dramatically his representational strategy with regard to this concept of fatal temporality at the heart of his late work. "In the last few weeks I've been studying the writings of Blanqui," Benjamin writes to his friend Fritz Lieb just before Christmas 1937, "to which I owe great insights" (*GB*, 5:631). The book he was reading was Blanqui's last, *L'Éternité par les astres*, written by the professional conspirator and radical revolutionary in a dank cell in the notorious island-prison of Taureau, where he was held to prevent his leading the Paris Commune in 1871. The work is a piece of cosmological speculation, and its central hypothesis, ten years before Nietzsche would write *Thus Spoke Zarathustra*, is an eternal return of the same. "Every human being is thus eternal at every second of his or her existence. What I write at this moment in a cell of the Fort du Taureau I have written and shall write throughout all eternity—at a table, with a pen, clothed as I am now, in circumstances like these."[16] Benjamin's discovery of this alternate version of an eternal return of the same immediately amplified its role in his conceptions. What in the exposé of 1935 had been one insight among many became, by the time Benjamin rewrote the exposé in French in 1939, the culminating point of the introduction and the centerpiece of the conclusion.

Blanqui's book shows Benjamin that Nietzsche's eternal return of the same is not simply a particular doctrine specific to that philosopher but is something "in the air" at the time.

> In the idea of the eternal recurrence, the historicism of the nineteenth century capsizes. As a result, every tradition, even the most recent, becomes the legacy of something that has already run its course in the immemorial night of the ages. Tradition henceforth assumes the

form of a phantasmagoria in which ur-history enters the scene in ultramodern get-up. (AP, 116; GS, 5:174)

Moreover, the political implications that Nietzsche resisted were borne into the doctrine by Blanqui's revolutionary legacy. For Benjamin, Blanqui's cosmological doctrine is understood essentially as a capitulation. By proclaiming the eternal return of the same, Blanqui, the most revolutionary scion of the nineteenth century, surrenders the possibility of revolution to the triumph of reaction. "It represents unconditional submission," Benjamin wrote to Horkheimer, in a passage he excerpted into Convolute D, on "Boredom, Eternal Return," "but at the same time the most terrible accusation against a society that has reflected this image of the cosmos as a projection of itself onto the heavens" (CB, 548; GB, 6:10). And in his own summation, *Blanqui submits to bourgeois society. But he drops to his knee with such violence [Gewalt] that the throne begins to totter* (AP, 111; GS, 5:168).

The figure of Blanqui denouncing bourgeois society not directly but by objectifying its terrible judgment in his own unconditional surrender echoes Benjamin's earlier figure from the Trauerspiel book of the defiant tragic hero. *Blanqui appears as a tragic figure*, Benjamin notes in a later convolute; *his betrayal has tragic greatness; he was brought down by the enemy within* (AP, 375; GS, 5:474). But precisely the completeness of Blanqui's defeat, the incompatibility of this late doctrine with the entire revolutionary commitment of his earlier life, distinguishes his eternal return from Nietzsche's. Blanqui, the intellectually vulgar autodidact, reveals the infernal face of bourgeois time in spite of himself, embodies it as an intellectual sacrifice to the scientific spirit of the age. Nietzsche, by contrast, cannot be reduced to such an inadvertent theoretical position. Benjamin's discovery of Blanqui allows him to displace the eternal return into the more naive signature of the French revolutionary. At the same time, it prompts him to consider more closely Nietzsche's actual doctrine. And it is this reconsideration that leads Benjamin to Karl Löwith's book from three years earlier, *Nietzsche's Philosophy of the Eternal Recurrence of the Same.*[17]

There is much that Benjamin would have found amenable about Löwith's reading. For Löwith, Nietzsche's thought is "a system in aphorisms" (NER, 11; NEW, 11), a designation that resonates with Benjamin's remark in his dissertation from 1919, "The Concept of Art Criticism in German Romanticism," where he defended the coherence of Novalis's and Friedrich Schlegel's fragmentary writing by pointing to the example of Nietzsche.

> These days, the fact that an author expresses himself in aphorisms will not count for anyone as proving anything against his systematic intentions. Nietzsche, for example, wrote aphoristically, characterizing himself moreover as an enemy of system; yet he thought through his philosophy in a comprehensive and unitary manner in keeping with his guiding ideas, and in the end began to write his system. (*SW*, 1:136; *GS*, 1:42)

Like Benjamin's mature discussion of Nietzsche's tragic theory, Löwith's interpretation insists on the Romantic pedigree of Nietzsche's Hellenistic notion of myth. That Nietzsche's doctrine "repeats antiquity at the apex of modernity" (*NEW*, 113) fits nicely into Benjamin's own pursuit of an Ur-history within the nineteenth century. And indeed, most of Benjamin's notes in *The Arcades Project* are drawn from Löwith's fourth chapter, "The Repetition of Antiquity on the Peak of Modernity as the Historical Meaning of the Doctrine of the Eternal Return" and the preceding chapter titled the "The Double Equation for the Allegory of the Eternal Recurrence." Benjamin also notes several scattered remarks from earlier in the book, but chapters 7 and 8, where Löwith compares Nietzsche to Stirner and Weininger and summarizes Nietzsche's philosophy as an anachronistic and ultimately unsuccessful appeal to the Greek mean, figure less prominently.[18]

Yet, beneath these thematic congruencies, Löwith's account of Nietzsche's philosophy resonated tonally with Benjamin's evolving understanding of the philosopher. For Löwith, Nietzsche's philosophy is at bottom the reaction to an extreme disillusion. The historical triumph of nihilism is what Nietzsche confronts, and the eternal return of the same is his doomed attempt to overcome this collapse of transcendent values. Nietzsche's atheism "recognizes for the first time that the '*death of God*' means for man '*freedom toward death*.'" (*NER*, 38; *NEW*, 39). But this puts man

> in a problematic "*interim state*," and his nihilism can mean two things: It can mean a symptom of the enervation of the will of an emptied existence, but on the other hand, it can be a first sign of the strengthening of the will and of a willed destruction—a nihilism of passive weakness or of active strength. (*NER*, 50; *NEW*, 51)

The assertion of the eternal return of the same is Nietzsche's effort to transform the nihilistic loss of orienting values into the occasion for an active self-assertion. "As a result of this essential connection of the eternal recurrence and nihilism, Nietzsche's teaching has a double aspect: it is the 'self-overcoming of nihilism,' in which 'he who overcomes' and 'what is overcome' are one" (*NER*, 55–56; *NEW*, 56). This dual aspect of the eternal return, a nihilism that simultaneously overcomes itself, is explicitly historicized in Benjamin's account. The conceptually self-contradictory reflexivity in Löwith's interpretation becomes a stylistic self-overcoming.

> The idea of eternal return in Zarathustra is, according to its true nature, a stylization of the worldview that in Blanqui still displays its infernal traits. It is a stylization of existence down to the tiniest fractions of its temporal process. Nevertheless: Zarathustra's style disavows itself in the doctrine that is expounded through it. (*AP*, 557; *GS*, 5:691)

Yet the true value of Löwith's book for Benjamin lies less in its interpretation than in the extensive quotations from Nietzsche's own work that it contains. Like Bernoulli's vast reconstruction of Nietzsche's relation to Overbeck, if on a smaller scale, Löwith's interpretation is built around extensive, extended citations from Nietzsche's published and unpublished writings, and in his notes Benjamin is primarily interested in Nietzsche's language, not Löwith's.[19] Löwith's mastery of Nietzsche's notebooks spurred Benjamin to track down on his own some of Nietzsche's archival remarks, as the entries in convolute D show. In particular, Löwith's reference to a note of Nietzsche's that mentions the head of Medusa sent Benjamin back to the Musarion edition of Nietzsche's works, the latest version available to him. There, he noted a fragment from Nietzsche's notebooks of 1884, when he was working on the fourth part of Zarathustra, where the consequences of the "abysmal thought" (*TSZ*, 162; *KSA*, 4:205) of the eternal return of the same are at length to be presented. Benjamin notes: *On eternal recurrence: "The great thought as a Medusa head: all features of the world become motionless, a frozen death throe"* (*AP*, 115; *GS*, 5:175).[20] The frozen death throe brought about by the eternal return is the moment at which the temporality of the always new intersects with the unchanging temporality of fate in a form that allows reflection to discern the forces at work in it. Benjamin's own name for this is *dialectics at a standstill* (*AP*, 462; *GS*, 5:577). It is a notion he develops in complicity with Nietzsche.

Benjamin calls the eternal return *the fundamental form of the urhistorical, mythic consciousness (Mythic because it does not reflect)*

(*AP*, 119; *GS*, 5:177). As the temporality of fate, it carries a burden of guilt and death that only an extreme inversion can hope to overcome. At the same time, in the constellation formed by Nietzsche, Blanqui, and Baudelaire, the eternal return does bear a version of that ultimate hope. In Benjamin's late aphoristic sequence "Central Park," he indicates how this might be understood.

> Eternal recurrence is an attempt to combine the two antinomic principles of happiness: that of eternity and that of the "yet again."—The idea of eternal recurrence conjures the speculative idea (or phantasmagoria) of happiness from the misery of the times. Nietzsche's heroism has its counterpart in the heroism of Baudelaire, who conjures the phantasmagoria of modernity from the misery of philistinism. (*SW*, 4:184; *GS*, 1:682–83)

GLÜCK

Happiness is what never happens. In the second aphorism of *On the Concept of History* Benjamin evokes a happiness constituted by its absence: "This observation indicates that the image of happiness [*Glück*] we cherish is thoroughly colored by the time to which the course of our own existence has assigned us. There is happiness—such as could arouse envy in us—only in the air we have breathed, among people we could have talked to, women who could have given themselves to us. In other words, the idea of happiness is indissolubly bound up with the idea of redemption" (*SW*, 4:389; *GS*, 1:694). The impossibility of happiness is its theological reference in a profane universe whose very actuality calls out for redemption. The antagonism between happiness and time is what situates the former as the regulating notion of Benjamin's politics, the impossible telos of a "Teleology without Ultimate Goal" in the formula Benjamin devised for his early explorations of the metaphysical foundations of politics (*CB*, 169; *GB*, 2:109). If we try to imagine happiness positively, we are left with the fragility of hope: "On the portal, the 'Spes' [Hope] by Andrea de Pisano. Sitting, she helplessly extends her arms toward a fruit that remains beyond her reach. And yet she is winged. Nothing is more true" (*SW*, 1:471; *GS*, 4:125).

But the hostility toward the real that keeps happiness absent allows its negative manifestation: destruction. From a letter to Scholem we know that the model for Benjamin's 1931 thought-image "The Destructive Character" was Gustav Glück, the same Glück to whom he had dedicated the essay on Kraus. In the text itself, however, neither the name nor the concept appears. That the man Glück is not named may accord with the generalizability of a caricature; but that the concept of happiness does not appear is clearly intentional, for it provokes a number of circumlocutions to replace what would be its natural occurrence. That the destructive character is young and cheerful, always plunging into work, unconcerned with his reputation, never entrapped, indifferent to suicide—all of these qualities suggest the one culminating aspect of his being that organizes the panegyric tone, but remains unexpressed: his happiness, his *Glück*. What we see of the destructive character is his corrosive orientation in the present moment, his inverted sociability, in which he depends on a circle of witnesses whose reactions are of no concern to him, his dynamism and his iconoclasm. What we are not told is how the destructive character feels. And yet it is certain: He is happy.

The absence of *Glück* from "The Destructive Character" is an example of the fact that neither the character nor the concept leaves an expressive trace of itself. In confrontation with his antipodes, the Etui-person whose impressionable interiority registers the traces of the objects he encounters, "the destructive character obliterates even the traces of destruction" (*SW*, 2:542; *GS*, 4:398). To the extent that Gustav Glück is the model of the destructive character, we would not expect to find traces of his name in the text. Their very absence confirms the reference revealed by the letter. But this erasure holds as well for the concept the destructive character embodies. Happiness is this very movement of destroying the traces of its historical manifestation; this very unlocalizability is its essence. In this, happiness is more than a subjective attitude but the antithesis of the very connectivity that makes traces possible: the guilt-nexus of the living, fate. "Has fate any reference to good fortune, to happiness [*Glück*]? Is happiness, as misfortune doubtless is, an intrinsic category of fate? Happiness is, rather, what releases the fortunate man from the embroilment of the Fates and from the net of his own fate" (*SW*, 1:203; *GS*, 2:174). Happiness never happens—indeed, it is precisely the freedom from localizability that paradoxically defines it. The destructive character is a portrait of happiness because his portrait does not mention it.

The destructive character, like happiness, is necessarily viewed from without. Benjamin's thought-image makes clear from the start that a presentation of the destructive character depends precisely on the shock of one's recognized difference from him. "It could happen to someone looking back over his life," Benjamin begins,

> that he realized that almost all the deeper obligations he had endured in its course originated in people who everyone agreed had the traits of a "destructive character." He would stumble on this fact one day, perhaps by chance, and the heavier the shock [*Chock*] dealt to him, the better the chance of a presentation [*Darstellung*] of the destructive character. (*SW*, 2:541; *GS*, 4:396)

This presentational distance unfolds in the retrospective space between concrete bindings with others suffered or endured (*erlitten*), and the shock of their recognition in the present. This recognition is at least implicitly a return to collective evaluations: Everyone else, not the destructive characters themselves, agrees that these characters are destructive. And indeed, the very absence of expressive testimony from within the destructive character renders his exteriority as necessarily performative. "The destructive character does his work; the only work he avoids is creative. Just as the creator seeks solitude, the destroyer must be constantly surrounded by people, witnesses to his efficacy" (*SW*, 2:542; *GS*, 4:397). Yet those witnesses can hardly be reliable. "The destructive character has no interest in being understood," Benjamin insists. "Attempts in this direction he regards as superficial. Being misunderstood cannot harm him. On the contrary, he provokes it, just as oracles, those destructive institutions of the state, provoked it" (*SW*, 2:542; *GS*, 4:397). Benjamin speaks then as one of these witnesses, and the crystalizing shock that produces his exposition condenses, in his letter to Scholem that mentions the essay, into a caricaturing grain of salt. "The person I have been closest to for approximately one year has been Gustav Glück, the director of the foreign division of the National Credit Society. You will find a kind of portrait sketch of him—to be taken cum grano salis—in 'The Destructive Character' which I sent you" (*CB*, 386; *GB*, 4:62).

Cum grano salis, since no actual individual could embody the destructive happiness that echoes in Glück's name. That the escape from fatal imbrication could be borne by an onomastic accident: This, rather somberly expressed, is the humor of the piece. This humor is not a subjective attitude, no more than the happiness it rests in. It is the modality in which Benjamin's aphorisms span the distance between the historically specific Herr Glück and the impersonal necessity within a posture of happiness, a posture of survival. The outermost contours of this posture appear as a renunciation of any positive characterization of the future. "The destructive character sees no image hovering before him. He has few needs, and the least of them is to know what will replace what has been destroyed" (SW, 3:541; GS, 4:397). Since any practical coordination of disparate human efforts in the present must imply a communicable orientation toward the future, this renunciation of positive futurity manifests itself as the concomitant abjuration of understanding as a communicative ideal in the present. The grain of salt in his portrait precludes any ultimate characterization of his essence or guarantee of his existence.

It is thus in a fundamental sense a comedic shock the destructive character produces, borne not by his own chipper destructiveness, but registered in the fact that his presentation cannot be characterization, but must appear as caricature. For if "The Destructive Character" pursues no image, it is because his happiness beckons from beyond any conceivable reality, at the limit of thought marked by the eternal return. In his essay on "The Image of Proust," Benjamin had positioned *Glück* on an unpresentable boundary, generating two contradictory temporal systems: "There is a dual will to happiness, a dialectics of happiness [*Dialektik des Glücks*]: a hymnic form as well as an elegiac form. The one is the unheard-of, the unprecedented, the height of bliss; the other, the eternal once-again [*Nocheinmal*] the eternal restoration of the original, first happiness" (SW, 2:239; GS, 2:313). In this dialectic Benjamin clasps happiness in the destructive embrace of the new and always the same, the very temporality of hell.

The profane order should be erected on the idea of happiness [*Glück*], Benjamin wrote in the dense "Theological-Political Fragment." *The relation of this order to the messianic is one of the essential teachings of the philosophy of history. . . . The profane, therefore, though not itself a category of this* [*messianic*] *kingdom, is a decisive category of its most unobtrusive approach. For in happiness all that is earthly seeks its downfall* [*Untergang*], *and only in happiness is its downfall destined to find it* (SW, 3:305; GS, 2:203–4). The impossibility of happiness and the isolation of the destructive character with respect to human fate here converge in an *Untergang*, a down-going, that brings all of mortal reality into view, as a condition of an unimaginable alternative. And it is because happiness has this ultimate relation to a messianic alternative that the destructive character is no deformed misanthrope, *no Thersites*, as Benjamin remarks in a rough draft (*GS*, 4:999). Rather, the comprehensiveness of his unconcern renders him an Apollonian, and ultimately a Nietzschean, figure. "Really, only the insight into how radically the world is simplified when tested for its worthiness for destruction leads to such an Apollonian image of the destroyer. This is the great bond embracing and unifying all that exists" (*SW* 2:541; *GS*, 4:397). Zarathustra, at the edge of Nietzsche's and of Benjamin's signatures, shines forth in this image of self-destructive happiness, an index for the coming alternative that may eventually break the hold of mortal fate on life.

The perspective of happiness and the perspective of the deathday are congruent in every way but this slight exposure to a messianic transformation carried in the heart of the complicit destroyer. Not unrealized hope but impossible happiness rescues the destructive character from consequent self-destruction: "The destructive character lives from the feeling not that life is worth living but that suicide is not worth the trouble" (*SW*, 2:542; *GS*, 4:398).

NOW-TIME

Nietzsche moves across the face of Benjamin's final work, his aphorisms *On the Concept of History*. He is named, most obviously, as the source of an epigraph to one of the aphorisms, which bears a line from the second of Nietzsche's *Untimely Observations*: "We need history, but our need for it is different from that of the pampered idler in the garden of knowledge" (*SW*, 4:394; *GS*, 1:700 / *UO*, 85; *KSA*, 1:245). In the version of the text that was posthumously published, this excerpt from Nietzsche's early essay introduces the twelfth aphorism, in which "historical knowledge" is coordinated with vengeance for past wrongs as opposed to promises of future rights. A provocative conjunction, for Benjamin's text, endorsing as it does the motivating power of "the image of enslaved ancestors" over "the ideal of liberated grandchildren" would seem, prima facie, to be the epitome of the "spirit of resentment" Nietzsche denounces (*GM*, 74 et passim; *KSA*, 5:310). By leaving this different history and this different need unspecified, a merely negative contrast to a knowledge construed as distraction, the epigraph invests an expectation in the first person plural pronoun. Who are this "we" whose need for history is different from that of the idle horticulturalist? And indeed Benjamin has drawn these lines from the anticipatory "Preface" to the essay he gives as their source: Nietzsche's "On the Use and Disadvantage of History for Life." The quotation gestures negatively toward an unspecified contrast to idle historical knowledge, a dismissal of irrelevant history whose positive force has no other indication than the name that identifies its source. The call for a different history is a Nietzschean call; the pampered idlers are Nietzsche's target—the "cultivated philistines" and academic positivists against which "On the Use and Disadvantage of History for Life" was written. Benjamin's epigraph lets Nietzsche characterize the great need to which his own aphorisms respond.

In the simplest of circumstances epigraphs entertain an ambiguous relation to the texts they attend, and where Nietzsche draws attention to the epigraphs in the theses on history, their complexity soon becomes apparent. In the published version prepared after the war there is no epigraph for the work as a whole, but six of the short texts sport them, the fourth, seventh, ninth, twelfth, thirteenth, and fourteenth aphorisms. The irregularity of such a deployment is odd, and indeed unprecedented, in Benjamin's work. He is an unusually careful epigraphist, if we can bend that philological term to indicate an author's choosing and positioning of epigraphs. Where they stray from a universalist position beneath the title of an entire work, Benjamin's epigraphs are placed consistently at the next level of textual organization, introducing each numbered section of an essay. The "Metaphysics of Youth" displays the direction of its avant-garde exoticism in the orienting quotations from Hölderlin and Lao-Tse above first "Conversation" and then "Daybook." In the Goethe essay, Klopstock, Hölderlin, and George together project onto the tripartite exposition a historical trajectory from origin through historical crisis into the present. The Kraus essay, by contrast, deploys recurring quotations from Kraus himself to reinforce his relevance to an interpretation that passes through demonic citation into a critique of the entire present moment in human history. This unifying function is performed, mutatis mutandis, by the epigraphs to the large sections of *The Origin of German Trauerspiel*, all of which derive from German Baroque sources. This tendency toward interior epigraphs reaches its apotheosis in the exposés to *The Arcades Project*. In the 1935 exposé the epigraphs are proliferating beyond the individual sections, interrupting and redirecting the exposition within these larger categories. One of the notable differences between this early version and the 1939 French exposé is a regularization of these epigraphs, which now adorn every subsection of every section. The staggered use of epigraphs in the final aphorisms on history fly in the face of their structural situation elsewhere.

The new edition of *On the Concept of History* in volume 19 of the *Werke und Nachlass* reveals the palimpsest character of this final text, which survives in several versions. Oldest is the manuscript Benjamin gave to Hannah Arendt; in this version the ninth aphorism, which describes the subject of historical knowledge as the avenger of past injustice, has no epigraph. In Benjamin's personal typescript, which philology suggests is next in order of composition, this aphorism has become the twelfth, and the Nietzsche epigraph now appears above it. This makes the epigraph the first of three attending three sequential aphorisms, a brief dialogic modulation in the midst of the sequence as a whole. Nietzsche's demand is followed in the thirteenth aphorism with Wilhelm Dietzgen's epitome of social-democratic complacency: "Every day our cause becomes clearer and people get smarter" (*SW*, 4:394; *WuN*, 19:39), which introduces Benjamin's ruthless critique of the concept of progress. And then the fourteenth aphorism, which bears the resonant phrase from Kraus: "Origin is the goal." This aphorism responds to the Nietzschean demand by identifying the temporality at stake in history: "History is the subject of a construction whose site is not homogeneous, empty time, but time filled full by now-time [*Jetztzeit*]" (*SW*, 4:395; *WuN*, 40).

The French manuscript, which the editors place next in the order of composition, dispenses with all of the epigraphs except one, Nietzsche's complaint about useful history now translated into French. "Ils nous faut l'histoire; mais il nous la faut autrement qu'à celui qui, désœuvré, flâne dans les jardins de l'érudition" (*WuN*, 19:65). That Benjamin retains this epigraph alone suggests its importance to the entire conception of the work. A further piece of philological evidence confirms this, for when it seemed to Benjamin and his sister Dora that the French post could no longer be trusted with the unexpurgated sequence, they prepared another typescript from which the more politically compromising passages had been removed. This involved changing the occurrences of "historical materialist" to "historical dialectician," as well as suppressing the twelfth aphorism entirely, which mentions Spartacus explicitly, and where Nietzsche's sentence had been perched. Yet rather than dispensing with the Nietzsche citation, Benjamin has removed it to the seventh aphorism, on the relation of barbarism to culture, which had in earlier versions carried an epigraph by Brecht. This too suggests that he was unwilling to see the sequence on history without it.

Aphorism 12 of *On the Concept of History* addresses "the subject of historical knowledge," which it identifies as "the struggling, oppressed class itself." The aphorism continues:

> Marx presents it as the last enslaved class—the avenger that completes the task of liberation in the name of generations of the downtrodden. This conviction, which had a brief resurgence in the Spartacus League, has always been objectionable to Social Democrats. Within three decades they managed to erase the name of Blanqui almost entirely, though at the sound of that name the preceding century had quaked. The Social Democrats preferred to cast the working class in the role of a redeemer of *future* generations, in this way cutting the sinews of its greatest strength. This indoctrination made the working class forget both its hatred and its spirit of sacrifice, for both are nourished by the image of enslaved ancestors rather than by the ideal of liberated grandchildren. (*SW*, 4:394; *GS*, 1:700)

Benjamin's claim that the subject of historical knowledge is the struggling, oppressed class itself cannot be taken to suggest a proletarian metaconsciousness. To the extent that historical knowledge appears, it will be vested in a collective subject, but it will be vested by an individual author. Not Marxism, but Marx himself presents the subject of history as a vengeful class, performing its historical work in the name of the preceding generations of the oppressed. To the extent that Marx's theory identifies the proletariat as the objectively necessary agent of revolutionary change, Benjamin has little sympathy with it. "Nothing," his prior aphorism had asserted, "has so corrupted the German working class as the notion that *it* was moving with the current" (*SW*, 4:393; *GS*, 1:698). It is far more Marx's vehement, uncompromising polemical tone than his theory that is at work here. It is this radical tone that has always discomfited social democracy, so that their deviance from Marx is not understood as theoretical revisionism, but as the obliteration of the memory of Blanqui. That Blanqui's revolutionary theory was less sophisticated than Marx's is thus irrelevant: It is Blanqui's tone that has been forgotten, his implacable hatred of the class into which he was born, the extremity of his political posture. By repressing this, social democracy reveals a betrayal not merely of the theory of Marx, but of its entire motivation. Blanqui, and by extension Marx, understood revolution as the long-awaited payback for untold centuries of suffering. In *On the Concept of History* the term "generation" marks a specific contemporaneaity, a field in which the indexical "now" can be culturally recognized. Generation situates its present as an actual element in a process of transmission between vanished parents and potential children. Not its biological provenance, which merely dislodges it from institutional commitments, but its temporal discontinuity moves Benjamin to adopt it.

For Kant, the domains of space and time were distinct and irreducible. For Benjamin (and for Nietzsche as well), such an absolute distinction was untenable, and any discussion of temporality was bound to involve spatial metaphors, just as any discussion of space could not escape temporal contrasts. But this mutual involvement does not in turn imply equivalence. The spatial language of *Aura*, with its dynamic of nearness and distance, is, from this perspective, a metaphor to characterize an immanent duplicity in the now-time. "The mystical 'instant' [*Nu*] becomes the 'now' [*Jetzt*] of contemporary actuality; the symbolic becomes distorted into the allegorical" (*OT*, 183; *GS*, 1:358). The immediate moment encounters history not by expanding into a mystical totality, but in a transitory distortion that, while a potential in every present, is realized only in the most tenuous and rarefied occasions. The difference between the potential truth residing in the present as such, and its potential realization in any given present moment produces Benjamin's early formula, the *Now of Knowability*. This notion governs the earliest notes to *The Arcades Project*: *Real time enters the dialectical image not in natural magnitude—let alone psychologically—but in its smallest gestalt*, Benjamin writes there. ——*All in all the temporal moment* [*Zeitmoment*] *in the dialectical image can be determined only through confrontation with another concept. This concept is the 'now of knowability'* [*'Jetzt der Erkennbarkeit'*] (*AP*, 867; *GS*, 5:1038). In *The Arcades Project*, Benjamin explores this notion further, granting it a fundamental place in his methodology. The now of knowability is the modality of the historical perception he intends to explore; and in intending to explore it he must surrender intention for the sake of truth.

> These images are to be thought of entirely apart from the categories of the "human sciences," from the so-called habitus, from style, and the like. For the historical index of the images not only says that they belong to a particular time; it says, above all, that they attain

> to legibility only at a particular time. And indeed this acceding "to legibility" constitutes a specific critical point in the movement at their interior. Every present day is determined by the images that are synchronic with it: each "now" is the now of a particular knowability. In it, truth is charged to the bursting point with time (This point of explosion, and nothing else is the death of the intentio, which thus coincides with the birth of authentic historical time, the time of truth.) (AP, 462–63; GS, 5:578)

The now of knowability thus identifies a receptive position in the present as it relates to the past. Since truth cannot relinquish its relation to time, the now of knowability marks the conjunction of logic and temporality, and its possibility is in contrast with all timeless "validity." These explicit reflections emerge in Benjamin's early notes.

> *The two tasks facing the theory of knowledge are:*
> *1) The constitution of things in the now of knowability and*
> *2) the limitation of knowledge in the symbol.*
> *Regarding point 1. The sentence: Truth belongs in one sense or another to the perfected state of the world, grows catastrophically to that other sentence, grows by the dimension of the "now": the world is knowable now. Truth resides in the "now of knowability." Only in this is there a [systematic, conceptual] nexus [Zusammenhang]—(a nexus between existing things and also with the perfected state of the world.) The now of knowability is logical time, which has to replace that of timeless validity.* (SW, 1:276; GS, 6:46).

But if the now of knowability is logical time, it cannot survive as content in the inscription that enables it. We, in our own now, must take responsibility for our own knowledge. The radicalness of this surrender is the Ur-political implication of Benjamin's encounter with Nietzsche. It is this encounter that unapologetically emphasizes Benjamin's revolutionary commitments and their communist provenance, and insists on their relevance for the postcommunist present. In the most general terms, the meaning *for us* of Benjamin's political engagement is not dependent on the continuing accuracy of his terms in their received significance. They can become anachronistic, and indeed must become anachronistic, since this anachronism testifies to Benjamin's historical imbrication in the twentieth century. His politics does not reduce itself to a program that could be evaluated from an ahistorical position in terms of timeless validity, could be confirmed or debunked by subsequent historical events. Benjamin's prescience, or lack thereof, is not at issue. Rather, his transience, and within that transience, his posture. This posture, however, is not simply an admirable attitude that could be transplanted into our own historical milieu mutatis mutandis. It is not a matter of sharing Benjamin's sympathies. It is rather a matter of preparing the past in the light of the destruction of the present. It is a matter of collaborating with the destruction of the present, not in the name of a vision of future bliss—all such visions being part of the present and complicit with its continuation. It is a matter of destroying the entire present, together with its compensatory dreams and frantic excuses, in the name of an absolutely indeterminate future.

This is not Caesarism, for no intellectual confronts the entire present. But it does mean that a consequently revolutionary writing at any time must attack the present, and its own conditions of possibility, wherever it descries them. This, then, is the posture that emerges in our present from a temporary conjunction of Benjamin and Nietzsche: to produce with the tools of the dominant culture a cultural product that accelerates the destruction of that culture, appearing useless and superfluous to the proponents of culture while presenting the enemies of that culture with unexpected potentials. In Benjamin's time, the most implacable and resolute enemy of his own culture is the proletariat. It is not naïveté that Benjamin's communist sympathies betray; Benjamin is sympathetic not to the grim reality of Russian totalitarianism but to the unrealized alternative to capitalism animating the totalizing ambition of Bolshevism. It is because—and here events have proven him quite prescient—when all hope of a radical transformation of the present moment in history has been sacrificed on the altar of a mad maturity, the decency and humanity that seem to appear are in fact infantile and bloodthirsty, the implacable nemesis of any genuine adulthood. It is revolution, not communism, that remains for Benjamin and for us in the future. And however distant revolution may appear today, it is the service to revolution that marks the final extreme of contiguity and divergence between this book and its objective problem, the relation between Benjamin and Nietzsche. Only to the infinitesimal extent that it promotes an absolute transformation of our contemporary world does it approach the now of knowability.

There is an old student joke at Nietzsche's expense, presented in the form of juxtaposed graffiti: "'God is dead'—Nietzsche. 'Nietzsche is dead'—God," it runs. On the wall of the University of Muri, the statements is reversed, "'Nietzsche is dead'—God. 'God is dead'—Nietzsche," and this, in the end, displays precisely Benjamin's deepest response to Nietzsche. The overcoming of Nietzschean nihilism is borne not by an affirmation of divinity, but as a translation of their reciprocal deaths into written quotations, upon whose material surfaces reside in the insubstantial form of possibility a redemption beyond nihilism. That translation is borne not by the questionable intellectual content of the joke, but by its tone, by the fact that it is a joke, a nihilistic inversion of Nietzsche's most nihilistic insights that aims not at blank despair but wry amusement. And it is the possibility of this tone that, paradoxically, Benjamin receives from the Nietzsche he thereby overcomes.

Conclusion

Friedrich Nietzsche, Walter Benjamin

> Above me shone the stars for the night was very clear. I felt a certain sense of friendly comfort in their twinkling. All the old constellations had gone from the sky, however: that slow movement which is imperceptible in a hundred human lifetimes, had long since rearranged them in unfamiliar groupings.... Through that long night I held my mind off the Morlocks as well as I could, and whiled away the time by trying to fancy I could find signs of the old constellations in the new confusion.
>
> —H. G. WELLS, *The Time Machine*

TRANSCENDENTAL MEDICINE

In January of 1886, as Friedrich Nietzsche struggled to negotiate the private printing of forty-five copies of *Zarathustra*'s final book, the Scotch author Robert Louis Stevenson brought out a hugely successful story: *Strange Case of Dr. Jekyll and Mr. Hyde*. Its germ, like the germ of Mary Shelley's *Frankenstein*, had come to him in a vivid dream. Countless cinematic visualizations have hardly exhausted the force of the tale's central image: the accomplished if stuffy doctor imbibing a volatile tincture and transforming into his snarling alter ego. The birth of the bestial protégé, in an obscene induced masculine labor, seems to embody the cautionary moral of the story of Jekyll (Stevenson preferred the long 'e') and Hyde, seems to encapsulate the direction of its critique. In every Jekyll lurks a Hyde; individual moral integration is always incomplete, and bears an inextinguishable nostalgia for brute asocial indulgence: "I felt younger, lighter, happier in body, within I was conscious of a heady recklessness, a current of disordered sensual images running like a mill race in my fancy, a solution of the bonds of obligation, an unknown but not an innocent freedom of the soul."[1]

The "Full Statement of the Case" that concludes the narrative, and from which these words are taken, presents the tale from the doctor's perspective, and this version, with Jekyll as narrator, has informed its many cinematic translations. Thus they present the transformation from Jekyll into Hyde, for this subjective immoral emancipation is what is immediately expressed in Jekyll's physical alteration. Recounting, the doctor sidesteps the technical particulars of his discovery in order to characterize it in phrenological terms, as a communicative inscription in his physical presence.

> Enough, then, that I not only recognized my natural body from the mere aura and effulgence of certain of the powers that made up my spirit, but managed to compound a drug by which these powers should be dethroned from their supremacy, and a second form and countenance substituted, none the less natural to me because they were the expression, and bore the stamp, of lower elements in my soul. (49-50)

This immediate amoral expressiveness of Hyde's body, and particularly his face, is the emphatic condition of possibility of Stevenson's narrative. It has provoked, and licensed, the persistent visualizations of the story because it inhabits the original. And yet, it is precisely those visualizations that obscure the peculiarity of Stevenson's actual presentation. *Strange Case of Dr. Jekyll and Mr. Hyde* must pass through two prior narrative positions before it reaches the doctor's first person perspective; and the tale of the miscreant scientist conditions the even stranger case of Mr. Utterson and Dr. Lanyon.

The story is initially filtered through the awareness of Dr. Jekyll's lawyer. As Mr. Utterson encounters the case, the scandal of a reduction of the morally antithetical individuals Jekyll and Hyde to a sequential oscillation between Jekyll-states and Hyde-states appears not in the immediacy of corporeal transformation, but approaches as a collection of puzzling endorsements. The mystery Utterson attempts to explain is embodied in a series of signed contractual commitments with Hyde into which the respected doctor has entered. In particular, "a document endorsed on the envelope as Dr. Jekyll's Will" irritates the attorney. This holograph testament

> provided not only that, in case of the decease of Henry Jekyll, M.D., D.C.L., LL.D., F.R.S., etc., all his possessions were to pass into the hand of his 'friend and benefactor Edward Hyde'; but that in case of Dr. Jekyll's 'disappearance or unexplained absence for any period exceeding three calendar months,' the said Edward Hyde should step into the said Henry Jekyll's shoes without further delay. (12-13)

The unadorned name "Edward Hyde" at first means nothing to Mr. Utterson, but the very form of such a contract repulses him. "It

Conclusion

offended him both as a lawyer and as a lover of the sane and customary sides of life, to whom the fanciful was the immodest" (13). He determines to seek out the man behind this named beneficiary: "'If he be Mr. Hyde,' he had thought, 'I shall be Mr. Seek'" (15).

When he does encounter Mr. Hyde, Mr. Utterson's immediate aversion obscures the visual particulars of the man's appearance. The object of his observation disperses immediately into a subjective reaction to his presence. "He was small, and very plainly dressed; and the look of him, even at that distance, went somehow strongly against the watcher's inclination" (16). The mechanisms of this reaction cannot be articulated; it does not reside in the causal traces of particular moral actions, the marks of debauchery, red nose or wasted skin. The very expressiveness of Hyde's body pushes it out of representation.

> "There must be something else," said the perplexed gentleman. "There *is* something more, if I could find a name for it. God bless me, the man seems hardly human! Something troglodytic, shall we say? [...] or is it the mere radiance of a foul soul that thus transpires through, and transfigures, its clay continent? The last, I think; for O my poor old Harry Jekyll, if ever I read Satan's signature upon a face, it is on that of your new friend." (17)

Mr. Utterson vests the discursively resistant expressiveness in an infernal signature, and it is his professional faith in this stability of signatures that, in the end, prevents his own investigations from directly revealing to him the mystery of Jekyll and Hyde. The case gains urgency when Hyde is witnessed bludgeoning to death Sir Danvers Carew, "an aged and beautiful gentleman with white hair" (21), and Member of Parliament.

> The newsboys, as [Mr. Utterson] went, were crying themselves hoarse along the footways: "Special edition. Shocking murder of an M.P." That was the funeral oration of one friend and client; and he could not help a certain apprehension lest the good name of another should be sucked down in the eddy of the scandal. [...] And, self-reliant as he was by habit, he began to cherish a longing for advice. (27)

It is here that he turns to his clerk Guest, "a great student and critic of handwriting" (27), who brings him as close to the solution as he comes, when he compares a sample of Hyde's autograph with Jekyll's fortuitously received invitation to dinner.

> "One moment. I thank you, sir;" and the clerk laid the two sheets of paper alongside and sedulously compared their contents. "Thank you, sir," he said at last, returning both; "it's a very interesting autograph."

> There was a pause, during which Utterson struggled with himself.
> "Why did you compare them, Guest?" he inquired suddenly.
> "Well, sir," returned the clerk, "there's a rather singular resemblance; the two hands are in many points identical: only differently sloped."
> "Rather quaint," said Utterson. (28)

Though deeply troubled, the lawyer cannot break with the singularity of the signature, and must resort to the notion of forgery to reconcile the difficulty. "'What!' he thought. 'Henry Jekyll forge for a murderer!' And his blood ran cold in his veins" (28). But of course, the strangeness of the case here is that neither autograph is forged. The differing slopes reflect the physical transmutation between Hyde and Jekyll, while the "many points [that are] identical" embody graphologically their inner continuity. "Then I remembered that of my original character, one part remained to me: I could write my own hand," Jekyll-as-Hyde-as-Jekyll will paradoxically recall at story's end (58-59). But in the realm of stable signatures, the transgressive incarnation of the natural body cannot be directly detected, but must appear as forgery.

As a "case," the story of Jekyll and Hyde had from the start been inscribed within an ambiguity between law and medicine. And the long train of institutional titles that attends Jekyll's name — "Medicinae Doctor," "Doctor of Civil Law," "Legum Doctor," "Fellow of the Royal Society of London for the Promotion of Natural Knowledge" — license the ambiguity. These public certifications attached to Jekyll's signature anchor the public congruity between scientific inquiry and judicial respectability. So a powerful logic had, at the outset, impelled Mr. Utterson, "the last reputable acquaintance and the last good influence in the lives of down-going men" (7), "in the direction of Cavendish Square, that citadel of medicine, where his friend, the great Dr. Lanyon, had his house and received his crowding patients. 'If anyone knows, it will be Lanyon,' he had thought" (13). The visit had been a failure: this instinctive alliance between Mr. Utterson, as the guardian of legally binding signature, and Dr. Lanyon, as the guardian of recognized scientific achievement, ("for these two were old friends, old mates both at school and college" [6]) is precisely what Jekyll's experiment has ruptured. "I see little of him now," Lanyon tells his friend.

> "Indeed!" said Utterson. "I thought you had a bond of common interest."

Conclusion

> "We had," was the reply. "But it is more than ten years since Henry Jekyll became too fanciful for me. He began to go wrong, wrong in mind; and though, of course, I continue to take an interest in him for old sake's sake as they say, I see and I have seen devilish little of the man. Such unscientific balderdash. (14)

Beneath an onomastic constancy that still has suasive force, Jekyll's own scientific researches have transformed him. Parallel to the fanciful testament that unites him to an indescribable body and its affectual resonance, Jekyll's scientifically fanciful interests have isolated him from the investigative community. But as Mr. Utterson's fiduciary investigations languish, it is upon the unsuspecting Dr. Lanyon that the narrative burden is foisted. And even here, before he has assumed it, Dr. Lanyon's words echo, beyond his intention, a description of the "devilish little" Hyde. Faced for the first time with the unaccountable villain in person, however, Dr. Lanyon's diagnostic description repeats in positivist terms the same reflective swerve Mr. Utterson's had performed.

> He was small, as I have said; I was struck besides with the shocking expression of his face, with his remarkable combination of great muscular activity and great apparent debility of constitution, and — last but not least — with the odd, subjective disturbance caused by his neighborhood. This bore some resemblance to incipient rigor, and was accompanied by a marked sinking of the pulse. (44)

The appeal that involves Dr. Lanyon directly, and that leads to his interview with Mr. Hyde, is contained in "a registered envelope, addressed in the hand of my colleague and old school-companion, Henry Jekyll" (41), and asks that he retrieve a container of chemicals from Jekyll's chambers and deliver them at midnight to an unknown man who will call on him at home. The request strikes the doctor as mad. "Upon the reading of this letter, I made sure my colleague was insane; but till that was proved beyond the possibility of doubt, I felt bound to do as he requested. [...] An appeal so worded could not be set aside without a grave responsibility" (43). The obligation Jekyll invokes is a reciprocal commitment that transcends scientific differences.

> Dear Lanyon, — you are one of my oldest friends; and although we may have differed at times on scientific questions, I cannot remember, at least on my side, any break in our affection. There was never a day when, if you had said to me, 'Jekyll, my life, my honour, my reason, depend upon you,' I would not have sacrificed my fortune or my left hand to help you (41-42)

But in fact, as we learn from Jekyll's own narrative, this plea was written by Mr. Hyde, desperate to escape from execution for the murder of Carew into Dr. Jekyll's unquestionable respectability.

These appeals to unbroken affection cannot be taken at face value, then. Moreover, as we eventually learn from the doctor's confession, Hyde is nothing more than the manifestation of the professional resentment that alienates Dr. Jekyll from Dr. Lanyon. "Had I approached my discovery in a more noble spirit," Jekyll recounts,

> had I risked the experiment while under the empire of generous or pious aspirations, all must have been otherwise, and from these agonies of death and birth I had come forth an angel instead of a fiend. The drug had no discriminating action; it was neither diabolical nor divine [...]. At that time my virtue slumbered; my evil, kept awake by ambition, was alert and swift to seize the occasion; and the thing that was projected was Edward Hyde. (51-52)

It is this professional resentment that invades Dr. Lanyon's chambers at midnight to retrieve the requested chemicals. Gloating over his verifying experiment, the simian murderer taunts Lanyon's curiosity until the positivist doctor agrees to witness his achievement. "Lanyon, you remember your vows: what follows is under the seal of our profession." The binding professional vows, publicized in Jekyll's institutional titles, but here invoked by the heretical, unsituated Mr. Hyde, are exactly congruent with the legal vacancy the signature on Jekyll's obscene will occupies. "And now, you who have so long been bound to the most narrow and material views, you who have denied the virtue of transcendental medicine, you who have derided your superiors — behold!" (46-47). What Lanyon sees dissolves his positivism into a stew of terrified affect, so that, when Mr. Utterson sees the great man afterwards, "he had his death-warrant written legibly upon his face" (29). "My life is shaken to its roots; sleep has left me; the deadliest terror sits by me at all hours of the day and night; I feel that my days are numbered, and that I must die; and yet I shall die incredulous" (47).

This, then, was the image that appeared in Stevenson's dream: As opposed to the cinematic visualizations, the transformation that embodies the catastasis and reveals the mystery is not that of Jekyll into Hyde, but the reverse. It is Mr. Hyde we see quaff the solution, Dr. Jekyll who emerges.

> He put the glass to his lips, and drank at one gulp. A cry followed; he reeled, staggered, clutched at the table and held on, staring with injected eyes, gasping with open mouth; and as I looked there came,

Conclusion

> I thought, a change — he seemed to swell — his face became suddenly black, and the features seemed to melt and alter — and the next moment I had sprung to my feet and leaped back against the wall, my arm raised to shield me from that prodigy, my mind submerged in terror.
> "O God!" I screamed, and "O God!" again and again; for there before my eyes — pale and shaken, and half fainting, and groping before him with his hands, like a man restored from death — there stood Henry Jekyll! (47)

Robert Louis Stevenson literalizes the insight that Nietzsche and Benjamin both recognized in its full metaphysical destructiveness: Beneath the signature that sutures life to the surface of the inscriptions authorizing the humane regimes of law and science, an insurrectionary, misanthropic force lies hidden. That force, which must always appear to public existence as a stunted, repulsive homicide, is history itself.

THE PAWNSHOP

At least once, almost a century ago, the now-time of history within which Friedrich Nietzsche and Walter Benjamin converge touched the surface of the world directly and was caught in the photographic emulsion of a moving picture. The year was 1916; the film Charlie Chaplin's two-reeler *The Pawnshop*. We know that Benjamin saw the film. In a letter to Horkheimer from March of 1940, mere months before his final flight from Paris, Benjamin mentions the psychoanalytically inspired autobiography of Michel Leiris, *L'Age d'homme*. "I admit myself," Benjamin writes in French,

> that the book reminds me of that gag of Chaplin's if you know it, in which he plays the role of a pawnshop employee. Seeing a client present an alarm-clock that he would like to pawn, he examines the object suspiciously, and then, just to be sure, he painstakingly disassembles the mechanism only in the end to sweep the detached pieces into the client's cap and announce that he is not able to put a price on such an object. I have heard that when [Alfred] Polgar saw the film he cried out "it's the spitting image of psychoanalysis." (*GB*, 6:407)

The routine, in which Chaplin renders Albert Austin's alarm clock worthless in the course of trying to determine its value, is one of the highlights of the unforgettable film. *The Pawnshop* is set in the traditionally Jewish milieu of a pawnbroker's establishment in an urban ghetto; the pawnbroker himself, Henry Bergman, is dressed in typically Jewish attire, although Chaplin makes nothing further of the ethnic associations. An absolute absence of anti-Semitism is a striking feature of Chaplin's entire persona. Here as Benjamin noted, he plays an incompetent clerk, ceaselessly scrapping with his fellow clerk (John Rand) behind the back of the shop's owner. The skirmishes move the pair through the four spaces within which the movie takes place: From the street with its storefront and policeman, through the shop floor where business is transacted, into the back room where pawned articles are stored, and finally to the kitchen, where Edna Purviance, Chaplin's love interest, embodies a domestic ideal. The pawnshop setting provides Chaplin with a host of disconnected props, and the comic "business" he undertakes with them makes it one of Chaplin's most inventive and surreal early films. The destruction of the alarm clock is one such episode.

Chaplin's twelve comedies for the Mutual company, made during the years 1916 and 1917, represent a provisional culmination in his astonishing career. "Fulfilling the Mutual contract, I suppose," he would recall later in his autobiography, "was the happiest period of my career. I was light and unencumbered, twenty-seven years old, with fabulous prospects and a friendly, glamorous world before me. Within a short time I would be a millionaire—it all seemed slightly mad."[2] The contract that had lured him from his earlier Essanay studio for an unprecedented sum was international news. Chaplin recounts, "That evening I stood with the crowd in Times Square as news flashed on the electric sign that runs round the Times building. It read: 'Chaplin signs with Mutual at six hundred seventy thousand a year.' I stood and read it objectively as though it were about someone else."[3]

Having come to the United States from England on tour with Fred Karno's vaudeville troop in 1912, Chaplin left the stage and began working with Mack Sennett's Keystone Studios the next year. There he learned the fundamentals of film production at the time, and in particular, was able explore in a restricted format the potentials of the rectangular spatial frame. In these early shorts and in the Essanay comedies that followed them, Chaplin worked with a limited number of camera setups mostly linked by immediate spatial continuity. Indeed, throughout his career, Chaplin rarely used either of the two great editing innovations of his contemporary D. W. Griffith: suspenseful crosscutting between distant scenes or emotional close-ups on significant details. Chaplin's art was, from the beginning,

Conclusion 257

The Pawnshop (Charles Chaplin, 1916). Film still courtesy of Film Preservation Associates.

geometric, exploiting the possibilities of recognition and misrecognition, interpolation and obscurity, of three-dimensional perspective in a two-dimensional frame. The later sentimentality associated with his longer feature films was melodramatic material grafted onto the dispassionate geometric structure of Chaplin's visual imagination.

Chaplin's films reached Germany relatively late,[4] but when they did, Walter Benjamin was particularly sensitive to this aspect of Chaplin's work. *His unique significance,* Benjamin remarked in a note from 1935, *lies in the fact that, in his work, the human being is integrated into the film image by way of his gestures—that is, his bodily and mental posture. The innovation of Chaplin's gestures is that he dissects the expressive movements of human beings into a series of minute innervations* (SW, 3:94; GS, 1:1040). It is just such a gesture that brings the now-time to the surface in *The Pawnshop*. Not the disassembling of the alarm clock but an earlier play with the measurement of temporality. The "Little Fellow" with his bowler hat and bamboo cane arrives at work with his typical jaunty irresponsibility. The title card reads: "Late—as usual." He is scolded by his boss, the pawnbroker, to whom he tips his hat ingratiatingly and shrugs. And then, as if to justify himself, Chaplin removes his pocket watch and checks it against the wall calendar.

Chaplin's gesture is minute. Yet in the incongruity between the cyclical time of the watch and the sequential time of the calendar, the full dislocation of mankind in temporality is contained. Such an incongruity is generally nothing more than nonsense; only the expressively charged environment of Chaplin's film world can briefly suspend it in visibility. The milieu of the silent film or the streets of the revolution. Chaplin's gesture is the comedic inversion of the revolutionary gesture Benjamin recounts in "On the Concept of History."

> What characterizes revolutionary classes at their moment of action is the awareness that they are about to make the continuum of history explode. The Great Revolution introduced a new calendar. The initial day of a calendar presents history in time-lapse mode. And basically it is this same day that keeps recurring in the guise of holidays, which are days of remembrance. Thus calendars do not measure time the way clocks do; they are monuments of a historical consciousness of which not the slightest trace has been apparent in Europe, it would seem, for the past hundred years. In the July Revolution an incident occurred in which this consciousness came into its own. On the first evening of the fighting, it so happened that the dials on clocktowers were being fired at simultaneously and independently from several locations in Paris. (SW, 4:395; GS 1:701–2)

Until the force of revolution reemerges in the present, the now-time of history will find refuge in such infinitesimal dislocations as *The Pawnshop*. Nietzsche and Benjamin are heralds of this tiny and catastrophic nuance.

THE END OF ALL THINGS

Kant's essay from 1794, "The End of All Things," an intervention in teleological debates among the learned readership of the *Berliner Monatsschrift*, draws its initial orientation from a theological characterization of the death of the other: "It is a common expression, especially when speaking piously, for a dying man to say that he is *passing from time into eternity*."[5] The pious expression, Kant recognizes, is inexact. Already the subjunctive mood posits it at the intersection of two utterly incompatible perspectives; the eulogistic farewell by the living toward the dead but, inversely, the mysterious perspective of the dying man himself. The incompatibility of these two perspectives will move through the essay, scuttling any epistemological claims it might seem to put forward. Their only reconciliation is not abstract knowledge (which cannot truly touch or be touched by death) but generalized death, an apocalyptic end to phenomenal reality as such. In clarifying the expression, Kant is thus pushed toward this apocalyptic conjunction, for a leave-taking from time conjures the possibility of an end to time itself, and the death of the other falls into a general death. The end of time is not an object that can be conceptualized but a site where reasonable reflection and immediate awareness no longer merge into knowledge. The best that can be derived in this domain is a reasonable preference for one internally coherent hypothesis over another, in terms of the practical consequences on moral behavior of adopting it. The end of time is sublime; repellent, "for it leads to an abyss, from which there is no possible return for whosoever falls into it"; attractive, "for one cannot cease from returning one's frightened eyes to it."[6] At the end of all things is the strange attractor of a singular departure and the compulsive return of a fascinated gaze.

What Trauerspiel manifests in its own generalization of the death of the other is a crisis beneath the Enlightenment's banishment of final cause as an *explanatory* principle to the interiority of subjective intentions. This teleological crisis is manifested not in the retrospective explanation of events but rather at the level of objective expression itself, as the collapse of resolution. The crisis is visible, Benjamin says, in modern drama's emancipation from the odd-numbered act structure still anachronistically conditioning Trauerspiel. "These dramas should not have had an odd number of acts, as was the case in imitation of the drama of the Greeks; an even number is much more appropriate to the repeatable actions which they describe.... With its emancipation from the three-act and five-act scheme, modern drama has secured the triumph of one of the tendencies of the baroque" (OT, 137–38; GS, 1:316). But as the introduction of fatal history into representation, this crisis is not limited to dramatic construction. The emancipation from resolution into implicit repetition apparent in modern drama can be recognized as a feature of all contemporary culture, from the repeat-and-fade non-cadences in rock songs to the sequels of action and horror movies to the episodic form of the television series.

That these contemporary sensory manifestations of the process of making sense of death all tend toward this dissolution of resolution into repetition is not the mark of their subordination to material interests within capitalism as a collective arrangement of individual human effort, as a social form; if we follow Benjamin, it registers at a far deeper level the collapse of meaning that materializes history in the object word. It is this historical materialization of the object that Benjamin will come to call "*Kapitalismus*"; commodities are not explanatorily dependent on capitalism, as the form the object of labor assumes when its production is appropriated for surplus value. Rather, capitalism is explanatorily dependent on the commodity, as the historical epoch within which such an object could appear. Cultural expressions participate in capitalism not merely at the level of human interest and intention, but because they share with it the temporal deep structure of the commodity; they are simultaneously new and always the same, returning eternally. The commodity's lack of resolution is implicit in its static dynamism. Like Trauerspiel, like mortal life, the commodity too cannot resolve.

No more can Nietzsche or Benjamin. Beyond their intersection and the precarious suspension it performs, neither thinker concludes, but both lives push the terminal moment into the contingent and arbitrary slough of historical change. But if these collapses and deaths, these escapes into nonexistent eternity, are meaninglessness, they are not thereby irrelevant. Benjamin's suicide, Nietzsche's madness project this meaninglessness back through their writing, which remains "essentially" incomplete: call, request, rebuttal, challenge. These philosophies produce meaning not through significant closure but by outrunning nonsense with perpetual explosive inventiveness. The truthful writer, the writer engaging a materialized history haunted by the unrealized hopes for happiness calling from the vanished lives of the past, operates, Benjamin says, under the imperative "never disappoint." His homologies with the destructive character, however, who operates under the imperative "never create," suggest an analogy outside the epistemological disappointment of the skeptical tradition. The "never disappoint" guiding Benjamin's philosopher is not so far away from the stand-up comedian's dictum to "keep it fresh." Successful comedians exhibit something called "timing," a word that gestures in temporal terms toward an extremely heterogeneous array of specifics of delivery, an array that appears as such only in their provisionally teleological relation to the immediate reaction of laughter. What is addressed and what laughs in such an encounter is not in the first instance an individual consciousness, but the "house." A stand-up monologue addresses itself to collective laughter. Alone, in his or her own name, with at best a few physical props, the stand-up comedian must create the demonic atmosphere of the laughing house, in which any mention of a recognizable feature of the common environment dissolves into spontaneous uproar. This congruence is not the manifestation of a clownish archetypal continuity beneath history, but is merely the effect of a contemporary cultural realization on the historical potentials buried in these earlier expressions. What appears behind the performance of stand-up comedy in the face of death is that aspect of Benjamin's conception that is a humorous inversion of the melancholy earnestness in its most obviously powerful expressions. It reminds us that if the destructive character isn't obviously funny, Walter Benjamin quite often is, and that his nihilism also flashes into a wide variety of amusements scattered throughout the constant catastrophe of history, a potential localized in the anecdotes on Kant he collected, the children's plays he wrote, the University of Muri he administered, and that must be heard as well in the spaces between the last reflections on the historical materialist. That potential can translate without loss of tragic insight the most terrifying aspects of Nietzsche's and of Benjamin's thought. But it will be borne by an alternate angel of history, loosed from the Spirit of Gravity, and speaking not to us, but to those who may come after us.

So this absence of resolution, as Benjamin and Nietzsche both struggled to show, can be thought as the paradoxical condition of an absolute revolution, when affirmed in the right manner. "Das es 'so weiter' geht, *ist* die Katastrophe." That things go on as before *is* the catastrophe, Benjamin says in "Central Park" (*SW*, 4:184; *GS*, 1:683). And yet, after seeing Chaplin's *The Circus*, Benjamin is struck most powerfully by the ending of the film.

> *The most wonderful part is the way the end of the film is structured. He strews confetti over the happy couple, and you think: This must be the end. Then you see him standing there when the circus procession starts off; he shuts the door behind everyone, and you think: This must be the end. Then you see him stuck in the rut of the circle earlier drawn by poverty, and you think: This must be the end. Then you see a close-up of his completely bedraggled form, sitting on a stone in the arena. Here you think the end is absolutely unavoidable, but then he gets up and you see him from behind, walking further and further away, with that gait peculiar to Charlie Chaplin; he is his own walking trademark, just like the company trademark you see at the end of other films. And now, at the only point where there's no break and you'd like to be able to follow him with your gaze forever*—just here the film ends! (*SW*, 2:200; *GS*, 6:138)

NOTES

PREFACE

1. Theodor W. Adorno. "Charakteristik Walter Benjamins," 1950, in *Gesammelte Schriften*, 20 vols., ed. Rolf Tiedemann. vol. 10.1 (Frankfurt am Main: Suhrkamp, 1997), 241. Translated into English by Samuel Weber and Shierry Weber as "A Portrait of Walter Benjamin," in Theodor W. Adorno, *Prisms* (Cambridge, Mass.: MIT Press, 1982), 231.

2. For an excellent overview of Nietzsche reception in the United States after the Second World War and the outsized roles played first by Walter Kaufmann and then by Jacques Derrida in creating a Nietzsche who would be at home in the specialized research university, see Jennifer Ratner-Rosenhagen, *American Nietzsche: A History of an Icon and His Ideas* (Chicago: University of Chicago Press, 2012), particularly chapters 5 and 6.

3. Helmut Pfotenhauer, "Benjamin und Nietzsche," in *"Links hatte noch alles sich zu enträtseln": Walter Benjamin im Kontext*, ed. Burkhardt Lindner (Frankfurt am Main: Syndikat, 1978), 111.

4. Irving Wohlfahrt, "Resentment Begins at Home: Nietzsche, Benjamin, and the University," in *On Walter Benjamin: Critical Essays and Recollections*, ed. Gary Smith (Cambridge, Mass.: MIT Press, 1988), 224–59.

5. Renate Reschke, "Barbaren, Kult und Katastrophen: Nietzsche bei Benjamin: Unzusammenhängendes im Zusammenhang gelesen," in *Aber ein Sturm weht vom Paradiese her: Texte zu Walter Benjamin*, ed. Michael Opitz and Erdmut Wizisla (Leipzig: Reclam, 1992), 303–39.

6. Stéphane Moses, "Benjamin, Nietzsche et l'idée de l'éternel retour," *Europe, revue littéraire mensuelle* 74, no. 804 (1996): 152.

INTRODUCTION: WALTER BENJAMIN, FRIEDRICH NIETZSCHE

1. Curt Paul Janz, *Friedrich Nietzsche,* 3 vols. (Munich: Carl Hanser Verlag, 1978), 3:224.

2. The meaning of the German word Förster being "forester," a Förster-Haus would be a gamekeeper's lodge.

3. The reference is in fact to the fairy-tale "Riffraff" ["*Lumpengesindel*"] in the collection by the Brothers Grimm, in which a rooster and a hen climb a hill to gather nuts before the squirrel can haul them away.

4. "*Nietzsches Leben ist typisch für die bloße Fernenbestimmtheit, die das Verhängnis der höchsten unter den fertigen Menschen ist.*"

5. *Urgeschichte*, Benjamin's term, first appears in the tragic theory of *The Origin of German Trauerspiel*. There Benjamin is contrasting tragic drama with the epic saga (*Sage*) that is the older form in which mythic content appears. "Tragic poetry is opposed to epic poetry as a tendentious re-shaping of the tradition," Benjamin writes there, ". . .The reshaping of the saga is not motivated by the search for tragic constellations, but it is undertaken with a tendentious purpose which would lose all its significance if the tendency were not expressed in terms of the saga, the primordial history [*Urgeschichte*] of the nation" (*OT*, 106; *GS*, 1:285). What distinguishes epic ur-history from tragedy is not its mythic content but the disinterested and impersonal presentation of that mythic material. The tendentiousness of tragedy is its defiant denunciation of mythic judgment; in the saga, "the streams of tradition, which surge down violently, often from opposite directions, have finally come to rest beneath the epic surface which conceals a divided, many-armed river-bed" (*OT*, 106; *GS*, 1:285).

At this point Benjamin is using the term *Urgeschichte* in its ordinary sense, to indicate the archaic narratives that precede any documented historical individuals. It is only later, in his overlooked essay on the French American writer Julien Green that Benjamin's own idiosyncratic use of the word begins to develop. It is the virtue of Green's novels, Benjamin claims, to depict the distinctly modern form of mythic suffering. Green's characters are destroyed by external chance, not by their internal drives, and "Chance is the figure of Necessity abandoned by God" (*SW*, 2:332, *GS*, 2:330). Thus the figures in Green's stories unite a sharply observed historical objectivity with the unsettling timelessness of mythic sanction.

> Inflexible as the mask-like personae of tragedians, [Green's characters] live out their lives in small French towns. Their clothes and their daily lives are stunted and old-fashioned, but in their gestures survive age-old rulers, evildoers, fanatics. . . . The merging of the old-fashioned with ur-history, the trauma of seeing one's parents in a dual perspective—one that is both historical and part of ur-history—is the abiding motif of this author. (*SW*, 335; *GS*, 2:333)

Ur-history converges with history in the parental generation; more important, it *disturbs* history. By the time of *The Arcades Project,* ur-history has become a *terminus technicus*, most emphatically in remarks from convolute N.

> "Ur-history of the nineteenth century"—this would be of no interest if it were understood to mean that forms of ur-history are to be recoverd among the inventory of the nineteenth century. Only where the nineteenth century would be presented as originary form of ur-history—in a

form, that is to say, in which the whole of ur-history groups itself anew in images appropriate to that century—only there does the concept of an ur-history of the nineteenth century have meaning. (AP, 463; GS, 5:579)

6. The term is from Benjamin's dissertation. As he himself notes of its genitive tergiversation: "The ambiguity of the designation [i.e., "Reflexions-medium"] in this case entails no lack of clarity. For, on the one hand, owing to its continuous context, reflection itself is a medium, and, on the other hand, the medium in question is one such that reflection moves within it—for reflection, as the absolute, moves within itself" (SW, 1:189; GS, 1:36).

7. Curt Paul Janz, *Friedrich Nietzsche*, 3 vols. (Munich: Carl Hanser, 1978), 1:629.

8. Ibid., 1:630.

9. Henry Wadsworth Longfellow, *The Works of Henry Wadsworth Longfellow* ed. Samuel Longfellow, 14 vols., vol. 1: *Voices of the Night, Poems on Slavery, The Belfry of Bruges, etc.* (Boston: Houghton, Mifflin, 1886), 79.

10. Ibid., 1:79–80.

1. MORTAL YOUTH

1. The small essay, titled "Did Grillparzer Farm with Goethe's Plough," already addresses the question of cultural continuity.

2. Thus in Benjamin's first letter to Ludwig Strauß, when he closes by inviting Strauß to contribute to a planned collection of pedagogically critical writings he and his colleagues are organizing, he gives a hint of his attitude toward juvenilia when he suggests he wants to publish not only essays but letters by Gymnasium students: "Moreover, I intend to collect school-boy letters [*Schülerbriefe*]. It's important to get documents of the school-boy life [*Schülerleben*] that novels and novellas basically distort" (GB, 1:65). Already here we see the documentary emphasis that will come to animate Benjamin's adult commitment to the material, archival, unintentional dimension of cultural transmission.

3. Theoretically, not philologically, impossible. The efforts made to reconstruct the context around these writings, many since Tiedemann's remark, are hardly futile, and undergird the present analysis. Examining the role of Judaism in the youth movement experiences of Benjamin, and so responding to different (though not incompatible) emphases in these texts is Astrid Deuber-Mankowsky's indispensable and sensitive study *Der frühe Walter Benjamin und Hermann Cohen: Jüdische Werte, Kritische Philosophie, vergängliche Erfahrung* (Berlin: Verlag Vorwerk, 2000). Her discussion is specified and complemented by Gabriele Guerra's *Judentum zwischen Anarchie und Theokratie: Ein religionspolitische Diskussion am Beispiel der Begegnung zwischen Walter Benjamin und Gershom Scholem* (Bielefeld: Aisthesis Verlag, 2007). A focus on the Youth Culture Movement in particular, as a part of the larger youth movement that grew out of the Wandervogel, is the topic of Peter Dudek's *Fetisch Jugend: Walter Benjamin und Siegfried*

Bernfeld—Jugendprotest am Vorabend des Ersten Weltkrieges (Bad Heilbrunn: Julius Klinkhardt, 2002) and Hans-Ulrich Wipf's *Studentische Politik und Kulterreform: Geschichte der Freistudenten-Bewegung 1896–1918* (Schwalbach: Wohenschau Verlag, 2004). The historiography of the youth movement still takes its impetus from Walter Laqueur's *Young Germany: A History of the German Youth Movement* (New York: Basic Books, 1962). And yet it cannot be denied that by hoisting Benjamin's early expressions seamlessly into the company of his adult precedents and contemporaries, these studies betray Benjamin's own intent at the time, which was less to engage these adults as interlocutors than to interrupt them in the name of a radically heterogeneous authority, "youth," which to their adult perspective must appear as juvenile naïveté and childish fantasy.

4. If anything, Elisabeth's interpolations into Nietzsche's oeuvre, in particular her distortions of his correspondence, reiterated and emphasized his hostility in particular to the anti-Semitism of her husband. For a useful corrective to the widespread postwar attribution of Nietzsche's politically reactionary consequences to his sister's bowdlerization, see Robert C. Holub, "The Elisabeth Legend: The Cleansing of Nietzsche and the Sullying of His Sister," in *Nietzsche, Godfather of Fascism? On the Uses and Abuses of a Philosophy*, ed. Jacob Golomb and Robert S. Wistrich (Princeton: Princeton University Press, 2002), 215–34.

5. As Aschheim remarks, with reference to Richard Frank Krummel's monumental and indispensable bibliographical registry of the Nietzschean explosion: *Nietzsche und der deutsche Geist*, "during these years [viz., 1890s] an encounter with Nietzsche—at least for the intelligentsia—was virtually mandatory" (Steven Aschheim, *The Nietzsche Legacy in Germany, 1890–1990* [Berkeley: University of California Press, 1992], 19).

6. Thomas Herfurth, "Zarathustras Adler im Wandervogelnest: Formen und Phasen der Nietzsche-Rezeption in der deutschen Jugendbewegung," *Jahrbuch des Archivs der Deutschen Jugendbewegung* 16 (1986/87): 82.

7. Christian Niemeyer, *Nietzsche, die Jugend und die Pädagogik: Eine Einführung* (Weinheim: Juventa Verlag), 103.

8. Hans-Georg Gadamer, "Nietzsche—Der Antipode: Das Drama Zarathustras," in *Gesammelte Werke 4: Neuere Philosophie II* (Tübingen: Mohr, 1987), 449.

9. For two academic years, from 1905 to 1907, Benjamin attended the progressive *Landerziehungsheim* in the tiny town of Haubinda, Thuringia. His experience at this educational institution was dominated by Gustav Wyneken, who taught philosophy at the school until 1906, when—in the midst of Benjamin's brief tenure—conflict with its founder forced him to leave. Wyneken's educational philosophy was frankly elitist, aimed at promoting the independence of exceptional students. In Haubinda Benjamin found this "English" approach much more congenial than the traditionalism of the Prussian Gymnasium curriculum even in its relatively modernized form. Wyneken's expulsion from Haubinda interrupted any preliminary relation between teacher and pupil, but Benjamin returned to the Kaiser-Friedrich-Schule a self-conscious representative of these progressive attitudes. The

founder of the Haubinda institution, Hermann Lietz, intended with it to replace an "Unterrichtsschule" with an "Erziehungsschule," a "school of lessons" with a "school of upbringing." "In his [viz., Lietz's] residential schools he attempted to realize the idea of upbringing [*Erziehung*] through communal living and to reinvigorate that power of upbringing that had disappeared from the family. In order to protect youth from damaging urban influences, the new school had to be set in the country, where it was possible to raise youth in immediate proximity to nature. In the *Landerziehungsheimen* the teachers and students lived together in comradely community" (Hinrich Jantzen, *Jugendkultur und Jugendbewegung: Studie zur Stellung und Bedeutung Gustav Wynekens innerhalb der Jugendbewegung*, [Frankfurt am Main: Dipa-Verlag, 1963], 15).

10. Gustav Wyneken, *Schule und Jugendkultur*. 2nd ed. (Jena: Eugen Diederichs, 1914), 63.

11. This inversion of hermeneutic authority between the mentor and his disciple is what restricts our consideration of Nietzsche's role to its immediate manifestation in Benjamin and spares us the task of charting in detail the immensely complex contours of antebellum avant-garde Nietzscheanism. The particular emphases in his writings brought out by self-consciously Jewish Nietzscheans, both Zionists and not, is the relevant context for Benjamin's first discussions of the philosopher. We will in part touch on the matter when considering his letters to Ludwig Strauß. But in general there is an absence of sophisticated interpretations of Nietzsche in Benjamin's youthful milieu, even acknowledging the efforts, far more respectable than Wyneken's, of "Mynona," or Salomo Friedländer, a passionate disciple and prolific expositor of Nietzsche, whom Benjamin thought highly of in this regard (*SF*, 58; *GF*, 63). The paucity of substantive Nietzsche interpretations is an example of Benjamin's more general intellectual isolation in these early years, an isolation that was noted by his associates almost as soon as he reached intellectual maturity with the First World War.

12. This Nietzsche, too, has affinities with contemporary interpretations that, while not immediately deriving from it, also react to the ontological bias characteristic of Nietzsche's more sophisticated interpretations in the 1930s, and so also develop a more tactical and performative image of the philosopher. Here Sarah Kofman's and Eric Blondel's work deserve particular notice.

13. The canonical account from Benjamin's hand is his letter from 10 October 1912 to Ludwig Strauß. "The decisive influence was this: in a Landeserziehungsheim in which I spent 1¾ important years my teacher was the man who would later found the Freie Schulgemeinde Wickersdorf, Dr. Wyneken" (*GB*, 1:70).

14. Wyneken has suffered the compound misfortune of having in Heinrich Kupffer an unsympathetic and a competent biographer. Kupffer describes the general pattern of Wyneken's reformist engagement as follows: "At first Wyneken would be dissatisfied with a given situation and develop a revolutionary plan aimed at bringing about an entirely new order. He would win over accomplices who were enthusiastic about his ideas, and

together they would battle the opposed group of conservatives. Finally after partially succeeding in their attempts Wyneken would break with his allies, who would then distance themselves from him, so that he would again be, as at first, alone in opposition. And now the same movement would recommence" (Heinrich Kupffer, *Gustav Wyneken* [Stuttgart: Ernst Klett, 1970], 64.). Under Wyneken's leadership, his embodied idea in its new site at Wickersdorf was caught up in further turmoil. Though the school Wyneken and his colleague Paul Geheeb had established flourished, the two men fell out between themselves. Geheeb was removed acrimoniously in 1909, but by 1910 parental complaints and his own intransigence had cost Wyneken, too, his position as director of the school he had cofounded four years before. The directorship of Wickersdorf now fell to a formerly trusted younger colleague, and Wyneken's example was exiled from its native field of operation. Benjamin would rejoin Wyneken only after this severance from his institutional achievement had taken place, and he would break with his mentor well before Wyneken managed to recapture administrative ascendancy over Wickersdorf. Thus throughout the five years Benjamin was associated with him, Wyneken was in intellectual exile, trying to regain control of his expropriated experiment. Wickersdorf, as the lost but extant site of his pedagogic innovations, monopolized Wyneken's understanding of school reform; any compromise with other educational projects seemed to pull him further from an eventual return.

15. Although the group abjured any overt confessional identity, a large percentage of its members were Jewish despite Wyneken's own lack of interest in Jewish influences in German society (a lack of interest that would in turn offer his opportunism little moral resistance, despite his broadly leftwing political sympathies, when the Nazis came to power).

16. Erdmut Wizisla, "'Fritz Heinle war Dichter': Walter Benjamin und sein Jugendfreund," in *"Was nie geschrieben wurde, lesen," Frankfurter Benjamin-Vorträge,* ed. Lorenz Jäger and Thomas Regehly (Bielefeld: Aisthesis Verlag, 1992), 115–31. For a detailed account of the *Sprechsaalbewegung,* which rapidly expanded to Prague, Munich, Stuttgart, Freiburg, Heidelberg, and other major urban centers, see Dudek, *Fetisch Jugend,* 121–48.

17. The most detailed and influential reading of the "Metaphysics of Youth" can be found in Sigrid Weigel's *Body- and Image-Space: Rereading Walter Benjamin,* trans. Georgina Paul with Rachel McNicholl and Jeremy Gaines (London: Routledge, 1996). There, in a central chapter on the transformation of images to dialectical images, Weigel submits the text to a careful consideration and discovers a host of "curious ways" in which "Metaphysics of Youth" connects to the Arcades Project and Benjamin's last reflections. For Weigel, who is centrally concerned with rescuing the neglected or simplified implications in Benjamin's work for theoretical appropriations of gender, the "Metaphysics of Youth" displays with naive brio the elements of a complicated gendering of thought that persists—despite all the subsequent changes—throughout the thought-images structuring Benjamin's mature reflections on modernity.

18. The Night beyond its edge turns out to be, in point of fact, the nocturnal dimension of Benjamin's mature thought, as it is expressed in the essays on Kafka and Karl Kraus.

19. This anticipatory posture is primordial in Benjamin's work. "On a journey one ought not to wear his worst outfit, since a journey is an international cultural act: one steps forth from his private existence into the public realm" (*GS*, 6:232). So begins Benjamin's boyhood travel-diary from April 1911. What is here remarked at the most literal level, a responsibility attendant upon the emergence into public visibility, will accompany the juvenilia throughout its development. Three and a half years later, in his discussion of Hölderlin, the resonances will have expanded immeasurably, but the moment will still be recognizable: "Drum, mein Genius, tritt nur / Bar ins Leben und sorge nicht!" ["Therefore, my genius, simply enter / Naked into life and have no care!"] Benjamin quotes Hölderlin, and then exposits: "Here 'life' lies outside poetic existence; in the new version it is not the precondition but the object of a movement accomplished with a mighty freedom: the poet *enters into* life; he does not wander forth in it" (*SW*, 1:28; *GS*, 2:116).

20. It is here that we must take issue with Weigel's characterization of Benjamin's gender politics in this text. The Genius and the Prostitute are indeed "counterparts," as she suggests (Sigrid Weigel. *Body- and Image-Space: Rereading Walter Benjamin.* Translated by Georgina Paul et al. [London: Routledge, 1996], 84), but only because both of them are essentially silent. Both the Genius and the Prostitute are transfigured by pure passivity in the face of culture; they contrast with the everyday active "thinkers and women" who haunt the café. That a passive prostitute exists as an ideal potential in every active woman and a passive genius as ideal potential in every active thinker does not permit an equation between these two manifestations, since the active thinkers and women fall on the side of the blaspheming speaker, while the passive genius and prostitute embody the ideal side of the validating listener.

21. The later complexity of Benjamin's figure of the whore, with its Baudelairean provenance, its political implications, and its relation to the gendered situation of Benjamin's text as a whole, are ably explored by Weigel, particularly pages 86–89. As Weigel notes, the later thought-figure is associated with a terminological change from *Dirne* to *Hure* in *The Arcades Project* notes, where we find reflections on *the dialectical function of money in prostitution* (*AP*, 492; *GS*, 5:614), or the systematization of fetishes it produces (*Prostitution opens a market in feminine types* [*AP*, 515; *GS*, 5:641]). At the same time, the fundamental aspects of Benjamin's relation to the prostitute continue to operate even here: that she is a position of identification (*Love for the prostitute is the apotheosis of empathy with the commodity* [*AP*, 511; *GS*, 5:637]), and that she marks a site of ambiguous suspension (*It is not only from the thresholds of these gates of imagination that lovers and friends like to draw their energies; it is from thresholds in general. Prostitutes, however, love the thresholds of these gates of dream* [*AP*, 494; *GS*, 5:617–18]). This latter aspect is what binds the prostitute to gambling in general.

22. "She [viz., the prostitute] expels Nature from her ultimate sanctuary, sexuality," Benjamin writes to Blumenthal. In the context of the youthful facies, this is unmitigated praise, and it would be anachronistic to understand it in terms of a Habermasian colonization of the life-world through alienating, instrumental reason.

23. *Let two mirrors reflect each other*, Benjamin would write in the earliest notes of *The Arcades Project* in 1927; *then Satan plays his favorite trick and opens here in his way (as his parner does in lovers' gazes) the perspective on infinity* (*AP*, 877; *GS*, 5:1049).

24. This motif of a conjunction of immortality and death survives in the more challenging messianic context of the "Theologico-Political Fragment."

25. Strauß would in fact eventually become Buber's son-in-law.

26. Richard Frank Krummel, *Nietzsche und der deutsche Geist, vol. 1: Ausbreitung und Wirkung des Nietzscheschen Werkes im deutschen Sprachraum bis zum Todesjahr: Ein Schriftumsverzeichnis der Jahre 1867–1900* (Berlin: de Gruyter, 1998), 123.

27. The historical context informing this antebellum encounter between the young Benjamin and Buber's existential Zionism is definitively presented in terms of modern German-Jewish Messianism in Rabinbach's *In the Shadow of Catastrophe: German Intellectuals between Apocalypse and Enlightenment*. The immediate issue grew up between Strauß and Benjamin through the *Kunstwart* debate, a literary controversy over Jewish participation in German cultural traditions and the imperative to develop specifically Jewish cultural expressions. Strauß had published on the controversy, and the possibility of a joint journalistic enterprise that would develop the perspectives opened up thereby was what motivated Benjamin and Strauß's initial correspondence.

28. Martin Buber, *Drei Reden über das Judentum* (Frankfurt am Main: Rütten and Loening, 1911), 60–61.

29. Indeed, it is not hard to identify the Zionist Strauß in the "Dialogue on the Religiosity of the Present": "I could well imagine speaking with someone who had an outlook very different from yours," Benjamin's "I" interjects suddenly, two-thirds of the way through the dialogue. "For him, the social would have been an experience [*Erlebnis*] that first violently tore him out of his most naive and unbroken integrity. He would have represented the mass of the living [*Masse der Lebenden*], and he belongs in the widest sense to the historical religions" (*EW*, 76; *GS*, 2:31).

30. Johann Wolfgang von Goethe. *Werke. Hamburger Ausgabe in 14 Bänden*, ed. Erich Trunz et al. (Munich: Deutscher Taschenbuch Verlag, 1988), 3:23 (*Faust I*, l.489–90).

31. Bernd Witte sees the relation of German to Jew behind the contrast: "Much speaks for the fact that Benjamin saw in this confrontation the archetypical realization of his idea of a pure spiritual community and hence at the same time his desired symbiosis of German and Jew. For him Heinle was the productive one, the poet, who could speak in the name of Love, whereas he himself identified with the role of a literatus who intended to decipher the spiritual in all manifestations of life" (Bernd Witte, *Walter Benjamin:*

Mit Selbstzeugnissen und Bilddokumenten [Reinbek bei Hamburg: rororo-Rowohlt, 1985], 25). Witte's remarks conflate the posthumous asymmetry in the relation with its earlier commutative dynamic, and thus obscure the transformative meaning of death in the friendship. That the tortured history of German Jewish relations played into the relation between Heinle and Benjamin is certainly the case, but the fatal distribution of roles that fixed Heinle as Speaker and Benjamin as Addressee occurred against the brutal interruption of a dated and individual suicide, and did not grow out of collective archetypal soil. And even should we wish to search for recognizable referents behind these undefined terms, given the commutative symmetry in Benjamin's letter (which Witte must here read as politically compensatory idealization), a more relevant cultural opposition than Jew to German would be Jew to Catholic. Neither Benjamin nor Heinle were practicing members of these respective religions, but the intellectual milieu within which they met was beholden to a Catholicism that inflected the political anti-Semitic discrimination at work in Wilheminian Germany but cannot be reduced to it. The move from Freiburg to Berlin was also a move from a Thomistic, institutionalized milieu to a Lutheran, pietistic milieu. Against this background, the alliance of Heinle and Benjamin that founds the *Sprechsaal* in Berlin is an alliance between two theological positions outside the dominant milieu, one of which represents the oldest continuous church institution on the planet, and the other of which represents the oldest continuous monotheistic religion on the planet. The symmetry between Heinle and Benjamin rests in part, from this perspective, on symmetries between Catholic/Protestant in a Protestant culture, and Jewish/Christian in a Christian culture. That Catholicism is Jewish apostasy and Protestantism Catholic heresy—this unstable parallelism positions both Benjamin and Heinle in Berlin as representatives of older religious continuities surviving in a culture that has rebelled against them. In general, the role of pre- and post-Reformation Catholicism in Benjamin's thinking has not been sufficiently considered in its own terms, all too often being reduced to Romanticism and thus stripped of its theological vitality. No doubt Romanticism inflected Benjamin's understanding of Catholic dogma. But it is to reverse the order of implication, should one forget that the institution of these dogmas, and their reasonable elaboration, is a theological, and not an aesthetic, reality. The usurpation of the "Symbol" by Romantic art theory of which the Trauerspiel book speaks is illegitimate precisely on account of this reversal, which can only come about through a forgetting of what is at stake in theology: salvation from death. This amnesiac posture toward salvation is in fact the very regress of forgetting itself: To forget is also to forget that you have forgotten. The fact that the promise made by the Catholic Church is mendacious, and that those who die in its arms are as dead as everybody else, does not render Catholic theology irrelevant, but centralizes it as the paradigmatic model of visible authority. Benjamin's Judaism is, needless to say, complex. But throughout his career it has theological force as a specifically pre- and anti-Catholicism, and not merely in opposition to undifferentiated "Christianity" or the immediate national identifications this term disguises. In short, to the extent that this opposition between "love" and "symbol" in Benjamin's letter can be coordinated with recognizable commitments, it seems far more likely that these commitments involved the encounter of Jew and Catholic, not Jew and German.

32. "For if it is the danger of the daybook as such to lay bare prematurely the germs of memory in the soul and prevent the ripening of its fruits, the danger must necessarily become fatal when the spiritual life expresses itself only in the daybook," as Benjamin remarks in Goethes Wahlverwandtschaften (*SW*, 1:338; *GS*, 1:178).

33. In his 1917 appropriation of neo-Kantian terminology, "On the Program of the Coming Philosophy," Benjamin gestures toward this subversive conceptual possibility: "But besides the concept of synthesis, another concept, that of a certain nonsynthesis of two concepts in another, will become very important systematically, since another relation between thesis and antithesis is possible besides synthesis." If we mark this possibility with the formula "continual subversion," it is merely a provisional convenience, for this certain nonsynthetic relation between concepts, Benjamin notes, "can hardly lead to a fourfold structure of relational categories, however" (*SW*, 1:106; *GS*, 2:166).

34. The essay on Wieland, for instance, is an exception.

35. "The concept of the poetized is in two respects a limit-concept. It is first of all a limit-concept with respect to the concept of the poem.... At the same time, however, it [the poetized] is a limit-concept with respect to another functional unity, ... the idea of the task, corresponding to the idea of the solution as which the poem exists.... For the creator, this idea of the task is always life.... Thus, the poetized emerges as the transition from the functional unity of life to that of the poem" (*SW*, 1:19–20; *GS*, 2:107).

36. Immanuel Kant. *Kritik der reinen Vernunft*, in *Werke* (Akademie-Ausgabe), ed. the Royal Prussian Academy of Sciences, 11 vols. (Berlin: Walter de Gruyter, 1968), 79 (A58/B82).

37. Georg Wilhelm Friedrich Hegel, *The Phenomenology of Spirit*, trans. A. V. Miller (Oxford: Oxford University Press, 1977), 19. *Die Phänomenologie des Geistes*, 1806, *Werke*, vol. 3. ed. Eva Moldenhauer and Karl Markus Michel (Frankfurt am Main: Suhrkamp Verlag, 1970), 36.

38. In this regard, we draw attention to Werner Hamacher's essay on Celan, "The Second of Inversion." "By virtue of the mediating and converting character of the substantial subject, a meaning attaches itself to each linguistic sign it posits—we indeed 'want to name' this unreality (even after a certain hesitation) death—and this meaning remains indispensable for the interaction between the sign, what it signifies, and the communicative interaction between different speakers" (Werner Hamacher, "The Second of Inversion: Movements of a Figure through Celan's Poetry," in *Premises: Essays on Philosophy and Literature from Kant to Celan*, trans. Peter Fenves [Stanford: Stanford University Press, 1996], 341). Hamacher's point, that negativity relates to significance only by passing through, as death, a subject already mastering it, may hold for Hegel (though Derrida's remarks on the figure of the tomb and its economy of death in Hegel's semiology suggest that the story even here is more complicated than this allows). For Benjamin,

and for Nietzsche, such a passage is impossible; death is never mastered by the reflecting subject, but always exceeds it, leaving philosophy to assume a theological space once congruent with the infinite deity: the sense, from one perspective, of the formula "Gott ist tot." It becomes the principle of signification not merely by temporizing the encompassing subject, but by exceeding and destroying any formulation that subject produces, so that there always must be more significance, more language.

39. Thus Benjamin's motive for transcribing much later in his *Passagen-Werk*, with these particular ellipses, the following Nietzschean observation: *On suicide as signature of modernity*. "*One cannot sufficiently condemn Christianity for having devalued the value of such a great purifying nihilistic movement, as was perhaps already being formed . . . through continual deterrence from the deed of nihilism, which is suicide*" (*AP*, 370; *GS*, 5:467, in Nietzsche, *KSA*, 13:222). Benjamin is noting this from a citation in Löwith. In its context in Löwith's interpretation the citation indicates a point of contrast between Christianity and its fraternal twin version of nihilism, Buddhism. Both religions express the "will to nothing" whose only antidote is the Eternal Return, but Christianity, in addition, bears a positive responsibility for hindering the benefits that might have resulted from the cultural developments with which its triumph interfered. Löwith takes this to imply that Nietzsche's own doctrine is an attempt to reinvigorate that antique non-Christian cultural development: "It is the intention of Nietzsche's teaching to set free this purifying movement in Europe" (*NER*, 114; *NEW*, 108). Thus Benjamin is noting an interpretation of Nietzsche's passage that situates its relevance between, roughly, Constantine and Nietzsche himself. (Löwith's discussion is in the chapter on the anti-Christian repetition of antiquity at the summit of modernity.)

2. PRESENTATION

1. Thomas Mann, "Nietzsche's Philosophy in the Light of Contemporary Events," in *Thomas Mann's Addresses Delivered at the Library of Congress, 1942–1949* (Washington: Library of Congress, 1963), 99.

2. The anticipatory dimension of Nietzsche's production, which we here merely evoke and do not claim to define or describe, and which is also its irreducibly "prejudicial" dimension, governs its profound affinity for phenomenological inquiry, as well.

3. Already here in this early methodological distinction we can see how Benjamin's thinking divorces the significance of historical documents from their obvious relevance, which is borne by the continuous history relating them to the present. The point perhaps remains latent in this case, because Benjamin is talking about Goethe, whose public profile has never faltered since he produced his works. But the fact that what mattered about a work is merely the condition and never the content of what matters about it now is what allows Benjamin to begin to conceptualize and make operational a notion of *dis*continuous history. And even here, Benjamin's reading is far more sensitive to the historically conditioned "strangeness" of Goethe's late

productions, a strangeness that must strike any unprepared, naive contemporary reader.

4. In the appendix to his dissertation, for instance, where a discussion of Goethe's metaphysics rests on an analysis that distributes a priori artistic substance (*Gehalt*) into a plurality of "pure contents" ("*reine Inhalte*"). See *GS*, 1:111–12; *SW*, 1:179 (though the contrast between *Gehalt* and *Inhalt* is lost through their common translation as "content").

5. In developing his method of reading through the contrast between a positivist philological discipline and a speculative reaction to that disciplined object, Benjamin is continuing the essential division that defines philology as an intellectual enterprise. As long ago as Friedrich Schleiermacher's development of "hermeneutics" in the wake of Kantian critique and the Romantic rediscovery of the classical heritage, philology found itself negotiating a breach between a "higher" and a "lower" version of its inquiry. For Schleiermacher, the distinction reduces to a contrast between intentional and unintentional distortions introduced into the textual record: the "lower," "documentary," or "nonarbitrary" emendations eliminating unintentional mistakes of transcription, while the "higher," "divinatory," "arbitrary" sort of critique appears "everywhere there is a presupposition that between the document as it lies before us and the original fact an arbitrary [*willkürliche*] act has intervened and altered the relation of the former to the latter." The mission of this higher, hermeneutical philology is "to determine as completely as possible the intervening act and to present the reasons and intentions and provenance of the forgery" (Friedrich Schleiermacher, "Über Begriff und Einteilung der philologischen Kritik" [1830], in *Hermeneutik und Kritik*, ed. Manfred Frank [Frankfurt am Main: Suhrkamp, 1977], 359).

6. "In the course of this duration, the concrete realities rise up before the eyes of the beholder all the more distinctly the more they die out in the world" (*SW*, 1:297; *GS*, 1:125). Benjamin's word "*Realien*" is the common term for the anachronistic referents philology is called upon to explicate. But the word disappears from his discussion immediately, once the referential dimension of Goethe's novel has surrendered to the more profound sense of material content as Myth.

7. This fundamentally *diagnostic* relation to Goethe by way of Kant is the posture Benjamin adopts from Georg Simmel, who must be understood to structure the essay at a profound level. Throughout Simmel's career the juxtaposition of Kant and Goethe served an extensive expository function, and he returned to it again and again, from "Kant und Goethe" of 1899 to the essay of the same name from 1906 to an essay "Über Goethes und Kants moralische Weltanschauung" from 1908 to the "Fragmente eines Goethe-Buches: Aus dem Kapitel über Goethe und Kant" of 1909 to the Goethe book itself, from 1918, that Benjamin cites explicitly in his own analysis. Simmel's constant motif is that these two figures represent two utterly antithetical postures toward man's relations to what transcends himself—the subject or unchanging law in Kant's case versus the object or protean nature in Goethe's. Despite an essay by Fredric Jameson that draws out the relation between Benjamin and Simmel in very general terms in order primarily to

criticize the impasses of Simmel's thought, his role specifically in Benjamin's image of Goethe remains to be explored. Cf. Fredric Jameson, "The Theoretical Hesitation: Benjamin's Sociological Predecessor," *Critical Inquiry* 25, no. 2 (1999): 267–88.

8. "Jener scheussliche Hexentrank aus Wollust und Grausamkeit" (*BT*, 40; *KSA*, 1:33); "that horrible witches' brew of sensuality and cruelty." The translator Kaufmann has added scare-quotes around the metaphor, a distancing not in the original, and a fine example of the domesticating gesture that compromises Kaufmann's hugely well-informed and sympathetic Americanization of Nietzsche.

9. The critique of Nietzsche's aestheticism is a recognizable descendant of Benjamin's juvenile critique of pantheism. There, harmless "Übermenschentum" accompanied a complacent acknowledgment of the morally indifferent immanent natural totality, *deus sive natura*, an acknowledgment that failed to take the demonic aspects of mortal nature seriously. The loss of positive religious transcendence, the historical condition any genuine new religiosity must countenance, appears initially in this pretentious and insufficient way, as the reduction of moral seriousness to aesthetic appreciation. What is truly at stake in pantheism is not presented by its proponents themselves but appears indirectly in those "*Literaten*" who exhibit a self-destructive commitment to transcendent values despite the historical anachronism of those values. So too Nietzsche's philological skepticism, his refusal to acknowledge the contemporary availability of tragic significance, is the condition for any genuine insight into tragic meaning. But the mere affirmation of that negative condition is the recipe for a superficial posture that is, in its own way, as objectionable as the pious humanist tradition. Yet the historical dimension Benjamin's mature theory introduces alters the terms of the debate fundamentally: The disingenuous acceptance of nihilistic superficiality is itself an interpretable event in the past, so its negative, critical function can be retained even as its self-important posturing is rejected. This makes possible a conflation, as different phases of the same extended process, of the diagnostically valuable "*Literaten*" who anachronistically agitate for impossible transcendence and the theoretically accurate pantheist who asserts the irrevocability of immanence. Nietzsche the Wagnerian is thus the disillusioning if superficial advocate of immanence, while Nietzsche's rejection of Wagner as nihilist (for the characterization Benjamin relies on here is Nietzsche's own, if a later Nietzsche) aligns the philosopher with the symptomatic man of letters.

10. Georg Lukács, *Die Seele und die Formen: Essays* (1911; Neuwied: Luchterhand Verlag, 1971), 227. Translated as *Soul and Form* by Anna Bostock (Cambridge, Mass.: MIT Press, 1974), 182.

11. Lukács, *Soul and Form*, 175; *Die Seele und die Formen*, 218.

12. Lukács, *Soul and Form*, 184; *Die Seele und die Formen*, 230.

13. Lukács, *Soul and Form*, 197; *Die Seele und die Formen*, 248–49.

14. In the essay on Goethe's *Elective Affinities*, Benjamin describes "the relation between myth and truth. This relation is one of mutual exclusion. There is no truth, for there is no unequivocalness [*Eindeutigkeit*]—and

hence not even error—in myth" (*SW*, 1:325–26; *GS*, 1:162). In the Trauerspiel book, Benjamin develops this insight in terms of the demonic: "The tragic is to the demonic what the paradox is to ambiguity [*Zweideutigkeit*]. In all the paradoxes of tragedy . . . ambiguity, the stigma of the demonic, is in decline" (*OT*, 109; *GS*, 1:288). Between equivocation and ambiguity the possibility of intentional deception attends the notions of myth and of daemon, bringing the meaning of the German "*Zweideutigkeit*" into proximity with the English "duplicity."

15. The importance of the notion of myth in Benjamin has long been noted; "The reconciliation of myth [*Versöhnung des Mythos*] is the theme of Benjamin's philosophy," as Adorno put it in 1950 (*AGS*, 10:244), and in this spirit Winfried Menninghaus has devoted a treatise to Benjamin's "doctrine of thresholds" as a theory of myth. Nonetheless, without denying the importance of this notion to Benjamin's thought, it is essential to recognize that the "reconciliation of myth" is in fact the theme of Adorno's, not Benjamin's, philosophy. In particular, the antimythological role that theology plays in Benjamin can be understood only with the greatest difficulty, if at all, when religion is assimilated to myth through their common opposition to Enlightenment reason. A "dialectic of Enlightenment" in the sense in which Horkheimer and Adorno develop it in the 1940s, as mythic domination at the horizon of a transparent reason ostensibly hostile to it, is quite alien to the emphases of Benjamin's concerns, regardless of the various congruencies that can be made to appear between them. Despite the oft-quoted remark in convolute N on the *whetted ax of reason* (*AP*, 456; *GS*, 5:570), and despite the seriousness of his epistemology, Benjamin does not see in "*Vernunft*," reason, a particularly useful category. The idealist heritage burdens the term with an ineradicable complacency, importing into the definition of collective thought the transparency to redemptive truth that it is in fact the task of a far more tenuously collective thought only to *prepare*, a humble assignment nonetheless already almost beyond its powers.

Menninghaus, for instance, in adopting this Adornian perspective, is forced into a series of misreadings that draw him well away from Benjamin. Despite Menninghaus's claims, Benjamin's thought does not evince a period shift between an early, wholly negative notion of myth and a later revision in which "the negative accents of the concept of myth are 'dialectized' by positive ones"; nor does Benjamin ever situate myth "in the first instance among motifs of social theory" (Winfried Menninghaus, *Schwellenkunde: Walter Benjamins Passage des Mythos* [Frankfurt am Main: Suhrkamp, 1986], 111). What is here attributed to Benjamin is in fact the difference between his extreme conception and Adorno's sociological concentration. Menninghaus's attempt to understand Benjamin by relating his notion of myth to his notion of threshold, however many complementary theories of myth it enlists to explain the connection, remains perhaps a helpful catalogue of quotations from Benjamin's scattered works but falls short of any understanding of these notions, since it can neither decide which of the two, mythos or threshold, is explicans or explicandum, nor, more importantly, convey in any way the *urgency* of Benjamin's conception. Menninghaus is aware of this last shortcoming, as his self-effacing conclusion indicates: "Does the rank of Benjamin's writings lie in their fundamental concepts and motifs at all, here in the myth/anti-myth schema? Or is it rather that in their detailed efforts they forget and even transcend the 'identical' fundamental motifs?" (114). The urgency of Adorno's thought is indissolubly linked to the Shoah, and interpretations of Benjamin that begin from Adorno's perspective tend to assume that a similar relation holds, anachronistically, for Benjamin—a reading that is primed for disappointment, as Derrida's "Force of Law" prominently illustrates. Benjamin's conceptions can, of course, help us encounter the Shoah, but this is our urgency, not his.

16. In particular, Benjamin's letter to Rang of 20 January 1924, asking "what evidence is there for a derivation of tragedy from the *agon* outside of the word 'protagonist,'" documents the help Rang provided on this point. But the perspective is far from alien to Benjamin, whose entire theoretical posture can be said to be antagonistic, destructive in the extreme.

17. Franz Rosenzweig, *Der Stern der Erlösung* (1921; Frankfurt am Main: Suhrkamp Verlag, 1988), 83. English: *The Star of Redemption*, trans. Barbara E. Galli (Madison: University of Wisconsin Press, 2005), 85. Further references to Rosenzweig's work are given in the text to these editions. The translation of this sentence quoted by Benjamin follows the translation of Benjamin's treatise. The reference there is (*OT*, 108; *GS*, 1:286–87).

18. In its original context in Rosenzweig's exposition, prerevelation silence will prove in the event to contrast with a postrevelation liturgical silence, a silence that, unlike tragic defiance, harbors the promise of redemption. "There is a *Schweigen* here," Rosenzweig writes in the introduction to the third part of the treatise, "that is unlike the speechlessness of the primordial world that has no words yet, but a silence that no longer needs words. It is the silence of perfect understanding. Here, a glance says everything" (*SR*, 313; *SE*, 328). In Benjamin's theory there is no place for such a satisfied collective silence, and the illusion of perfect comprehension within a human collective is precisely what tragic defiance so purely challenges. Beyond Benjamin's tragic silence *conceptually* there lies only an unimaginable messianic transformation, something far different from what lies *after* tragic silence *historically*. For Rosenzweig, tragic silence passes over into the order of revelation outside of history, through the miracle, whereas in Benjamin tragic silence collapses into the irony of a figure barely present in Rosenzweig's treatise, the figure of Socrates. "The martyr-drama was born from the death of Socrates as a parody of tragedy" (*OT*, 113; *GS*, 1:292). The pure silence of the tragic hero dissolves into an antibiotic punch line, a sarcastic cock for Asclepius.

19. As Jane Newman has shown in her careful reconstruction of the literary-historical debates around the German Baroque in the early years of the twentieth century, the distinction between Renaissance and Baroque was at this time anything but an innocent question of periodization, but mediated profound questions of national origin and identity. The Renaissance stood in for an "imitative," derivative movement and the Baroque for an original and nationally distinct phenomenon. Shakespeare, an author of the English Renaissance appropriated by nineteenth- and twentieth-century German

nationalists as part of the particularly German literary tradition, and more specifically the "Germanic" tragedy *Hamlet*, became a privileged site of contention for these debates. Cf. Jane O. Newman, *Benjamin's Library: Modernity, Nation, and the Baroque* (Ithaca: Cornell University Press, 2011), esp. 115–54.

20. Years later, Benjamin would say of *The Arcades Project* in a letter to Scholem, "I have had to expand the ideas of the project more and more. I have thus had to make it so universal within its most particular and minute framework that it will take possession of the *inheritance* of surrealism in purely temporal terms and, indeed, with all the authority of a philosophical Fortinbras" (*CB*, 342; *GB*, 3:420). The object endorses the philosophical work that attends it the way Hamlet grants succession to Fortinbras. The author is implicated only secondarily.

21. Benjamin's privilege of writing over speech in the understanding of language has made him, from a contemporary perspective, an important forerunner of deconstruction. And yet the differences between Benjamin's allegorical perspective and the deconstructive intervention in signifying processes ought not to be too quickly reduced. With Derrida, writing is a privileged object of reflection because it is inscribed as a phenomenological potential in all signifying practices. The gap between signifier and signified that constitutes the sign in its generality is reflected in writing more visibly than it is in speech, where the living voice seems to bear an intention that would bind the two aspects of the sign into a vital unity. Benjamin's writing is the physical manifestation of living meaning, and the allegorical perspective is thus a leveling of writing and nature, the latter understood as the realm of physical objects exterior to subjectivity. Not that the concept "nature" is caught in an endless interplay of differences that disseminate its stabilizing referential function is Benjamin's point, but that the physicality of writing returns it to the opaque ipseity of the natural object. "The more meaning, the more subjection to death [*Todverfallenheit*], because death digs most deeply the jagged demarcation line between physical nature and meaning. But if nature has always been subject to the power of death, so has it also always been allegorical" (*OT*, 166; *GS*, 1:343).

22. Bertrand Russell, *Introduction to Mathematical Philosophy*, 1920 (New York: Dover, 1993). "When you have taken account of all the feelings roused by Napoleon in writers and readers of history, you have not touched the actual man; but in the case of Hamlet you have come to the end of him. If no one thought about Hamlet, there would be nothing left of him; if no one had thought about Napoleon, he would have soon seen to it that some one did. The sense of reality is vital in logic, and whoever juggles with it by pretending that Hamlet has another kind of reality is doing a disservice to thought" (169–70). That there are not two kinds of reality does not, of course, tell us whether reference to it is closer to the posthumous Napoleon or the imaginary Hamlet. For a thoughtful attempt to use the theory of reference and its impasses to bridge "postmodernist" and "postanalytic" directions in contemporary theoretical discourse, see Christopher Norris's *Fiction, Philosophy and Literary Theory: Will the Real Saul Kripke Please*

Stand Up? (London: Continuum, 2007), esp. chap. 5, which gives the book its subtitle.

23. See the section on "Muri," below.

24. This aphorism sits at a critical juncture in that book. The antepenultimate aphorism of book 4, it precedes the famous first presentation of the eternal return, "the greatest weight," and the concluding description of Zarathustra's descent, text-identical with the opening of *Thus Spoke Zarathustra*. "I admire the courage and wisdom of Socrates in everything he did, said—and did not say," the aphorism begins. But this admiration for Socratic reticence finds a boundary at the moment of his death. "I wish he had remained taciturn also at the last moment of his life; in that case he might belong to a still higher order of spirits" (*GSc*, 272; *KSA*, 3:569). Socrates' last words in the *Phaedo*, "Crito, we owe a cock to Asclepius; make this offering to him and do not forget" (118a), reveals, Nietzsche says, that at the final instant the philosopher viewed life as an illness, and left it with a vengeful insult on his lips. "Did a Socrates need such revenge? Did his overrich virtue lack an ounce of magnanimity?—O friends! We must overcome even the Greeks!" (*GSc*, 272; *KSA*, 3:570).

25. This portrait of Socrates is, at the biographical level, a mask for Benjamin's settling of accounts with his earlier teacher Gustav Wyneken. "What is most barbaric about the figure of Socrates is that this unartistic [*unmusisch*] human being constitutes the erotic center of the relationships of the platonic circle," Benjamin begins his discussion. "If, however, his love of the general capacity to communicate dispenses with art, then by what means does he render it so effective? By means of will. Socrates makes Eros a slave to his purposes. This sacrilege is reflected in the castratedness [*Kastratentum*] of his person. For in the last analysis, this is what the Athenians abhor; their feeling, even if subjectively base, is historically in the right. Socrates poisons the youth; he leads them astray" (*SW*, 1:52; *GS*, 2:129). The louche undertone to these words captures a distinct aspect of Wyneken's pedagogic persona, one potential version of "pädogogische Eros" that would eventually end Wyneken's public career in sexual scandal.

26. The distance of the *Phaedo* from the first-person perspective is emphasized in the dialogue itself by its explicit exclusion of Plato from the events it describes (*Phaedo* 59b).

27. "For these are not so much plays which cause mourning," Benjamin will write of Trauerspiele in the *Habilitation*, "as plays through which mournfulness finds satisfaction: plays for the mournful [*Spiel vor Traurigen*]" (*OT*, 119; *GS*, 1:298).

28. Thus Benjamin's approving observation of Kafka: "Kafka's Sirens are silent. Perhaps because for Kafka music and singing are an expression or at least a token of escape" (*SW*, 2:799; *GS*, 2:416).

29. For Michel Foucault, this recursive reencounter with his own philological site of articulation sets Nietzsche at the origin of the linguistic orientation of all contemporary philosophy: "Language did not return into the field of thought directly and in its own right until the end of the nineteenth century. We might even have said until the twentieth, had not Nietzsche the

philologist—and even in that field he was so wise, he knew so much, he wrote such good books—been the first to connect the philosophical task with a radical reflection upon language" (Michel Foucault, *The Order of Things: An Archaeology of the Human Sciences*, a translation of *Les Mots et les choses* [New York: Vintage Books, 1994], 305). Foucault's celebrated claim that man is over, "he is a quite recent creature, which the demiurge of knowledge fabricated with its own hands less than two hundred years ago" (308), is a projection into humanist discursive regularities of the asyndeton between the adjectives in Nietzsche's title, *Human, All Too Human*, which makes visible the necessary suspension between incompatible evaluative perspectives that allows for the stabilization of any concept of "man." From our perspective, more revealing than the specific authority Foucault here invokes, is his recourse to Nietzschean hyperbole in citing it. The discursive lucidity of Foucault's analyses meets up with the Nietzschean explosion by briefly participating in it at this critical juncture—with sincere irony, one might say. In the narrative of *The Order of Things*, philology is but one of the human sciences, a transitional moment in the movement from preclassical grammars to modern linguistics. But as the principle of responsible reading and writing, it is simultaneously the moment where Nietzschean clarity and the style it produced can expand into all of philosophical reflection, and subordinate the question of truth to a notion of language. The restricted canon philology explicitly addressed domesticates these implications in Foucault's larger text, and allows the larger structural movement between epistemes to be described. But it is not surprising that Foucault's trajectory eventually returned him to philological speculation explicitly, the ground beneath his feet, as it were, recognized as the still smoking battlefield where bodies encounter the normative force of reading, and technologies of selfhood can be objectified and combated.

30. The necessity that Wagner's music be both present and absent from Nietzsche's book is something other than a mere reversal of Dionysian and Apollonian priorities, if these are understood as operating within an encompassing textuality. It is the outside of the text that is here at issue, a site registered in Nietzsche as contending authorities. The danger of textualizing this exteriority shows clearly in the strangely morose reading of *The Birth of Tragedy* provided by Paul de Man. De Man reads *The Birth of Tragedy* as riven between a pathos-laden manifest philosophical content anchored in and promoting historical continuities (between classical Greek and German nationalism), and a rhetorical (largely metaphoric) presentational practice that undermines the possibility of such continuities of content. This conflict turns the authoritative voice against itself: "The narrator who argues against the subjectivity of the lyric and against representational realism destroys the credibility of the other narrator, for whom Dionysian insight is the tragic perception of original truth" (De Man, *Allegories of Reading*, 98).

These two narrators are not distributed among the statements composing the text, but meet in a more elusive domain, "between, on the one hand, metalinguistic statements about the rhetorical nature of language and, on the other hand, a rhetorical praxis that puts these statements into a question" (98). Rhetoric is not ornamental in *The Birth of Tragedy*, but emerges to preserve the historical continuities supporting its philosophical arguments, purchasing their plausibility at the price of restricting itself to an audience already coordinated pathologically into a sympathetic "we." The emotional harmony is the mystification defining this restricted public. But by having recourse to this strategy, Nietzsche's performance demolishes the priority of truth over metaphor. Perceiving this domain is not a matter of reorganizing the heterogeneous claims the book makes, but of bringing to bear a literary sensibility precisely upon its philosophical presentation. From this perspective, suspended between philosophy and literature, "philosophy turns out to be an endless reflection on its own destruction at the hands of literature" (115). This is the "residue of meaning that can, in its turn, be translated into statement, although the authority of this second statement can no longer be like that of the voice in the text when it is read naïvely. The nonauthoritative secondary statement that results from the reading will have to be a statement about the limitations of textual authority" (99). But authority is not so easily evaded. By staging *The Birth of Tragedy* as a struggle between the abstract genres of philosophy and literature, with their respective elements of concepts and tropes, de Man suppresses the actual discipline within which *The Birth of Tragedy* unfolds. That discipline is, of course, philology. The sympathetic "wir" toward which *The Birth of Tragedy* is directed appears explicitly not in order to ground a literary genre, but in order to interrupt a scientific practice. The esoteric meaning of *The Birth of Tragedy* is not a semiotic skepticism performed as hyper-Romantic irony, but lies in its implications for the specific scientific practice within which it operates. Philological authority, which in fact regulates the interstitial space between philosophy and literature that de Man identifies, is what is at issue in *The Birth of Tragedy*. It is this authority that the specific enthusiasm behind Nietzsche's tropes and concepts challenges. This authority does not evaporate into a "nonauthoritative secondary meaning," but resides in the philologist. It is the philologist who is characterized by skeptical withdrawal, and this withdrawal is precisely the meaning of Socratic optimism, even when manifested in de Man's own tone of melancholy precision. This is the nihilistic danger, appearing tonally upon the text at a site that cannot be comprehended through the opposition of rhetorical generalizations to conceptual abstractions. The very taxonomy of rhetorical tropes that allows the comparison is already invested in conceptual transparency: The question of style invades the practice of rhetorical description, and so evades its conceptualized result. Style is not operative in an abstract textual realm, provisionally formalized via the endlessness of concrete repetitions, but arises among those specific repetitions themselves in the mortal history that surrounds the text, a site for Nietzsche not of resignation before necessary collapse, but of inspiration and maneuver in the active toppling of the anonymous authority masquerading as that necessity.

31. *BT*, 105; *KSA*, 1:109.

3. INSCRIPTION

1. As interest in formal paradoxes grew in the twentieth century, a large secondary literature developed around these precedent Scholastic discussions. The expositional and translational work of Paul Vincent Spade is exemplary in this regard. His entry in the online *Stanford Encyclopedia of Philosophy* is a very clear and convenient consideration of the medieval formulations and their antique sources (Paul Vincent Spade, "Insolubles," *Stanford Encyclopedia of Philosophy (Fall 2005 Edition)*, ed. Edward N. Zalta. http://plato.stanford.edu/archives/fall2005/entries/insolubles/). Historically, although Paul's reference is the oldest clearly recognizable formulation, it played no role in the Schools, which instead referred to Aristotle's *Sophistical Refutations* 25 [at 180a27–b7], where something approximating the liar is presented: "He who swears that he will break his oath" and does so.

2. The relationship between the liar's paradox and these metamathematical impasses is not, of course, self-evident or uncontroversial, even if Gödel himself drew the connection in his 1931 paper. For a helpful contemporary overview, György Serény has recently brought together these notions in his essay "Gödel, Tarski, Church, and the Liar," *Bulletin of Symbolic Logic* 9, no. 1 (2003): 3–25. From the perspective of our investigation, Rudolf Carnap is an additional irreducible reference point in conceptualizing the logical limits of meaning.

3. W. V. O. Quine, "The Ways of Paradox," in *The Ways of Paradox and Other Essays, Revised and Enlarged Edition* (Cambridge, Mass.: Harvard University Press, 1976), 6. Further references provided in the text.

4. This is the point Hegel makes early in *The Phenomenology of Spirit*, with reference to the formal shifters "I," "Here," and "Now" (G. W. F. Hegel, *Phenomenology of Spirit*, trans. A.V. Miller [Oxford: Oxford University Press, 1977], 60; G. W. F. Hegel, *Phänomenologie des Geistes*, vol. 3 of *Werke*, 20 vols., ed. Eva Moldenhauer and Karl Markus Michel [Frankfurt am Main: Suhrkamp, 1986], 84). The sentence "Now is Night" becomes false at dawn, which undermines its relation to the Absolute but does not imply that it is not true when uttered at night or false when uttered in the day. The liar's paradox, in contrast, undermines the very relevance of logical form.

5. The formula is originally Goethe's but had been emphasized by Simmel. Another example of the influence of Simmel's vision of a definitive Goethe/Kant opposition on the Goethe of Benjamin's *Elective Affinities* essay (as opposed to the Goethe of his Soviet Encyclopedia article).

6. Johann Wolfgang von Goethe, *Werke: Hamburger Ausgabe in 14 Bänden: 11: Autobiographische Schriften III (Italienische Reise 1817)*, ed. Erich Trunz (Munich: Deutscher Taschenbuch Verlag, 1988), 454. Translated by Christine Shuttleworth Robert R. Heitner, ed. Thomas P. Saine and Jeffrey L. Sammons under the title *Italian Journey*, vol. 6 of *Goethe's Collected Works* (New York: Suhrkamp, 1989), 364.

7. Jodi Cranston, "Tropes of Revelation in Raphael's 'Transfiguration,'" *Renaissance Quarterly* 56, no. 1 (2003): 6.

8. The specific relations vary. Thus Kaufmann is content to let the narrative of Nietzsche's life lend psychological plausibility to a systematized *Will to Power*. Jaspers, by contrast, interprets the aphoristic expressions as a coherent existential posture, an active philosophizing. More radical still is Pierre Klossowski, whose reading operates across an indiscriminate space of letters, notes, and published texts by Nietzsche and those who knew him, for the valetudinary distinctions that would segregate these texts are precisely what the vicious circle demolishes. The particularities of our investigation draw our attention in directions Klossowski does not pursue, but the space of his reading is Benjamin's, is ours, as well.

9. A failure to recognize this complementary dimension, producing in Benjamin's terms an "aestheticist," insubstantial Nietzsche entirely self-involved, is the πρῶτον ψεῦδος of a range of English-language domestications of Nietzsche, for which Alexander Nehamas's diagnostically incoherent account in *Nietzsche: Life as Literature* can be taken as exemplary, if not responsible. The transposition of philosophy into literature is understood there as a modification in Nietzsche's understanding of truth-claims, and against the threat of an epistemological relativism, his doctrine is produced as "perspectivism." This doctrine, together with an aestheticism that takes literary texts as the most accurate model of reality, integrates Nietzsche's project not by merely constructing an abstract system around an abstract intention named Nietzsche, but by attributing a second-order intention to the display of this first intention, an intention that maintains aesthetic perspectivism by insisting on the particularity of Nietzsche's truth-claims. Thus the intention to create a site of articulation that cannot be forgotten by the reader—whether in the process of reading, as it sometimes seems, or more problematically, in the process of "writing" the "free" life made possible by this message—is the ultimate object behind the signature "Nietzsche." But the question of style cannot be reduced to content so easily. The compromise that the book itself enacts between analytical rigor and pathological (in the Kantian, but perhaps also the Nietzschean, sense of "pathological") report undermines the gestures that would make its philology philosophical: Nietzsche's writing is diverted from a frightening intervention in operative values into an impotent skepticism toward truthful description, and in the irreducible ambiguity attending the figure of Socrates (cf. Alexander Nehamas, *Nietzsche: Life as Literature* [Cambridge, Mass.: Harvard University Press, 1985], 30), Nehamas's own ambivalent presentation is ensconced. For what is not ambiguous is Nehamas's own attitude toward Nietzsche's ambivalence. That ambivalence is exemplary, presenting a "commendable and undogmatic" (39)—posture toward the world. It is difficult to see how a lack of dogmatism does anything but support what is already commendable, adding at best a narcissistic metapreference for further examples of its own ambivalence, further demonstrations of absence of dogmatism. The experience of ostensible epistemological clarity where error can be confidently refuted is the experience of any absence of ambivalence. But dogmatism in this sense, as a commitment by axiomatic thought to the irreducibility of certain orienting principles of explanation, has been on the defensive for two

hundred years, and if Nietzsche's objections to dogmatism exhaust themselves in this critique, his resort to the governing figure of hyperbole can hardly be justified. The gesture that would free the eternal recurrence from its cosmological vulnerabilities, by reducing it to an hypothesis "C) If my life were to recur, then it could recur only in identical fashion" (153), obscures the return of its own reactive posture toward this abysmal thought by constituting it as an idle, empathetically based reaction to Nietzsche's own life. Nehamas forgets that not only has philosophy been presented "in the most various styles imaginable" (13), it has also been propounded in the most various places, by the most various authorities, and that a figure defined as saying "more than is strictly speaking appropriate" (31) cannot do more than appropriate Nietzsche's text into a normative set of strict, not free, reactions. Philosophy as Nietzsche understands it is, of course, conveyed from the lectern, discussed in the seminar. But it is also inscribed into bodies by the executioner, shouted into crowds by the demagogue, pronounced into duty by the legislator, incanted into dreams by the priest. In these contexts, there is little enough "hyperbolic" about Nietzsche's isolated, if careening, career. In its entire effort to preserve the Apollonian distinction between "World" and "Self," the very scaffold of its exposition, Nehamas's book surrenders to the nihilism it hopes to outrun, and erects the "monumental" and "antiquarian" Nietzsche philology must necessarily produce at the cost of neutralizing the Dionysian philosopher who explodes beyond the signature that serves as Nehamas's title.

10. Carl Albrecht Bernoulli, *Franz Overbeck und Friedrich Nietzsche: Eine Freundschaft*, 2 vols. (Jena: Eugen Diederichs, 1908), 2:162–65. The exchange is also reproduced in Richard Frank Krummel, *Nietzsche und der deutsche Geist*, 3 vols. Monographien und Texte zur Nietzsche-Forschung 3. (Berlin: Walter de Gruyter, 1998), 1:126–27.

11. Bernoulli, *Franz Overbeck und Friedrich Nietzsche*, 2:162–63. Krummel, *Nietzsche und der deutsche Geist*, 1:126–27.

12. Bernoulli, *Franz Overbeck und Friedrich Nietzsche*, 2:165. Krummel, *Nietzsche und der deutsche Geist*, 1:126.

13. The most famous of these provisional titles is certainly the notorious "Will to Power." Walter Kaufmann remarks in the introduction of his translation of the book produced by Nietzsche's sister under this heading: "Nietzsche himself had contemplated a book under the title *The Will to Power*. His notebooks contain a great many drafts for title pages for this and other projected works, and some of the drafts for this book suggest as a subtitle: *Attempt at a Revaluation of All Values*. Later on Nietzsche considered writing a book of a somewhat different nature (less aphoristic, more continuous) under the title *Revaluation of all Values*, and for a time he conceived of *The Antichrist*, written in the fall of 1888, as the first of the four books comprising the *Revaluation of All Values*" (*WP,* xvii). It is not quite clear how Kaufmann derives the formal variations among these differing conceptions, but that he considers these various projects preliminary, and not provisional, is clear. What he describes here in terms of *Will to Power* and *Revaluation of All Values* characterizes Nietzsche's entire production: it is always swelling

up beneath titles that cannot control it, and they do not represent stable if uncompleted projects but reflective limits of authorial self-conception. Thus their tendency toward contentless rhetorical forms: asserting and simultaneously debunking (*Human, All too Human*); pleonastically reiterating (*Will to Power*, i.e., Will to the ability to Will); paradoxically generalizing (*Revaluation of All Values, Beyond Good and Evil*). Since Kaufmann is committed to a stable hierarchy between published and unpublished writing, he mislocates the titles that mediate this gap, situating them in Nietzsche's intention, when the opposite picture is more appropriate: Writing forces titles upon Nietzsche, ever new titles; the ones that "take" and are published retrospectively mark not merely a book, but a self-overcoming.

14. This is the fundamental distortion that mars David Farrell Krell's recent attempt to enter the notebooks productively. The effort to find the origins of the Eternal Return in notebook M II 1 becomes an attempt to transform this label into a title. (David Farrell Krell, "Eternal Recurrence—of the Same? Reading Notebook M III 1," in *Infectious Nietzsche* [Bloomington: University of Indiana Press, 1996], 157–76.). The title of notebook M II 1, however, is plural and distributed throughout its pages: *Die Erziehung des Genius; Das Theater und das böse Gewissen; An die Moralgläubigen; Kur des Einzelnen.*

15. That this discrepancy between articulating authorities and their respective horizons informs the Observation procedure is evident even in the first appearance of the phrase "Bayreuth Horizon Observations" as the title for an individual lecture, in the earlier notebook P I 20b, fragment 19[274]. The phrase titles an outline for a hypothetical lecture whose opening already indicates the two authorities contending within "untimeliness": Wagnerian art and scientific philology.

Bayreuth Horizon Observations.

1. Pentecost in Bayreuth. Enormous lack of understanding all around. Gathering of philologists in Leipzig. The war and the University of Starsbourg. (UW, 84; KSA, 7:505)

A slightly later fragment (19[303]) formalizes the title:

Bayreuth's Horizon

The Horizon of Bayreuth

Bayreuth Horizon Oberservations. (UW, 91; KSA, 7:512)

Nietzsche is working not so much with the specificity of Bayreuth as with the formal metaphor of a *horizon*, with its perspectival and relativizing implications. "Untimeliness" labels a skeptical attitude that can no longer be conceptualized in terms of an explicit concept of "horizon."

16. In fact, the "observation" procedure is inherently adversarial: Its situation is in each case guaranteed by a localized polemical reference. Indeed, it is the incorporation of this polemical reference that establishes Untimeliness as a posture, and the shifts between the four published *Betrachtungen* can

be charted against the delocalization of this point of polemical contact (1. Strauss, 2. Hartmann, 3. Germany, 4. what is not-Wagner).

17. Raymond J. Benders et. al., *Friedrich Nietzsche: Chronik in Bildern und Texten,* Stiftung Weimarer Klassik (Munich: Deutsche Taschenbuch Verlag, 2000), 305.

18. This is, in fact the germ of the letter, deriving directly from a passage in the letter of 18 October 1873 to Erwin Rohde that first described the project. To give Rohde an impression of the assignment, which has not yet been undertaken, Nietzsche improvises on the international motif: "3. Comparison with other Nations: If a man in France or in England or in Italy, after he had defied all public powers and opinions and given the theater five works of unique stature and powerful style that had been ceaselessly praised and in demand from north to south—if such a man were to cry: the current theater does not fit the spirit of the nation, it is as public art a disgrace! Help me prepare a setting for the national spirit! would not everyone come to help him, even if only from a sense of honor? etc. etc." (*SB,* 4:167).

19. See the title-page reproductions in William H. Schaberg. *The Nietzsche Canon: A Publication History and Bibliography* (Chicago: University of Chicago Press, 1995), 34, 37, 43, 50, and then 62, where Schaberg remarks, "another innovation could be noted on the title page—this is the first instance where the cover of a book listed Nietzsche by his name only, omitting his title as professor at Basel."

20. The topic was in fact suggested by Wagner. Janz recounts: "On 7 February 1873 Cosima noted: 'Dinner with the Wesendoncks, argument over the book by Strauß, "The Old and New Faith," which Richard and I find terribly shallow but that Mrs. Wesendonck admires.' The discussion was still vehement when Nietzsche arrived in Bayreuth in April. Wagner used the opportunity—he had an old account to settle with David Friedrich Strauß—and assigned his devoted young friend as topic number one a polemic against the liberal theologian, to whom Nietzsche had however up until then been somewhat drawn. But he mastered himself" (Curt Paul Janz, *Friedrich Nietzsche,* 3 vols. [Munich: Carl Hanser, 1978], 1:533).

21. "From this we can explain," Schopenhauer had written in his essay on university philosophy, "how the age when Kant philosophized, Goethe wrote, and Mozart composed, could be followed by the present one of political poets and even more political philosophers, of hungry men of letters who earn a living in literature by falsehood and imposture, and of ink-slingers of all kinds who wantonly ruin the language. It calls itself with one of its home-made words, as characteristic as it is euphonious, the 'now-time'; now-time indeed, in other words, because one thinks only of the Now and does not venture to glance at the time that will come and condemn. I wish I could show this 'now-time' in a magic mirror what it will look like in the eyes of posterity" (Arthur Schopenhauer, "Über die Universitäts-Philosophie," in *Sämtliche Werke,* ed. Wolfgang Frhr. Von Löhneysen. 5 vols. [Frankfurt am Main: Suhrkamp, 1986], 4:213–14; "On Philosophy at the Universities," in Schopenhauer, *Parerga and Paralipomena: Short Philosophical Essays, vol. 1,* trans. E. F. J. Payne. [Oxford: Clarendon Press,

1974], 173). Already the term is positioned as an autobaptism, disowned by the author who cites it.

22. Thus to the much-commented texts of Benjamin's on the status of theology in his thought, the remark in *The Arcades Project* (*My thinking is related to theology as blotting pad is related to ink* [*AP*, 471; *GS*, 5:588;]) and the first of the *Theses on the Concept of History*, where the wizened dwarf theology animates the chess machine of historical materialism, should doubtless be added Benjamin's Muri review of the travel writer Theodor Däubler's nonexistent *Athos and the Atheists*, which reveals, on the basis of "fragmentary inscriptions from Athos, undeniable archeological testimonies, deciphered painstakingly from weathered slabs" that "the Atheists—that is, 'Those from Athos'—were a sect of ardent ecstatics formerly resident all over the island, second to none in the bitterness of their self-chastisements, who were denounced in the 11th century by a scribe in the pay of the Greek patriarch Euthymios on the basis of vulgar Greek and no doubt intentionally falsified etymology with the name of deniers of God and thereby delivered over to the persecutions of the authorities" (*GS*, 4:442–43).

23. "Nowhere during the Wilhelmine era was the mobilization of provincial philistinism [*Spießertum*] that is bearing its political fruits today more sedulously prepared than in the [Nietzsche] Archive" (*GS*, 3:324).

24. The perspective is sociological only to the extent that sociology, whose object—the *socios*—emerges at the turn of the twentieth century from behind the nations and states constructed by the prior disciplines of economics and political history, is understood to be situated in the last analysis theologically. As a vision of collective existence beyond the conceptual framework of nation, people, state, or economy, the object of "sociology" is ultimately an abandoned congregation.

25. This shift in perspective that brings a site of immediate concentration into discernible view is not mere psychological introspection, but has metaphysical implications. Benjamin found this shift explicated in great detail by Henri Bergson. Defining metaphysics as "the science which claims to dispense with symbols," Bergson is led to distinguish between knowledge by analysis and knowledge by intuition. But these two different epistemological modalities do not condense into Kantian faculties, but occupy two disparate temporal orders. The crucial difference between knowledge by analysis and knowledge by intuition is that the latter exists only for as long as it is happening. The "kind of *intellectual sympathy* by which one places oneself within an object in order to coincide with what is unique in it and consequently inexpressible," as Bergson defines intuition (Henri Bergson, *Oeuvres*, ed. André Robinet [Paris: Presses Universitaires de France, 1959], 1395; *An Introduction to Metaphysics*. trans. T. E. Hulme [Indianapolis: Hackett, 1999], 23–24), is not the production of fixed conceptual recognitions, but a much more tenuous effort of concentration that is "extremely difficult," Bergson writes.

> The mind has to do violence to itself, has to reverse the direction of the operation by which it habitually thinks, has perpetually to revise, or rather to recast, all its categories. But in this way it will attain to fluid concepts, capable of following reality in all its sinuosities and of

adopting the very movement of the inward life of things. (Bergson, *Oeuvres*, 1421–22; *Introduction to Metaphysics*, 51–52)

The reflective dynamic of this intellectual sympathy with duration, which separates philosophical truth from any symbolic mediation precisely by tying it to the changing present *at the site of reading*, is what prompts the elaborate evocative similes in which Bergson's philosophy is conducted. Within Benjamin's contemporary intellectual milieu, Bergson is the philosopher Benjamin integrated most deeply into his own expression. Benjamin's "Bergsonism" does not establish explicit agreements between their respective speculations but rather shares a series of common astonishments, which then move in very different directions. But the intellectual scaffolding of Benjamin's mortalism (unlike, say, the critical theory of Horkheimer or Adorno's negative dialectics) is not provided by Husserl, Marx, or Freud, and is relatively free of the Schopenhauerian pessimism that weights the recognized tradition of critical theory. Benjamin resists pessimism by means of nihilism. This is his Nietzschean dimension. But the basic strategies he adopts can, throughout his career, always be illuminated by the early work of Bergson.

26. Nietzsche saw this prospect in exactly the opposite way: *Horrifying danger*, he remarks in an 1873 notebook entry from the time of "We Philologists": *that the American-political industry [Getreibe] and the unmoored scholarly culture fuse together* (KSA, 7:423).

27. One can only speculate on the state of the affair when Benjamin considered the title "Street Closed!" (*GB*, 3:161).

28. That the physical appearance of the text has relevance for its interpretation is a point made in *One-Way Street* itself. "The typewriter will alienate the hand of the man of letters from the pen," Benjamin writes, "only when the precision of typographic forms has directly entered the conception of his books." And he even comes close to anticipating contemporary word-processing. "One might suppose that new systems with more variable typefaces would then be needed. They will put the innervation of commanding fingers in place of the pliant hand" (*SW*, 1:457; *GS*, 4:105).

29. The Schlechta edition of Nietzsche's works reconstructs a text beneath this title, which has been translated into English, but it is an impressionistic bundle of *Nachlaß* entries, itself philologically worthless.

30. The *ad hominem* enthymeme is central to Nietzsche's arguments, arising in the complex interplay of tragic significance, musical presentation, critical relevance. In Gilles Deleuze's reading, it informs the notion of "dramatisation." "This method . . . is itself the *tragic method*. Or, more precisely, if we remove from the word 'drama' all the Christian and dialectical pathos which taints it, it is the method of *dramatisation*. 'What do you will?' Ariadne asks Dionysus. What a will wants—this is the latent content of the corresponding thing" (Gilles Deleuze, *Nietzsche and Philosophy*, trans. Hugh Tomlinson [New York: Columbia University Press, 1983], 78).

31. *It is true, humanism and Enlightenment have made an alliance with antiquity. And so it's natural that the enemies of humanism should be*

hostile to antiquity. Except for the fact that antiquity was badly understood and wholly falsified by humanism. Clearly understood, it's evidence against humanism, against the notion that human-nature is essentially good, etc. The enemies of humanism are wrong when they fight against antiquity, in which they have a powerful ally. (WC, 359; KSA, 8:58)

32. The German Reformation cuts us off from the ancient world: was this necessary? It revealed anew the old contradiction of "paganism, Christianity." At the same time it was a protest against the decorative culture of the Renaissance; it was a victory over the same culture that was defeated in Christianity's beginnings. (WC, 351; KSA, 8:47)

33. Human and All Too Human.
Paths toward the Liberation of the Spirit.
The Alleviation of Life.
Woman and Child.
State and Society. (KSA, 8:308)

34. Free and Bound Spirits.
Woman and Child.
Ranks and Occupations.
Alleviation of Life.
Human and All Too Human. (KSA, 8:313)

35. This emphasis on the ultimate opacity of significance lies at the heart of Wittgenstein's later philosophy. "How does one teach anyone to read to himself? How does one know if he can do so? How does he himself know that he is doing what is required of him?" (Ludwig Wittgenstein, *Philosophical Investigations*, trans. G. E. M. Anscombe [New York: Macmillan, 1858], 116, #375). The questions are unanswerable. And in particular, recourse to a notion of subjective representation dissolves into irrelevance: "It is no more essential for the understanding of a proposition that one should imagine anything in connexion with it, than that one should make a sketch from it" (Wittgenstein, *Philosophical Investigations*, 120, #396).

36. The philological project to which Nietzsche devoted much of his early academic career had to do with attribution, the reconstruction of the canon of works of Democritus. Later, Nietzsche would marshal much of this research in his lectures on "Philosophy in the Tragic Age of the Greeks," again where he attempts to determine an overriding philosophical intention at work in the pre-Socratic philosophers on the basis of their fragmentary textual remains. For a fascinating exploration of this aspect of Nietzsche's thought, an aspect much neglected and most important, see James I. Porter. *Nietzsche and the Philology of the Future* (Stanford: Stanford University Press, 2000).

37. Widmann would in fact publish a Trauerspiel some seven years later with the title *Beyond Good and Evil*, whose character can be gleaned from a synopsis he provided in a letter. "A modern professor (an art historian who is writing a history of Malatesta von Rimini) neglects his good and beautiful wife for the sake of a coquettishly clever baroness," Widmann described his device.

And he does this ever more in the consciousness that for the strong everything is permitted; he identifies himself involuntarily with his hero, the terrible and spectacular Sigismondo Malatesta. I won't reveal here how it is arranged that he falls asleep; it is no ordinary sleep. In this sleep he dreams the second drama inserted in the modern one. For now we have Sigismondo Malatesta before us, who strangles his spouse Polissena . . . for love of the beautiful Isotta. Naturally the same actors act in the embedded play as in the framing one. . . . In the end of the medieval play Malatesta, in the full enjoyment of his successful stratagems, is cast down by his awakened conscience. At this moment the modern play picks up again; Malatesta awakes as a professor and savours the happiness of not being the terrible man he dreamed himself to be. He is cured, reconciled with his spouse. . . . It is directed against Nietzsche's philosophy and shall end with Goethe's words: "Noble is man, helpful and good." (Richard Frank Krummel, *Nietzsche und der deutsche Geist*. 3 vols. [Berlin: Walter de Gruyter, 1998], 1:262)

38. An asyndeton that will inform a host of related philosophical gestures toward significance and its significant interruption: from prosody, caesura; from syntax, parataxis; from phonetics, hiatus; from music, dissonance. These terms are not synonymous labels for a common underlying phenomenon but analogous intrusions in incompatible signifying systems.

39. It is Jacques Derrida who has put one version of the concept of signature at the heart of an interpretation of Nietzsche. He probes into the concept in a series of readings deeply indebted to Heidegger's *Nietzsche I & II*. "To stage signatures, to make an immense bio-graphical paraph out of all that one has written on life or death—" Derrida muses in "Otobiographies: The Teaching of Nietzsche and the Politics of the Proper Name," a discussion from the early 1980s, "this is perhaps what [Nietzsche] has done and what we have to put on active record" (Jacques Derrida. *The Ear of the Other: Otobiography, Transference, Translation*, ed. Christie McDonald, trans. Peggy Kamuf [Lincoln: University of Nebraska Press, 1985], 7). That the unity and uniqueness of Nietzsche's thought derives from the inherent unity of Western metaphysics and Nietzsche's liminal position with regard to it—this Heideggerian thesis prompts Derrida to reflect on the name that identifies that edge of thought. "Nietzsche" as a name for metaphysics at its ambiguous and ambivalent limit is how Derrida, following Hiedegger, locates the philosopher, in order then to call the unity implicit in limitation per se into question by emphasizing the ambivalence and ambiguity manifested in the gesture that signs his name, Friedrich Nietzsche.

Nietzsche's signature as a universal *problem* comes most sharply into focus at the historical limit of his oeuvre in the strangely self-reflective final book *Ecce Homo: How One Becomes What One Is*. The baroque exaggerations and disavowals to which Nietzsche's signatory authority is subjected there produce in that name a discontinuous but persistent distortion in the processes of authorized historical transmission. As the suture between metaphysical responsibility per se and an irreducibly local biography through which that responsibility bequeaths itself to historical successors, Nietzsche's

Notes

signature performs the gesture of philosophical authority itself in its presentational self-alienation and ultimate vacuity. The signature and Nietzsche behind it are thus simultaneously void of authority and omnipotent, which is to say he cannot be reliably located among the hierarchies organizing our actual cultural transmission. From the perspective of *Ecce Homo*, Nietzsche's signature raises a question that Derrida then situates in a particular institutional context: the university. Nietzsche's philosophical signature calls into question the communicative practices in the institution charged with overseeing and certifying the transmission of culture.

This overtly political dimension of the signature is no surprise. The gestural, iterative character of signatures can be pursued, as Derrida elsewhere discusses in some detail, into the entire authorizing framework of linguistic performativity. And yet in a strange way, for all the internal shifts and displacements of authority that Derrida traces through Nietzsche's signature—between the law of the dead father and the life of the surviving mother, between Polish nobility and German venality, between posthumous birth and contemporary acclaim—the signatory gesture itself remains constant and iteratively self-identical. The legacy of Heidegger's ontological totalization of Nietzsche's philosophical position at the limit of metaphysics points Derrida toward a specifically poststructuralist conception of a recalcitrant distortion in an abstractly persistent structure. Derrida's exposition can leap from the terminal enthusiasm of *Ecce Homo* to Nietzsche's early lectures on educational institutions because the implications of their shared signature effect both texts equally. Thus with the same move that opens up Nietzsche's signature as a textual problem at the limit of knowledge, Derrida risks closing off a consideration of Nietzsche's signature as a differential system *within* his oeuvre.

The "signature/tomb" in the closing section of Derrida's *Spurs: Nietzsche's Styles* that fails to seal a meaning into the fragment from 1881 "*I have forgotten my umbrella*" (KSA, 9:587), opens more nearly onto this internal perspective. But even here the iterability of the signature dissolves it before it can gain any traction on the text, "the signature and the text fall out with each other. No sooner are they iterated than they are secreted, separated, excreted" (Jacques Derrida. *Spurs: Nietzsche's Styles*, trans. Barbara Harlow [Chicago: University of Chicago Press, 1978], 161), and the fragment is left as a bare remnant of the uninterpretable textuality that undermines any historical determination. The enduring virtue of Derrida's reading of the signature is to have emphasized the problem of its own authority as constitutive of Nietzsche's oeuvre. And indeed this too is Heidegger's great question to Nietzsche: By what right do you speak?

The provisional signatures and titles in the *Nachlaß* illuminate the problem of Nietzsche's signature from a different angle. This internal problematic is illuminated more directly by Michel Foucault, in his essay "What Is an Author" from 1969. There Nietzsche appears as an example of what is a more immediately practical problem inscribed into the philological telos of the authoritative edition. "The problem is both theoretical and practical," Foucault writes there.

If we wish to publish the complete works of Nietzsche, for example, where do we draw the line? Certainly, everything must be published, but can we agree on what "everything" means? We will, of course, include everything that Nietzsche himself published, along with the drafts of his works, his plans for aphorisms, his marginal notations and corrections. But what if, in a notebook filled with aphorisms, we find a reference, a reminder of an appointment, an address, or a laundry bill, should this be included in his works? Why not? These practical considerations are endless once we consider how a work can be extracted from the millions of traces left by an individual after his death. Plainly, we lack a theory to encompass the questions generated by a work, and the empirical activity of those who naively undertake the publication of the complete works of an author often suffers from the absence of this framework (Michel Foucault, "What Is an Author," in *Language, Counter-Memory, Practice: Selected Essays and Interviews*, ed. Donald F. Bouchard [Ithaca, N.Y.: Cornell University Press, 1977], 118–19).

This is a general question, and Nietzsche serves Foucault here as a familiar example. But his case is, we are arguing, singular. For Nietzsche in particular, the principle of the signature is never abstracted from the process of his self-articulation: His name operates as a signature only for as long as his text operates on the reader. The Nietzschean signature cannot be encompassed either by philosophy (Derrida) or by philology (Foucault), but positions the historical possibility of a distinction between these two truth principles.

40. "What is unpleasant and disturbs my modesty is that I am at bottom every name in history; also the children that I have set into the world make me wonder with a certain mistrust, whether everyone who enters *into* 'God's Kingdom' also comes *out* of God. This autumn I was present, dressed in as little as possible, two times at my funeral" (*SB*, 8:578).

41. Samuel Weber, in a recent reading of "Capitalism as Religion," points out that Benjamin is here, whether intentionally or not, altering a familiar French phrase that he would have encountered in Baudelaire, "*sans trêve ni merci*," without truce or grace (Samuel Weber, "Closing the Net," in *Benjamin's –abilities* [Cambridge, Mass.: Harvard University Press, 2008], 255).

4. COLLABORATION

1. Alenka Zupančič, *The Shortest Shadow: Nietzsche's Philosophy of the Two* (Cambridge, Mass.: MIT Press, 2003), explores this motif in a metaphysical register indebted to Alain Badiou and Slavoj Zizek.

2. Karl Löwith, *Nietzsche's Philosophy of the Eternal Recurrence of the Same*, trans. J. Harvey Lomax (Berkeley: University of California Press, 1997). Translation of *Nietzsches Philosophie der ewigen Wiederkunft des*

Gleichen (Berlin: die Runde, 1935). The phrase "der systematische Grundgedanke in Nietzsches Philosophie" is the title of chapter 3, page 27 in both editions.

3. The closing letter printed in the *Gesammelte Schriften* was removed by Benjamin before the book's publication, which ended with Overbeck's letter to Nietzsche. The terminal position of this letter is significant, and we insist upon it here; but this is not to deny that *Deutsche Menschen* is merely part of a much larger epistolary project that Benjamin pursued in potentia both before and after the *Frankfurter Zeitung* publication of the series. This renders the Nietzschean endpoint provisional, but this contingency is redeemed by the *principled* incompleteness of the book. It is constitutive of the meaning of the letters there assembled that they point beyond themselves to an indefinite number of further testimonies, that any testimony in this medium is necessarily incomplete, for it is conducted essentially across death.

4. Theodor W. Adorno, "Zu Benjamins Briefbuch 'Deutsche Menschen'" in *Noten zur Literatur: Gesammelte Schriften*, vol. 11, ed. Rolf Tiedemann (Frankfurt am Main: Suhrkamp, 1997), 686. Translated by Shierry Weber Nicholsen under the title "On Benjamin's Deutsche Menschen, a Book of Letters," in *Notes on Literature*, vol. 2 (New York: Columbia University Press, 1992), 328.

5. Peter Szondi, "Hoffnung in Vergangenen: Über Walter Benjamin," 1961, in *Schriften in 2 Bänden*. ed. Wolfgang Fietkau, 2:294. Translated as "Hope in the Past: On Walter Benjamin," trans. Harvey Mendelsohn. *Critical Inquiry* 4, no. 3 (1978): 505.

6. The placement of these texts in the English translation of Benjamin's work reflects a conjectural dating that would have "German Letters" preceding the composition of "On the Trail of Old Letters." The philological question would be settled most convincingly on the basis of archival comparisons of paper and penmanship, but from the point of view of content, the dating of "German Letters" to 1933, subsequent to "On the Trail of Old Letters," reflects more accurately Benjamin's changing attitude toward the question of a book publication. The primary evidence for the earlier dating is simply that Benjamin was engaged at that time in what I am calling the newspaper project; but from my perspective, which attempts to distinguish between the Weimar Republic's newspaper project and the book that appeared in Nazi Germany, this is closer to counterevidence for the earlier date.

7. "Von Ehre ohne Ruhm / Von Größe ohne Glanz / Von Würde ohne Sold" (*SW*, 3:167; *GS*, 4:150).

8. Walter Benjamin, *Illuminations: Essays and Reflections*, ed. and with an introduction by Hannah Arendt, trans. Harry Zohn (New York: Schocken, 1968), 265.

9. "Not as though the path of critique should be staked out in advance by the author's statements; yet the more critique removes itself from them, the less will it want to evade the task of understanding them, too, on the basis of the same hidden jurisdictions as the work" (*SW*, 1:309; *GS*,

1:141). Myth is the name of the domain in which these hidden jurisdictions operate.

10. A recent book has explored the performative permanence of Zarathustra's death in ways quite pertinent to the analysis here. See Paul S. Loeb, *The Death of Nietzsche's Zarathustra* (Cambridge: Cambridge University Press, 2010).

11. William Shakespeare, *The Tragedy of Julius Caesar*, in *The Norton Shakespeare*, ed. Stephen Greenblatt (New York: Norton, 1997), 1538 (1.2.143–48).

12. Max Weber, *Wirtschaft und Gesellschaft: Grundriss der verstehenden Soziologie*, 5th ed. (Tübingen: J. C. B. Mohr, 1976), 142.

5. MAD MATURITY

1. A detailed investigation of the relations between Benjamin's philosophy and speech act theory is performed by Werner Hamacher in his essay "Afformative, Strike." The general Austinian terminology of speech act theory is there arranged to posit a new term, "afformative event" in contrast with "performative act." The contrast between act and event is a dispersal within the description of the intention that grounds agency. The afformative event "does not posit, it 'deposes'" (Werner Hamacher, "Afformative, Strike: Benjamin's 'Critique of Violence,'" in *Walter Benjamin's Philosophy: Destruction and Experience*, ed. Andrew Benjamin and Peter Osborne [London: Routledge, 1994], 115). There is, of course, a self-deprecating irony at work in the act of proposing a neologism to characterize this aspect of Benjamin's thought, for the "afformative" is outside of all positing, as the eventual singularity into which the dialectic of violent generalization and its enforcement intrude. Indeed, for Hamacher—and this seems right—Benjamin's political ontology reverses the entire Enlightenment tradition of reflection on these "political" matters, by centering his conceptualization of the political not on a foundational act, of either concord or domination, but around a moment of passivity—the (proletarian) strike. But on the terminological wings of afformation, the proletarian strike is able to spread through the entire sphere of language, so that "whoever speaks of the strike cannot be sure that he is not already affected by it, that he is not already participating in it" (126). True enough. But Benjamin, in contrast to Hamacher, did not forget that however universally the potential for the proletarian strike is distributed through history, only the proletariat, and those who have allied themselves with it explicitly, are likely to get their heads smashed for their participation in it. The weight of this recognition on Benjamin's part grows substantially, of course, in the years after "The Critique of Violence," the text Hamacher is reading. But even there, the utopian tenor of an absolutely revolutionary passivity is mitigated by the stakes, for the proletarian general strike is positioned in history in contrast not to an act of abstract positing, but to the defining act of sovereign power: *Todesstrafe*, the death penalty, and its institutional materialization in the state: *die*

Polizei, the police. Hamacher's startling claim that "pure violence" includes resolutely nonviolent resolution of conflict misses the undeniably insurrectionary, aggressive tone of Benjamin's essay. As an answer to the political theater of sovereign execution, and the mobile, spectral threat of the police, neither of which Hamacher dwells on, Benjamin's tone is more plausible and his use of the term "Gewalt," violence, less arbitrary. In fact, it is not entirely easy to read Benjamin's description of "pure mediacy," from which "pure violence" is derived, as including such comforting principles as "sympathy, peaceableness, trust." Benjamin continues his mention of these subjective presuppositions for nonviolent conflict resolution with the observation that "unalloyed [*reine*] means are never those of direct solutions but always those of indirect solutions. They therefore never apply directly to the resolution of conflict between man and man, but apply only to matters concerning objects" (*SW*, 1:244; *GS*, 2:191).

2. Speech-act theory of the Anglo-American sort elides this lacuna into a coherent subjective intention guiding the convention-bound action. This is, in Benjaminian terms, to situate truth entirely in the simultaneous terrain between speaker and audience, entirely in the conversational locus. Such a perspective can only produce continuities through time, and so misses the force of history. The temporal rupture between prepared text and public presentation is no less volatile when it falls within the identical signature. The daybook dimension of expression operates here. The proper realization of the composed text will open it to an inexpressible truth that will itself constitute its audience, among which the speaker must be included as a fundamentally receptive or passive instance. Thus, for Benjamin, the performative dimension of expression serves to open the force of articulation to influences beyond any individual intention. Benjamin shares with speech act theory the perspective that for something to be an expression, it must do something to its world, transform it and those participating in it in some way. But he has no temptation to situate the sources of this effect in implicit conventions guiding collective behavior among the currently living. The source of expressive effectiveness lies in its openness to temporal objectivity, to life understood as survival. At the same time, J.L. Austin's original positing of the terminology of a "theory of the performative," in the self-consciously performative medium of the William James Lectures, is not insensitive to these questions: "One could say that part of the procedure is getting oneself appointed. When the saint baptized the penguins, was this void because the procedure of baptizing is inappropriate to be applied to penguins, or because there is no accepted procedure of baptizing anything except humans?" (J. L. Austin, *How to Do Things with Words* [Cambridge, Mass.: Harvard University Press, 1975], 24). The undecidability of this question from our human perspective, perched between penguin and saint, is, in Benjamin's terms, mythic ambiguity. Again, on the details of this comparison, the reader is referred to Hamacher's "Afformative, Strike."

3. No doubt it is for this reason that "The Task of the Translator" has proved so attractive to deconstructive critics. Peter Fenves, for instance, delineates his defining notion of arrested/arresting language in its terms, while

Carol Jacobs uses it to demonstrate the abysmal inescapability of Benjamin's textuality. Though both recognize the challenge to authority presented by the essay, neither stops to consider its unusual devotion to the canon, and so both render the authority in question a disinterested propositional claim to truth. These, too, could there be such things, would be debunked by Benjamin; but the authority in question in his writing is not propositional, it is a matter of life and death.

4. "The superior intriguer is all intellect and will-power," Benjamin says in the Trauerspiel book. "And as such he corresponds to an ideal which was first outlined by Machiavelli and which was energetically elaborated in the creative and theoretical literature of the seventeenth century" (*OT*, 95; *GS*, 1:274).

5. In assembling these heterogeneous signatures and provoking an expressive posture from among them, Nietzsche is returning to a motif that had first arisen at the end of *The Gay Science*, in the aphoristic sequence "We Fearless Ones." Among the constellation of collective designations that sequence explores, Nietzsche retreats in aphorism 365 into the voice of the "hermit," to describe from this extremity of isolation new principles of sociability:

> But there are also other ways and tricks when it comes to associating with or "passing among" men: for example, as ghost,—which is altogether advisable if one wants to get rid of them quickly and make them afraid. Example: One reaches out for us but gets no hold of us. That is frightening. Or: we enter through a closed door. Or after all lights have been extinguished. Or after we have died. The last is the trick of *posthumous* people par excellence.

The adjective "posthumous" emerges from a series of metaphors that describe the evasive and transgressive advantages of appearing insubstantial to one's contemporaries. In this context, it marks a subtle violation of that metaphoric principle. The first three advantages use gothic traditions to enact a denunciatory translation, so to speak, of Greek "*metaphysics*" into the Latin "*supernatural*." But a ghost is by definition posthumous, and when the aphorism proceeds to specify this as a particular advantage, death exceeds the metaphoric framework. An insubstantial and invisible way of occupying the living present mutates into a literal existence after death. To be posthumous here is to speak suddenly from a different point, to a different audience. Thus the aphorism concludes in a parenthesis, in which the posthumous voice emerges from an ambiguous grave:

> ("What did you think?" one of them once asked impatiently, "would we feel like enduring the estrangement, the cold and quiet of the grave around us, this whole subterranean, concealed, mute, undiscovered solitude that among us is called life but might just as well be called death, if we did not know what will *become* of us,—and that it is only after death that we shall enter *our* life and become alive, oh, very much alive, we posthumous people!"). (*GSc*, 321; *KSA*, 3:613–14)

The lively gothic encounters of the first half of the aphorism reverse at the parenthesis into premature burial and a voice from the tomb. The parentheses themselves are transformed into silent psychopomps at the edge of the sepulchre. The title of the aphorism, "The hermit speaks once more," which initially tied it to the preceding aphorism, "The hermit speaks," now gains a second sense, as the record of this displaced consolation, a consolation that floats between extremes of isolation and engagement, between Nietzsche's voice alive in 1883, at the moment he is writing, and a ghostly rebirth in the future, at the instant in which he is read.

6. The text was written in collaboration with Benjamin's friend Günther Anders. "Today I could no longer decide which statements were from him and which from me," Anders admits (*GS*, 6:730).

7. Perhaps the epitome of Benjamin's extremism is the so-called "Theological-Political Fragment," where, under the sign of nihilism, Benjamin advocates the very self-destructiveness of happiness itself in order to solicit indirectly a messianic transformation of the world.

8. Samuel Weber, "Taking Exception to Decision: Walter Benjamin and Carl Schmitt," in *Benjamin's -abilities* (Cambridge, Mass.: Harvard University Press, 2008), 179.

9. Lukács himself would later repudiate this aspect of the book, calling it "messianic utopianism" (*HCC*, xviii; *GKB*, 18). For a thorough excavation of Benjamin's political thinking at this time, see Uwe Steiner, "The True Politician: Walter Benjamin's Concept of the Political," in *New German Critique* 83 (Spring/Summer 2001): 43–88.

10. The material for understanding this central friendship in Benjamin's life has been carefully and revealingly assembled and contextualized by Erdmut Wizisla in *Benjamin und Brecht: Die Geschichte einer Freundschaft: Mit einer Chronik und den Gesprächsprotokollen des Zeitschriftenprojekts "Krise und Kritik"* (Frankfurt am Main: Suhrkamp, 2004). Translated by Christine Shuttleworth under the title *Walter Benjamin and Bertolt Brecht: The Story of a Friendship* (New Haven: Yale University Press, 2009).

11. The transformation effected by the deathday in Benjamin's writing practice renders the two principles Conversation and Daybook, in the youthful facies separate ideals, two dialectical extremes, which represent in isolation complementary *dangers*. "For if it is the danger of the daybook as such to lay bare prematurely the germs of memory in the soul and prevent the ripening of its fruits, the danger must necessarily become fatal when the spirtual life expresses itself only in the daybook," as Benjamin remarks in *Goethe's Elective Affinities* (*SW*, 1:338; *GS*, 1:178).

12. Bertolt Brecht, "Über Nietzsches 'Zarathustra,'" in *Die Gedichte von Bertolt Brecht in einem Band* (Frankfurt am Main: Suhrkamp, 1981), 613–14.

13. In particular, it is the language from the center of book 3 of *Thus Spoke Zarathustra* that Brecht is echoing, the discourse "On Passing By" where Zarathustra reacts to the contemporary metropolis. Upon his approach to "the great city" (*TSZ*, 175; *KSA*, 4:222), Zarathustra is accosted by a "foaming

fool" who warns him away from the gates. "Why do you want to wade through this mire? . . . Spit on the great city which is the great swill room where all the swill spumes together" (*TSZ*, 176–77; *KSA*, 4:222–24). The fool is Zarathustra's Ape, "for he had gathered something of his phrasing and cadences and also liked to borrow from the treasures of his wisdom" (*TSZ*, 175–76; *KSA*, 4:222), and Zarathustra is offended by his hebephrenic critique. His quarrel is not with the substance of the denigration, but with the fact that it is uttered.

14. *Paris, Capital of the Nineteenth Century*, his working title from 1935 to 1939, indicates Benjamin's negative distance from any conventional urban sociology, and in particular the Marxist critical tradition. Paris, here, is not the capital of a spatial territory, but of a temporal epoch. This shift of registers, from space to time, separates the potential work organized by this title from the history it would present. Despite our contemporary tendency to "think globally and act locally," there is nothing obvious about such a transposition, which is itself historically conditioned. The internationalism that could make a territorial notion such as "capital" intuitively compatible, beyond any constitutive national boundaries, with a temporal designation such as "nineteenth century" is guaranteed throughout the nineteenth century not by Paris, but across the English Channel by London as the administrative center of the British Empire.

In Marxist terms, in particular, the "capital" of the nineteenth century could only be London, and its status as such is established for Marxism not least by the exiled situation of the author of *Das Kapital* itself. And indeed, Benjamin's "Marxism" always passes through the mortal figure of Karl Marx. In Benjamin's political engagement, his title situates the base/superstructure distinction that preserves Marxist materialism as the tendentious and tenuous priority of Paris over against Marx's own London, of the Bibliothèque nationale over the British Museum, as sites of exiled reflection. This is Benjamin's "revisionism": not the relinquishing of revolutionary intensity in favor of gradualism, but just the contrary: a preservation of revolutionary energy in contemporary historical conditions by reforming—or better, deforming—the past, in order to free those revolutionary energies within it that the past did not, itself, manage to exploit. That a century dominated in all of its material interactions by a British Empire administered from London could nonetheless have its "capital" in Paris does not reflect an abstract realignment of the relative importance of culture and economy. London's almost total absence from Benjamin's pictures of the nineteenth century (the one exception is a quotation from Shelley's *Peter Bell the Third*, that "Hell is a city much like London") does not imply that, despite appearances, Paris had "really" been the capital all along. It is, rather, to situate Marxist reflection in the present through the mortality of Marx himself. When Marx labored in the London archives of British imperialism, he was not mistaken or misdirected as to their central importance "at the time." It is only in the twentieth century that Paris becomes the capital of the nineteenth century, as the redemption of its secondary status in a transformed actual economic milieu. This is not to suggest that biographical contingencies did not play a role in Benjamin's attitude, but that the resistance manifested by his reluctance to visit England, or to learn English, even when he was married to a translator from that language, loses its theoretical resonance as soon as it is irretrievably deposited into Benjamin's particular vanished sensibility.

15. Benjamin repeats the formula in his *Elective Affinities* essay, as well: *SW* 1:307; *GS*, 1:138.

16. Auguste Blanqui, *L'Éternité par les astres* (1871), with a foreword by Jacques Rancière (Paris: Les Impressions Nouvelles, 2002), 107. Nietzsche himself knew Blanqui's book, or knew of it. The author and title appear as a fragment in notebook N VI 6 from the fall of 1883. Cf. *KSA*, 10:560.

17. Karl Löwith, *Nietzsches Philosophie der ewigen Wiederkunft des Gleichen*. Berlin: Verlag die Runde, 1935. Translated by J. Harvey Lomax under the title *Nietzsche's Philosophy of the Eternal Recurrence of the Same*. Berkeley: University of California Press, 1997. Because the translation is of the second edition from 1955, not every quotation Benjamin uses appears there.

18. Evidence for the completeness of Benjamin's reading appears in a letter to Adorno (*GB*, 6:157). Benjamin informs him that he is mentioned at an important place in the book. This doubtless refers to a footnote keyed to the first chapter (*NEW*, 18), where Adorno's Kierkegaard book is called to witness for the possibility of a philosophical language that transcends the opposition between truth and poetry. But he does not mention the second Adorno reference, on page 155, where Kierkegaard's "aesthetic" version of the eternal return is identified — in contrast to Nietzsche — via Adorno as a "'mythical repetition." It is unlikely, then, that he read these chapters carefully.

19. One citation Benjamin does transcribe concerns the confluence of antique and contemporary in Löwith's understanding of Nietzsche: *On the problem: modernity and antiquity*. *"The existence that has lost its stability and its direction, and the world that has lost its coherence and its significance, come together in the will of the 'eternal recurrence of the same' as the attempt to repeat—on the peak of modernity, in a symbol—the life which the Greeks lived within the living cosmos of the visible world"* (Karl Löwith, *Nietzsche's Philosophy of the Eternal Recurrence of the Same* (Berlin 1935), 83 [*AP*, 116; *GS*, 5:174]). Benjamin has here extracted the central thesis of Löwith's book, in Löwith's own words, as an illumination of the dialectical categories of modernity and antiquity. That this conflation of past and present would appeal to Benjamin's own understanding of redemptive time is understandable, but Löwith's two eras are far too literal to accommodate Benjamin's ontologically revisionary view of time.

20. The citation from Nietzsche, which is prefaced with *In Zarathustra 4* and does not explicitly mention the eternal return, can be found at *KSA*, 11:360.

CONCLUSION: FRIEDRICH NIETZSCHE, WALTER BENJAMIN

1. Robert Louis Stevenson, *Strange Case of Dr. Jekyll and Mr. Hyde*, ed. Katherine Linehan, Norton Critical Edition (New York: W. W. Norton, 2003), 50. Further references given in the text.

2. Charles Chaplin. *My Autobiography* (London: Penguin Books, 2003), 188.

3. Ibid., 178–79.

4. For a useful résumé of Chaplin's remarkable impact on Weimar intelligentsia, particularly on the political left, see Sabine Hake, "Chaplin Reception in Weimar Germany," *New German Critique* 51. (1990): 87–111.

5. Kant, Immanuel. "The End of All Things" (1794), in *Perpetual Peace and Other Essays on Politics, History, and Morals*, trans. Ted Humphrey (Indianapolis: Hackett, 1983), 93; *AA*, 8:327.

6. Kant, "End of All Things," 93; *AA*, 8:327.

BIBLIOGRAPHY

Adorno, Theodor W. *Gesammelte Schriften*. Edited by Rolf Tiedemann. 20 vols. Frankfurt am Main: Suhrkamp, 1997.

———. *Prisms*. Translated by Samuel Weber and Shierry Weber. Cambridge, Mass.: MIT Press, 1982.

Agamben, Giorgio. *Language and Death: The Place of Negativity*. Translated by Karen E. Pinkus with Michael Hardt. Theory and History of Literature 78. Minneapolis: University of Minnesota Press, 1991. Translation of *Il linguaggio e la morte: Un seminario sul luogo della negatività*. Turin: Guilio Einaudi, 1982.

———. "Walter Benjamin and the Demonic: Happiness and Historical Redemption." In *Potentialities: Collected Essays in Philosophy*, translated by Daniel Heller-Roazen, 139–59. Stanford: Stanford University Press, 1999.

Andreas-Salomé, Lou von. *Nietzsche in seinen Werken*. 1895. Frankfurt am Main: Insel, 2000.

Ansell Pearson, Keith, ed. *A Companion to Nietzsche*. West Sussex: Wiley-Blackwell, 2009.

———. *Nietzsche* contra *Rousseau: A Study of Nietzsche's Moral and Political Thought*. Cambridge: Cambridge University Press, 1991.

Aschheim, Steven E. *The Nietzsche Legacy in Germany, 1890–1990*. Weimar and Now: German Cultural Criticism 2. Berkeley: University of California Press, 1992.

Assoun, Paul-Laurent. *Freud and Nietzsche*. Translated by Richard L. Collier Jr. New York: Continuum, 2002. Translation of *Freud et Nietzsche*. Paris: Presses Universitaires de France, 1980.

Austin, John L. *How to Do Things with Words*. Cambridge, Mass.: Harvard University Press, 1975.

Badiou, Alain. "Who Is Nietzsche?" *Pli* 11 (2001): 1–11.

Benders, Raymond J., and Stephan Oettermann, eds. *Friedrich Nietzsche:*

Chronik in Bildern und Texten. Stiftung Weimarer Klassik. Munich: Hanser, 2000.

Benjamin, Andrew. "Shoah, Remembrance and the Abeyance of Fate: Walter Benjamin's 'Fate and Character.'" In *The Actuality of Walter Benjamin,* edited by Laura Marcus and Lynda Nead, 135–55. London: Lawrence and Wishart, 1998.

———, ed. *Walter Benjamin and Art.* New York: Continuum, 2005.

———. *Walter Benjamin and History.* New York: Continuum, 2005.

Benjamin, Andrew, and Peter Osborne, eds. *Walter Benjamin's Philosophy: Destruction and Experience.* London: Routledge, 1994.

Benjamin, Walter. *Gesammelte Briefe.* Edited by Christoph Gödde and Henri Lonitz. 6 vols. Frankfurt am Main: Suhrkamp, 1995–2000.

———. *Gesammelte Schriften.* Edited by Rolf Tiedemann and Hermann Schweppenhäuser. 7 vols. Frankfurt am Main: Suhrkamp, 1992.

Bennett, Benjamin. "Bridge: Against Nothing." In *Nietzsche and the Feminine,* edited by Peter J. Burgard, 289–315. Charlottesville: University Press of Virginia, 1994.

Bergson, Henri. *Matter and Memory.* Translated by N. M. Paul and W. S. Palmer. New York: Zone Books, 1991. Translation of *Matière et Mémoire,* 1896.

———. *Ouevres,* ed. André Robinet. Paris: Presses Universitaires de France, 1959.

———. *Time and Free Will: An Essay on the Immediate Data of Consciousness.* Translated by F. L. Pogson. Montana: Kessinger. Translation of *Essai sur les données immédiates del la conscience,* 1889.

Bernoulli, Carl Albrecht. *Franz Overbeck und Friedrich Nietzsche: Eine Freundschaft.* 2 vols. Jena: Eugen Diederichs, 1908.

Blanqui, Auguste. *L'Éternité par les astres.* 1871. With a foreword by Jacques Rancière. Paris: Les Impressions Nouvelles, 2002.

Blondel, Eric. *Nietzsche: The Body and Culture: Philosophy as a Philological Genealogy.* Translated by by Seán Hand. Stanford: Stanford University Press, 1991. Translation of *Nietzsche le corps et la culture* (Paris: Presses Universitaires de France, 1986).

Bloom, Harold. *The Anxiety of Influence: A Theory of Poetry.* 1973. 2nd ed. New York: Oxford University Press, 1997.

———. *Kabbalah and Criticism.* New York: Continuum, 1975.

Brecht, Bertolt. *Die Gedichte von Bertolt Brecht in einem Band.* Frankfurt am Main: Suhrkamp, 1981.

Brodersen, Momme. *Walter Benjamin: A Biography.* Translated by Malcolm R. Green and Ingrida Ligers. New York: Verso, 1996. Translation of *Spinne im eigenen Netz. Walter Benjamin—Leben und Werk.* Bühl-Moos: Elster Verlag, 1990.

Brogen, Walter. "Zarathustra: the Tragic Figure of the Last Philosopher." In *Philosophy and Tragedy*, edited by Miguel de Beistegui and Simon Sparks, 152–66. London: Routledge, 2000.

Buber, Martin. *Drei Reden über das Judentum.* Frankfurt am Main: Rütten and Loening, 1911.

Campioni, Giuliano, et. al. *Nietzsches persönliche Bibliothek.* Supplementa Nietzscheana, Vol. 6. Berlin: Walter de Gruyter, 2003.

Chaplin, Charles. *My Autobiography.* London: Penguin Books, 2003.

Corngold, Stanley. *Complex Pleasure: Forms of Feeling in German Literature.* Stanford: Stanford University Press, 1998.

Cranston, Jodi. "Tropes of Revelation in Raphael's 'Transfiguration.'" *Renaissance Quarterly* 56, no. 1 (2003).

Deleuze, Gilles. *Nietzsche and Philosophy.* Translated by Hugh Tomlinson. New York: Columbia University Press, 1983. Translation of *Nietzsche et la philosophie* (Paris: Presse Universitaires de France, 1962).

De Man, Paul. *Allegories of Reading: Figural Language in Rousseau, Nietzsche, Rilke, and Proust.* New Haven: Yale University Press, 1979.

Derrida, Jacques. *Margins of Philosophy.* Translated by Alan Bass. Chicago: University of Chicago Press, 1982. Translation of *Marges de la philosophie* (Paris: Les Editions de Minuit, 1972).

———. "Otobiographies: The Teaching of Nietzsche and the Politics of the Proper Name." Translated by Avital Ronell. In *The Ear of the Other: Otobiography, Transference, Translation*, edited by Christie McDonald, 1–38. Lincoln: University of Nebraska Press, 1988.

———. *Spurs: Nietzsche's Styles.* Translated by Barbara Harlow. Chicago: University of Chicago Press, 1978.

———. *Who's Afraid of Philosophy? Right to Philosophy I.* Translated by Jan Plug. Stanford: Stanford University Press, 2002. Translation of *Du droit à la philosophie* (Paris: Editions Galilée, 1990).

Deuber-Mankowsky, Astrid. *Der frühe Walter Benjamin und Hermann Cohen: Jüdische Werte, Kritische Philosophie, vergängliche Erfahrung.* Berlin: Verlag Vorwerk, 2000.

Dudek, Peter. *Fetisch Jugend: Walter Benjamin und Siegfried Bernfeld—Jugendprotest am Vorabend des Ersten Weltkrieges.* Bad Heilbrunn: Julius Klinkhardt, 2002.

Eagleton, Terry. *Walter Benjamin: Or Towards a Revolutionary Criticism.* London: Verso, 1981.

Fenves, Peter. *Arresting Language: From Leibniz to Benjamin.* Stanford: Stanford University Press, 2001.

Foucault, Michel. *The Order of Things: An Archeology of the Human Sciences*. New York: Vintage, 1970. Translation of *Les Mots et les choses* (Paris: Editions Gallimard, 1966).

———. "What Is an Author?" In *Language, Counter-Memory, Practice: Selected Essays and Interviews*, edited by Donald F. Bouchard, 113–38. Ithaca, N.Y.: Cornell University Press, 1977.

Fuld, Werner. *Walter Benjamin: Eine Biographie*. Rev. ed. Reinbek bei Hamburg: rororo-Rowohlt, 1990.

Gadamer, Hans-Georg. "Nietzsche—Der Antipode: Das Drama Zarathustras." In *Gesammelte Werke 4: Neuere Philosophie II*, 448–62, Tübingen: Mohr 1987.

Goethe, Johann Wolfgang von. *Werke*. Hamburger Ausgabe in 14 Bänden. Edited by Erich Trunz et al. Munich: Deutscher Taschenbuch Verlag, 1988.

———. *Italian Journey*. Translated by Robert R. Heitner. Vol. 6 of *Goethe's Collected Works*. 12 vols. New York: Suhrkamp, 1989.

Guerra, Gabriele. *Judentum zwischen Anarchie und Theokratie: Ein religionspolitische Diskussion am Beispiel der Begegnung zwischen Walter Benjamin und Gershom Scholem*. Bielefeld: Aisthesis Verlag, 2007.

Hake, Sabine. "Chaplin Reception in Weimar Germany." *New German Critique* 51 (1990): 87–111.

Hamacher, Werner. "Afformative, Strike: Benjamin's 'Critique of Violence.'" In *Walter Benjamin's Philosophy: Destruction and Experience*, ed. Andrew Benjamin and Peter Osborne, 110–38. London: Routledge, 1994.

———. "The Gesture in the Name: On Benjamin and Kafka." In *Premises: Essays on Philosophy and Literature from Kant to Celan*, translated by Peter Fenves, 294–336. Stanford: Stanford University Press, 1996.

———. *Premises: Essays on Philosophy and Literature from Kant to Celan*. Translated by Peter Fenves. Stanford: Stanford University Press, 1996.

———. "The Second of Inversion: Movements of a Figure through Celan's Poetry." In *Premises: Essays on Philosophy and Literature from Kant to Celan*, translated by Peter Fenves, 337–87. Stanford: Stanford University Press, 1996.

———. "The Word *Wolke*—If It Is One." In *Benjamin's Ground: New Readings of Walter Benjamin*, 147–76. Detroit: Wayne State University Press, 1988.

Hansen, Miriam. "Benjamin, Cinema and Experience: 'The Blue Flower in the Land of Technology.'" *Film Quarterly* (1985): 179–224.

Hanssen, Beatrice, and Andrew Benjamin, eds. *Walter Benjamin and Romanticism*. New York: Continuum, 2002.

Hegel, Georg Wilhelm Friedrich. *Die Phänomenologie des Geistes*. 1806.

Werke, vol 3. Edited by Eva Moldenhauer and Karl Markus Michel. Frankfurt am Main: Suhrkamp Verlag, 1970. Translated by A. V. Miller under the title *The Phenomenology of Spirit*. Oxford: Oxford University Press, 1977.

Heidegger, Martin. *Nietzsche*. 2 vols. Pfullingen: Neske, 1961.

Holub, Robert C. "The Elisabeth Legend: The Cleansing of Nietzsche and the Sullying of His Sister." In *Nietzsche, Godfather of Fascism? On the Uses and Abuses of a Philosophy*, edited by Jacob Golomb and Robert S. Wistrich, 215–34. Princeton: Princeton University Press, 2002.

Jameson, Fredric. "The Theoretical Hesitation: Benjamin's Sociological Predecessor." *Critical Inquiry* 25, no. 2 (1999): 267–88.

Jantzen, Hinrich. *Jugendkultur und Jugendbewegung: Studie zur Stellung und Bedeutung Gustav Wynekens innerhalb der Jugenbewegung*. Frankfurt am Main: Dipa-Verlag, 1963.

Janz, Curt Paul. *Friedrich Nietzsche*. 3 vols. Munich: Carl Hanser, 1978.

Jennings, Michael W. *Dialectical Images: Walter Benjamin's Theory of Literary Criticism*. Ithaca, N.Y.: Cornell University Press, 1987.

———. "The Mortification of the Text: The Development of Walter Benjamin's Theory of Literary Criticism, 1912–1924." PhD diss. University of Virginia, 1981. Ann Arbor: UMI, 1981. 8208496.

Kafka, Franz. *Gesammelte Werke in zwölf Bänden*. Edited by Hans-Gerd Koch. Frankfurt am Main: Fischer, 1994.

Kambas, Chryssoula. "Walter Benjamin liest Georges Sorel: 'Réflections sur la violence.'" In *Aber ein Sturm weht vom Paradiese her: Texte zu Walter Benjamin*, edited by Michael Opitz and Erdmut Wizisla, 250–69. Leipzig: Reclam, 1992.

Kant, Immanuel. *Werke*. Akademie-Ausgabe. Edited by the Royal Prussian Academy of Sciences. 11 vols. Berlin: Walter de Gruyter, 1968.

———. "The End of All Things." 1794. In *Perpetual Peace and Other Essays on Politics, History, and Morals*, translated by Ted Humphrey, 93–105. Indianapolis: Hackett, 1983.

Klages, Ludwig. *Die psychologischen Errungenschaften Nietzsches*. 1926. Bonn: Bouvier Verlag Herbert Grundmann, 1977.

Klossowski, Pierre. *Nietzsche and the Vicious Circle*. Translated by Daniel W. Smith. Chicago: University of Chicago Press, 1997. Translation of *Nietzsche et le Cercle Vicieux* (Paris: Mercure de France, 1969).

Kofman, Sarah. *Explosion I: De l'"Ecce Homo" de Nietzsche*. Paris: Galilée, 1992.

Kofman, Sarah. *Explosion II: Les enfants de Nietzsche*. Paris: Galilée, 1993.

———. *Nietzsche and Metaphor*. Translated by Duncan Large. Stanford:

Stanford University Press, 1993. Translation of *Nietzsche et la métaphore* (Paris: Galilée, 1983).

Krell, David Farrell. *Infectious Nietzsche.* Bloomington: Indiana University Press, 1996.

Krummel, Richard Frank. *Nietzsche und der deutsche Geist.* 3 vols. Berlin: Walter de Gruyter, 1998.

Kupffer, Heinrich. *Gustav Wyneken.* Stuttgart: Ernst Klett, 1970.

Laqueur, Walter. *Young Germany: A History of the German Youth Movement.* New York: Basic Books, 1962.

Loeb, Paul S. *The Death of Nietzsche's Zarathustra.* Cambridge: Cambridge University Press, 2010.

Longfellow, Henry Wadsworth. *The Works of Henry Wadsworth Longfellow.* Edited by Samuel Longfellow, 14 vols. Vol. 1: *Voices of the Night, Poems on Slavery, The Belfry of Bruges, etc.* Boston: Houghton, Mifflin, 1886.

Löwith, Karl. *Nietzsches Philosophie der ewigen Wiederkunft des Gleichen.* Berlin: die Runde, 1935. Translated by J. Harvey Lomax under the title *Nietzsche's Philosophy of the Eternal Recurrence of the Same.* Berkeley: University of California Press, 1997.

Lukács, Georg. *Die Seele und die Formen: Essays.* 1911. Neuwied: Luchterhand, 1971. Translated by Anna Bostock under the title *Soul and Form.* New York: Columbia University Press, 2010.

———. *Geschichte und Klassenbewußtsein: Studien über marxistische Dialektik.* 1923. Darmstadt: Luchterhand, 1968. Translated by Rodney Livingstone under the title *History and Class Consciousness: Studies in Marxist Dialectics.* Cambridge, Mass.: MIT Press, 1971

Mann, Thomas. "Nietzsche's Philosophy in the Light of Contemporary Events." In *Thomas Mann's Addresses Delivered at the Library of Congress, 1942–1949.* Washington: Library of Congress, 1963.

Marcus, Laura, and Lynda Nead, eds. *The Actuality of Walter Benjamin.* London: Lawrence and Wishart, 1998.

Menninghaus, Winfried. *Schwellenkunde: Walter Benjamins Passage des Mythos.* Edition Suhrkamp Neue Folge 349. Frankfurt am Main: Suhrkamp, 1986.

———. *Walter Benjamins Theorie der Sprachmagie.* 1980. Rev. ed. Frankfurt am Main: Suhrkamp, 1995.

Missac, Pierre. *Walter Benjamin's Passages.* Translated by by Shierry Weber Nicholsen. Cambridge, Mass.: MIT Press, 1995. Translation of *Passage de Walter Benjamin* (Paris: Editions du Seuil, 1987).

Moses, Stéphane. "Benjamin, Nietzsche et l'idée de l'éternel retour." *Europe, revue littéraire mensuelle* 74, no. 804 (1996): 140–58.

Nägele, Rainer. "Benjamin's Ground." In *Benjamin's Ground: New Readings of Walter Benjamin*, 10–37. Detroit: Wayne State University Press, 1988.

———, ed. *Benjamin's Ground: New Readings of Walter Benjamin*. Detroit: Wayne State University Press, 1988.

Nehamas, Alexander. *Nietzsche: Life as Literature*. Cambridge, Mass.: Harvard University Press, 1985.

Newman, Jane O. *Benjamin's Library: Modernity, Nation, and the Baroque*. Ithaca, N.Y.: Cornell University Press, 2011.

Nietzsche, Friedrich. *Fruhe Schriften*. Edited by Hans Joachim Mette, Karl Schlechta, and Carl Koch. 5 vols. Beck'sche Ausgabe Werke. Munich: Deutscher Taschenbuch Verlag, 1994.

———. *Kritische Studienausgabe*. Edited by Giorgio Colli and Mazzino Montinari. 15 vols. Berlin: Walter de Gruyter, 1988.

———. *Sämtliche Briefe*. Edited by Giorgio Colli and Mazzino Montinari. 8 vols. Berlin: Walter de Gruyter, 1984.

Norris, Christopher. *Fiction, Philosophy and Literary Theory: Will the Real Saul Kripke Please Stand Up?* London: Continuum, 2007.

Outhwaite, William. "Nietzsche and Critical Theory." In *Nietzsche: A Critical Reader*, edited by Peter R. Sedgwick, 203–21. Oxford: Blackwell, 1995.

Pestalozzi, Karl. "Nietzsches Baudelaire-Rezeption." *Nietzsche-Studien: Internationales Jahrbuch für die Nietzsche-Forschung* 7 (1978): 158–88.

Pfotenhauer, Helmut. "Benjamin und Nietzsche." In *"Links hatte noch alles sich zu enträtseln": Walter Benjamin im Kontext.*, edited by Burkhardt Lindner, 100–126. Frankfurt am Main: Syndikat, 1978.

Podach, E. F. *Nietzsches Zusammenbruch: Beiträge zu einer Biographie auf Grund unveröffentlichter Dokumente*. Heidelberg, Niels Kampmann, 1930.

Polczyk, Peter. "Physiognomien der Humanität—Ordnung der Schrift: Walter Benjamins *Deutsche Menschen*." *Wirkendes Wort. Deutsche Sprache und Literatur in Forschung und Lehre* 2, no. 88 (1988): 214–34.

Porter, James I. *The Invention of Dionysus: An Essay on* The Birth of Tragedy. Stanford: Stanford University Press, 2000.

———. *Nietzsche and the Philology of the Future*. Stanford: Stanford University Press, 2000.

Pütz, Peter. "Nietzsche im Lichte der kritischen Theorie." *Nietzsche-Studien: Internationales Jahrbuch für die Nietzsche-Forschung* 3 (1974): 175–91.

Quine, Willard van Orman. "The Ways of Paradox." In *The Ways of Paradox and Other Essays, Revised and Enlarged Edition*, 1–18. Cambridge, Mass.: Harvard University Press, 1976.

Ratner-Rosenhagen, Jennifer. *American Nietzsche: A History of an Icon and His Ideas*. Chicago: University of Chicago Press, 2012.

Reijen, Willem van, and Herman van Doorn. *Aufenthalte und Passagen: Leben und Werk Walter Benjamins. Eine Chronik*. Frankfurt am Main: Suhrkamp, 2001.

Reschke, Renate. "Barbaren, Kult und Katastrophen: Nietzsche bei Benjamin: Unzusammenhängendes im Zusammenhang gelesen." In *Aber ein Sturm weht vom Paradiese her: Texte zu Walter Benjamin*, edited by Michael Opitz and Erdmut Wizisla, 303–39. Leipzig: Reclam, 1992.

Rosenzweig, Franz. *Der Stern der Erlösung*. 1921. Frankfurt am Main: Suhrkamp Verlag, 1988. Translated by Barbara E. Galli under the title *The Star of Redemption*. Madison: University of Wisconsin Press, 2005.

Rrenban, Monad [Brendan Moran]. *Wild, Unforgettable Philosophy: in Early Works of Walter Benjamin*. Lanham: Lexington Books, 2005.

Russell, Bertrand. *Introduction to Mathematical Philosophy*. 1920. New York: Dover, 1993.

Sallis, John. *Crossings: Nietzsche and the Space of Tragedy*. Chicago: University of Chicago Press, 1991.

Schaberg, William H. *The Nietzsche Canon: A Publication History and Bibliography*. Chicago: University of Chicago Press, 1995.

Schiller, Friedrich. *Werke: Nationalausgabe*. Edited by Julius Petersen and Hermann Schneider. 43 vols. Weimar: Hermann Böhlaus Nachfolger, 1949–66.

Schleiermacher, Friedrich. "Über Begriff und Einteilung der philologischen Kritik." 1830. In *Hermeneutik und Kritik*, edited by Manfred Frank, 347–60. Frankfurt am Main: Suhrkamp, 1977.

Scholem, Gershom. *Walter Benjamin: Die Geschichte einer Freundschaft*. Frankfurt am Main: Suhrkamp, 1975. Translated by Harry Zohn under the title *Walter Benjamin: The Story of a Friendship*. New York: New York Review Books, 1981.

Schopenhauer, Arthur. *Sämtliche Werke*. Edited by Wolfgang Frhr. Von Löhneysen. 5 vols. Frankfurt am Main: Suhrkamp, 1986.

———. "On Philosophy at the Universities." In Arthur Schopenhauer, *Parerga and Paralipomena: Short Philosophical Essays*, vol. 1, translated by E. F. J. Payne. Oxford: Clarendon Press, 1974.

Schöttker, Detlev. *Konstruktiver Fragmentarismus: Form und Rezeption der Schriften Walter Benjamins*. Frankfurt am Main: Suhrkamp, 1999.

Schulte, Christian. *Ursprung ist das Ziel: Walter Benjamin über Karl Kraus*. Würzburg: Königshausen and Neumann, 2003.

Seiffert, Johannes. "*Deutsche Menschen*: Vorlaufiges zu Walter Benjamins Brief-Anthologie." *Jarbuch des Instituts fur deutsche Geschinte*, 1 (1972): 159–70.

Serény, György. "Gödel, Tarski, Church, and the Liar." *Bulletin of Symbolic Logic* 9, no. 1 (2003).

Shapiro, Gary. *Nietzschean Narratives*. Bloomington: Indiana University Press, 1989.

Sparks, Simon. "Fatalities: Freedom and the Question of Language in Walter Benjamin's Reading of Tragedy." in *Philosophy and Tragedy*, edited by Miguel de Beistegui and Simon Sparks, 193–218. London: Routledge, 2000.

Staten, Henry. *Nietzsche's Voice*. Ithaca, N.Y.: Cornell University Press, 1990.

Steiner, Uwe. *Die Geburt der Kritik aus dem Geiste der Kunst: Untersuchungen zum Begriff der Kritik in den frühen Schriften Walter Benjamins*. Würzburg: Königshausen and Neumann, 1989.

———. "The True Politician: Walter Benjamin's Concept of the Political." *New German Critique* 83 (Spring–Summer 2001): 43–88.

Stevenson, Robert Louis. *Strange Case of Dr. Jekyll and Mr. Hyde*. 1886. Edited by Katherine Linehan. Norton Critical Edition. New York: W. W. Norton, 2003.

Stroux, Johannes. *Nietzsches Professur in Basel*. Jena: Frommannsche Buchhandlung (Walter Biedermann), 1925.

Szondi, Peter. "Hoffnung in Vergangenen: Über Walter Benjamin," 1961, in *Schriften in 2 Bänden*. ed. Wolfgang Fietkau, 2:275–294. Translated by Harvey Mendelsohn under the title "Hope in the Past: On Walter Benjamin." *Critical Inquiry* 4, no. 3 (1978): 491–505.

Volz, Pia Daniela. *Nietzsche im Labyrinth seiner Krankheit: Eine medizinisch-biographische Untersuchung*. Würzburg: Königshausen and Neumann, 1990.

Waite, Geoff. *Nietzsche's Corps/e: Aesthetics, Politics, Prophecy, or, the Spectacular Technoculture of Everyday Life*. Durham, N.C.: Duke University Press, 1996.

Weber, Max. *Die protestantische Ethik und der Geist des Kapitalismus*. 1920. In *Gesammelte Aufsätze zur Religionssoziologie I*. Tübingen: J. C. B Mohr Verlag, 1988. 17–206. Translated by Talcott Parsons under the title *The Protestant Ethic and the Spirit of Capitalism* (1930; London: Routledge, 1992).

———. *Wirtschaft und Gesellschaft: Grundriss der verstehenden Soziologie*, 5th ed. Tübingen: J. C. B. Mohr, 1976.

Weber, Samuel. *Benjamin's -abilities*. Cambridge, Mass.: Harvard University Press, 2008.

Weigel, Sigrid. *Body- and Image-Space: Re-reading Walter Benjamin*.

Translated by Georgina Paul with Rachel McNicholl and Jeremy Gaines. London: Routledge, 1996.

———. *Entstellte Ähnlichkeit: Walter Benjamins theoretische Schreibweise.* Frankfurt am Main: Fischer Taschenbuch Verlag, 1997.

Wilamowitz-Möllendorff, Ulrich von. "Zukunftsphilologie! eine erwidrung auf Friedrich Nietzsches ord. professors der classischen philologie zu Basel 'Geburt der Tragödie.'" 1872. In *Der Streit um Nietzsches "Geburt der Tragödie": Die Schriften von E. Rohde, R. Wagner, U. v. Wilamowitz-Möllendorff*, 27–55. Hildesheim: G. Olms, 1969.

Witte, Bernd. *Walter Benjamin: Mit Selbstzeugnissen und Bilddokumenten.* Reinbek bei Hamburg: rororo-Rowohlt, 1985.

Wittgenstein, Ludwig. *Philosophische Untersuchungen.* Leipzig: Reclam 1990. Translated by G. E. M. Anscombe under the title *Philosophical Investigations.* New York: Macmillan, 1958.

Wizisla, Erdmut. *Benjamin und Brecht: Die Geschichte einer Freundschaft. Mit einer Chronik und den Gesprächsprotokollen des Zeitschriftenprojekts "Krise und Kritik."* Frankfurt am Main: Suhrkamp, 2004. Translated by Christine Shuttleworth under the title *Walter Benjamin and Bertolt Brecht: The Story of a Friendship* (New Haven: Yale University Press, 2009).

———. "'Fritz Heinle war Dichter': Walter Benjamin und sein Jugendfreund." In *"Was nie geschrieben wurde, lesen," Frankfurter Benjamin-Vorträge*, edited by Lorenz Jäger and Thomas Regehly, 115–31. Bielefeld: Aisthesis Verlag, 1992.

Wohlfahrt, Irving. "Resentment Begins at Home: Nietzsche, Benjamin, and the University." In *On Walter Benjamin: Critical Essays and Recollections*, edited by Gary Smith, 224–59. Cambridge, Mass.: MIT Press, 1988.

Wyneken, Gustav. *Schule und Jugendkultur.* 2nd ed. Jena: Eugen Diederichs, 1914.

Zupančič, Alenka. *The Shortest Shadow: Nietzsche's Philosophy of the Two.* Cambridge, Mass.: MIT Press, 2003.

INDEX

Abitur (Benjamin), 16
Abstand (interval), 64, 66, 205
abstinence, 22
activism, student, 21, 23
activity, 28, 209
actuality, 29, 218
ad hominem, 149–51, 159, 161, 288n30
Adorno, Gretel. *See* Karplus, Gretel
Adorno, Theodor W., vii, viii, 7, 180–81, 230, 233
Aeschylus, 90, 99–100, 144
aesthetics: performance and, 209; satisfaction in, 109; science of, 99, 143; Socratism, 90
aestheticism, 76, 78, 112, 275n9
Aesthetics of the Tragic (Volkelt), 75
"Afformative, Strike" (Hamacher), 294n1, 295n2
afterlife, 210
Against the Writer David Strauss (Nietzsche), 127
L'Age d'homme (Leiris), 255
agon, 79, 218
Albert-Ludwigs-Universität, 21
allegory, 84, 87–89, 204, 226
ambiguity, 79
American Revolution, 12
Amtliches Lehrgedicht (Scholem, Gershom), 130
anachronism, 64, 192, 211–13, 217–18, 246, 275n9
analytical formalism, 104
Anders, Günther, 297n6
"André Gide: La porte étroite" (Benjamin), 56
antagonism, 14, 197, 218; class, 222; temporalities, 26
Antebellum youth movement debates, 22
The Antichrist (Nietzsche), 153–54, 211, 284n13
anti-Dreyfusards, 220

antihumanism, 49
anti-Semitism, 127, 220, 256
aphorisms, 26
Apollo, 76, 90, 109, 144–45, 200
Apparat, 187
The Arcades Project (Benjamin), viii, 71, 205, 219, 223, 227–29, 231–33, 235, 245, 264n5, 268n17, 269n21, 270n23, 278n20, 287n20
"Archimedean point," 76, 101
Arendt, Hannah, 191, 223, 243
ark, metaphor of, 181–82
art, 36–37, 44, 53, 143–44; criticism of, 72; of science, 152; theory, 271n31
artists, 37, 47
l'art pour l'art, 44
ascent, 14, 197
asceticism, 158
Aschheim, Steven, 19, 266n5
astronomy, 36
As You Like It (Shakespeare), 83
asyndeton, 146, 155–61, 176f., 205, 280n29
atheism, 235
Athos and the Atheists (Benjamin), 287n22
atonement, 77
Attempt at a Revaluation of All Values (Nietzsche), 284n13
Attic tragedies, 76, 82
audience, 209
Aufgabe, 211; *endlose*, 87
aura, 6, 65, 245, 250
das Ausdruckslose. See the expressionless
Ausland, 123
Austin, Albert, 255
Austin, J. L., 295n2
"The Author as Producer" (Benjamin), 186, 188

authority, 20, 35, 117–18, 127, 164, 177, 215; dependent, 216; of original, 213–14; of performance, 209; political, 206; of translation, 212; of university, 138
Autrui (Levinas), 58
awareness, 32, 143, 144

Bachofen, Johann Jakob, 133
Badiou, Alain, 292n1
Bailyn, John Fred, xi–xii
"The Ball" (Benjamin), 25
ballad stanza, European, 13
Balzac, Honoré de, 232
baptism, 55, 57
barbarism, 244
Baroque drama, 96
Baroque Trauerspiel, 74
Baudelaire, Charles, 8, 141–42, 209, 212, 228, 269n21
Bayreuth, 19, 112, 120–22, 126–27
Bayreuth Horizon Observations (Nietzsche), 120
beam, 30
beauty, 57; truth and, 108
Beethoven, Ludwig van, 215
Beinecke Rare Book and Manuscript Library, 130
Belmore, Herbert. *See* Blumenthal, Herbert
"Benjamin, Nietzsche, et l'idée de l'éternel retour" (Moses), x
"Benjamin und Nietzsche" (Pfotenhauer), ix
Benjamin, Dora (sister), 181, 243
Benjamin, Dora née Kellner (wife), 195
Bentley, Richard, 147
Bergman, Henry, 256
Bergson, Henri, 287n25
Berlin Childhood around 1900 (Benjamin), 14
Berlin Chronicle (Benjamin), 51, 53
Bernoulli, C. A., 5, 116, 179, 236
Berufsverschwörer, 223
Beyle, Marie-Henri. *See* Stendhal
Beyond Good and Evil (Nietzsche), 5, 115, 129, 157, 163, 169, 172
The Bible, 213, New Testament, 111, 116, 200
Bildungsroman, 54
birthday celebration, 55
The Birth of Tragedy (Nietzsche), viii, 75–76, 96, 99–102, 142–44
Blanqui, Auguste, 71, 233–34, 244
blessings, 154
Blondel, Eric, 267n12

Blumenthal, Herbert, 23, 28, 43, 52, 54, 60, 270n22
Body- and Image-Space: Rereading Walter Benjamin (Weigel), 268n17
Bolshevism, 247
Bonaparte, Napoleon. *See* Napoleon
"Boredom, Eternal Return (Benjamin), 234
bourgeois: cultural history, 230; society, 223, 234
Brandes, Georg, 126
Brecht, Bertolt, 6, 7, 187, 222, 224–25, 227
British Museum, 136
Brothers Grimm, 184
Brutus, Lucius Junius, 202
Buber, Martin, 33, 38, 39
Büchner, Georg, 184
Buddhism, 273n39
Burckhardt, Jacob, 161, 292n40

Caesar, 202–7
Caesarism, 247
cafés, 30
Calderón, Pedro de la Barca, 83, 87, 167
capitalism, 162–65, 247, 260
"Capitalism as Religion" (Benjamin), 162–165, 292n41
caricature, 238–40
Cartesian theater, 31
The Case of Wagner (Nietzsche), 5
catastrophe, 67, 261
catatonia, 2, 3
Catholicism, 220, 271n31
"Central Park" (Benjamin), 223, 237, 261
Chaplin, Charlie, 255–58, 261, 300n4
childhood, of Benjamin, 14, 16
Christ, Jesus, 111, 112, 201
Christianity, 49, 156, 189, 273n39; Catholicism, 220, 271n1; Judeo-Christian culture, 201; Passion, 80; Protestantism, 271n31
The Circus (film), 261
classical heritage, 274n5
class struggle, 221
coeducation, 22
coffeehouses, 30
Cohen, Hermann, 67
Cohn, Jula, 29, 195
collaboration, 223
collective logic, 143
collective response, 208
collective silence, 277n18
collective singular nouns, 185
collective unconscious, 230

Index

Collenbusch, Samuel, 184
Colli, Giorgio, ix
comedy, 260–61
commodity, 260
The Competition (Nietzsche), 120
complacency, social-democratic, 243
complicity, 218, 219, 227
comprehensibility, 96
"The Concept of Art Criticism in German Romanticism" (Benjamin), 234–35
concrete realities, 73
confessional deception, 105
consciousness: of God, 39; historical, 232; mythic, 236
"Conspiracies, *Compagnonnage*" (Benjamin), 223
conspiracy, 223–24
constellation, vii, 8, 11, 13, 66, 75, 208, 224–25, 229–30, 237, 264n5, 296n5
contemporary institutions, 136
continued life, 210
controlled empirical psychology, 1
"The Convalescent" (Nietzsche), 198
Conversation (*Gespräch*) (Benjamin), 25–29, 242
"Conversation on Love" (Benjamin), 43, 44
convivial sayings, 152
Corngold, Stanley, xi
correspondence, 180–90. *See also* letters
courage, 61; poetic, 63
Cranston, Jodi, 112
The Cretan, 103–5, 107
"The Criminal" (Benjamin), 25
Crisis and Criticism (journal), 222–23
critical efforts, of Benjamin, 56
criticism: of art, 72; of Nietzsche, 40–41; of philology, 147, 150
"Cry of Distress" (Nietzsche), 178
cultivated philistines, 242
culture, 187; barbarism and, 244; bourgeois cultural history, 230; Greek, 146; Judeo-Christian, 201; mediating between, 191; Wilhelminian, 18–19, 62. *See also* Youth Culture Movement
Culture-Zionism, 34
cycle, 25; life cycle, 94

danger, 35–37, 77, 157, 210, 224–25, 272n32
Dasein (Heidegger), 58
Däubler, Theodor, 287n22
"David Strauss, the Confessor and the Writer" (Nietzsche), 129, 146

Daybook (*Tagebuch*) (Benjamin), 25–26, 30–31, 242
"Daybook from the Seventh of August Nineteen-Thirtyone to my Deathday" (Benjamin), 55
Daybreak (Nietzsche), 5, 153
death, 26, 32–33, 55, 65, 78, 79, 210–11, 258–59; of God, 163, 235; of hero, 80–81; language and, 58; of Nietzsche, 68; philosophy of, 57; of Socrates, 92–93; of tragedy, 93; of Zarathustra, 198–201, 207
deathday, 55, 62, 64, 241, 297n11
Death of Empedocles (Hölderlin), 201
deceptive confession, 105
defiance, 79, 81, 92; silence and, 94
Deleuze, Gilles, viii, 288n30
de Ligne, Charles-Joseph, Fürst, 172
de Man, Paul, 280n30
Derrida, Jacques, ix, 263n2, 272n38, 278n21, 290n39
Descartes, René, 106
destruction, 237–38, 239–40
"The Destructive Character" (Benjamin), 237, 240
"Detachment for School Reform," 22
Deuber-Mankowsky, Astrid, 265n3
Deussen, Paul, 156
Deutsche Menschen: A Series of Letters (Benjamin), xi, 71, 179–83, 186–88
dialectics at a standstill, 236
"Dialogue on the Religiosity of the Present" (Benjamin), 18, 43–44, 47–51, 270n29
"Did Grillparzer Farm with Goethe's Plough" (Benjamin), 265n1
Dietzgen, Wilhelm, 243
Dionysus, 76, 144–45, 200–201
direct influence, 225
discontinuity, 193
discussion forum, 23
display, 88
"Distance and Images" (Benjamin), 172
divinity, 248
doctrine of thresholds, 276n15
dogmatism, 283n9
Dostoevsky, Fyodor, 33, 56
"The Double Equation for the Allegory of the Eternal Recurrence" (Löwith), 235
drama of fate, 83
dramatisation, 288n30
dreaming collective, 230
dreams, 144, 229
Drei Reden über das Judentum (Buber), 38

drug experiments, 1–2
Dudek, Peter, 265n3
duplicity, 276n14

Earth-Spirit, 46
Ecce Homo (Nietzsche), 101, 113, 155–57, 204, 207, 211
education, 21–22; coeducation, 22. *See also specific schools and universities*
egalitarianism, politics, 226
egalitarian political premise, 137
Elective Affinities (Goethe), 39, 74, 183, 194–95, 275n14
elite, 136
Elizabethan theater, 83
Emerson, Ralph Waldo, 103
endless task, 87
endlose Aufgabe (endless task), 87
"The End of All Things" (Kant), 258–61
enemy, 32
Enlightenment, 45, 73, 150, 259, 276n15
entertainment, of reader, 118
epigraphs, 242–43, 244
Epimenides, 103, 104, 105
"Epistemo-critical Preface" (Benjamin), 137
epistemological relativism, 221
Erkenntnis (knowledge as precise discernment), 169
Ernst, Paul, 77–78
eroticism, 28–29, 138
esotericism, 139, 142
Essanay Studios, 257
etching, of Nietzsche, 2
Eternal Return, viii, 129, 200–201, 227–37, 240, 273n39
L'Éternité par les astres (Blanqui), 233
ethical transparency, 41
Euripides, 90
European ballad stanza, 13
evolution, dogma of, 39
excelsior, 12–14, 197
"Excelsior" (Longfellow), 10, 11–12
exceptionality, 140
"Exhortation to the Germans" (Nietzsche), 121–23, 124–26
exile, 173
"'Experience'" (Benjamin), 43, 59
"Experience and Poverty" (Benjamin), 172
expiration, 211
explicitness, 162
expression, 27
the expressionless, (*das Ausdruckslose*) 109
exterior history, 213

externalization, 177, 204
extracurricular reform, 22
extremism, 220, 297n7

Die Fackel. See *The Torch*
failure, 14
fascism, vii, 71, 188
fashion, 232
fatal history, 259
fate, 86, 231; drama of, 83; temporality of, 236–37
"Fate and Character" (Benjamin), 231
feeling, 45
Feind (enemy), 26
Fenves, Peter, 295n3
Fernenbestimmtheit, 68, 179
Fetisch Jugend: Walter Benjamin und Siegfried Bernfeld-Jugendprotest am Vorabend des Ersten Weltkrieges (Dudek), 266n3
feuilleton, 233
fidelity, 197; translation and, 210
finitude, 78
first-person, 105–7, 221
"Five Prefaces to Five Unwritten Books" (Nietzsche), 70
flâneur, 233
form, 78
formalism: analytical, 104; logical, 103
Förster, Bernd, 19
Förster House, 4, 15
Förster-Nietzsche, Elisabeth, ix, 3, 18–19, 132–33
Foucault, Michel, ix, 279n29
Fränkel, Fritz, 1
Frankenstein (Shelley), 10, 249
Frankfurter Allgemeine Zeitung, 140, 182, 188–89, 190
"Franz Kafka" (Benjamin), 226
Franz Overbeck und Friedrich Nietzsche (Bernoulli), 5, 116
freedom of reason, 176
Free Student Movement, 21, 60, 63
French Revolution, 62
Friedländer, Salomo, (Mynona) 267n11
Friedrich-Wilhelm-Universität, 22
Friedrich Wilhelm IV, 113
friendship, 40–43, 50, 52
Fritzsch, E. W. (publisher), 161
"From High Mountains" (Nietzsche), 169
Der frühe Walter Benjamin und Hermann Cohen: Jüdische Werte, Kritische Philosophie, vergängliche Erfahrung (Deuber-Mankowsky), 265n3
Fuchs, Eduard, 141

functionalized agencies, 26
future religiosity, 45
future rights, 241

Gadamer, Hans-Georg, 19
Gaines, Jeremy, 268n17
Gast, Peter. *See* Köselitz, Heinrich
The Gay Science (Nietzsche), 5, 13, 91, 158, 163, 202
Geliebte (beloved), 26
gender politics, 269n20
Genealogy of Morals (Nietzsche), 38
genius, 28
Genossenschaft (Wyneken), 41
George, Stefan, 61, 184
Germans, 121, 125; mourning play, 75; music of, 98; philosophy of, 98; Romanticism, 6
German Gymnasien, 59
"German Letters." *See Deutsche Menschen*
Germany, secret, 184–86
Gersdorff, Carl von, 122, 128
Gesammelte Schriften (Benjamin), viii
Gesamtkunstwerk (Wagner, R.), 98, 144
Gespräch, 25, 29
Gide, André, xi
Glück. See happiness
Glück, Gustav, 237–41
God: consciousness of, 39; death of, 163, 235
Gödel, Kurt, 103, 282n2
Goethe, Johann Wolfgang von, 72–74, 147, 194–95, 215, 274n7; beautiful semblance and, 108; essay on, 109; youth and, 18
Goethe's Elective Affinities (Benjamin), 56
Golgotha, 87
Görres, Joseph, 184
gradualism, 298n14
Greeks, 121, 149; culture of, 146; music of, 99; tragedy of, 75, 77, 79–80, 200–201
Greek and German (Nietzsche), 120
Green, Julien, 264n5
Griffith, D. W., 257
Grillparzer, Franz, 16
Grimm (brothers), 184
Guerra, Gabriele, 265n3
guilt, 77

Haas, Willy, 131
Habilitation (Benjamin), 132
Hahn, Barbara, xii
hallucination, 3–4

Hamacher, Werner, 272n38, 294n1
Hamlet (Shakespeare), 67, 83–89, 278n19
happiness, 237–41
von Hardenberg, Friedrich. *See* Novalis
Haubinda (*Landeserziehungsheim Haubinda*), 21
Hebel, Johann Peter, 55
Hegel, Georg Wilhelm Friedrich, 57, 272n38, 282n4
Heidegger, Martin, viii, 21, 58
Heinle, Christoph Friedrich, 23, 32, 49–58, 86, 205, 270n31
Heinle, Wolf, 134
Herfurth, Thomas, 19
hermeneutics, 274n5
heroes, 79–81
hierarchy, papal, 113
history, 62, 219; bourgeois cultural, 230; exterior, 213; fatal, 259; meaningless, 113; Ur-history, 8, 235, 264n5
historical consciousness, 232
historical dialectician, 243
historical distance, 183–85
historical knowledge, 241, 243, 244
historical materialist, 243
historical newness, 233
History and Class Consciousness (Lukács), 220–21
Hobbes, Thomas, 108
Hofmannsthal, Hugo von, 4, 139
Hölderlin, Friedrich, 32, 39, 56, 63, 67, 201, 213, 242
Holub, Robert C., 266n4
Homer, 213
"Hope in the Past" (Szondi), 181
Horkheimer, Max, 234, 255
House of Despair, 164
Hulme, T. E., 287n25
Human, All Too Human (Nietzsche), 5, 113, 119, 151–52, 158, 177–78
humanism, 197; antihumanism, 49
Human to Superman (Nietzsche), 160

"I," 30–31, 45, 46
Ibsen, Henrik, 48
ideals, 27; collapse of, 65; receptivity, 29; of youth, 24, 67
The Idiot (Dostoevsky), 89
"'The Idiot' by Dostoevsky" (Benjamin), 56
Illuminations (Benjamin), 191
"The Image of Proust" (Benjamin), 240
immortality, 58, 270n24
imperialism, 206
"Imperial Panorama" (Benjamin), 134

independence of the soul, 202
individualism, 67
influence, 7–8, 15, 19; direct, 225; plurality of, 164
Inhalt, 73
innovation, 228–29
inscription, ix, 31, 58, 88–89, 103, 114–15, 130, 139–42, 155
insolubilia, 103
instability, 16
"Intellect" (Emerson), 103
Intellect, reviving of, 7
intentionality, 30
interlinguistic translation, 209
international perspective, 123
interpretation, 17
In the Shadow of Catastrophe: German Intellectuals between Apocalypse and Enlightenment (Rabinbach), 270n27
intoxication, 144
Introduction to Mathematical Philosophy (Russell), 88
Italian Journey (Goethe), 112

Jacobs, Carol, 296n3
James, William, 295n2
Jameson, Fredric, 274n7
Janz, Curt Paul, 2
Jaspers, Karl, viii, 21, 283n8
Jay, John, 12
Jennings, Michael, xi
Jetztzeit. See now-time
Journal of Social Research, 229
Judaism, 127, 181–82, 255–56, 268n15, 270n31; anti-Semitism, 127, 220, 256; Jewish renewal, 33–34; Youth Culture Movement and, 265n3
Judentum zwischen Anarchie und Theokratie: Ein religionspolitische Diskussion am Beispiel der Begegnung zwischen Walter Benjamin und Gershom Scholem (Guerra), 265n3
Judeo-Christian culture, 201
Jugend, 54
Julius Caesar (Shakespeare), 201–4
Jung, Carl, 230
juvenilia, 16–17, 24, 25, 32, 33, 44

Kafka, Franz, 6, 39, 55, 165, 232, 269n18, 279n28; essay on, 225; readings of, 141
Kaiser-Friedrich-Schule, 21
Kameradschaft (Nietzsche), 41
Kant, Immanuel, 73–74, 98, 143, 258–61, 274n5; ethical transparency and, 41; neo-Kantianism, 71; philosophy of, 57; space and time and, 245
"Kant und Goethe" (Simmel), 274n7
Kapitalismus, 260
"Karl Kraus" (Benjamin), 190–91, 193–94
Karplus, Gretel, (later Gretel Adorno) 29, 180, 224
Kaufmann, Walter, 263n2, 275n8, 283n8, 284n13
Keller, Gottfried, 131, 133
Keystone Studios, 257
Kierkegaard: Construction of the Aesthetic, (Adorno), 67, 299n18
"Kingdome of Darknesse" (Hobbes), 108
Kippenberg, Anton, 55
Klassik Stiftung Weimar, 114
Klossowski, Pierre, 283n8
Des Knaben Wunderhorn (collection of German folk poems), 15
knowability, now of, 245–46
knowledge, 143; historical, 241, 243, 244; as precise discernment, 169
Kofman, Sarah, 267n12
Kölnische Zeitung, 167
Korporationen, 21
Köselitz, Heinrich, (Peter Gast) ix, 156
Kracauer, Siegfried, 140, 181
Kraus, Karl, 8, 39, 141, 190–93, 208, 269n18
Krell, David Farrell, 285n14
Krise und Kritik (Crisis and Criticism) (magazine), 222–23
Krummel, Richard Frank, 266n5
Kupffer, Heinrich, 267n14

Lacis, Asja, 29, 138, 220
Landeserziehungsheim Haubinda, 21
Landschaft (landscape), 31
language: death and, 58; historical distance in, 185; mortal boundary of, 192–93; nature and, 95; scientific, 137; semantic transfer between, 210; theory of, 36
Lao-Tse, 242
Laqueur, Walter, 266n3
Latin, 12–13
law, 252
lectures: of Nietzsche, 59–60; William James Lectures, 295n2
Leiris, Michel, 255
Leopardi, Giacomo, 147, 232
Lesskow, Nikolai, 141
letters: of Benjamin, 4, 33, 43; men of, 34

Index

letter project, 180, 182–83, 186
Levinas, Emmanuel, 58
Lieb, Fritz, 233
Lietz, Hermann, 267n9
life, 210; cycle, 94
"The Life and Activity of Delivery-Men to the Court" (Wilamowitz-Moellendorff), 132
Life Is a Dream (Calderón), 83, 167
"The Life of Nietzsche: Volume VII: Burial and Grave-Tending" (Förster-Nietzsche), 132
"The Life of Students" (Benjamin), 18, 24, 33, 59–62, 65–66, 131
Literarische Welt (Haas), 131
"Literary History and the Study of Literature" (Benjamin), 142
Literaten (men of letters), 34, 48
"The Little Hunchback" (Benjamin), 14–15
logic, 246; collective, 143; truth-functional, 104
logical formalism, 103
logical insight, 144
loneliness, 42
Longfellow, Henry Wadsworth, 10–12
love, 29, 51, 196
Löwith, Karl, 174, 205–6, 234, 236
Lukács, George, 76–78, 80, 82, 89, 220–22, 297n9

Machiavelli, Niccolò, 215
"Man Alone with Himself" (Nietzsche), 158
manifest contradictions, 229
Mann, Thomas, 69
Männliche Briefe (Benjamin), 185
Mark Antony, 202, 205
marriage, 195–96
Marx, Karl, 244, 298n14
Masculine Letters (Benjamin), 185
mass psychology, 230
material content, 73–74, 183
maturity, 67
El mayor monstruo, los celos (Calderón), 83
McFarland, Thomas, xii
McNicholl, Rachel, 268n17
meaning: music and, 97; tragedy and, 95
"The Meaning of Language in Trauerspiel and Tragedy" (Nietzsche), 93
medicine, transcendental, 249–55
mediocrity, 140
Meditations (Descartes), 106
Meinecke, Friedrich, 21
melancholy, 84–86, 93, 166, 204

"Memorial Issue for Goethe's 100th Deathday" (Benjamin), 55
Menninghaus, Winfried, 276n15
men of letters, 34
mescaline, 1–2
messianic utopianism, 297n9
Messianism, 270n27
metaphysics, 287n25, 296n5
"Metaphysics of Youth" (Benjamin), 24–26, 32–33, 43, 55, 242, 268n17
methodological extremism, 220
misrecognition, 42, 170
Mitleid (pitying sympathy), 199
modernity, 228
"Molière: The Hypochondriac" (Benjamin), 56
Mommsen, Theodor, 133
montage, 186, 187
Montinari, Mazzino, ix, 200
"Monument to a Warrior" (Benjamin), 192, 193
Moor, Karl, 18
moral integration, 249
mortalism, 56, 166, 210, 288n25
mortality, 56
Moses, Stéphane, x
mourning play. *See* Trauerspiel
Muri, Switzerland, 130–31
"Muri: Verlag der Universität [1928]", 130
music, 95, 96; German, 98; Greek, 99; meaning and, 97; opera, 96–98, 100; subordination of, 100
Mutual Film Corporation, 256
Mynona. *See* Friedländer, Salomo
myth, 235, 276n15; Teutonic, 98; tragedy and, 79
mythic consciousness, 236

Nachlaß (Nietzsche), 114, 118–20, 147, 168, 199, 207, 227
Nachtlied (Nietzsche). *See* "Nightsong"
name day, 55
Napoleon, 88–89, 215, 278n22
National Credit Society, 239
national perspective, 123
National Socialism, viii, 182
natural cries, 94–95
naturalism, 48, 67
Nazism, vii, 184
Nehamas, Alexander, 283n9
neo-Kantianism, 71
neologism, 18, 217, 218, 294n1
Neue Schweitzer Rundschau, 167
Newman, Jane, 277n19
newness, 229–32; historical, 233
newspapers, 186–87

Niemeyer, Christian, 19
Nietzsche: Life as Literature (lehamas), 283n9
"Nietzsche and the Archive of His Sister" (Benjamin), 132
Nietzsche Archive, ix, 3, 18, 133
Nietzsche et la philosophie (Deleuze), viii
Nietzsche's Philosophy of the Eternal Recurrence of the Same (Löwith), 174, 234
Nietzsches Zusammenbruch (Nietzsche's Breakdown) (Podach), 3
"Night: The Ball/The Criminal" (Benjamin), 25
"Night-Song (*Nachtlied*)" (Nietzsche), 35, 36, 42
nihilism, 8, 71, 81, 220, 297n7; self-overcoming and, 236; skepticism and, 222
notebooks, 69, 119, 199
Novalis, (Friedrich von Hardenberg), 235
now of knowability, 245–46
now-time (*Jetztzeit*), 129–30, 140, 146, 166, 241–48, 286n21

objectification, 176
objective semblance, 112
observation, 120, 121, 285n16
Offenbach, Jacques, 190, 208
Öffentliche Akademische Gesellschaft, 59
"Official Didactic Poem" (Scholem, Gershom), 130
Olde, Hans, 2
One-Way Street (Benjamin), 54, 132, 134, 137–39, 141–42, 192
"On Great Events" (Nietzsche), 178
"On Love of One's Neighbor" (Nietzsche), 16
"On Nietzsche's 'Zarathustra'" (Brecht), 226
On Reading and Writing (Nietzsche), 120, 129
"On Semblance" (Benjamin), 109
On the Aesthetic Education of Man (Schiller), 109
On the Concept of History (Benjamin), 29, 219, 237, 241, 243–45
On The Future of our Educational Institutions (Nietzsche), 59–62, 120, 129, 291n39
On the Genealogy of Morals (Nietzsche), 158
"On the Return of Hofmannsthal's Deathday" (Benjamin), 55

"On the Trail of Old Letters" (Benjamin), 183, 293n6
"On the Use and Disadvantage of History for Life" (Nietzsche), 5, 18, 20, 126, 128, 242
"On the Vision and the Riddle" (Nietzsche), 14
opera, 96–97; philology and, 100; Wagnerian, 98
optimism, 93
origin, 218
original document, 212–14
original speech, 214
The Origin of German Trauerspiel (Benjamin), viii, 39, 68, 81, 86–87, 92–94, 141–42; *Hamlet* and, 84; tragedy and, 74–75, 78, 112
"The Other Dancing Song" (Nietzsche), 198
"Otobiographies: The Teaching of Nietzsche and the Politics of the Proper Name" (Derrida), 290n39
"Outline of the Psychophysical Problem" (Benjamin), 6
Overbeck, Franz, 71, 115–16, 118, 179, 188–90, 236

Pana (disciple of Zarathustra), 199
pantheism, 45–46, 275n9
papal hierarchy, 113
paradox, 17, 52, 103–6, 149, 170, 282n2; of dependent authority, 216; esotericism and, 139; formal, 282n1
Passagenarbeit. See Arcades Project
passivity, 28, 81, 209
Paul, Georgina, 268n17, 269n20
The Pawnshop (film), 255–58
pedagogy, 148–49
performance, 30, 208, 209
performative act, 294n1
permanence, 74
personal totality, 64
perspective, 110, 112, 123, 258; scientific, 149
perspectivism, 283n9
Peter Bell the Third (Shelley), 298n14
Pfotenhauer, Helmut, ix–x
Phaedo (Plato), 92, 279n26
Phenomenology of Spirit (Hegel), 57
philistines, cultivated, 242
philistinism, 44
philology, 72, 74, 127, 145, 151–55; criticism of, 147, 150; opera and, 100; origin of, 148; philosophy and, 154; science and, 100, 155, theology and, 154

"Philology of the Future!" (Wilamowitz-Moellendorff), 91, 133
The Philosophers of the Tragic Age (Nietzsche), 120
philosophy: of Benjamin, 56–57; of death, 57; German, 98; of Kant, 57; of Nietzsche, 7–8, 37, 155, 157, 165, 235; philology and, 154; Platonic, 90, 92; post-Hellenic, 175; scholastic, 103; Socrates and, 91–92
"Philosophy in the Tragic Age of the Greeks" (Nietzsche), 145, 158, 175, 289n36
photographs, of Nietzsche, 2
physiognomy, 17
pitying sympathy, 199
Plato, 18, 28, 93
Platonism, 90, 92
plurality, 26, 185; of influence, 164; of students, 65
Podach, E. F., 3, 166, 179
"Poet" (Hölderlin), 63
poetic courage, 63
poetry, 10
Poetry and Truth (Goethe), 194
political theology, 93,
politics, 221–22, 241; authority and, 206; egalitarianism and, 137, 226; gender, 269n20; reactionary, 220; of weakness, 219, 223
"A Portrait of Walter Benjamin" (Adorno), vii
possession, 211
posthumous revitalization, 218
posthumous status, 214–16
Powers, Benjamin, xi
prayers, 154
preface. *See Vorrede*
prejudice, 70
presentation, 92–93; science and, 137; textual, 209
present tenses, 184
prior institutions, 136
Prisms (Adorno), vii
privacy, 162
progress, 243
proletariat, 221–22, 244, 247
prostitute, 26–28, 54, 269n20, 269n21
Protestantism, 271n31
Proust, Marcel, 39, 141
pseudomenon, 103–13
psychology: controlled empirical, 1; mass, 230
"Psychophysical Problem" (Benjamin), 68

public speakers, 208, 209
pure contents, 274n4
pure word, 94, 95
Purviance, Edna, 256

Quine, Willard Van Orman, 104, 105

Rabinbach, Anson, 38, 270n27
"The Rainbow" (Benjamin), 43, 44
Rang, Florens Christian, 277n16
Raphael, 111, 112
Räumen (clearing away), 240
ray, 30
reactionary discourse, viii
reader, entertainment of, 118
reading, 140, 150, 153–54
Realien, 274n6
reason, 209, 276n15; freedom of, 176
receptivity, ideal, 29
recognition, 41
reconciliation, 181
redemption, 29
Rée, Paul, 150
reference, 105; onomastic, 89; theory of, 88
reflection, 265n6
Reformation, 150
rejection, 170
relativism, epistemological, 221
religion, 164–65. *See also specific religions*
religiosity, 44; authentic, 37; future, 45
Renaissance, 203, 277n19
"The Renewal of Judaism" (Buber), 38
renunciation, 12–13, 65
"The Repetition of Antiquity on the Peak of Modernity as the Historical Meaning of the Doctrine of the Eternal Return" (Löwith), 235
representation, 88; tragedy and, 78, 89
Reschke, Renate, x
Rettung (rescuing), 181
revisionism, 298n14
revolution, 245
revolutionary theory, 223, 244
Rhythm (Nietzsche), 120
Rickert, Heinrich, 21
"Riffraff" (fairy-tale), 4, 15, 264n3
"The Ring of Saturn or, Some Remarks on Iron Construction" (Benjamin), 232
Ritschl, Friedrich Wilhelm, 154
The Robbers (Schiller), 18
Rohde, Erwin, 59, 115–18, 286n18
Romanticism, 18, 84, 235; art criticism of, 72; art theory, 271n31; German, 6

"Romanticism" (Benjamin), 43
Rorschach tests, 1
Rosenzweig, Franz, 76, 81–82, 89, 91, 202, 277n18
Rowohlt, Ernst (publisher), 132, 141
Russell, Bertrand, 88, 278n22
Rychner, Max, 194

Sachgehalt. *See* material content
Sachs, Franz, 23
sacrifice, 39, 79–81, 84–85, 89, 207, 234
Salome, Lou, 13
Sappho, 29
"Sappho" (Grillparzer), 16
satanic success, 197
satirists, 208
Schein. *See* semblance
Schelling, Friedrich Wilhelm Joseph, 62
Schicksalsdrama (drama of fate), 83
Schiller, Friedrich, 18, 97, 109
Schiller Archive, 114
Schlechta, Karl, ix
Schlegel, Friedrich, 62, 235
Schleiermacher, Friedrich, 274n5
Schmitt, Carl, 220
Schoen, Ernst, 5, 195
scholastic philosophy, 103
Scholem, Arthur, 130
Scholem, Gershom, 4–7, 25, 34, 130–31, 208, 220, 223, 237
Schopenhauer, 98, 129, 215
Schriften (Benjamin), 7
Schweppenhäuser, Hermann, viii
science: of aesthetics, 99, 143; art of, 152; form of appearance of, 137; inquiry and, 134; language and, 137; perspective and, 149; philology and, 100, 155; presentation and, 137; theological condition of, 134
Seal of the State of New York, 12
"The Second of Inversion" (Hamacher), 272n38
Second Reich, 71
secret Germany, 184–86
"Secret Signs" (Benjamin), 162
Seiffert, Johannes, 181
self-annihilation, 203
self-assertion, 17
self-dramatization, 30
self-evidence, 134
self-overcoming, 41, 236
self-realization, 174
self-recognition, 41, 43
self-reflection, 177
self-relation, 176

Seligson, Carla, 22, 36, 43, 50, 53, 54
Seligson, Rika, 23, 53
semblance, 107, 109–12; beautiful, 108; objective, 112
Sennett, Mack, 257
Serény, György, 282n2
set theory, 104
sexuality, 54
shadows, 178
"Shakespeare: As You Like It" (Benjamin), 56
Shakespeare, William, 67, 83, 87, 201–4, 208, 213, 215
shame, 37–38, 40
Shea, Mark, xi
Shelley, Mary, 10, 249, 298n14
"Short Shadows" (Benjamin), 167–68, 171, 172
Siglo de Oro drama, 83
signature, xviii, 17, 24, 30–33, 42, 48, 58, 63–66, 67, 88, 92, 113–14, 119–24, 126–28, 141, 144, 146, 148, 152–53, 158–61, 166, 168, 193, 204, 207, 215–16, 228, 234, 251–55, 273n39, 290n39
"signature of essence," 88
silence (*Schweigen*), 26–27, 93–102; 161, 191, collective, 277n18; defiant, 94; tragedy and, 82, 95
Simmel, Georg, 74, 274n7, 282n4
Skovsbostrand, Denmark, 224–25
"Sleeping Beauty" (Benjamin), 17–18
sociability, 296n5
social democracy, 244
social-democratic complacency, 243
socialism, 23; nationalism, viii, 182
sociology, 287n24
Socrates, 89–93, 279n25
solidarity, 222
Sophocles, 111
Soul and Forms (Lukács), 76
"Souterrain" (Benjamin), 54
space, 245
Spade, Paul Vincent, 282n1
speech act theory, 294n1, 295n2
Spieltrieb, 109
Spinoza, Baruch, 18, 45
spirit, 209
Spirit of Gravity, 14–15, 197, 261
"Spirits of the Primal Forest" (*Urwaldgeister*) (Benjamin and Heinle), 53
Spitteler, Carl, 37
spouses, 196–97
Sprechsaal (discussion forum), 23–24, 29, 44, 49–51, 67
stand-up comedy, 260–61

The Star of Redemption (Rosenzweig), 76, 81–82
status quo, 220
Stendhal, (Marie-Henri Beyle), 215
Stevenson, Robert Louis, 249–50, 254–55
"The Stillest Hour" (Nietzsche), 38, 162
Stirner, Max, 235
The Story of a Friendship (Scholem, Gershom), 131
Strahl (beam/ray), 30
Strange Case of Dr. Jekyll and Mr. Hyde (Stevenson), 249–55
Strauß, David (David Strauss), 120, 127–28, 265, 267n11, 267n13, 270n27
Strauß, Ludwig, 4, 33–34, 37, 39, 40, 43
Strindberg, August, 18, 47, 156
student activism, 21, 23
Studentische Politik und Kulterreform: Geschichte der Freistudenten-Bewegung 1896–1918 (Wipf), 266n3
student reform movement, 61
"Studies" (Brecht), 226
sublime, 259
subversion, continual, 55
suicide, 55, 58, 198, 201
Superbus, Tarquinius, 202
superhumanity, 47; confidence, 38–39, 67; striving, 46
superman, viii, 20, 38–40, 46, 49, 69, 160, 163–65, 200
supernatural, 296n5
surrender, 14
survival, 78, 92, 205, 210–13, 223, 239, 295n2
Sussman, Henry, xi
symbol, 51, 84
Symposium (Plato), 28
synaesthesia, 98
synchronous unity, 147
Szondi, Peter, 181

Tagebuch (daybook), 25, 29
Tasso, Torquato, 18
Taureau (prison), 233
"Teaching Aid" (Benjamin), 139
"Teleology without Ultimate Goal" (Benjamin), 237
temporality, 145, 228–29, 246; antagonism and, 26; fatal, 231; of fate, 236–37
temporal relation, 31
terminology, of Nietzsche, 67
Teutonic myth, 98

textual categories, 187
textual presentation, 209
theology, 135, 154, 287n22
theological condition of science, 134
"Theological-Political Fragment" (Benjamin), 241, 297n7
theoretical dialogue, 43
Theses on the Concept of History, 287n22
Thieme, Karl, 180, 185
"Thirteen Theses against Snobs" (Benjamin), 140
thought-image, 54, 162, 168, 171, 237–38
Three Discourses on Judaism (Buber), 38
Thus Spoke Zarathustra (Nietzsche), 5, 35, 119, 160–62, 178, 233; books of, 200; rhetorical strategies of, 37
Tiedemann, Rolf, viii, 17, 265n3
time, 57, 175, 206, 245, 246
The Time Machine (Wells), 249
timidity, 63
timing, 260
title, 42, 51, 56, 65, 84, 113–14, 119–21, 126–130, 141–42, 146, 148, 151–52, 159–61, 168, 183, 185, 203–4, 207, 216, 242, 252
title-aphorisms, 168
der Tod (death), 26
"To Live without Leaving Traces" (Benjamin), 172
topoi, 24
The Torch (Die Fackel) (Kraus), 190
Torquato Tasso (Goethe), 18
totalitarianism, 247
totality, 64
totalizing principle, 93
"La Traduction—le pour et le contra" (Benjamin), 216
tragedy, 74–82, 112; antique, 74; Attic, 76, 82; birth of, 90; classical, 75–76; death of, 93; elements of, 76; form and, 78; Greek, 75, 77, 79–80, 200–201; as identity, 145; meaning and, 95; myth and, 79; representation and, 78, 89; sacrifice and, 79–81, 85, 89; silence and, 82, 95; Socrates and, 90; theory of, 76–77, 83, 101, 264n5
"Tragedy and Trauerspiel" (Nietzsche), 93
Trampedach, Mathilde, 9–11, 13
transcendental medicine, 249–55
transcription, 155
Transfiguration (Raphael), 111

transgressive incarnation, 252
transience, 246
translation, 211–15, 218; anachronism in, 217; authority of, 212; fidelity and, 210; interlinguistic, 209; theory of, 216, 217
transparency, 138; ethical, 41
"Transvaluation of All Values" (Nietzsche), 161
Trauerspiel, 74–75, 83, 85–87, 93, 96, 101, 259, 260
"Trauerspiel and Tragedy" (Benjamin), 83
triadic structure, 194
The Trial (Kafka), 232
Trotz (defiance), 79, 81, 92
true awareness, 32
truth, 26–27, 29, 47, 57, 110; beauty and, 108; nature of, 138; of theology, 135; time and, 246
truth content, 72–74, 183
truth-functional logic, 104
Twilight of the Idols (Nietzsche), 126, 156, 214
"Two Poems by Friedrich Hölderlin" (Benjamin), 56

"Über Goethes und Kants moralische Weltaunschauung" (Simmel), 274n7
Übermenschentum (superhuman striving), 46, 275n9
university, 61; authority of, 138; theology and, 135. *See also specific universities*
University of Muri, 131–32, 134
untimeliness, 113–30, 146, 158, 285n15
Untimely Observations (Nietzsche), 5, 20, 113, 120, 126–27, 145, 159
Ur-history, (*Urgeschichte*) 8, 234–35, 264n5
"Urwaldgeister" (Benjamin and Heinle). *See* "Spirits of the Primal Forest"

van Hoddis, Jakob, (Hans Davidsohn), 53
"veritable witches," 2
Vernunft (reason), 276n15
La vida es sueño (Life is a Dream) (Calderón), 83, 167
Villa Silberblick, 2
virtue, 202
vitalism, 210
vocabulary, 25
Volkelt, Johannes, 75
Voltaire, 147
von Meysenbug, Malwida, 157

von Senger, Hugo, 9–11
Vorrede (preface), 70, 153, 160–61, 185, 242
Vorurteil, 70, 164

Wagner, Cosima, 59, 122, 124–25, 188, 280n30, 286n20; Bayreuth propaganda of, 19; opera and, 98
Wagner, Richard, 5, 9, 11, 70, 90, 99–102, 124
"Wagner in Bayreuth" (Nietzsche), 158–59
Wahrheitsgehalt. See truth content
Walter Benjamin: The Story of a Friendship (Scholem, Gershom), 6
Wanderer, 174–77
"The Wanderer and His Shadow" (Nietzsche), 173
War to the Death against the House of Hohenzollern (Nietzsche), 113
"we," 143–44, 221
weakness, politics of, 219, 223
Weber, Max, 162, 165, 207
Weber, Samuel, 220, 292n41
"We Fearless Ones" (Nietzsche), 296n5
Weigel, Sigrid, 29, 268n17, 269n21
Weimar Republic, 182
Weininger, Otto, 235
Weissbach, Richard, 56
Wells, H. G., 249
"We Philologists" (Nietzsche), 145–49, 151
"We Scholars" (Nietzsche), 129, 157
Wesendonck, Mathilde, 11
whore. *See* prostitute
Wickersdorf (school), 21
Widmann, J. V., 157–58, 289n37
Wilamowitz-Moellendorff, Ulrich von, 59, 89, 91, 132–33, 179
Wilhelminian culture, 18–19, 62
William James Lectures, 295n2
The Will to Power (Nietzsche), ix, 9, 227, 284n13
Wipf, Hans-Ulrich, 266n3
wisdom of Silenus, 93, 111
witches' brew, 76
Witte, Bernd, 270n31
Wittgenstein, Ludwig, 289n35
Wizisla, Erdmut, 268n16, 297n10
Wohlfahrt, Irving, x
women, 269n20
writing, 114, 140; mature, 36, 67; privilege of, 278n21; transformation of, 115
Wyneken, Gustav, 20–22, 40–41, 266n9, 267n14, 268n15, 279n25

Index

Yale University, 130
"you," 177
Young Germany: A History of the German Youth Movement (Laqueur), 266n3
youth, 18, 34; commitment to, 35; ideal of, 24, 67; paradigm of, 50
"Youth" (Benjamin), 16, 22, 23
Youth Culture Movement, 17, 19–21, 33, 49, 62; antebellum debates of, 22; goals of, 22; Judaism and, 265n3; *Sprechsaal* and, 23–24
youthful facies, 17, 21–22, 24–25, 28, 32, 41, 51, 208
youthful works approach theory, 208
youth-life, 17, 32

Zarathustra: apotheosis of, 8; death of, 198–201, 207; discourse of, 41, 49, 129; friendship and, 40–42; hour of, 169, 171–72, 175; madness and, 166; reference to, 168; shame and, 38; Spirit of Gravity and, 14–15
Zeitschrift für Sozialforschung (Journal of Social Research), 229
Zionism, 22, 23, 33–34, 267n11, 270n27, 270n29
Zizek, Slavoj, 292n1
zu Grunde gehen (expiration), 211
"*Zukunftsphilologie!*" (Wilamowitz-Moellendorff), 91
Zunft, 152
Zweideutigkeit (ambiguity), 79, 276n14

www.ingramcontent.com/pod-product-compliance
Lightning Source LLC
Chambersburg PA
CBHW022030290426
44109CB00014B/812